*Policing the*

Policing the Roman Empire

Soldiers, Administration, and Public Order

CHRISTOPHER J.
FUHRMANN

OXFORD
UNIVERSITY PRESS

OXFORD
UNIVERSITY PRESS

Oxford University Press is a department of the University of Oxford.
It furthers the University's objective of excellence in research, scholarship,
and education by publishing worldwide.

Oxford   New York

Auckland   Cape Town   Dar es Salaam   Hong Kong   Karachi
Kuala Lumpur   Madrid   Melbourne   Mexico City   Nairobi
New Delhi   Shanghai   Taipei   Toronto

With offices in

Argentina   Austria   Brazil   Chile   Czech Republic   France   Greece
Guatemala   Hungary   Italy   Japan   Poland   Portugal   Singapore
South Korea   Switzerland   Thailand   Turkey   Ukraine   Vietnam

Oxford is a registered trade mark of Oxford University Press
in the UK and certain other countries.

Published in the United States of America by
Oxford University Press
198 Madison Avenue, New York, NY 10016

Library of Congress Cataloging-in-Publication Data
Fuhrmann, Christopher J.
Policing the Roman Empire : soldiers, administration, and public order / Christopher J. Fuhrmann.
p. cm.
Includes bibliographical references and indexes.
ISBN 978-0-19-973784-0 (hardcover); 978-0-19-936001-7 (paperback)
1. Police—Rome—History.   2. Soldiers—Rome—History.   3. Magistrates, Roman—History.
4. Social control—Rome—History.   5. Rome—History—Empire, 30 B.C.-476 A.D.
6. Rome—Politics and government—30 B.C.-476 A.D.   7. Rome—Social conditions.
8. Roman provinces—History.   9. Roman provinces—Politics and government.
10. Roman provinces—Social conditions.   I. Title.
DG109.F84   2011
937'.06—dc22   2011009168

To Tiffany

Contents

Preface

WHEN I ONCE told an eminent ancient historian that I was working on police forces in the Roman provinces, his snap reaction was, "But there weren't any!" After a moment of reflection, he conceded, "Well, I suppose there were eirenarchs. And *stationarii*..." It was a revealing exchange, which demonstrated that a modern study of imperial Roman policing and public order was long overdue. This book is intended to remedy that neglect. I have tried to make it accessible to anyone interested in the ancient world or the history of policing, while also contributing to the academic dialogue of fellow specialists.

In the following pages, I quote a broad range of ancient sources. Biblical passages are from the New Revised Standard Version. Quoted translations of papyri are usually those of the specified edition, when these included an English translation. Otherwise most translations from Greek and Latin sources are my own; exceptions are specifically noted. In translating, I have often consulted published translations as a rough guide. In every case, my analysis is based on the original Greek and Latin, and I vouch for all of the following translated passages, even when they are not my own. My understanding of material in other ancient languages, such as Aramaic or Coptic, depends entirely on the cited translator.

Acknowledgments

THIS BOOK HAS come together over a lengthy period of development. As a result, my debts are numerous.

Two people deserve much of the credit for whatever in the following pages is good. It was Richard Talbert who suggested the topic to me when I was a new graduate student in the History Department of the University of North Carolina at Chapel Hill. Over the next six years, he was a generous mentor and ideal dissertation supervisor. The more perspective I gain in this profession, the more I realize how lucky I was to have worked with him. As a reader for Oxford University Press, Michael Peachin made ample comments that alternatively encouraged me and challenged me to improve weak points. As a reader, I used to disdain the omnipresent statement in acknowledgments, "none of the people I just thanked should be blamed for any of my book's shortcomings," as too obvious. Richard Talbert's and Michael Peachin's generosity forces me to say it anyway.

I have benefited greatly from the guidance and input of other esteemed scholars. From my time at UNC, Leanne Bablitz, Hilary Becker, Lee Brice, Jayendra Chhana, Tom Elliott, George Houston, Jerzy Linderski, and Daniëlle Slootjes contributed significantly. So did Tolly Boatwright and Kent Rigsby of Duke University. Werner Riess's model of erudition and intellectual ambition was a great boon. John Bauschatz has been a partner in crime; his work on Ptolemaic Egypt helped keep me excited about policing in the ancient world. I warmly thank my friend and colleague Dean M. Cassella for his indispensable advice on translation, topography, and much else. Benjamin Kelly, Charlotte Roueché, Sara Saba, and Dorothy Thompson kindly sent me work in advance of publication. So many others assisted by reading drafts, helping me at key moments, sharing a reference, or providing feedback that I must resort to a bare (and probably incomplete) list: Cédric Brélaz, Christopher Browning, Melissa Bullard, Mike Campbell, Guy Chet, Serena Connolly, Michael Crawford, Henry Eaton, Garrett Fagan, Bruce Frier, Joseph T. Fuhrmann, Richard Golden, Edward Harris, Deborah Kamen, Noel Lenski,

Michael Maas, Herwig Maehler, Marilyn Morris, Fred Naiden, Aaron Navarro, Christopher Netek, the late John Oates, Zlatko Pleše, Stephen H. Rapp, Walt Roberts, Cornelia Römer, Joshua Sosin, Philip Stadter, Laura Stern, Geoff Wawro and the UNT Military History Center, Richard Weigel, and Jaren Wilkerson. Some of these fine scholars probably do not even realize how a chance remark or a difficult question pushed me to rethink weak assumptions or gain a new insight. I sincerely apologize if I have inadvertently omitted anyone.

The help and support of my colleagues in the History Department of the University of North Texas has been instrumental, especially Adrian Lewis and Rick McCaslin, my former and current chairs, respectively. Departmental staff helped keep me (and everyone) sane: Stephanie Friday, Denece Gerlach, Kayla Hunt, Donna Morgan, Gina Pumphrey, Shannon Sacks, and Sue Samples-Sinkular. Student workers fielded onerous and esoteric photocopy requests: Shae Gerlach, Jeff Hartsock, Janie Martinez, and Jared Ridgley. My students James Baker, Kristan Ewin, Melissa Hendrick, Marshall Lilly, Javier Lopez, Corey Newman, Warren Wheatley, and Nik Overtoom helped me in various ways and pointed me toward pertinent material in their own work. The graduate students in my spring 2010 Roman Empire course kindly critiqued some chapters.

Other institutions that deserve acknowledgment include the provost's office, College of Arts and Sciences, and Center for the Study of Interdisciplinarity of the University of North Texas, for four crucial grants to support my research. The UNC History Department supported early phases of this work and hosted me as a visiting scholar during the revision process. I have also benefited from the excellence of the Classics and Religious Studies faculties of both UNC and Duke. I thank Rudolf Habelt GMBH and *Greek Roman and Byzantine Studies* for kindly allowing me to reproduce their images of *paraphylakes* and UNC's Ancient World Mapping Center and its director, Brian Turner, for diligently and patiently creating this book's custom-made map (terrain depiction calculated from Environmental Systems Research Institute; SRTM shaded relief on ESRI Data & Maps 2006 [DVD-ROM], Redlands, Calif.). I am grateful again to Rick McCaslin and the UNT History Department for covering the cost of the map.

I thank the Association of Ancient Historians and its president, Lindsay Adams, for a subvention grant; audience critiques of my work at the 2006 Stanford and the 2009 Vancouver meetings of the AAH were most fruitful. I am also grateful to audiences at Baylor University, Southern Methodist University, the University of North Carolina at Chapel Hill, the University of North Texas, and the 2005 meeting of the American Philological Association in Boston, for their questions and comments on elements of chapter 2.

Serious scholarship in the humanities is impossible without academic libraries and their staff. In my case, credit is due to the libraries of the American Academy in Rome, Duke University, Southern Methodist University, UNC Chapel Hill, and the University of North Texas (especially its Interlibrary Loan division, which I have relentlessly beleaguered).

The oldest debts become the largest. I must thank the Commonwealth of Kentucky for investing in me and giving me a free, formative education at the Murray Independent Schools, Governor's Scholar Program, Murray State University, and the University of Kentucky. I owe more than I can express here to UK's Departments of History and Classics, its Honors Program, and the Gaines Center for the Humanities. College degrees aside, I still feel that my real education came from two great high school teachers, Mark Etherton and the late Sue Spann.

As senior classics editor at Oxford University Press, New York, Stefan Vranka has been unfailingly patient and supportive. I also thank his helpful assistants, Deirdre Brady and Sarah Pirovitz. The anonymous reader for the Press offered useful comments. Three undergraduate assistants made completing this book easier: LauraLee Brott helped by scanning images, Christopher Rios checked my Greek, and Carl Foster ably edited some chapters. As graduate assistant in 2005–06, Chase Machen pointed me toward good material and has helped clarify my thoughts since then. Dr. Machen also lent a former police officer's eye to this project, as did my former colleague J. Laurence Hare and my former student S. Kris Kawucha.

Our friends generously gave their support at critical times; among them are Nell Baker, Sheila Connolly, Holly Karlen, Bryan and Betsy Kempter, Nichole and Shahram Khosraviani, Kathleen Marks, Pam McElhinney, and Karen Schockmel. I feel so fortunate for the love and support of my sister, Maria; my parents, Joe and Mary; and (last but not least) my in-laws Delaney and Chris Kirk, and Don, Frances, and Jimmy Lloyd. My daughters, Istra and Elise, facilitated the last phase of work by assuming more family duties than I ever had at their age. It was always a pleasure discussing ideas with Istra, who also helped with text formatting. Without Elise's unflagging cheer and generosity, this book could not have been finished. My son, Xavier, incited me to keep making steady progress (in other words, I tried to finish writing before he was born; I fear this won't be the last race I lose to him). I also thank him for being a rather contented baby.

My wife, Tiffany Lloyd Fuhrmann, has been a great partner in all ways. I lovingly dedicate this book to her and am so thankful that I have such a wonderful family to help keep me going.

Abbreviations

The abbreviations of ancient authors and texts in the notes follow Hornblower and Spawforth's *Oxford Classical Dictionary*, 3rd edition, although I have expanded some for greater clarity. Abbreviations for Judeo-Christian sources that are not included in the *OCD* list generally conform to the 1999 *SBL Handbook of Style for Ancient Near Eastern, Biblical, and Early Christian Studies*. Citations of papyri, ostraka, and tablets use the standard abbreviations of Oates et al., *Checklist of Greek, Latin, Demotic and Coptic Papyri, Ostraca and Tablets*, continuously updated at http://scriptorium.lib.duke.edu/papyrus/texts/clist.html.

Abbott & Johnson	F. F. Abbott and A. C. Johnson, *Municipal Administration in the Roman Empire*
Acta Alex.	H. Musurillo, ed., *The Acts of the Pagan Martyrs: Acta Alexandrinorum*
AE	*L'Année épigraphique*
ANRW	*Aufstieg und Niedergang der römischen Welt*
ARS	A. C. Johnson et al., eds., *Ancient Roman Statutes*
BAR	British Archaeological Reports, International Series
BASP	*Bulletin of the American Society of Papyrologists*
BAtlas	R. J. A. Talbert, ed., *Barrington Atlas of the Greek and Roman World*
BE	*Bulletin épigraphique*
BÉFAR	Bibliothèque des Écoles Françaises d'Athènes et de Rome
Bruns	C. G. Bruns et al., eds., *Fontes Iuris Romani Antiqui*, 7th ed.
CAH	*The Cambridge Ancient History*, 2nd ed.

CBI	E. Schallmayer et al., eds. *Der römische Weihebezirk von Osterburken I: Corpus der griechischen und lateinischen Beneficiarer-Inschriften des Römischen Reiches*
CÉFR	Collection de l'École Française de Rome
CIL	*Corpus Inscriptionum Latinarum*
Class. Phil.	*Classical Philology*
Crawford *RS*	M. Crawford, ed., *Roman Statutes*
Daremberg & Saglio,	*Dictionnaire* C. V. Daremberg and E. Saglio, eds., *Dictionnaire des antiquités grecques et romaines*, 2nd ed.
Dio	Cassius Dio, *Roman History*, Loeb Classical Library ed.
EDH	Epigraphische Datenbank Heidelberg (http://www.uni-heidelberg.de/institute/sonst/adw/edh/)
Ehrenberg-Jones	V. Ehrenberg and A. H. M. Jones, eds., *Documents Illustrating the Reigns of Augustus and Tiberius*, 2nd ed.
FAS	Forschungen zur antiken Sklaverei
FIRA	S. Riccobono et al., eds., *Fontes Iuris Romani Antejustiniani*
Fink *RMRP*	R. Fink, *Roman Military Records on Papyrus*
G&R	*Greece & Rome*
GRBS	*Greek, Roman, and Byzantine Studies*
HABES	Heidelberg Althistorische Beiträge und Epigraphische Studien
Hauken	T. Hauken, *Petition and Response: An Epigraphic Study of Petitions to Roman Emperors, 181–249*
Hist. E.	*Historia* Einzelschriften
IGBulg	G. Mihailov, *Inscriptiones Graecae in Bulgaria repertae*
IGLS	L. Jalabert, R. Mouterde, et al., *Inscriptions grecques et latines de la Syrie*
IGRR	R. Cagnat et al., *Inscriptiones Graecae ad res Romanas pertinentes*
IK	*Inschriften griechischer Städte aus Kleinasien*
ILAfr	R. Cagnat and A. Merlin, *Inscriptions latines d'Afrique (Tripolitaine, Tunisie, Maroc)*

ILBulg	B. Gerov, *Inscriptiones Latinae in Bulgaria repertae*
ILS	H. Dessau, ed., *Inscriptiones Latinae Selectae*, 2nd ed.
JARCE	*Journal of the American Research Center in Egypt*
Jones, *LRE*	A. H. M. Jones, *The Later Roman Empire, 284–602: A Social, Economic, and Administrative Survey*
JRS	*Journal of Roman Studies*
Lewis & Reinhold	N. Lewis and M. Reinhold, eds., *Roman Civilization: Selected Readings*, 3rd ed.
Lewis & Short	C. T. Lewis and C. Short, *A Latin Dictionary*
MAMA	*Monumenta Asiae Minoris Antiqua*
McCrum-Woodhead	M. McCrum and A. Woodhead, *Select Documents of the Principates of the Flavian Emperors*
MÉFRA	*Mélanges de l'École Française de Rome, Antiquité*
Millar, *ERW*	F. Millar, *The Emperor in the Roman World*
Musurillo	H. Musurillo, ed., *Acts of the Christian Martyrs*
OCD²	N. G. L. Hammond and H. H. Scullard, eds., *The Oxford Classical Dictionary*, 2nd ed.
OCD³	S. Hornblower and A. Spawforth, eds., *The Oxford Classical Dictionary*, 3rd ed.
OGIS	W. Dittenberger, *Orientis Graeci Inscriptiones Selectae*
Perry	B. E. Perry, ed., *Aesopica: A Series of Texts Relating to Aesop*
PBSR	*Papers of the British School at Rome*
PIR	*Prosopographia Imperii Romani Saeculi I, II, III*, 1st ed.
PIR²	*Prosopographia Imperii Romani Saeculi I, II, III*, 2nd ed.
P&P	*Past & Present*
RE	Pauly-Wissowa, *Real-Encyclopädie der classischen Altertumswissenschaft*
Rev. Phil.	*Revue de philologie, de littérature et d'histoire anciennes*, 3rd series
RIB	R. G. Collingwood and R. P. Wright, *The Roman Inscriptions of Britain*

Robert, *OMS*	L. Robert, *Opera Minora Selecta*
Rostovtzeff, *SEHRE*	M. Rostovtzeff, *The Social and Economic History of the Roman Empire*, 2nd ed., revised by P. M. Fraser
Samothrace	P. M. Fraser, *Samothrace. Excavations Conducted by the Institute of Fine Arts of New York University*, vol. 2, part I: *The Inscriptions on Stone*
SB	*Sammelbuch griechischer Urkunden aus Ägypten*
SEG	*Supplementum Epigraphicum Graecum*
Sherk, *Augustus*	R. K. Sherk, ed., *Rome and the Greek East to the Death of Augustus*
Sherk, *Hadrian*	R. K. Sherk, ed., *The Roman Empire: Augustus to Hadrian*
Sherk, *RDGE*	R. K. Sherk, *Roman Documents from the Greek East*
Smallwood, *Docs....Gaius*	E. M. Smallwood, ed., *Documents Illustrating the Principates of Gaius, Claudius, and Nero*
Smallwood, *Docs....Nerva*	E. M. Smallwood, ed., *Documents Illustrating the Principates of Nerva, Trajan, and Hadrian*
*Syll.*³	W. Dittenberger, *Sylloge Inscriptionum Graecarum*, 3rd ed.
Syme, *RP*	R. Syme, *Roman Papers*
TAM	*Tituli Asiae Minoris*
ZPE	*Zeitschrift für Papyrologie und Epigraphik*

Roman Emperors from Augustus to Julian

(Some minor emperors and usurpers omitted; dates do not cover joint reigns of fathers and sons.)

Augustus	27 BC–AD 14	
Tiberius	AD 14–37	
Gaius (Caligula)	37–41	Julio-Claudian dynasty
Claudius	41–54	
Nero	54–68	
Galba	68–69	
Otho	69	
Vitellius	69	
Vespasian	69–79	
Titus	79–81	Flavian dynasty
Domitian	81–96	
Nerva	96–98	
Trajan	98–117	
Hadrian	117–138	"Five Good Emperors"/
Antoninus Pius	138–161	Antonine dynasty
Lucius Verus	161–169	
Marcus Aurelius	161–180	
Commodus	180–192	
Pertinax	193	
Didius Julianus	193	
Septimius Severus	193–211	
Geta	211	
Antoninus (Caracalla)	211–217	
Macrinus	217–218	Severan dynasty
Elagabalus	218–222	
Alexander Severus	222–235	
Maximin Thrax	235–238	

Balbinus & Pupienus Maximus	238
Gordian I & Gordian II	238
Gordian III	238–244
Philip the Arab	244–249
Decius	249–251
Trebonianus Gallus	251–253
Valerian	253–260
Gallienus	260–268
Claudius II Gothicus	268–270
Aurelian	270–275
Tacitus	275–276
Probus	276–282
Carus	282–283
Carinus	283–285
Numerian	283–284
Diocletian	284–286

Divided empire

WEST		EAST	
Maximian	286–305, 307–310	Diocletian	286–305
Constantius I	305–306	Galerius	305–311
Maxentius	306–312	Maximin Daia	308–313
Constantine	306–324	Licinius	308–324

Constantine
(sole emperor)
324–337

WEST		EAST	
Constantine II	337–340	Constantius II	337-353
Constans	337–350		
Magnentius	350–353		

Constantius II
(sole emperor)
353–361
Julian
(sole emperor)
361–363

Map of the Roman Empire

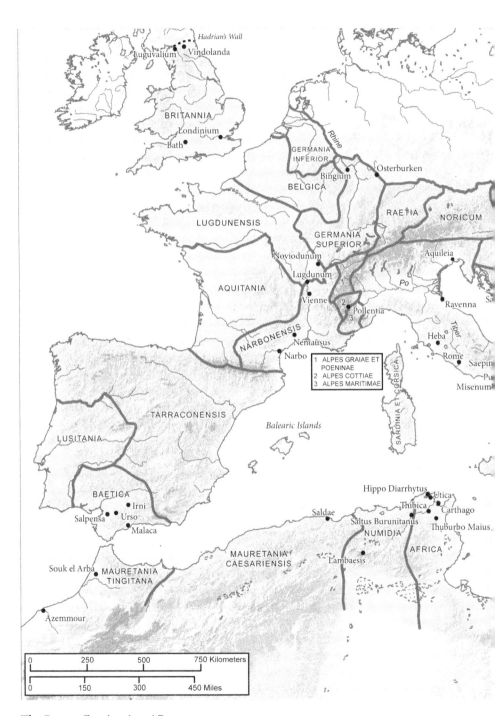

Hadrian's Wall
Luguvalium Vindolanda

BRITANNIA
Londinium
Bath

GERMANIA
INFERIOR   Osterburken
Bingium
BELGICA

Rhine

RAETIA   NORICUM

LUGDUNENSIS

GERMANIA
SUPERIOR

Noviodunum   Aquileia
Lugdunum   Po
AQUITANIA   Ravenna
Vienne
Pollentia
NARBONENSIS   Heba   Tiber
Nemausus   Rome
Narbo   Saepin
                                              Pu
1 ALPES GRAIAE ET   Misenum
   POENINAE
2 ALPES COTTIAE
3 ALPES MARITIMAE

TARRACONENSIS   Balearic Islands

LUSITANIA

SARDINIA ET CORSICA

Hippo Diarrhytus
Utica
BAETICA   Irni   Thibica Carthago
Salpensa Urso   Saldae   Thuburbo Maius
         Malaca   Saltus Burunitanus
                              NUMIDIA
Souk el Arba MAURETANIA MAURETANIA CAESARIENSIS AFRICA
              TINGITANA   Lambaesis

Azemmour

0   250   500   750 Kilometers

0   150   300   450 Miles

The Roman Empire circa AD 117.

DACIA

irmium

MOESIA INFERIOR

Marcianopolis

Tieion

ARMENIA

MOESIA SUPERIOR

Pizus

Byzantium

BITHYNIA ET PONTUS

GALATIA ET CAPPADOCIA

Samosata

MESOPOTAMIA

THRACIA

Nicomedia

Juliopolis

Skaptopara

Cyzicus

Prusa

PHRYGIA

Sülümenli

CILICIA

Philippi

Samothrace

Ioudda

LYDIA

Antioch

MACEDONIA

Thessalonica

Pergamum

ASIA

PISIDIA

Tarsus

SYRIA

Beroea

Smyrna

Aphrodisias

Aspendus

ISAURIA

ACHAEA

Thebes

Ephesus

CARIA

Boubon

Ovacık

Salamis

Hypata

LYCIA

Olympus

CYPRUS

Corinth

Athens

CRETA
(et Cyrene)

Tiberias
Nazareth

Tyre
Caesarea

JUDAEA

Qumran

Jerusalem

Alexandria

Nicopolis

ARABIA

Cyrene

Memphis

Bacchias

FAYUM

CYRENE

AEGYPTUS

Soknopaiou Nesos

Arsinoe

Karanis

Tebtunis

Cynopolis

Mons
Claudianus

Oxyrhynchus

Nile

Hermopolis

Apollonopolis Heptakomias

THEBAIS

Thebes

Gholaia (Bu Njem)

N
W   E
S

Policing the Roman Empire

I

Introduction

The Jews from Asia, who had seen [Paul] in the temple, stirred up the whole crowd. They seized him, shouting, "Fellow Israelites, help! This is the man who is teaching everyone everywhere against our people, our law, and this place; more than that, he has actually brought Greeks into the temple and has defiled this holy place." ... Then all the city was aroused, and the people rushed together. They seized Paul and dragged him out of the temple, and immediately the doors were shut. While they were trying to kill him, word came to the tribune of the cohort that all Jerusalem was in an uproar. Immediately he took soldiers and centurions and ran down to them. When they saw the tribune and the soldiers, they stopped beating Paul. Then the tribune came, arrested him, and ordered him to be bound with two chains; he inquired who he was and what he had done. Some in the crowd shouted one thing, some another; and as he could not learn the facts because of the uproar, he ordered him to be brought into the barracks. When Paul came to the steps, the violence of the mob was so great that he had to be carried by the soldiers. The crowd that followed kept shouting, "Away with him!" Just as Paul was about to be brought into the barracks, he said to the tribune, "May I say something to you?" The tribune replied, "Do you know Greek? Then you are not the Egyptian who recently stirred up a revolt and led the four thousand assassins out into the wilderness?" Paul replied, "I am a Jew, from Tarsus in Cilicia, a citizen of an important city; I beg you, let me speak to the people." When he had given him permission, Paul stood on the steps and motioned to the people for silence; and when there was a great hush, he addressed them in the Hebrew language.[1]

Suspicion, confusion, ethnic hostility—few passages in Roman imperial literature touch on as many complex troubles and explosive sensitivities as

---

1. Acts 21:27–40, slightly adapted from the NRSV. Cf. Acts 23:10. On the Egyptian revolutionary, see Josephus *BJ* 2.261–3.

this passage from Acts of the Apostles. In fact, there are eleven other incidents from Acts in which Paul's missionary activity nearly makes him a martyr, as he incited arrests, riots, attacks, and assassination attempts from various groups in several cities.[2] In this case, he was saved by the chance presence of Roman soldiers acting as keepers of the peace. But in many locales during the early empire, there was no visible Roman presence, and even where intractable problems hurt local communities, Roman officials were loath to entangle themselves in messy provincial affairs. We should remember how Paul's Messiah died. Although the procurator Pontius Pilate, according to our accounts, thought him innocent, he "washed his hands" of the whole affair and executed Jesus to placate an angry rabble.[3]

Contrary to the reputation of the *pax Romana*, the territory of the Roman Empire was anything but naturally peaceful, and governors often had great difficulty meeting their fundamental imperial mandate: to keep their provinces "pacified and quiet."[4] Threats to public order were plentiful in Italy and the provinces, from banditry and petty thefts to intercity rivalries and boundary disputes and even a large amphitheater riot between sports-crazed partisans of two Italian towns.[5] Hungry mobs threatened to immolate local leaders in times of famine.[6] Travel was risky, for both elite citizens and commoners. Jesus's parable of the Good Samaritan, who cared for a victim of bandits, surely resonated with its audience: bandit violence continually appears in novels, papyri, and contemporary tombstones marked "killed by brigands."[7]

---

2. Acts 9:23, 9:29, 13:50, 14:5, 14:19, 16:19–24, 17:5–9, 17:13, 18:12–17, 19:23–40, 20:3, cf. 20:19; usually, the author blames "the Jews." Cf. 2 Cor. 11:25–27: "Three times I was beaten with rods. Once I received a stoning…on frequent journeys, in danger from rivers, danger from bandits, danger from my own people, danger from Gentiles, danger in the city, danger in the wilderness, danger at sea." Cf. Wolff, "Le voyage et les juristes," 333–34.

3. Mark 15, Matt. 27, Luke 23, and John 18–19; contrast the proconsul Gallio's attitude in Acts 18:12–17. Pilate's hand washing is found only in Matt. 27:24 and is alluded to in the beginning of the extant fragment of the second-century *Gospel of Peter*.

4. Ulpian *Dig.* 1.18.13.pr.: *pacata atque quieta.*

5. Tac. *Ann.* 14.17, between residents of Pompeii and Nuceria in the year 59. Fagan (*Lure of the Arena*, 95) notes, "So far as we can tell, the Pompeii riot was a singular event in the history of the Roman *munera*." A fresco in a Pompeian home probably depicts the event: NM inv. 112222 from house I.iii.23.

6. Dio Chrys. *Or.* 46 (Prusa ad Olympum); Philostr. *VA* 1.15 (Aspendus in Pamphylia) and *VS* 1.23.1 (Athens). Even Claudius and Antoninus Pius were assaulted in Rome during grain shortages: Suet. *Claud.* 18.2 and *Epitome de Caes.* 15.9.

7. Elite victims: The *Laudatio Turiae* states that the wealthy wife's parents were apparently murdered in the countryside: ILS 8393.1.3–6. Pliny *Ep.* 6.25: "You write that the eminent Roman knight Robustus had traveled along with my friend Atilius Scaurus as

Christian literature from the provinces abounds in "like a thief in the night" imagery.[8] To be sure, the achievement of the Roman peace was quite real. The large area it covered had never enjoyed as much political and military stability as it did in the first two centuries AD, and future centuries have yet to match Rome's achievement. Yet keeping the imperial peace was not easy; an honest assessment of challenges to the Roman Empire should make us appreciate it more, not less.

Leaders in the Roman Empire had various means to stem the disorders they faced: community self-regulation, a well-developed tradition of civil law if that failed, the anxious supervision of local elites as a further safeguard, and, when necessary, the real threat of large-scale repercussions.

However, the absence of police in many episodes of disorder in the Roman Empire is striking. In modern society, we expect the police to ensure some modicum of security and saddle them with all sorts of duties: they pursue and arrest criminals, investigate crime, enforce laws, protect the community, regulate traffic, perform undercover operations, testify in trials, and even act as family counselors. Moreover, we expect our police to be professional, upright, and impartial. Critics might object that this is a comfortable, white, middle-class view, since in reality, poor and minority communities are often estranged from their local police forces. But pointing out various shortcomings of modern police draws on the same idealized expectations. While these high standards are never fully met, our high hopes for police seem to have nearly universal currency.

Rome's empire had no such police force, nothing as ambitious and wide-ranging that addressed all of these aspects with one institution. Although the word ultimately derives from *polis*, the ancient Greek word for a city-state, "police" is a modern idea, laden with modern expectations. The institution as we know it is rather recent: with various paramilitary and constabulary

---

far as Ocriculum, but then disappeared; you ask that Scaurus come and lead us in search of any trace of him, if he can. He will come, though I fear it will be in vain." The same letter mentions a centurion who suffered a similar fate. On humbler victims attacked by bandits, *ILS* 8504–08, Luke 10:30, and Gunnella, "Morti improvvise," 13–15. On the general prevalence of violence, see Fagan, "Violence."

8. E.g., 1 Thess. 5:2, Luke 12:39, 2 Pet. 3:10, Rev. 3:3 and 16:15. The *Gospel of Thomas* is particularly rich on this theme: "So I say, if the owner of a house knows that a thief is coming, he will be on guard before the thief arrives" (Saying 21); "Blessings on you if you know where the robbers will enter so you can wake up, rouse your estate, and arm yourself before they break in" (103; cf. Saying 35, Mark 3:27, Matt. 24:43). Translation from Barnstone and Meyer, *The Gnostic Bible*. Most scholars date the *Gospel of Thomas* to the second century AD.

antecedents in early modern Europe, the history of modern police properly begins with Robert Peel's "Bobbies" in London during the 1820s. It is important to avoid anachronistic thinking, and many historians altogether eschew the term "police" in connection with ancient society. (Specialists in ancient Egypt, on the other hand, have no qualms about using the word "police" to describe figures such as the *phylakitai* and *archephodoi,* so well attested in the papyri.) Neither Greek nor Latin has an equivalent concept or term. I use the word cautiously. Indeed, in the following pages, I often discuss Roman policing as a verb, rather than as a noun, focusing on the *activities* of groups that were armed and organized by the state to maintain public order within the empire. While acknowledging vast differences with modernity, it is fair to call some of the groups I treat here "police." It comes down to a matter of definitions.

Definitions and Levels of Police Authority

I define "police force" as any organized unit of men under official command whose duties involved maintaining public order and state control in a civilian setting. Here, "police work" or "policing" embraces the actions of men organized under state authority who attempted to impose public order by enforcing laws, state directives, and fundamental social mores with the threat of punishment. Specifically, these parameters (as I see them) include the following interrelated categories:

- Guard duty in all its varieties—bodyguards of officials, watches and patrols; the latter involves prevention of routine crimes such as burglary and arson.
- Mitigating disturbances (such as riots), whether by a show of force or by exemplary punishment of selected individuals.
- Police in the judicial process—investigating or documenting crime, for example, but especially their use of physical compulsion or the threat thereof: arresting suspects, serving summonses, searching for people who have gone missing (including pursuit of fugitive slaves and those accused of crimes), torturing and executing criminals.
- Political assassinations, enacting repressive measures against Christians and other targets, and further examples of police carrying out official orders.

Additional topics will be touched on only as they directly relate to policing. I have not exhaustively treated subjects whose broader aspects do not entail security and public order—for instance, the regulation of traffic.

Ordinary civilians carried out important quasi-policing tasks through private initiative and noninstitutional means (see chapter 3 below). But my focus throughout is on *institutional* policing, by which I mean police work done by men who held some kind of official status, from local municipal authorities to major Roman officials. A concurrent goal is to understand how state institutions (the emperor, provincial governors, the army, or town councils, for instance) had an impact on public order, law enforcement, and security.

I have largely left aside the looser meanings of the verb "police," such as in the "social policing of gender norms." For the most part, my treatment omits frontier forces, foreign conquest, and large-scale military reactions to major revolts and civil wars. Although I often transgress them, my general chronological parameters run from the start of the Augustan principate in 27 BC to the end of Valerian's reign in AD 260 (important texts concerning Valerian's persecution of Christians are the reason behind this end point). I cite occasional evidence from other societies to put the Roman Empire into the larger context of world history, but I do not claim to do so systematically or exhaustively.

The purpose of this book is to investigate how policing worked in the Roman world, focusing especially on the role of soldiers. The Romans' approach to policing and public order, in the words of one scholar, was "extremely mixed and hard to describe."[9] Variety is the keyword. A wide spectrum of civilian and military groups policed the Roman Empire, from the municipal slave serving as prison guard to the praetorian guardsman outposted to a north African military station. As much as possible, I differentiate the activities of these various groups and meanwhile take regional variations into account. Rather than just compiling a catalogue of attestations, my goal is to explain the origins, development, motives, social impact, and overall significance of policing in the Roman world.

I write partly in reaction to recent scholarship that claims that the Romans and other premodern societies did not have (or seek) recourse to state institutions for enforcement, relying instead on "self-help" or "community self-regulation" as noninstitutional means of conflict resolution and social control.[10] What, then, will we find if we comb the sources for instances of institutional policing? That question was the genesis of this project, and answering it leads to a more well-rounded view of Roman approaches to public order.

---

9. MacMullen, *Enemies of the Roman Order*, 164.

10. E.g., focusing on earlier periods, Nippel, *Aufruhr und "Polizei"* and *Public Order*; Riggsby, *Crime and Community*; cf. Hunter, *Policing Athens* (1994).

The fundamental argument of this work is that the self-help model often fails to fit the imperial-era evidence and that state policing significantly expanded in the first three centuries AD. This is especially true of policing on the part of soldiers of the Roman army, who, I maintain, were increasingly detached from their legions and outposted among civilians as police in the second and third centuries. These soldier-police, and the trends that pushed them into that role, are essential in this study. The African Christian writer Tertullian could claim circa 200 that "throughout all the provinces military stations are assigned to the hunting-out of brigands," with hundreds of attestations of soldiers working as police among civilians in the second and third century.[11] Several types of sources from all over the empire evidence this growth of military policing: inscriptions, papyri, histories, biographies, novels, and Judeo-Christian literature.

The expansion of policing occurred as a result of an accretion of the state's ad hoc responses to security needs in Rome, Italy, and the provinces. When we can reasonably infer the purposes of police arrangements, the evidence often suggests that they aimed primarily not at helping ordinary men and women but at safeguarding the position of elites and strengthening state power. On the other hand, at times, Roman policing made ordinary people's lives safer and more stable, and officials sometimes worked to protect lower-class people from abuse. We shall see that despite recurrent corruption, all levels of society valued institutional efforts to improve public order, even if the security benefits that police measures brought to ordinary people were sometimes incidental.

In the following pages, I address a number of difficult texts and problems, and I hope that my perspective on them will be useful for specialists and general readers alike. One key aim is to clarify the different *levels* of policing in the Roman Empire. First and foremost, there is a fundamental division between civilian policing and military policing, carried out by soldiers under the command of Roman authority.[12] Military policing itself operated on three levels: imperial, gubernatorial, and, finally, the hardest to define, quasi-independent military policing by soldiers temporarily detached from their legions and outposted among civilians as police.

---

11. Tert. *Apol.* 2.8: *Latronibus vestigandis per universas provincias militaris statio.* Cf. Suet. *Aug.* 32.1 and *Tib.* 37.1 on the imperial origins of military policing and Aelius Aristid. 26.101 on roads and security stations (σταθμοί = Latin *stationes*) in remote regions that supposedly made travel safe (all treated in detail below).

12. Riess makes similar distinctions between civilian and military policing in his 2001 monograph *Apuleius und die Räuber*; see esp. 200–216 on "Das duale System der Strafverfolgung."

Because Rome normally allowed provincial communities the autonomy to run their own local affairs, municipal governments generally had the scope to carry out limited security measures, from levying occasional citizen night watches to authorizing specialized "peace officer" magistracies. I define "civilian policing" as the security and law-enforcement functions of civilian militias, local magistrates and their subordinates, or groups of guards organized and administered by individual communities. This definition excludes any group under the direct command of Roman authorities (the emperor and officials working for him, such as governors or procurators), specifically anyone serving as a Roman soldier. We will see that civilian policing by provincial communities is marked by variety and, in many areas, sparseness. Most of western Europe, for instance, seems to have had no regular, standing civilian police institutions in Roman times. Egypt, by contrast, had a daunting array of police officials.

Before defining the remaining levels of policing, we must review some important facets of Roman law and law enforcement. First, in the first and second centuries, most inhabitants of the provinces did not have Roman citizenship, a privilege that protected one from rough forms of summary justice.[13] Most non-Roman citizens were citizens of a provincial town or city and thus under the jurisdiction of that urban center's magistrates. The titles and functions of these local magistrates followed local tradition and varied widely. The top local magistrates could use limited force to deter crime, arrest individuals, and set up trials for minor offenses, both within the town or city and within the surrounding countryside (*territorium* or *chôra*) consigned to the community's authority. But Roman law mandated that many major criminal cases be referred to the provincial governor, who would be an elite Roman chosen by the senate or the emperor (rather than a local leader chosen by the provincials).[14] Ordinarily, only the governor could impose the death penalty in his province, although naturally, the emperor (or his special representatives) had the same power. In addition, neither in Rome nor in the provinces do we

---

13. Note, e.g., the officials' surprise upon learning that Paul was a Roman citizen: Acts 16: 37–38 and 22:25–29. The legal distinction between Roman citizens and noncitizens became moot, for the most part, under Caracalla in 212, when the so-called *Constitutio Antoniniana* granted Roman citizenship to most inhabitants of the empire. Another distinction, however, was already in place and came to predominate, in which *honestiores* ("the more honorable") were privileged over *humiliores* ("the more humble").

14. Until Diocletian's reorganization of the provinces at the end of the third century, Italy was not considered a province and had no governor. The emperor, his praetorian prefects, and the urban prefect of Rome performed some of the duties carried out by provincial governors elsewhere. See chapter 5 below.

find specialized public prosecutors similar to our district attorneys or directors of public prosecution; some of the powers of modern legal officials were included in the purview of provincial magistrates and Roman officials, but bringing a prosecution to court and seeing it through depended greatly on private initiative.

Civilian policing aside, the remaining three levels of Roman policing all deal with facets of military policing, that is, policing carried out by Roman soldiers. We can approach the massive amount of evidence relating to military policing according to levels of command. First, there were special troops under the direct command of the emperor or troops at the disposal of those close to him, such as the imperial family and praetorian prefects. The importance of the emperor was not limited to the troops he commanded; by assessing the rhetoric of imperial peace produced by, or directed toward, Augustus and his successors, we will appreciate the emperor's significance as a symbol of public order. Moreover, the emperor truly had an impact on security conditions in the empire, both by mediating conflicts and issuing directives and by involving himself in ad hoc policing missions by the direct use of troops (usually from his own guard, the praetorians). In seeking the origins of the emperor's role (symbolic and real) in keeping public order, we will see that most facets of this important role ultimately go back to Augustus, the first *princeps*.[15]

The second level of Roman military policing was the provincial or gubernatorial level. Provincial governors were quintessential agents of security and law enforcement, aided by troops directly under their command whom they often employed as police. Sources from a variety of perspectives show how conscious both rulers and subjects were about the importance of the governor in keeping public order. One indispensable text for understanding the governor's role is the file of correspondence between the emperor Trajan and Pliny the Younger, when the latter served as a special governor of Bithynia-Pontus.

The third and final level of Roman military policing concerns outposted soldiers performing temporary police duties among civilians, a practice that was markedly increasing in the second and third centuries. Notionally, these detached-service or seconded soldiers were always under the command of a

---

15. *Princeps* ("leading citizen") was an unofficial but carefully promoted civilian title of the early emperors, most of whom sought to avoid offending traditional republican sensibilities. See Wallace-Hadrill, "*Civilis princeps*"; Momigliano and Cornell, *s.v.* "imperator," in *OCD*. The military term *imperator* (whence our word "emperor") connoted a victorious general and was widely used by a populace unconcerned with republican niceties. It was Vespasian who first successfully took *imperator* as an acceptable title, although *princeps* was also retained: Levick, *Vespasian*, 66.

superior (the emperor, a governor, or at least a legionary commander), but in reality, Roman soldiers outposted as police could often act freely, without close supervision. We will focus especially on the many military police who found themselves working somewhat independently, manning new military policing institutions, such as the *frumentarii*. We will also examine the practice of stationing outposted soldiers (*milites stationarii* and others) for minor, temporary policing tasks. By viewing soldier-police in a provincial context and in their own right, we can see them as members of a rising military police apparatus— at times almost bureaucratic—which functioned more and more separately from older, more traditional elements of Roman imperial governance.

Increased policing by soldiers had a considerable social impact, and we will see ancient policing at its best and at its worst. The sources amply illustrate how diverse elements of society all hoped for greater security; the state partly responded to people's hopes by expanding institutional policing. There is also the consistent, dark theme of limitations and failures at every level of policing in the Roman Empire. Some provincials consciously desired a police presence to make their lives more secure, but ironically, the very expansion of military policing increased soldiers' abuse of civilians, evident in several sources.

These four levels of policing (civilian, imperial, gubernatorial, and detached-service military) overlapped to some extent, but overall they serve as a useful schema by which to arrange the scattered evidence. The ensuing chapters will follow a loose chronology, in which we see less mature police institutions in the earliest imperial years, during which there was a greater reliance on noninstitutional self-remediation and civilian policing in much of the empire. The later principate saw heavier growth of institutional policing, especially on the part of Roman soldiers. We will also proceed according to the four policing levels described above, beginning with a survey of self-help and civilian policing (chapter 3). The remaining chapters concentrate on soldiers as police, first under the command of the emperor (chapters 4 through 6), then under the governor (chapter 7), and finally, soldiers who were detached from their units and outposted among civilians as police (chapter 8). Chapter 2, however, shows all policing levels clearly in action together, addressing the one issue where the Romans made concerted efforts to coordinate every level of police power: recovery of fugitive slaves. Exceptional police tactics here reveal much about Roman priorities.

While policing and security measures in the Roman Empire were never perfectly realized, it was not from failure of imagination. Both elites and non-elites had clear ideas about how security threats should be addressed, and while their multiple approaches to public order make the historian's work difficult, they certainly reveal the Romans' willingness to experiment. Although we must be wary of anachronism, we should not minimize the richness of policing in the Roman Empire by constantly comparing it unfavorably with modern police forces. (Those who do so tend to idealize modern policing, which is far from perfect.) Admittedly, the various levels of policing in the Roman Empire were unevenly scattered and typically uncoordinated. But in addition to fugitive-slave recovery, other policing efforts prove that the Romans were capable of making innovative and wide-ranging changes in policing, such as the capital city's rather full complement of security personnel or the *frumentarii* soldiers who provided links among emperors, governors, armies, and provincials.

Developments in policing highlight major trends in Roman imperial history, starting with the disorders of the republic's fall and the civil wars, from which Augustus forged a new order; on to increased militarization and the fading of genteel republican façades; from a tiny and amateurish administration to a bulkier and heavier-handed one; from emperors who were largely content to leave the provinces alone to ones who pushed the limits of state power by empire-wide persecutions of Christians. As the *pax Romana* fell on hard times in the third century, Roman rulers sought to increase state control, and the state that emerged under Diocletian and Constantine differed radically from the Augustan principate. Policing was a significant factor in the evolution of the Roman Empire.

Modern Historiography of Roman Policing

I am not the first scholar to notice the trends discussed here. Fergus Millar, for instance, observed in passing, "The evidence for the increased pressure of exactions by troops and officials in the second and third centuries is matched by similar evidence for the rapid spread, especially from around AD 200, of guard-posts for police purposes manned by soldiers in the Roman provinces."[16] Millar cites only one authority to support this statement: Otto Hirschfeld's 1891 article "Die Sicherheitspolizei im römischen Kaiserreich,"[17] a good work for its time, but many new documents and approaches have come to light since then. Valuable recent contributions tend to focus on a particular region of the empire or on a particular topic relating to public order (law, ban-

---

16. Millar, *The Roman Empire and Its Neighbors*, 242, also noting evidence of increased banditry in the same period; cf. Millar, "Condemnation to Hard Labour," n. 5; and Campbell, *War and Society*, 90–91.

17. Also note Hirschfeld's 1892 piece, "Die ägyptische Polizei."

ditry, or relations between soldiers and civilians, for example).[18] I owe a clear
debt to them. But when scholars seek to make general statements about the
way policing was practiced in the Roman Empire, the resulting shortcomings
and occasional errors in their observations highlight the need for a new and
up-to-date comprehensive treatment of policing in the Roman Empire.[19] More
than a century has now passed since anyone has attempted a comprehensive,
synoptic overview of policing in the Roman Empire and soldiers' involvement
therein. As Brent Shaw noted more than twenty-five years ago, "The whole
role of the army as an internal police force in the empire remains one of the
most neglected of subjects in works devoted to the institution."[20] My goal is
to fill the clear need for such a work, while also addressing broader Roman
approaches to public order.

In recent years, no one has advanced the discussion of public order in the
Roman world more thoughtfully than Wilfried Nippel. His work forcefully
demonstrates how our own modern preconceptions of police color our view of
Rome's more "flexible" approaches to law and order. Using sociological methods and armed with impressive comparative material, he highlights the importance of communal self-regulation. He thus helps us to understand and
appreciate Rome's style of policing (or, rather, in many cases, the lack thereof)
on its own terms. When Nippel discusses "Polizei" or "policing," he often
refers to general social procedures of "self-regulation" and "communal means
of enforcement." (Again, I avoid using the word this way, focusing instead on
police institutions.) Writing on the late republic, Nippel has argued that Rome
lacked "a strong and politically impartial police force" or a "specialized and

---

18. E.g., see the bibliography below for works by Alston, Bauman, Brélaz, Kelly, Pollard,
Riess, and Robinson. I consider Brélaz's regional study *La sécurité publique en Asie Mineure*
the best book of its kind. Legally focused studies tend to minimize institutional policing,
such as Robinson's *Penal Practice* and Harries's *Law and Crime in the Roman World*.

19. Policing in the Roman Empire has not been particularly well served by the standard
reference works for antiquity. Despite the heading "s(iehe) die Suppl." *ad locum* in the 1952
Band XXI.2 of Pauly-Wissowa's *Real-Encyclopädie*, no article for "Polizei" was ever published
in the *RE* supplements or in *Der Kleine Pauly*. (Of course, the *RE* has valuable offerings for
particular components of policing.) Nippel's *Der Neue Pauly*'s article on "Polizei" deals
almost exclusively with earlier periods. The same is true of Badian's and then Cornell's treatment in the second and third editions (respectively) of *The Oxford Classical Dictionary* and of
the 2006 *Cambridge Dictionary of Classical Civilization*'s entries for "Banditry," "Crime and
Criminals," and "Public Order" (there is no "Police" article). These say almost nothing about
institutional policing or the use of soldiers in Italy and the imperial provinces. Carrié's
"Police" entry in *Late Antiquity* is dismissive of the militarization of policing during the late
principate; I respond to his perspective in the concluding chapter of this book.

20. Shaw, "Bandits," 18.

impartial law-enforcement agency." In fact, the emperors did not create one later, Nippel claims, since such developments come from an "innovation of the eighteenth and nineteenth centuries."[21]

Nippel's work helps to illuminate the state and society of republican Rome. It is certainly an antidote to an earlier generation of scholarship based on faulty assumptions. Consider, for example, Edward Echols's statements from a 1958 article:

> Wherever there is organized government, there is law; and wherever there is law, there is inevitably an agency for the enforcement of that law, for Man has yet to devise a system of government which is able to dispense with the services of an adequate body of police. Thus kings, consuls, and emperors alike had at all times an agency for law enforcement on duty in the streets of Rome.[22]

Echols then employed a faulty method of scanning Roman literature for the generic term *custodes* ("guards"), whom he imagined serving as professional policemen, to maximize the supposed police presence at Rome. As if Rome must have had a police force akin to that of modern London, his assumptions tell us little about the real practices of law and order in ancient Rome. In short, the author was looking for something that was not there, telling the evidence what it should say, rather than listening to the sources.

Nippel's contribution is valuable because he argues effectively against two opposite extremes: those who naively assume that Rome had a police force along modern lines and those who claim that the lack of a modern-style police force was a fundamental weakness of the Roman state. I bring neither assumption to the table. In fact, the very substance of my study of public order differs from Nippel's. While he focuses on the city of Rome during the republic, I focus on the entire empire during the principate. The difference in temporal scope leads to conceptual differences, some of which derive from the available sources. From the literature of the republic, it is harder to glean anything but an elite perspective. The principate brings the benefit of many more inscriptions and papyri from humbler strata of the empire and an immense

---

21. Quotes are from the preface (ix) to Nippel's most recent contribution, *Public Order*. For his use of the word "Polizei" or "police," see the other two main works where he has developed his thoughts on the topic, "Policing Rome", 20; and *Aufruhr und "Polizei,"* 7–10. With the exception of the last chapter of *Aufruhr und "Polizei"* and the last chapter of *Public Order*, he focuses strictly on the republic.

22. Echols, "The Roman City Police," 377. Cf. Lanciani's *Ancient Rome*, 206.

body of Judeo-Christian literature from a provincial perspective, not to mention picaresque novels that indulge in low-life escapades.

Moreover, Nippel's minimizing of Roman policing partly depends on exaggerating the impact of modern police. Comparing ancient Rome to London, it is seen as only natural that the elder city had no *modern* police force, and contrasting the two cities leads Nippel into many qualifications: there was no police force in ancient Rome or the empire that was *impartial, specialized,* or *investigative.* Beyond these limitations, there was much policing in the Roman Empire. Nippel applies these traits to modern police but says little about problems of bias and corruption or their inability to solve or prevent many crimes. Few would want to live in a world without police protection, but police officers themselves readily admit that many factors constrain their ability "to serve and protect." Large parts of America and Europe, meanwhile, subsist on self-help and view police as a force to be feared.[23]

In any case, there was greater state involvement in public order than Nippel and others sometimes seem to suggest. Noting that self-help remained important under the emperors, Nippel cautions against thinking of the praetorian guard and urban cohorts in imperial Rome as modern police forces.[24] This may be true, but one must not underestimate the cumulative impact of the proliferation of institutional policing, especially in the second and third centuries. Nippel is surely right to see self-help and communal self-regulation as key factors in Roman society, since they have been important forces in every human society. But Roman approaches toward keeping order were not limited to noninstitutional means, even during the early republic, when magisterial authority was unambiguously communicated by the terrible rods and axes of the lictors' fasces (see chapters 3 and 4 below).

Sources and Methodology

The ravages of time have left us a bare minimum of what was written in the ancient world, with the result that the historical record for most decades of antiquity is extremely patchy. On the other hand, the texts generated in the first three hundred years of the Roman Empire offer compellingly diverse perspectives, and the challenge of using them is worthwhile. No single ancient

---

23. See, e.g., Fagan and Wilkinson, "Guns"; Rawlings, *Policing,* 221–23 (on the modern United Kingdom); Zedner, "Policing"; and Levi, "Making Counter-Law." Cf. Black's important paper, "Crime as Social Control."

24. Nippel, "Policing Rome," 29.

source or author provides a very full view of policing. Rather, we must synthesize a series of scattered suggestions, hints, and anecdotes into a larger picture.

In the past, historians have tended to focus on sources that they thought could yield "hard" data, especially histories (such as those written by Sallust or Tacitus), imperial biographies (Suetonius and a few others), epistolography (Cicero and Pliny), inscriptions, and legal collections. They gave less attention to sources deemed lacking in broad application (Egyptian papyri) or strict historicity (Christian writings, novels). I have sought to use the former, traditionally privileged class of texts to their full effect but also aim to advance scholarship by drawing on sources that have often been passed over or have been incompletely integrated into the historical record. Obviously, in terms of discovering ancient practices, not all sources are of equal value; a relevant anecdote from Tacitus or Suetonius is usually worth more historically than one couched in some discouraged Christian's apocalyptic fantasy.

Even "good" sources are difficult to use for our purposes. Historians rarely wrote without antipathy or partisanship. While modern historical writing is supposed to be factual and responsibly sourced, ancient historiography prioritized rhetoric, moralization, and literary emulation. Biographers might also show bias or scatter anecdotes in an unclear chronology. Whether from tendentious motives, simple incompetence, or the nature of their literary genre, some historians and biographers were quite loose with the truth, such as the elusive author of the *Historia Augusta* biographies. Even within the narratives of supposedly sound historians such as Tacitus and Dio, fictional elements crept in; we might be safer thinking of their work more as literature, on the same spectrum as poetry and oratory, rather than reportage of facts.[25]

---

25. Woodman's *Rhetoric in Classical Historiography* is fundamental; also note Wiseman, *Clio's Cosmetics* and "Lying Historians." For recent overviews, see Marincola, *Authority and Tradition*; Potter, *Literary Texts* (esp. 12–21, 138, 144–51); Damon, "Rhetoric and Historiography"; and Stadter, "Biography and History." On sources most relevant to policing, see Grünewald, *Bandits*, chap. 6 and pp. 163–66; Riess, *Apuleius und die Räuber*, 349–74; and Riess, "Between Fiction and Reality," 260–64, 278. Bowersock, *Martyrdom and Rome*, chap. 2, gives a guarded but positive appraisal of the martyr acts' historicity. On particularities of the biographical genre, Saller points out that "when modern scholars tap anecdotes for historical information, they are using them for a different purpose than the Romans who recited them" ("Anecdotes," 73). The reliability of the biographer Philostratus has been assessed by three first-rate scholars: Bowersock (*Greek Sophists*, chap. 1, esp. p. 15), C. P. Jones ("The Reliability of Philostratus"), and Swain ("The Reliability of Philostratus's *Lives*"). They generally agree that despite inaccuracies, Philostratus's *Lives* are based on good sources and are more factual than his novelistic *Life of Apollonius*.

The speeches delivered to various audiences by rhetors such as Dio Chrysostom provide important historical information, but we have their orations as written texts that may not accurately represent what was actually said, if they were delivered at all. In the case of state directives found in legal writings or inscriptions—an imperial letter against official corruption, for example—we cannot be sure how long-lasting, widespread, or effectively enforced the measures really were.

Ancient documents and letters on papyri from Roman Egypt involve some of the same difficulties encountered with inscriptions and legal texts. As with inscriptions, papyri usually preserve only part of an exchange of documents. Incomplete texts make interpretation difficult, tempting editors to make dubious restorations. It can also be difficult to contextualize papyri, especially private letters. Moreover, petitions from victims of crime are formulaic and probably tend to exaggerate the ills suffered by the petitioner.[26]

Yet Egyptian papyri offer a wealth of information that we cannot discount. Some modern scholars do just that, bewailing the paucity of our sources while ignoring the region that yields the most documents. They rationalize Egypt's exclusion because of its peculiar history, geography, and administration.[27] Eminent papyrologists have strongly defended the "Romanity" of the Egyptian province against its customary exclusion from general Roman history. By the early third century, Egypt had certainly become more like a typical Roman province.[28] While space does not permit an exhaustive papyrological study

---

26. Rathbone, "Poverty and Population," 106.

27. After Octavian (the future Augustus) seized Egypt from Cleopatra in 30 BC, Roman emperors held it as a special province, ruled by hand-picked equestrian prefects rather than senators (who could not even enter Egypt without permission). The geographical compactness of the rich Delta and Nile Valley gave pre-Roman Egypt a legacy of unity and centralized rule, starting from the Old Kingdom pharaohs at the dawn of civilization to the Greco-Macedonian Ptolemaic dynasty that died with Cleopatra. Unlike the case with other provinces, Romans found (and kept) Egypt subdivided into clear administrative subdistricts (nomes), administered by _stratêgoi_ and various lower officials. Egypt was also the only part of the Roman Empire with an ancient, continuous tradition of police institutions.

28. These developments began soon after Roman conquest and include forms of taxation, municipal administration, and social stratification familiar to Rome. Moreover, the prefect of Egypt behaved like other provincial governors. The Severan emperors further advanced the process in the early third century, when Septimius Severus let Egyptian cities have city councils and when his son issued the nearly universal grant of Roman citizenship. Some institutions peculiar to Egypt persisted, such as the administrative nome and its subdivisions. See N. Lewis, "The Romanity of Roman Egypt"; Bowman and Rathbone, "Cities and Administration"; Bagnall, _Reading Papyri_, 66–68. Millar stresses Egypt's peculiarities in "Redrawing the Map?" 494; note Jördens's sound and balanced assessment, _Statthalterliche Verwaltung_, 24–58.

here, Egyptian papyri highlight issues of crime and policing attested to elsewhere in the empire, from "wanted" posters for runaway slaves to soldiers stealing pack animals. Such cross-references show that Egyptian society was not a wholly separate world unto its own but shared important traits with the rest of the Roman world. Egypt belongs in the picture.

The following analysis draws on a wide variety of texts, and some are more challenging than others for historical purposes. Novels richly illustrate daily life and offer fertile ground for studying policing, but bandits and the forces that fight them are subordinate tools of the plot. Accepting the novels' bandit (or pirate) tales at face value would be akin to assuming that most Americans have daily run-ins with the Mafia, based on the popularity of *The Sopranos* and Mario Puzo's novels. The Mafia is real; so was banditry. But popular culture exaggerates. In any case, the ancient novels remain indispensable for suggesting social and institutional possibilities. This is especially true of the Latin novels, Petronius's *Satyrica*, and, in particular, Apuleius's *Metamorphoses* (also known as *The Golden Ass*). Despite various mythic elements and far-fetched episodes, their impressive literary realism provides crucial insight for the historian. While Apuleius clearly hit his readers with events that many would find fantastic (a man turning into a donkey is the central plot point), he wove such episodes into a realistic tapestry of everyday life in the provinces. Within this tapestry, it is unlikely that Apuleius and other storytellers would conjure new security arrangements that would strike readers as inauthentic.[29]

Jewish and Christian writings supply valuable insights, despite the prevalence of ahistorical or supernatural forces.[30] In early commentaries on the Hebrew scriptures, second- and third-century rabbis described current social conditions in Palestine and diaspora communities, sometimes touching on security and policing. Those of us (like myself) not trained in the difficult philology of these texts are further deterred by problems of dating and obscurities that even befuddle experts. We should nevertheless explore what they can teach us about life in the Roman Empire. Rabbinic sources do not deal solely with Jewish affairs but often reflect tense relations with Gentiles and agents of the Roman imperial order in mixed communities such as Tiberias and Caesarea. Jewish sources certainly have more to tell us than what I could

---

29. On realism, note Millar's classic, "The World of the *Golden Ass*," and cf. Hopkins's comments about using the "lies" of the Aesop novel as a launching point for the social history of slavery in "Novel Evidence." Riess reveals the historical implausibility of the *Metamorphoses'* most violent bandit episodes: *Apuleius und die Räuber*, esp. 247–348.

30. Of course, many "pagan" sources also feature supernatural forces.

include here, but it is a start in incorporating a unique provincial perspective often absent in Roman studies.

Some historians also overlook Christian texts, unfortunately. The New Testament is a problematic historical source, and I am familiar with the many challenges in using it as such. Still, the Christian Bible was written in the Roman Empire and reflects attitudes and conditions there. Gospels are at least as useful as the novels, with the added benefit of some historical structure. The same is true of martyr literature, which lends key details about arrests, detentions, trials, and executions. Despite contradictions and unanswered questions in our texts, Paul's career clearly catalyzed Christianity's encounters with state authority. Patristic essays and letters elucidate various conflicts that deserve our attention. Among modern classicists and historians, the most neglected Christian sources are apocryphal and heretical tracts, such as the *Gospel of Judas* and the *Gospel of Thomas*, to name only the highest-profile exemplars. We have these two works in Coptic—another linguistic hurdle—but there are extensive texts in Greek and Latin (such as the apocryphal acts of various apostles) that have undergone little historical analysis. Some of these texts are tedious, clumsy, or altogether esoteric, but they reveal some provincials' worldviews, conflicts, and attitudes toward authority. In America, at least, they are rarely studied outside of seminaries and religious studies departments, despite their historical value. Our disciplinary blinders serve no one well.

We are lucky to have such a diverse and interesting patchwork of sources (including some art and archaeological findings), from a broad range of perspectives: commands of emperors, desires of governors, and the hopes of the humble; the views of imperial and urban elites and of alienated religious minorities. While it is never easy to recapture the perspective of ancient non-elites, we will see tantalizing glimpses of it in novels, inscriptions, papyri, and other texts.

The same variety can render synthesis difficult. Another factor that makes work in this field both exciting and potentially frustrating is that any day, a new discovery could throw everything into a state of flux. Indeed, the following discussion is largely shaped by the uneven distribution of sources, which suggest, for instance, that Egypt had many police but northern Gaul only a few. If conditions of climate and the habits of documentation were friendlier for the survival of texts in western Europe, then perhaps more police institutions there would come to light. Some scholars have become increasingly ambitious in employing social-science methodology and comparative evidence from better-documented periods and places to "fill in gaps" in ancient sources. I have drawn on some comparative material, both pre- and post-Roman, when it seemed particularly apt. But since the scope of this book is ambitious enough, I have felt it necessary to base my main conclusions entirely on sources directly relevant to the first three centuries of the Roman Empire.

Some sources are better than others, and no source is wholly trustworthy on its own. Yet we can build a fairly firm foundation by accumulating imperfect sources, which Keith Hopkins called the "wigwam argument: each pole would fall down by itself, but together the poles stand up, by leaning on each other; they point roughly in the same direction, and circumscribe 'truth.'"[31] We will question the truthfulness of specific sources or episodes as we meet them in the following chapters. And while no source is perfect, the cumulative weight of policing attestations in inscriptions, papyri, histories, biographies, legal writings, novels, oratory, and Judeo-Christian literature provides enough material for a significant analysis of how public order and policing operated in the Roman Empire.

---

31. Hopkins, *Conquerors and Slaves*, 20.

2

"Arrest me, for I have run away":
Fugitive-Slave Hunting
in the Roman Empire

THE PURSUIT AND recapture of runaway slaves is a paramount concern in all slaveholding societies. Cicero, for instance, while in transit to his eastern governorship, intended to go to great lengths to apprehend a slave of his friend Atticus; as governor, Cicero besieged an obscure Cilician mountain town for eight weeks, in large part because it was harboring fugitives.[1] Five years later, in 46 BC, he wrote to his friend P. Sulpicius Rufus, then a military commander in Illyricum:

> On account of our friendship, I…beg you to take pains for me in another matter: Dionysius, a slave of mine, entrusted with the care of my valuable library, has stolen many books and run away to avoid punishment. He is in your province. My close associate Marcus Bolanus and many others have spotted him in Narona, but when he claimed I had manumitted him, they believed him. If you could see to it that he is returned to me, I cannot tell you how grateful to you I would be. It's a small matter in itself, but it has greatly vexed me.[2]

Centuries later, we can compare a parallel case from another *pater patriae*. On September 1, 1796, President George Washington wrote to Oliver Wolcott, his secretary of the Treasury:

---

1. Cic. *Att.* 5.15 (August 51 BC); siege of Pindenissum (October 51, location unknown): *Fam.* 15.4.10. Cicero did not specify that these Cilician fugitives were slaves, but the word *fugitivus* commonly serves as a substantive for "runaway slave(s)": *TLL* II.A.1.a. Shackleton Bailey's (SB *F.*110) translation "deserters" seems unlikely; Cicero would have likely commented more about such circumstances in an episode he discussed at length to enhance his own thin military record. Cf. Tac. *Ann.* 14.29.

2. Cicero, *Fam.* 13.77.3; cf. 5.9, 5.11.3, and *Q. Fr.* 1.2.14.

Enclosed is the name and description of the Girl I mentioned to you last night. She has been the particular attendant on Mrs. Washington since she was ten years old; and was handy and useful to her.... We have heard that she was seen in New York by someone who knew her, directly after she went off. And [she was seen] since [then] by Miss Langden, in Portsmouth.... Whether she is Stationary at Portsmouth, or was there *en passant* only, is uncertain; but as it is the last we have heard of her, I would thank you for writing to the Collector of that Port...to recover, and send her back....I am sorry to give you, or anyone else trouble on such a trifling occasion, but the ingratitude of the girl, who was brought up and treated more like a child than a Servant (and Mrs. Washington's desire to recover her) ought not to escape with impunity.[3]

American historians have noted that white slave owners probably invested more resources in the recovery of fugitive slaves than in any other aspect of slavery.[4] Slave flight was no less a concern in antiquity than it was in early America. In fact, because ancient slaves had no particular skin color or ethnicity, attempted escapes may have been more common, and successful, in the Roman Empire. As a result, the determination of many Roman masters to prevent slave flight bordered on the obsessive.[5] Both Cicero and Washington seemed outraged at the insulting betrayal of a household slave, who, in fact, would have lived comfortably compared with most other slaves.[6] Both men sought help from important state associates, although recovering fugitive slaves was certainly not among Wolcott's or Sulpicius Rufus's proper duties.

One difficulty for both of these powerful slave-owners, and especially Cicero, was that there was no effective, specialized police force that could easily cross boundaries to pursue runaway slaves. (In fact, neither

---

3. Fitzpatrick, ed., *The Writings of George Washington*, vol. 35, 201–2.

4. Jordan, *White over Black*, 107.

5. Finley, *Ancient Slavery and Modern Ideology*, 110 (= p. 179 of Shaw's 1998 expanded edition); Bradley, *Slavery and Society*, 118–20, 129–30. Bradley's book is the best single treatment of Roman slavery and the control and resistance it involved; see also his *Slaves and Masters* and, on the republican era, *Slavery and Rebellion*. The fundamental work on slave flight is Bellen's *Studien zur Sklavenflucht*. For further background on ancient runaways, see Kudlien, "Zur sozialen Situation des flüchtigen Sklaven"; and Schumacher, *Sklaverei*, 284–7.

6. Compare the moral outrage in Seneca *Ep.* 107. Even the enslaved characters in Plautus's *Captivi* (line 209) pretend to be taken aback when it is suggested they might *fugitivos imitari* ("act like runaways").

Dionysius nor Oney Judge, Washington's *fugitiva*, were ever apprehended, it seems.[7]) It is true that Rome had a class of professional fugitive slave hunters, the *fugitivarii*, but they were notoriously corrupt private contractors, who would often conspire with slaves to finagle their escape. Late Republican and imperial legislation fought this practice, apparently with limited success.[8]

Servitude and freedom became essential elements of Roman thought. The first substantial point the jurist Gaius raised in his second-century textbook is that "the most fundamental distinction in the law of persons is this: that all men are either free men or slaves."[9] To the best of their ability, Roman elites strictly enforced this dichotomy between "slave" and "free," intolerant of any blurring of this distinction by runaway slaves. Also repugnant was the opposite extreme, the illegal enslavement of free people. This injustice was most often effected by piracy and banditry, which was at its worst in the late republic, was ameliorated somewhat during the principate, only to worsen again in the third-century and later empire.[10]

As Octavian emerged from the disorder of the late republic and consolidated his power as *princeps* Augustus, he paid careful attention to both ends of this spectrum. He invested considerable military resources to stop the rampant kidnapping of Italian citizens, who were then confined in conditions of forced labor.[11] At the other end of the spectrum, Augustus boasted in

---

7. See Cic. *Fam.* 5.9, 5.11, and 5.10a. Oney Judge successfully evaded a botched scheme to arrest her and return her to Mount Vernon. She last entered the historical record in January 1797, living as a free woman in New Hampshire, where she was able to contract a legal marriage. See Hirschfeld, *George Washington and Slavery*, 112–17.

8. See Daube's classic "Slave-Catching"; Watson, *Roman Slave Law*, 64–66; Rivière, "Recherche et identification," 183–91; *Dig.* 12.5.4.4, 21.1.58.2, 48.15; and *Pauli sententiae* 1.6a.1–2, 5.30b. Freedom did not have to be the only goal of flight; runaways might have to settle for servitude under another master—still a violation of status boundaries, as choosing where one would work was a free person's prerogative.

9. Gai. *Inst.* 1.3.9 (= *Dig.* 1.5.3); cf. *CTh* 10.10.33.

10. Pompey's extraordinary command against the pirates in 67 BC improved security in the Mediterranean, although piracy was not suppressed until the consolidation of Augustus's power, after which it would not reach a critical level until the late third century. For piratical kidnapping in late antiquity, see Augustine, *Ep.* 10* (Divjak; *CSEL* 88), and Schipp's "Der Raub freier Menschen." Even during the principate, banditry was endemic in many areas, and kidnapping remained a source for new slaves. This sort of enslavement likely bore basic parallels to African enslavement in the early modern epoch; cf. chap. 2 of *The Interesting Narrative of the Life of Olaudah Equiano* (1789), although some scholars recently have questioned if the African experiences described here were the author's own.

11. Suet. *Aug.* 32.1 and *Tib.* 8; App. *BC* 5.132, discussed further in chapter 4 below.

his autobiographical *Res Gestae* of returning thirty thousand fugitive slaves to their masters for punishment.[12] Family tradition may have encouraged such activity. One of the few facts we know about Augustus's biological father, Gaius Octavius, was that in 60 BC, the senate gave him a special commission to battle runaway slaves around Thurii in southern Italy. We are reasonably certain that when Augustus was a youth, his name featured the cognomen "Thurinus" by virtue of this victory, the last phase of the terrible slave revolts that shook Rome in the late republic.[13] Romans long remembered the menace of Spartacus and other slave rebels. Fear of a large-scale slave uprising was probably a significant motive behind the Roman state's measures against slave flight.[14]

Maintaining the legal rights of masters and rectifying the distinction between slave and free remained essential to the ethos of the imperial regime. Under Augustus, legislation was enacted that provided for the torture and execution of all slaves in a house where a master seemed to have been killed by a slave (in one controversial case under Nero, more than four hundred slaves were executed); this law was amended and reconfirmed by later emperors.[15] Pliny's Bithynian correspondence with Trajan reveals the continued imperial concern that slaves must not illegally escape their servile condition.[16] About a century later, Septimius Severus instructed his prefect of the night watch in Rome to use the *vigiles* watchmen he commanded "to seek out fugitive slaves and return them to their masters."[17] The issue is rife in the legal

---

12. *RGDA* 25; cf. App. *BC* 5.131 and Dio, who tells us (49.12.4) that slaves whose masters could not be found were crucified.

13. Suet. *Aug.* 3.1 and 7.1, with Carter's commentary in *Suetonius: Divus Augustus*, 92–93 and 95. Suetonius specifies that these runaway slaves were residue from Spartacus's uprising in the late 70s BC and from Catiline's in the late 60s. Augustus's father was an ambitious "new man" (*novus homo*) who died in 58 BC, before he could stand for consul.

14. Of course, Romans could not know that they would never again have to face a slave insurrection on the scale of Spartacus's uprising. The threat remained very real. Note Tac. *Ann.* 3.43, 3.46, 4.27 (cf. *ILS* 961), 15.46; Dio 77.10; SHA *Gallien.* 4.9.

15. On the *senatus consultum Silanianum* (which may have clarified earlier laws and traditions), see Tac. *Ann.* 14.42–45; *Dig.* 29.5, passim; and Buckland, *The Roman Law of Slavery*, 94–97. Cf. Pliny *Ep.* 3.14.

16. Pliny *Ep.* 10.29–30, 65–66, 74. Cf. Claudius's letter to the Alexandrians (*P.Lond.* 6.1912 = *CPJ* 2.153), lines 53–57.

17. Ulp. *Dig.* 1.15.4. On the militarization and police duties of the *vigiles* by this point in time, see chapter 5 below. Bellen (*Studien zur Sklavenflucht*, 13–14) notes the probability that governors' *mandata* (instructions from the emperor) contained similar orders.

tomes, which often specify the high-level interest of emperors, governors, and magistrates.[18]

Hatred of the runaway slave found its way into the Latin language. Much as with the term *latro* ("bandit"), a Roman might call someone a *fugitivus* to denote an utter scoundrel.[19] Spartacus and other slave rebels were likewise called *fugitivi*, denying them any respect, despite their rather effective challenge to Roman power. Even the firebrand wretch Catiline, Sallust carefully pointed out, refused to allow fugitive slaves into his rebel army.[20] Roman abhorrence of runaways is ironic, considering that their own foundation myths had Romulus populating his new city by opening an asylum, specifically taking in fugitive slaves and other unseemly refugees.[21] Later Romans

----

18. E.g., Gaius *Inst.* 1.52; *Dig.* 4.2.8.1 (on the importance of documents proving free status), 6.1.36, 11.3–4, 12.1.11.2, 12.5.4.4, 13.6.21.1, 14.5.8, 17.1.22.9 ("Titius" is akin to our generic John Doe, sometimes suggesting scenarios that are more academic than real-world), 17.2.60.1, 18.1.5, 19.5.18, 21.1.58 (and *Dig.* 21 passim), 24.3.25.3, 29.5.3.17, 30.39.pr., 30.47, 30.84.10, 31.8.pr., 32.82, 39.4.12–13, 39.4.16.4, 40.7.14.1, 40.12.10–12, 41.2.15, 44.38, 46.3.19, 46.3.34.5, 47.2.17.3, 47.2.36, 47.2.61, 47.2.63, 48.15.2, 49.16.4.15, 50.16.225, 50.17.23; *CJ* 11.48.12; cf. SHA *Macr.* 12.10 and Reinhold, "Usurpation of Status," esp. 296–97. Ulp. *Dig.* 21.1.1.17 covers definitions; some thought taking two steps in flight made a slave a runaway (21.1.17.9). The jurists sympathized with slaves whose masters were excessively cruel: Gaius *Inst.* 1.53; Ulp. *Dig.* 1.6.1–2 (citing Antoninus Pius and Hadrian), 2.14.50, 11.3.5.pr., 21.1.17.12; Paulus *Dig.* 21.1.43.1; cf. Papinian *Dig.* 48.3.2.1 and Pliny *Ep.* 3.14. Slaves often ran away at change of owners and other times of confusion: Ulp. *Dig.* 17.1.8.10; Paulus 21.1.58; cf. Dio Chrys. 45.10; Apul. *Met.* 8.15; and Biezunska-Małowist, "Les esclaves fugitifs." Sellers were legally bound to disclose if a slave was (or was prone to be) a runaway, vagabond (*erro*), or criminal: Gell. 4.2.1; *Dig.* 21.1.1.1 (from the edict of the curule aediles); Crook, *Law and Life*, 183–85; and Tomlin, "'The Girl in Question'"; cf. *Life of Aesop* 26 and Rivière, "Recherche et identification," 122–31.

19. Cicero frequently used the word this way. See Nippel, *Public Order*, 73.

20. Spartacus et al.: Grünewald, *Bandits*, 57–71. Catiline: Sall. *Cat.* 56.5, but also note 24.4, 30.2, 44.5–6, 46.3, and Cic. *Cat.* 3.7, with Bradley's careful reading of the evidence in "Slaves and the Conspiracy of Catiline." It was a topos to condemn using slaves for military service. Velleius Paterculus damned Sextus Pompey for accepting "slaves and runaways into the number of his army" (2.73.3; cf. App. *BC* 5.72). But this was often necessary. Suetonius noted (*Aug.* 16.1) that Augustus himself freed twenty thousand slaves to train as rowers against Sextus Pompey's very force. He later excuses the emperor's military use of servile manpower by stressing that he made sure they were legally free before serving: 25.2. The *Historia Augusta* (*Marc. Phil.* 21.6–9) justifies Marcus Aurelius's enrollment of slaves, bandits, and gladiators by stressing the military challenges, effects of the plague, and Marcus's humane funding from his own pocket.

21. Livy (1.8–9) and Plutarch (*Rom.* 9.3) both specify runaway slaves as a significant part of Rome's earliest populace. Dionys. Halic. (2.15.3–4) cleaned this up, claiming that slaves were barred. See Rigsby, *Asylia* 575–9; Dench, *Romulus' Asylum* 1–25; and Ver Eecke, *La République et le roi*, 71–80. On origins of the myth, Dench notes (15), "The story of the asylum is much harder to track before the late Republic," where our sources are very thin; Rigsby points out (575) that Fabius Pictor seems to have known the story in the late third century BC. Cf. Polyb. 12.5–6 on a similar etiology of Locri Epizephyrii in south Italy.

remembered this unsavory origin with discomfort, with Cicero calling the urban plebs of his day *faex Romuli* ("Romulus's shit") in a private letter, and none other than the brash Juvenal seemed embarrassed by his people's roots.[22]

Fugitive slaves populate the literary tradition of Rome and its empire, from beginning to end. The misbehaving slave was a stock character in the comedies of Plautus, our earliest fully extant Roman author (ca. 200 BC). In particular, his *Captivi* offers a plot featuring kidnapping, enslavement, chaining, direct discussion of flight, and torturous punishments for it that were extreme enough to serve as an example to other slaves.[23] Slave flight was essential to the plot of the Latin novels, alluded to in fables, and a common concern of people depositing curse tablets, consulting dream interpreters, or visiting oracles, asking, "Will I find the fugitive?" and "Is my runaway escaping?"[24] Nearly four hundred years after Plautus, the Greek writer Lucian spurned roguish philosophers as runaways in his parody *Fugitivi*.

---

22. Cic. *Att.* 2.1.8; Juv. 8.272–75; cf. Augustine *De civ. dei* 4.5.1. The story of the *rex nemorensis*—a runaway slave who ruled the sacred Latin grove of Diana at Aricia until he was murdered by a successful successor—reveals further dissonance amid Roman hostility toward *fugitivi*. The sources for the *rex nemorensis* depict the institutions as ongoing in their own time: Strabo 5.3.12; Statius *Silv.* 3.1.52–60; Suet. *Calig.* 35.3; Pausanias 2.27.4; Servius *Ad Aen.* 6.136; see Green's ambitious but speculative work, *Roman Religion and the Cult of Diana*, esp. part 2.

23. Note lines 110–28, 205–10, 254, 691, 723–31, 752–60, 962, 972, 998–1001, 1119–21. The *Captivi* is based on an unidentified Greek model, but the material is adapted to a Roman audience: Grimal, "Le modèle et la date des *Captivi*," 299–314.

24. Among fables, the most famous concerns Androclus (or Androcles) and the lion, as told by Aulus Gellius (*NA* 5.14) and Aelian (*De natura animalium* 7.48); also note Phaedrus *App.* 20 (= Perry 548), Plut. *Advice on Marriage* 41.144a (= Perry 440); and cf. Hezser, *Jewish Slavery*, 354–55. The novels will be discussed in detail below. Curse tablets: e.g., Jordan *GRBS* 26.2 #60 = Gager *Curse Tablets* #75 (second century, Amorgos). Dreams: Artemidorus *Oneirocrit.* 1.26, 1.56, 2.11, 2.19–20, 2.35, 4.1, 4.5, 4.56, all from a master's perspective; from a slave's perspective, 2.49, 2.53–54, and 2.68 (on literal flight). Oracles: Lucian *Alex.* 24; the cited oracular questions are *Sortes Astrampsychi* 36 and 89. The first question generates (randomly, by a "mystically" complicated but mathematically straightforward system) five possible positive responses and five negative ones (e.g., 23.6 in the text's *ecodosis altera*, or alternate edition, specifies that the slave will not be found because ἔπλευσεν ["he sailed away"]). The second cited question (89) offers a much better chance (nine in ten) of eventually finding the runaway. Cf. question 46, "Am I reconciling with my masters?" as the type of question a *runaway* might ask the oracle; 74 asks an important question for a slave considering flight: "Am I getting sold?" These *Oracles of Astrampsychus* originated in the second or early third century AD and were adapted and expanded throughout late antiquity, the Middle Ages, and the modern era. See Hansen's discussion in *Anthology of Ancient Greek Popular Literature*, 285–91; and Stewart, "The Textual Transmission of the *Sortes Astrampsychi*." On magic against runaways, see Pliny *HN* 28.3.13 and Rivière, "Recherche et identification des esclaves fugitifs," 115–16.

One might glean a more positive attitude toward runaways in Christian literature. The premise of Paul's brief letter to Philemon is that Paul's friend should reconcile with his slave Onesimus, who had left his master and come to Paul in prison.[25] In later antiquity, there was sympathy for Christians who were kidnapped on frontiers but escaped enslavement by running away. Most famous is Saint Patrick, who described his entrance into, work in, and escape from slavery in Ireland. Jerome also wrote what purports to be an oral history of a Syrian monk enslaved by Saracen raiders near the eastern frontier, and his harrowing escape. Patrick and Jerome provide rare direct accounts of slave flight in Roman times.[26]

But in none of this do Christian authorities allow slaves to run away or forgive slaves who chose flight. Early Christians challenged some elements of the dominant social order, yet most remained eager to advertise themselves as law-abiding subjects of the emperor. Much like Paul, the writer of the New Testament epistle 1 Peter (2:13–21) exhorted Christians to obey emperors and governors; the author then told slaves to follow the example of Christ and "accept the authority of your masters with all deference, not only those who are kind and gentle but also those who are harsh." There were no crusaders for universal abolition at this time; while an ancient Christian (or a Stoic) might esteem a slave as a brother, revolutionary efforts to end slavery were never on the table.[27]

---

25. For recent work on Philemon, see Barth and Blanke, *The Letter to Philemon*; Dunn, *The Epistles to the Colossians and to Philemon*, 294–349; and Nordling's Concordia commentary, *Philemon*. Arzt-Grabner argues that legally Onesimus was best described not as a *fugitivus* but as an *erro*, a wandering slave; "Onesimus erro" (but note *Dig.* 11.4.5). Cf. Pionius's companion, the celebrated *fugitiva* martyr Sabina: *Martyrdom of Pionius* 9, datable to AD 250 (Robert, *Le martyre de Pionios*, pace Euseb. *Hist. eccl.* 4.15).

26. Patrick was kidnapped in Britain around the year 400, when he was sixteen: *Confessio* 1 and 16–19; cf. his *Epistola ad Coroticum* on general enslavement of free people in Britain and Ireland. Much legend surrounds Patrick, but these two works are considered genuine. Jerome wrote *Vita Malchi monachi captivi* ("Life of Malchus, the Captive Monk") in 391, when he was in his forties, having heard the tale from the source when he was young and Malchus was old, thus placing the events in the early or middle fourth century. Cf. Jav. *Dig.* 49.15.27. On changing asylum practices in late antiquity, see Bellen, *Studien zur Sklavenflucht*, 8–9, 74–78, 124–25; Barone-Adesi, "*Servi fugitivi in ecclesia*"; Melluso, "In tema di *servi fugitivi in ecclesia*"; and Schumacher, *Stellung des Sklaven*, 37–43.

27. Quoted is 1 Pet. 2:18, on which see Glancy, *Slavery in Early Christianity*, 148–51. Paul on secular authority: e.g., Rom. 13:1–7. Some Jews of the Essene and Therapeutae sects were against slavery on principle, but this was one of several traits that made them look like fringe utopians; see Garnsey, *Ideas of Slavery*, 28, 78–79, 140–41. The Dead Sea Scrolls community (which I think was Essene: Magness, *The Archaeology of Qumran*) may have owned some slaves; see Hezser, *Jewish Slavery*, 236–37, 291–92, 300. The Stoic philosopher Epictetus, a former slave himself, dispassionately discussed runaways with neutrality, if not sympathy: Epict. *Diss.* 1.9.8 and 1.29.59–60; Glancy's reading of Epictetus is more negative: *Slavery in Early Christianity*, 89 (citing *Diss.* 1.29.63 and 3.26.1–2).

Moreover, the word *fugitivus* retained its negative force even in late antique Christianity, and the distinction between slave status and freedom remained essential.[28]

Methods of Fighting Slave Flight

In the American South, scent hounds were among the most effective, and fearsome, weapons used by masters to recapture runaway slaves. Some professional slave catchers kept fierce packs of dogs that were specially trained to "catch negroes," and sometimes the animals' masters had trouble keeping the beasts from mauling runaways to death.[29] This method of recapturing fugitive slaves was used in various times and places but apparently not in the Roman Empire, which is somewhat surprising. The Greeks and Romans certainly understood the concept of scent and appreciated dogs' special tracking abilities. We distinctly see this in the hunting literature, which catered to the elites' preoccupation with this form of leisure sport.[30] Moreover, there are a few suggestions of dogs being sent to track down people. Plutarch conjectured that Romans depicted tutelary deities with canine adornments because dogs "hunt out and attack wicked men." Writing in the late second century

---

28. E.g., Augustine *Conf.* 7.21; cf. John Chrys. *De Lazaro* 6 (Migne, *PG* 48.1038). Lactantius (*Div. inst.* 5.18.14 = *CSEL* 19, 460) still thought that runaways merited whips, chains, and even crucifixion. The mid-fourth-century Council of Gangra (canon 3) specifically anathematized any Christian who told a slave to leave his or her master; cf. Basil's *Asceticon magnum* (*Regulae Fusius tract.*, or *Longer Responses*), Question 11 (*PG* 31.948); and canon 4 of the Council of Chalcedon (AD 451). Glancy (*Slavery in Early Christianity*, 90) raises the possibility that some fringe Christians harbored runaway slaves, perhaps influenced by Deuteronomy 23:15–16: "Slaves who have escaped to you from their owners shall not be given back to them. They shall reside with you, in your midst, in any place they choose in any one of your towns, wherever they please; you shall not oppress them."

29. See Franklin and Schweninger, *Runaway Slaves*, 160–64. Outside the United States, dogs were used in the Caribbean (Franklin and Schweninger, 161) and in Brazil, where tradition holds that plantation owners developed the Fila Brasileiro breed as specialized canine slave hunters. These dogs are so aggressive that a 1991 act of Parliament made it illegal to own Filas in Great Britain. On specialist breeders and trainers of slave-tracking dogs in Cuba, see Ballou's 1854 *History of Cuba*, 177–80. In seventeenth-century Italy, sheriffs (*borgelli*) and their deputies (*sbirri*) used fierce dogs to track fugitive outlaws: Hughes, "Fear and Loathing in Bologna and Rome," 101–2.

30. Dogs may have been domesticated as early as 12,000 BC; their use in hunting certainly predates recorded history by millennia (Johns, *Dogs*, 9). Grattius, in his Augustan-era poem, calls canines the hunter's primary concern—the rest is mere minutiae: *Cynegeticon*, lines 150–51. On scent hounds, also note Xenophon *Cynegeticus* 4.9–5.7; Oppian *Cynegetica*, lines 451–513 (early third century AD); cf. Apul. *Met.* 8.4; Hull, *Hounds and Hunting*, 67–68; Anderson, *Hunting in the Ancient World*, 44 and 134.

AD, Polyaenus claimed that Philip, Alexander the Great's father, located barbarian warriors hiding in thickets by sending out several hunting dogs against them.[31] But if the idea to turn this canine weapon against runaway slaves ever occurred to the Romans, it was not practiced widely enough to enter the source record clearly.[32]

What we do see in Roman fugitive-slave hunting is a great amount of cruelty and concerted effort. Masters, who bore the basic onus of recovering their runaways, employed harsh methods to deter the escape of slaves who were considered disobedient or flight risks. These measures might include heavy chaining, permanent disfigurements from identifying brands, intentional scars, and—most commonly—tattooed letters, which our sources call *stigmata*. In extreme cases, masters might tattoo "Arrest me, I am running away" in large letters across a slave's face or forehead, a practice alluded to in Petronius's novel.[33] Other masters forced slaves to wear humiliating iron collars, inscribed with messages such as *tene me quia fugi* ("Arrest me, for I have run away"), commonplace enough to remain recognizable as the abbreviation *TMQF*. Some such collars were inscribed with

---

31. Plut. *Quaest. Rom.* 51 (276f-277a, on the *Lares*) and Polyaenus *Strat.* 4.2.16 both used the same verb for canine tracking, ἐξιχνεύω; cf. Plut. *Pomp.* 27 and (pseudo?) Plutarch's *Parallela minora* 21 (310e–f, suggesting a hunting milieu for Polyaenus's Philip anecdote). M. Argentarius's (Augustan era?) poem in *Greek Anthology* 5.16 mentions sending "Aphrodite's silver hounds" after a missing lover, but this is merely a hunting metaphor.

32. The closest our sources come to having dogs hunting fugitives is an allegorical dream interpretation in Artemidorus's *Oneirocrit.* 2.11: dreaming of hunting paraphernalia is "a good omen only for those pursuing runaways and for those seeking something which has been lost; (hunting gear) means speedy discovery of these things." A few lines later (and bracketed by modern editors as an interpolation): Dreams of "hunting dogs going out against their prey are good omens for everybody . . . but bad for those in flight." In Chariton's novel (4.2, mid-first century?), captives in a chain gang broke out one night, murdered their overseer, then tried to flee, "but they didn't get away, for dogs betrayed them by barking. So they were found that night, and fettered more carefully in wooden stocks." Here the dogs spoiled the stealth of the original crime, alerting others to the escape; no canine pursuit or tracking is mentioned. Apuleius (*Met.* 8.17) and Aelian (*VH* 13.28) have dogs brutally attacking runaway slaves as wandering strangers far from home, that is, by chance, not because their masters were tracking them.

33. Petron. *Sat.* 103.1-5, 105.11–106.1; and C. P. Jones, "*Stigma*." Jones argues (140–41, 154–55) that the stigmata mentioned in Greek and Roman authors are almost always tattoos, not brands, and suggests that the Romans adopted servile tattooing from Greeks, who had learned it from the Persians (in fact, the practice is found in pre-Persian Mesopotamian sources of various eras and is also attested in early China: see Reiner, "Runaway—Seize Him"). The slave's forehead usually bore the tattoo: Jones 143–49. Jones adduces the message of the tattoo from a Byzantine scholium on Aeschines 2.79: κάτεχέ με, φεύγω. Cf. Diod. Sic. 34.2.1 (Photius), 34.2.27, 34.2.32, 34.2.36 (Constantine Porphyrog.) on tattooing and the origins of the Sicilian slave revolt of 135–132 BC. See now Kamen, "A Corpus of Inscriptions."

Christian symbols.[34] In fact, these collars were most common after the Christianization of Rome, showing that the Romans' fixation on runaways survived major changes in religion and society.

Of course, it is not surprising that Romans were intolerant of slave flight, considering the inherent economic loss involved. (Besides stealing themselves, as it were, runaway slaves would naturally filch supplies for their escape.[35]) Indeed, Rome was not the first ancient society to take action against slave runaways. Papyri from Ptolemaic Egypt preserve several appeals from offended owners, demanding that government officials help them recapture their slaves. Treaties between Hellenistic cities in Asia Minor included provisions for the arrest and return of fugitive slaves. Evidence from classical Athens suggests both vigilantism and state involvement against runaways. And nearly four millennia ago, the Babylonian Code of Hammurabi mandated the death penalty for anyone aiding or harboring a runaway slave.[36] The Romans were not exceptional for their attitude toward runaways, which was neither new for its time nor unique in world history; it is their particular coordinated methods that prove exceptional.

Coordinated Efforts to Recover Runaway Slaves

In the context of Roman imperial policing, what is most significant about fugitive-slave hunting are the connections among the four levels of institutional

---

34. *TMQF*: e.g., *ILS* 9454. See *CIL* 15.2.1, 7171–99 for fourth- and fifth-century samples from the city of Rome (7184, 7188, 7190, 7192 are among those showing clear Christian symbols). Thurmond, in "Some Roman Slave Collars in *CIL*," posits that collars became more common as Christian leaders became less comfortable with face tattoos, believing that the face must not be disfigured since it bore the "celestial beauty" of God's image (*CTh* 9.40.2 = *CJ* 9.47.17; Constantine, noting that limbs remained liable to penal tattoos); cf. Bellen, *Studien zur Sklavenflucht*, 27–29. Rivière argues ("Recherche et identification," 146–64 and 193–96, *pace* Thurmond) that masters used inscribed collars and tags more to prevent kidnapping than to prevent flight; I do not think the evidence quite bears this out. As Rivière himself admits (163), collars or tags could be removed. In fact, the changeability of collars may have been an advantage over tattoos, since addresses, owners, and occupations (information included on some collars) could be updated as necessary.

35. Epict. *Diss.* 3.26.1–2; Paulus *Dig.* 21.1.58; cf. Apul. *Met.* 8.15 and Cicero's aforementioned librarian (*Fam.* 13.77.3). In his discussions of Paul's letter, John Chrysostom assumed that Philemon's slave Onesimus stole "many things" from his master before running away: *Laud. Paul.* 3.8 (Migne, *PG* 50.486; cf. 62.701 and further examples quoted in M. Mitchell, "John Chrysostom on Philemon").

36. Relevant Ptolemaic papyri include *P.Diosk.* 9; *P.Hib.* 1.54 and 71; *P.Hib.* 2.198; *BGU* 8.1774 and 1881; *P.Rein.* 2.94; *PSI* 4.359, 4.366, and 6.570; *P.Tebt.* 3.2.904; *P.Zen.Pestm.* 24, 36, and 43; *SB* 5.7569; *UPZ* 1.69 and 1.121 (= *P.Paris* 10). Hellenistic cities: *Milet* 1(3), 150 (= *Syll.*[3] 633).96–99, an early second-century BC *isopoliteia* treaty between Miletus and Heraclea ad Latmum (*BAtlas* 61 F2). Athens: E.g., *IG* I[3] 45 (ca. 445 BC); Lysias 3 and 23.9–11; Dem. 59.37–40. Code of Hammurabi: laws 15–16; note Snell, *Flight and Freedom*.

policing introduced previously: civilian, imperial, gubernatorial, and military. We will see that the Romans were typically content to let policing operate within these four divisions of authority, with minimal connections among them. But the Roman authorities were so intolerant of slave flight that they made radical exceptions to their normal approach to law and order. We see this most clearly in a single title of Justinian's *Digest*, 11.4, *De fugitiviis* ("On fugitive slaves"), much of which deals with Italy.

Fugitive-slave hunting in Italy presented great challenges. Especially in the south, enormous plantations (*latifundia*) had grown in the late republic, and the members of slave gangs who worked these estates outnumbered free citizens in many areas. Furthermore, because Italy was not a subject province, there was no single governor holding power, and large landowners would have been wary of having their property and financial dealings intruded upon. But what we see immediately in Ulpian's first two paragraphs of *Digest* 11.4 is the active involvement of the highest levels of the Roman state, the senate and the emperor:

1. The senate has decreed that *fugitivi* must not be allowed into woodlands (of estates), or be protected by the estate owners' overseers and managers; in addition, the senate established a fine (for this offense). The senate has granted pardon to those overseers and managers who, despite any previous misconduct, return runaways to their owners or produce them before the (local) magistrates within twenty days. Moreover, the same senate decree then grants impunity to someone who finds fugitive slaves on his land and hands them over to their owner or to the magistrates, within the aforesaid time.

2. This senatorial decree also gives a soldier or civilian the right to enter the estates of senators or civilians in order to search for a runaway, which the *lex Fabia* and the senatorial decree passed in Modestus's consulship also provided for, (and mandates) that those wanting to search for runaway slaves are to give letters to the magistrates, and institutes a fine of 100 gold coins for magistrates if they fail to help the searchers after receiving their letters. It also set the same penalty against anyone who prevents his own property from being searched. There is also a general letter from the deified Marcus and Commodus, in which it is declared that provincial governors, magistrates, and *milites stationarii* (outposted soldiers) must help a master who is searching for *fugitivi*, and that they must return the runaways after they find them, and that the people with whom they hid must be punished, if a criminal offense was involved.[37]

---

37. Ulp. *Dig.* 11.4.1.1: *Senatus censuit, ne fugitivi admittantur in saltus neque protegantur a vilicis vel procuratoribus possessorum et multam statuit: his autem, qui intra viginti dies fugitivos vel dominis reddidissent vel apud magistratus exhibuissent, veniam in ante actum dedit: sed et*

In order to coerce cooperation from local elites, the law put abettors of fugitives on a par with bandits[38] and further encouraged compliance by the threat of a fine. It specifies that *fugitivi* cannot even enter estates, much less make illicit arrangements with the servile overseers and managers of the estate. Paragraph 2 sets up a system to allow anyone, soldier or civilian, legitimately searching for fugitive slaves to enter another's property to search for runaways. All that is required is to submit a letter to the local magistrate, who is required to cooperate, under threat of a stiff financial penalty. Since they are thus admonished, it is reasonable to suspect that some magistrates were crooked or were themselves involved in an illegal slave trade. The general letter from Marcus Aurelius and his son Commodus reveals imperial concern over the issue of slave flight, and their directive applied to Italian and provincial authorities alike. Whatever qualms the emperors and senators might have had about the honesty of local magistrates, much is demanded of them in the recovery of runaways:

> 8a: The runaways' names, identifying features (including scars), and owner should be reported to the magistrates, so that the *fugitivi* can be more easily identified and seized: the same law applies whether this information is displayed publicly in writing, or if you display it on a temple.[39]

---

deinceps eodem senatus consulto impunitas datur ei, qui intra praestituta tempora, quam repperit fugitivos in agro suo, domino vel magistratibus tradiderit. 11.4.1.2: *Hoc autem senatus consultum aditum etiam dedit militi vel pagano ad investigandum fugitivum in praedia senatorum vel paganorum (cui rei etiam lex Fabia prospexerat et senatus consultum Modesto consule factum), ut fugitivos inquirere volentibus litterae ad magistratus dentur, multa etiam centum solidorum in magistratus statuta, si litteris acceptis inquirentes non adiuvent. sed et in eum, qui quaeri apud se prohibuit, eadem poena statuta. est etiam generalis epistula divorum Marci et Commodi, qua declaratur et praesides et magistratus et milites stationarios dominum adiuvare debere inquirendis fugitivis, et ut inventos redderent, et ut hi, apud quos delitescant, puniantur, si crimine contingantur.* The *Digesta* is a collection of Roman legal writings published in 533, under the Byzantine emperor Justinian. Most of its substance comes from much earlier periods, and particularly important here are the extracts from the books of Ulpian, who died in 223. The identity of Modestus and the date of his consulship are uncertain. Mommsen (note *ad locum* in his *Dig.* edition) thought he was probably a suffect consul under Domitian in AD 82 (*PIR*² M 657).

38. *Dig.* 11.4.1 is headed by the brief *principium*, "he who conceals a runaway slave is a thief"; compare *CJ* 6.1.4. On potential monetary rewards for disclosing where a slave is hiding, see Ulp. *Dig.* 19.5.15.

39. Ulp. *Dig.* 11.4.1.8a: *Eorumque nomina et notae et cuius se quis esse dicat ad magistratus deferantur, ut facilius adgnosci et percipi fugitivi possint (notae autem verbo etiam cicatrices continentur): idem iuris est, si haec in scriptis publice vel in aedes proponas.* A graffito from Pompeii (*CIL* 4.5214) states only the name and exact date on which a certain slave absconded; no other information was probably needed if he was well known in the neighborhood.

The public advertising of a wanted individual's name and identifying features was a commonsense tactic to recover a missing slave and has some attestations in Roman fiction and Egyptian papyri, which we will discuss shortly. However, such routine facets of Roman crime control are often obscured in our scattered sources. The level of specificity here is striking. The mention of scars also reminds us of the brutality of Roman slavery; ironically, the injuries and beatings that would have driven many slaves to flee also made it easier to identify and return them for punishment. Thousands of ugly modern parallels can be seen in the runaway-slave advertisements from the antebellum American South. One Virginia master's advertisement noted that scars on his runaway slave woman's torso would "prove her to be an old offender."[40] Many Roman masters were no less cruel.

The last short paragraphs of *Dig.* 11.4.1 lay out a careful process of arrest and detention for runaway slaves, whereby arrested *fugitivi* were kept under careful guard by the magistrates:

3. Everyone who apprehends a runaway must produce him in public.
4. Magistrates are justly warned to keep them in custody diligently, lest they escape....
6. "To be produced in public" means that they have been handed over to municipal magistrates or their staff (*publica ministeria*).
7. "Diligent custody" permits chaining.
8. They are kept in custody until they are presented to the prefect of the *vigiles* or the provincial governor.[41]

---

40. *Virginia Gazette*, June 22, 1782: "RAN AWAY from the subscriber, near Hanover-Town, on the 15th of May last, two Negroes; one a fellow named WILL, about 30 years of age, of a sluggish appearance, and remarkable for a large scar behind one of his ears and down the side of his neck....The other a wench named KATE, Virginia born, about 26 or 27 years of age, has many scars about her neck and breast...her back will prove her to be an old offender, and I am told she has lost a piece of one of her ears." Kate and Will's master offered a fifteen-dollar reward if his runaways were taken within thirty miles of his house, more if farther away. We do not know if his search was successful. From Windley, *Runaway Slave Advertisements*, vol. 1, 339–40. Slave hunters clearly benefited from their quarry's physical mutilations, occasioned not only by beatings but also by the grueling nature of their work. These newspaper advertisements often noted uneven gait, bad posture, missing toes, and other disfigurements obviously derived from horrid work conditions. The quality of life for slaves in the Roman Empire could have been no better: Bradley, *Slavery and Society*, esp. 107–31.

41. Ulp. *Dig.* 11.4.1.3: *Unusquisque eorum, qui fugitivum adpraehendit, in publicum deducere debet.* 11.4.1.4: *Et merito monentur magistratus eos diligenter custodire, ne evadant....*11.4.1.6: *In publicum deduci intelleguntur qui magistratibus municipalibus traditi sunt vel publicis ministeriis.* 11.4.1.7: *Diligens custodia etiam vincire permittit.* 11.4.1.8: *Tamdiu autem custodiuntur, quamdiu ad praefectum vigilum uel ad praesidem deducantur.*

The *publica ministeria* who served as staff for municipal magistrates would have been either magisterial attendants (*apparitores*) or public slaves (*servi publici*) owned by the community. Both *apparitores* and *servi publici* were significant elements in civilian policing. As for the latter, it might seem ironic that it was often other slaves who guarded recaptured runaways, but public slaves enjoyed a privileged position in the slave hierarchy and were vested in a number of official functions.[42]

The growth of military policing in the second and third centuries is further reflected in fragment 4 of the same *Digest* title, quoting the early-third-century jurist Paulus:

> Harbor masters (*limenarchae*) and outposted soldiers (*milites stationarii*) should hold arrested *fugitivi* in custody. Municipal magistrates should transfer arrested *fugitivi* to the support staff (*officium*) of the province's governor or proconsul.

Paulus's additional mention of *milites stationarii* points to the greater prevalence of this important type of soldier-police, discussed extensively in chapter 8 below. *Limenarchae* ("harbor masters"), about whom little is known, were included because escaping slaves sometimes sought to board outbound ships, as had Cicero's runaway librarian.[43] Other sources attest to the military's involvement in processing recaptured slaves.[44]

Further Evidence for Police Coordination

It is particularly striking that in this single *Digest* title alone, we have the mention of every significant level of state authority: emperor, senate, provincial

---

42. *Servi publici* dealt with the general upkeep of public buildings and temples and endured the drudgery of service as guards, doormen, and porters. Evidence shows that public slaves took part in search-and-arrest parties, guarded prisoners, and acted as torturers and executioners. See chapter 3 below.

43. Paulus *Dig.* 11.4.4 (= *Pauli sententiae* 1.6a.3): *Limenarchae et stationarii fugitivos depraehensos recte in custodiam retinent. Magistratus municipales ad officium praesidis provinciae uel proconsulis conpraehensos fugitivos recte transmittunt.* Lewis & Short's lexicon incorrectly suggests that *limenarcha* might be a Latin-Greek hybrid word from *limen* and ἄρχω, yielding some sort of border guard. They were civilian port officials, clearly more aquatic than terrestrial (note the first-century *limenarcha Cypri* of *CIL* 6.1440 and Alciphron's comical use of the word as a fisherman's name in *Ep.* 1.20); the limenarch's agent in *P.Wisc.* 2.80 (AD 114, Bacchias) checked a long list of imports; cf. *P.Giss.* 1.10 (AD 118, Apollonopolis Heptakomias), *Dig.* 50.4.18.10, and *CJ* 7.16.38 (AD 294). See further Raschke, "New Studies," 778.

44. Note, e.g., Arrius Menander *Dig.* 49.16.4.15, *P.Oxy.* 51.3616 (3rd century?), and Pliny *Ep.* 10.74 (a complicated case). Soldiers on the frontiers received and held runaways who had escaped the empire's boundaries: *Ostraca de Bu Njem* 71 (mid third century).

governors, Roman magistrates, and local magistrates; for policing authorities, we have private estate bailiffs, magisterial attendants, public slaves, and out-posted soldiers. These people rarely functioned together in such a way. Indeed, to my knowledge, no other concise passage in Roman literature gathers so many separate powers, bringing them to bear on one problem: the recovery of runaway slaves.[45] This case truly stands apart from typical Roman police practice. In fact, sometimes the authorities actively resisted having different types of police work together.[46]

But how trustworthy is this legal evidence? One might argue that just be-cause this concerted police arrangement found its way onto paper, it does not necessarily mean that it was widely practiced. The senatorial decree discussed here was probably occasioned by a particular problem, and the efforts at solving it may have been a short-lived, failed experiment. However, a closer look at this and other texts shows that this general policing approach to the runaway-slave problem was probably fairly consistent, widespread, and persistent.

First of all, note the mention of precedents in *Dig.* 11.4.1.2, that some mea-sures of the new senatorial decree were reiterations of measures already ap-plied in the *lex Fabia* of the late republic and in the decree passed previously in Modestus's consulship. Moreover, in fragment 3 of the same *Digest* title, Ulpian describes a closely parallel scenario for fugitive-slave recovery, citing two separate imperial pronouncements in a provincial, empire-wide context:

> The deified [Antoninus] Pius issued a rescript stating that someone wishing to look for a *fugitivus* on another man's estate could approach the governor, who would issue him [an official] letter and, if the situa-tion calls for it, one of the governor's attendants as well, to enable the man to enter and search, and the governor should establish a punish-ment against anyone who does not allow [his estate] to be searched.
>
> Moreover, the deified Marcus, in a speech which he delivered in the senate, gave permission to those wishing to search for *fugitivi* the right

---

45. We will see that Romans and local communities also did some coordination of police powers in their constant fight against banditry; for now, see Grünewald, *Bandits*, 72; Riess, *Apuleius und die Räuber*, 174–236; and Wolff, *Les brigands*, 62–67, 177–219. While much of the policing evidence on bandits also derives from the *Digest*, it is more diffuse than *Dig.* 11.4 *De fugitivis*. There was significant overlap between brigandage and slave flight; I am not sure that a strict differentiation between *latrones* and *fugitivi* would make much sense to a Roman.

46. In Pliny *Ep.* 10.20, Trajan clearly instructed Pliny to cease using soldiers and public slaves together as prison guards in Bithynia's cities, fearing that they would blame their negligence on the other party.

to enter estates, whether those estates belong to the emperor, senators, or civilians, and to search the lairs and traces of the ones hiding.[47]

It is rather surprising that Marcus Aurelius demanded opening even imperial estates to private searches for runaways, further evidence of Roman determination versus *fugitivi*; the senators, moreover, were used to enjoying carefully guarded privileges that normally prevented this sort of interference.[48]

Earlier parallel practices show that the ambitious coordination of police authorities described in *Digest* 11.4 were not new. Papyri clearly reveal the same sort of process operating in Roman Egypt, with the involvement of each level of policing authority.[49] For example, a fragmentary papyrus from AD 151 shows an active, rather than passive, approach to recapturing Egyptian runaway slaves, with different local magistrates (nome *stratêgoi*) posting to one another descriptions of wanted fugitive slaves who might be in their area of jurisdiction.[50] A similar fragmentary missive (*P.Oxy.* 12.1422) from one nome *stratêgos* to another in AD 128 accuses a certain Achilleus of harboring a runaway; Achilleus himself had then gone missing. We have a number of third-century public notices and petitions describing the physical appearance of fugitive slaves from Oxyrhynchus in Middle Egypt: one of these posters specifies that the recovered slave should be brought "to the military post."[51] In the same century, a woman from the local elite petitioned the *stratêgos* of the Oxyrhynchite nome to help her recapture a slave suspected of theft; she requests the further involvement of a civilian policeman, an eirenarch ("peace

---

47. Ulp. *Dig.* 11.4.3: *Divus Pius rescripsit eum, qui fugitivum vult requirere in praediis alienis, posse adire praesidem litteras ei daturum et, si ita res exegerit, apparitorem quoque, ut ei permittatur ingredi et inquirere, et poenam eundem praesidem in eum constituere, qui inquiri non permisserit. Sed et divus Marcus oratione, qua<m> in senatu recitavit, facultatem dedit ingrediendi tam Caesaris quam senatorum et paganorum praedia volentibus fugitiuos inquirere scrutarique cubilia atque vestigia occultantium.*

48. Robert, "Documents d'Asie Mineure."

49. For imperial concern over slave flight in Egypt, see Claudius's letter to the Alexandrians: *P.Lond.* 1912 IV.9, lines 53–57. Private initiative and self-help were certainly also operative in Egypt; *P.Oxy.* 14.1643 (AD 298) apparently shows one private citizen appointing another private citizen as an agent to go to Alexandria and find his slave. However, following the potential seizure of the runaway, the text specifies the involvement of state authorities in punishing the slave and whoever harbored him. On slave flight in Egypt, see further Biezunska-Małowist, "Les esclaves fugitifs," and Rivière, "Recherche et identification," 166–73.

50. Llewelyn, "P. Harris I 62."

51. *P.Oxy.* 51.3616.5: ἐν τοῖς σίγνοις. Cf. *P.Oxy.* 51.3617, containing a thorough physical description.

officer").[52] A fourth-century document shows a member of the provincial governor's staff attempting to use all of the powers of his position to arrest one of his own slaves who had absconded.[53]

Moreover, the procedures laid out in *Digest* 11.4 were already in the popular imagination. Petronius's mid first-century novel *Satyrica* illustrates municipal authorities' involvement in the recovery of a runaway. In this episode, set in southern Italy, Ascyltos has just arrived at the rented lodgings of the narrator, Encolpius, looking for their mutual love interest, the slave boy Giton. A party of municipal officials accompanies him.

> At that point…a herald (*praeco*) came into the lodgings with a town-owned slave (*servus publicus*) and quite a crowd of others, shaking a torch which shed more smoke than light, and proclaimed, "Boy gone missing a little while ago from the bath, about sixteen years old, curly-headed, tender and pretty. Giton by name. If anyone is willing to return him or give the needed information, he will receive a thousand sesterces." Ascyltos stood there near the herald, dressed in richly colored garments and holding out the reward on a silver platter as evidence of his good faith. [Encolpius tells the boy to cling to the underside of the bed, like Odysseus evading the Cyclops.] Meanwhile, as Ascyltos was going through all the rooms with a town messenger (*viator*), he came to mine, and it gave him extra hope to see how the door was secured with extra diligence. [After the municipal slave pries the door open with an axe, Encolpius tries a ruse: he falls down at Ascyltos's feet and begs his estranged friend not to kill him. "Why else would you have brought axes?" he asks. Fooled, Ascyltos is touched and makes up with his friend, explaining that he only wants to find the fugitive slave.] But the municipal slave was not so dull. Taking a cane from the innkeeper, he poked it under the bed and looked everywhere else, even holes in the wall.[54]

Petronius lays out one possible scenario in which local magistrates use their authority to give a civilian permission to search private property for his runaway. Despite the bizarre, scalene love-triangle plot and the obvious play on Greek myth, the passage is imbued with a certain realism with the specific

---

52. *P.Turner* 41. On eirenarchs, see chapter 3 below.

53. *P.Oxy.* 12.1423.

54. Petron. *Sat.* 97–98. Because of one of the text's many lacunae, it is hard to tell exactly what happens next. On the herald advertising a reward, see *Dig.* 19.5.15, Dio Chrys. *Or.* 7.123, and Lucian *Fugitivi* 27.

mention of the herald, the *viator* or messenger, and the public slave, all of which were actual categories of magisterial attendants and municipal employees who engaged in police work. All in all, Petronius neatly illustrates how local civilian officials might lend their police authority and resources to an offended slave owner. Ascyltos's pile of cash surely would have helped his cause. After all, much of the energy of Roman policing was focused on supporting the elites' interests. (Families of modest means regularly owned slaves, too, but assistance from the state was more available to the rich and well-connected, and in fact, flight from masters who owned only one or two slaves may have been relatively rare.[55])

Apuleius's second-century novel also specifically cites Roman slave-hunting procedure and police personnel in the Cupid and Psyche story, with wandering Psyche as the slave, Venus the enraged master, Mercury the herald, and Jupiter the magistrate. Aware of Venus's feverish search, the goddess Ceres threatened to take Psyche prisoner; when the girl begged for help from Juno, the goddess cited Roman law to her: "I am prohibited by the laws which forbid receiving others' fugitive slaves against their masters' will."[56] Next,

Venus immediately set out for the royal citadel of Jove, and demanded to borrow, with a haughty petition, the indispensable services of divine herald Mercury... to whom she anxiously spoke: "Arcadian brother, you surely know that I have never done anything without you there, and certainly you know how long now I've been unable to find my evasive maidservant. So there's nothing left to do but publicly advertise, with you as herald, a reward for the hunt. Go, then, hasten to perform my order (*mandatum*) and describe my incentives (*indicia*) for informants far and wide to anyone who might not know, lest anyone guilty of illegal concealment be able to defend himself by the excuse of ignorance." As she was saying this she handed him a public notification (*libellus*) consisting of Psyche's name and other essentials.... And Mercury obeyed, for he performed his duty of making the mandated proclamation far and wide, before all peoples: "He who can arrest from flight or reveal the hidden runaway slave princess, the maidservant of Venus named Psyche, meet the herald Mercury behind the Murcian

---

55. At least in rural Egypt: Biezunska-Małowist, "Les esclaves fugitifs," 77–81.

56. The search and Ceres: Apul. *Met.* 6.2–3; Juno: 6.4: *legibus quae servos alienos perfugos* [*profugos*, some mss.] *invitis dominis vetant suscipi prohibeor.* Venus first calls Psyche her *fugitiva* at 5.31. The Cupid and Psyche story features additional Roman legalese on matters such as marriage; see Osgood, "*Nuptiae iure civili congruae.*"

turning post (at the southeast end of Rome's Circus Maximus); he will receive the informer's reward from Venus herself: seven sweet kisses, plus one more made far sweeter by the gratifying caress of her tongue." With Mercury making his proclamation of so great an award in this way, lust inflamed the competitive zeal of all mortal men.[57]

Realizing that further evasion was now hopeless, Psyche delivered herself to Venus's door, where one of her household slaves (*famulitiones*) assailed her for causing so much trouble over the search. Venus calls on two specialist slave torturers of her household to scourge Psyche, but she eventually received Jupiter's pardon.[58]

In the novels, the cold policing procedure and legalese are part of the narrative's fun, setting a mock-serious tone inappropriate to the characters' circumstances. We cannot take them too seriously, but Venus's methods did work, and the search for Giton in Petronius's novel was almost successful. It is hard to determine how well the recovery process worked in real life; after all, once a runaway was returned to his or her owner, there was ordinarily no reason for the master to create durable documentation of the recovery for us to discover later. But if the process was vibrant enough to be noted in legal writings, papyri, and novels, slaves were probably aware of Roman tactics and would take them into account when weighing whether or not to take flight. This is the purport of a Roman-era fable, in which Aesop encounters a fellow slave who is just about to run away because of his master's cruelty. Without citing specifics, the text assumes successful pursuit and harsh punishment, for the wise Aesop persuades the errant slave to change his mind simply by asking, "If you suffer all these troubles when you've done nothing wrong, what if you *do* break the law (*peccare*)? What do you think you'll suffer then?"[59] Yet many slaves still chose to flee, and some certainly succeeded. Slavery was too widespread, and the desire for a better life too great, to deter all escapes, no matter what masters and their official allies did.

We do have hard evidence that outposted soldiers and municipal magistrates zealously worked together against runaway slaves—too zealously, in

---

57. Apul. *Met.* 6.7–8; some turns of phrase adapted from Hanson's 1986 Loeb translation. This episode echoes Hellenistic poems in which Eros is sought as a runaway slave: Moschus, "Eros the Fugitive" (Aphrodite as master); *Greek Anthology* 5.177 (Meleager).

58. Venus's household slaves are the minor deities Habit (*Consuetudo*, 6.8) and Trouble and Sadness (*Sollicitudo atque Tristities ancillae meae*, 6.9). See 6.22–23 on Jove's intercession. Cf. [Seneca?] *Apocolocyntosis* 15.

59. Phaedrus *App.* 20 (= Perry 548); cf. *Life of Aesop* 26.

fact. The problem is described in the Saepinum inscription from southern Italy, circa AD 170, preserving a subordinate's letter to an important imperial official (Cosmus, the financial secretary *a rationibus*):

> Written by Septimianus to Cosmus: The contractors of the sheep flocks under your care repeatedly complain to me in person that they are often injured on the paths of itinerant shepherds by outposted soldiers (*stationarii*) and the magistrates of Saepinum and Bovianum, because they detain in transit the pack animals and shepherds leased by the contractors, saying the shepherds are runaway slaves, and the pack animals stolen. Under this façade sheep belonging to the emperor are also disappearing amid this disorder. So it is necessary for us to write again (and ask them) to behave more peacefully, lest the emperor's affairs suffer. Since they persist in this same obstinacy, saying they will pay no attention either to my letters or to yours if you write to them, I ask you, sir, if it seems good to you, to notify the most eminent Praetorian Prefects Basseus Rufus and Macrinius Vindex to send letters to those same magistrates and outposted soldiers.

The rest is lost. It might seem surprising for the magistrates and soldiers to brush off the warnings of two imperial officials, but Septimianus and Cosmus were both freedmen, highly placed but of low social status. The *a rationibus* Cosmus was sufficiently influential to have Marcus Aurelius's praetorian prefects write to the magistrates of Saepinum, threatening legal investigation and punishment if they did not restrain themselves.[60]

---

60. A rare case of a community posting a document that does not put it in a good light: *CIL* 9.2438: (III) *Script(ae) a Septimiano ad Co/smum. <Cum> conductores gregum oviaricorum qui sunt sub cura tua, in re pr(a)esenti / subinde mihi quererentur per itinera callium frequenter iniuria(m) / se accipere a stationaris et mag(istratibus) Saepino et Boviano eo quod in tra<n>situ / iumenta et pastores, quos conductos habent, dicentes fugitivos esse et / iumenta abactia habere, et sub hac specie oves quoque dominicae / [diffu]giant in illo tumultu, necesse habe<b>amus etiam scribere quietius ag/erent ne res dominica detrimentum pateretur; et cum in eadem contumacia / perseverent, dicentes non curaturos se neque meas litteras neque si tu eis / scrips[isses] litter[a]s, t[e] rogo, domine, si tibi videbitur, indices Basseo Rufo / et Macrin<i>o Vindici pr(aefectis) pr(aetorio) e(minentissimis) v(iris), ut epistulas emittant ad eosdem mag(istratus) et stati/onarios [- - -]...factum est.* I have consulted the translation and interpretation of Corbier, "Fiscus and Patrimonium." Saepinum and Bovianum are in the Apennines, a little more than one hundred miles southeast of Rome. The *stationarii* here have been mistaken for a municipal force (e.g., Bellen, *Studien zur Sklavenflucht*, 103–4, following Mommsen, *Römisches Strafrecht*, 307); we will see that such agents are soldiers. The praetorian prefects likely wrote separately to the soldiers, and the magistrates of Bovianum, too, but only the letter to Saepinum survives. The quoted passage is appended to the inscription that preserves a dossier of three letters on this matter. On the *a rationibus*, see Statius *Silv.* 3.3.

Perhaps the magistrates of Saepinum and Bovianum and the outposted soldiers went too far out of honest eagerness to enforce the law. Shepherds were typically slaves, but their free mobility along distant transhumance routes could allow fugitive slaves to mix in. The *Digest* title discussed above opens with the warning "He who hides a runaway is a thief," and shepherds were already regarded as likely criminals who regularly engaged in brigandage. This wariness partly reflects the tension between itinerant pastoralists and settled communities, and lying on major transhumance paths, Saepinum and Bovianum would have seen a lot of this disruptive traffic.[61]

Most likely, however, Septimianus's interpretation is right, and we are looking at a series of thefts and abuse of police power in the guise of fugitive-slave hunting. We will see several other cases of police corruption. The Saepinum inscription also introduces us to another persistent theme, lower officials' problems with their limited authority, which led to greater involvement from the top in policing matters. The matter was perhaps handled by Marcus Aurelius's assistants in Rome, because the emperor himself was often attending to northern wars in these years. (Incidentally, the involvement of the praetorian prefects here is a chapter in the growth of their power, which was never negligible. By the end of the third century, their administrative, judicial, and military roles had grown to such an extent that they essentially became assistant emperors; see chapter 5 below.) Finally, we are also reminded of the difficulties in recovering fugitive slaves and of maintaining general law and order. Roman authorities failed to enforce their laws perfectly, but this is true of all civilizations. It is as important to note their determined efforts against runaway slaves and their willingness to monitor and address problems such as the Saepinum-Bovianum episode.

Conclusion

Looking at fugitive-slave hunting in light of policing and public order introduces us to key themes that will recur throughout the following pages: the pivotal role of Augustus and the precedents he set, the importance of imperial ideology and order, the inadequacy of noninstitutional enforcement alone, the four levels of police authority, the growth of military policing, and the shortcomings of institutional policing.

---

61. Ulp. *Dig.* 11.4.1.pr.: *Is qui fugitivum celavit fur est.* On shepherds, see Varro *Rust.* 2.10.1–3; Shaw, "Eaters of Flesh" and "Bandits," 31–32; and Riess, "Hunting Down Robbers," 195–202. Plato may have alluded to runaways disguised as shepherds in *Crito* 53d (cf. Aristoph. *Clouds* line 72 for the dress of a goatherd).

Runaway slaves inflicted economic harm and social disruption; if unchecked, they could threaten the ancient social order with the terror of a large-scale revolt. For the Romans, slave flight also violated deeply held social norms, which guarded the distinction between servile status and freedom. Concerned slave owners fought flight with every means available to them, including noninstitutional approaches (oracles, magical curses, threats, tattoos, collars, and private slave catchers).

They also clearly sought help from every available type of institutional police, from civilian magistrates to outposted soldiers. The issue was important enough to garner the attention of governors, emperors, and the senate. The result was exceptional coordination of civilian, imperial, gubernatorial, and military authorities, who cooperated with owners to help recover their runaways. This fact reveals how Roman society prioritized safeguarding the legal rights and economic interests of slave owners, especially the social elites who had the most access to the powers that be. As the biggest slave owners in society, they also had the most to lose, and not just in the economic sense. They were further motivated by enormous fear of a servile population that might run away with stolen goods and perhaps even murder them in their sleep or challenge the social order by revolting against Rome. Everyone knew these things happened.

At the same time, the evidence does not accommodate a simple elites-versus-underclass schema. Landowners who received and abetted runaway slaves were a major part of the problem.[62] As we have seen above and will see further in the following chapter, slaves sometimes policed other slaves, preventing them from and punishing them for running away. Granted, these public slaves and estate bailiffs were very privileged compared with most slaves and were essentially arms of the elites they served. Yet slave flight could hurt the lower classes, too, mainly by feeding into criminal elements, which would be more likely to afflict the poor than the rich. Slaves at least belonged somewhere; runaways who did not have anywhere to go became outsiders without country or community. Many who could not find stable employment probably had little choice but to turn to banditry. The rich were largely insulated from such crime.

So a mix of fears and complaints may be behind Rome's policing measures against runaways, but most important were the concerns of cooperative elites.

---

62. See the mandates quoted above in *Dig.* 11.4 and Jordan *GRBS* 26.2, #60 = Gager *Curse Tablets* #75, a second-century curse tablet against someone who had enticed a man's slaves to escape. For landowners' collusion with outlaws, note Hopwood, "Bandits"; Nippel, *Public Order*, 103; and above all, Riess, *Apuleius und die Räuber*, esp. 162–64, 181, 278, 292.

They are probably the most important "target audience" here, since Rome could not run the empire without their help. Of course, Rome's effort to stem slave flight also benefited the state by reinforcing the imperial ideal of stability, lack of which could undermine the power and prestige of the emperor and his allies. The Roman authorities' anxiety over slave flight pushed them to forgo their usual policing tendencies, choosing instead an ambitious approach to coordinate several levels of police authority. While they did not develop focused strategies on a similar scale to counter other forms of illegality and disorder, we can judge from the available evidence on fugitive-slave hunting that they were capable of doing so.

We see these determined recovery processes most clearly in *Digest* 11.4, but they are also echoed in other documents and literature. Most of this material reflects the high point of institutional policing, in the second and early third centuries, when outposted soldier-police increasingly appear in our sources. Noninstitutional self-help, to which we turn next, was certainly employed by owners asserting their legal authority over their slaves. But again, self-help by itself was apparently not sufficient, for it is clear that offended slave masters called on every available level of state policing authority. They were not the only ones who hoped for more institutional policing to help them with their problems.

3

"Like a thief in the night": Self-help, Magisterial Authority, and Civilian Policing

PLINY, WRITING AS the governor of Bithynia to Trajan, clearly wanted to use Roman soldiers to police one of his province's cities. Realizing that precedents were important to the emperor, he began his request with one: "You acted most wisely, my lord, when you instructed the distinguished senator Calpurnius Macer to send a legionary detachment to Byzantium." Then, most politely, "Would you consider whether you might deem advisable a similar arrangement for the Juliopolitans?" he asked, citing the small size of the town, its supposedly precarious position, and its heavy traffic load. Pliny must have been disappointed when Trajan denied his request. While recognizing that Juliopolis might be in need, the *optimus princeps* feared setting a precedent whereby all other needy communities would come begging for Roman soldiers. The Juliopolitans were on their own.[1]

Despite this particular rejection of using soldiers for policing, it was around this very time that soldiers were increasingly drawn from their legions to serve as police among civilians in the provinces. Subsequent chapters will detail this expansion of military policing and Roman officials' related oversight of public order. This chapter briefly describes everything else—the security practices of communities without military police or imperial favor, such as Juliopolis.[2] From individual self-help to magistrates and specialized civilian police squads, these nonmilitary arrangements that did not directly depend on the Roman state are extremely significant, since soldiers and their commanders were never meant to provide permanent, ubiquitous law enforcement. Even at its height, military policing was just half of the picture.

---

1. Pliny *Ep.* 10.77f., treated further in chapter 8 below. See also Brélaz, "Pline le Jeune."

2. Because I intend to expand on these points in the future, the themes in this chapter are not treated exhaustively.

We start with noninstitutional tactics, moving on to citizen watches, militias, local magistrates, and civilian police forces.

Social Control and Religion

In terms of stemming crime and disorder, nothing is better than preventing such problems in the first place. Certain intangible social factors, while not absolute, may have encouraged overall stability: patron-client ties, traditional respect for authority, and weighty class distinctions. Traditionally, Roman society had a marked respect for law and maintenance of social order, without any expectation of recourse to police. Gossip and literature could make individuals think twice before doing something disreputable. No one wanted his or her name scrawled in slanderous graffiti, nor would anyone want to be a target of a malicious poet's poisonous pen. Catullus and Martial, for instance, both censured dinner guests for stealing napkins—one of their tamer accusations. The Romans even developed their own literary genre, satire, to impugn those worthy of censure.[3]

Religious belief significantly influenced people's behavior. As an outside observer in the middle republic, Polybius opined that superstitions about the gods and Hades' punishments kept the Roman polity orderly and law-abiding. Many Romans believed that earthly misdeeds would bring about an unpleasant afterlife, a belief heightened by multifarious eastern influences (Greek, Egyptian, Jewish, and Christian, among others).[4] By Jesus's time, some sects of Judaism had developed hell as a place of punishment for the wicked, which is fully evident in Christianity. While many of the New Testament's prescriptions on avoiding hell have nothing to do with crime per se, transgressions such as murder and theft were thought to destroy a soul's

---

3. Graffiti: e.g., *CIL* 4.1949 and 4.4764. Napkins: Catull. 12 and 25, Mart. 12.29. On the role of gossip, cf. Hunter, *Policing Athens*, 96–119. On public shame as social control, see Burrus, *Saving Shame*; on dishonor, see Lendon, "Social Control," 86, and *Empire of Honour*, 30–106; cf. Barton, *Roman Honor*, 199–269. On satire's function of criticizing men's foibles, Hor. *Serm.* 2.1.60–86, Persius 1.107–34, and Juv. 1.145–71, all citing the precedent of Lucilius (fl. late second century BC). In truth, the satirists were reluctant to attack living targets by name.

4. Polyb. 6.56.6–15; cf. Lucr. 3.28–29, Sall. *Cat.* 52.13, Verg. *Aen.* 6.535–627 (where ordinary sinners are punished in Tartarus, not just major mythological and political figures). Early eastern influences: Faulkner, *The Ancient Egyptian Book of the Dead*, 11–12, and Spell 125; Plato *Phaedo* 81b, 108b–c, 113d–114c; *Rep.* 1.330d–331b, and, reflecting popular belief, 2.364e–365a, 366a. On fear of postmortem punishment, atonement, purity, and afterlife, see Cumont, *Oriental Religions*, 39–43, and *After Life*, 26, 29, 37; Betz, "Fragments of a Catabasis Ritual"; Graf and Johnston, *Ritual Texts*, documents 6, 7, 9; Edwards, *Death in Ancient Rome*, 78–86 (on Lucretius and Cicero); and Smith, *Traversing Eternity*.

eternal bliss.⁵ It is impossible to gauge exactly how beliefs in the afterlife mitigated criminality, and indeed, traditional polytheism laid more stress on punishments for misdeeds in this life.

The rule of the Greco-Roman pantheon, though fickle, was not as amoral as it is sometimes made out to be. These gods punished oath breakers, murderers, and corrupters of justice.⁶ The potentially positive effect of such belief would be to scare individuals away from rampant criminality. The community as a whole shared a stupendous incentive to police itself, thereby avoiding nasty collective retributions meted out by an angry deity. For, as Hesiod pointed out circa 700 BC, "very often even a whole city suffers for the crime of one man." Romans shared this basic mentality, that misdeeds within a community bore collective divine punishment.⁷ Gods both protected and punished; cities had tutelary deities, as did homes and other places. Priapus commonly guarded gardens, for instance. Travelers invoked Hermes and other appropriate deities for a safe journey.⁸

Ghosts also played a major role. A man contemplating a sneaky murder would wonder if the victim's soul would plague him later. Greco-Roman culture was awash with such tales.⁹ One need not commit murder to have con-

---

5. Judaism: Sanders, *Judaism*, 298–303 (of course, divine punishment can come before death; e.g., Deut. 25:15 on market cheaters); cf. Sirach (Ecclesiasticus) 7. Christianity: Matt. 5:17–22 and 19:16–18; 1 Cor. 6:10; cf. James 2:11, all echoing the Ten Commandments. Also note *Didache* chaps. 2 and 5; Justin 1 *Apol.* 12; *Apocalypse of Peter* 5–7; and Meeks, *Origins of Christian Morality*, 175–79. The Christian notion of salvation by belief alone (faith, rather than good works and upright conduct), while detectable in the gospels (e.g., John 3:16), comes largely from Paul's letters. The New Testament does not offer a unified perspective on how to avoid hell, with some passages prioritizing right conduct over faith; e.g., Matt. 16:27, 25:31–46; James 2:14. Despite his faith-based soteriology, Paul stressed lawful behavior and utter obedience to secular authority; see esp. 1 Cor. 5–6 and Romans 5–6 and 13.

6. E.g., *inter alia multa*, Homer *Iliad* 3.275–79, citing as punishers of false oaths not just Zeus but also the sun god Helios, rivers, earth, and the dead; *Greek Anthology* 7.516 (sixth or fifth century BC) on Zeus. Cf. Grattius *Cynegeticon* 445–60 (Augustan era); *Life of Aesop*, Westermann ed., 109 (first or second century AD); Philostr. *VS* 556.

7. Hes. *Works and Days* 240. Compare grassroots persecutions of "atheist" Christians: Tertullian (*Apol.* 40) protested that pagans blamed Christians for every natural disaster; whether it was flood, earthquake, famine, or plague, the common cry was "Christians to the lion!" Cf. Babrius 117 (= Perry 306).

8. Note, e.g., Cic. *Cat.* 1.11 and 3.29 on Jupiter or Livy 5.21–52 passim on Juno. The ubiquitous Roman cults of the *di Penates* and *Lares* (see *OCD* on both) involved protecting the household. Priapus's monstrous "tool" inspired later levity in art and literature, but at its roots, Roman culture (like many others) endowed the penis with apotropaic powers: Adams, *Latin Sexual Vocabulary*, 4–5; Clarke, *Looking at Laughter*, 63–73.

9. E.g., Suet. *Nero* 34.4, *Otho* 7.2; Apul. *Met.* 8.8, 9.31; Lucian *Philops.* 29; Kittredge, "Armpitting."

tact with ghosts. There was a wider notion that the spirits of the dead interacted everywhere with those still living; as one second-century lecturer noted, they "assist the worthy, succor the wronged, and punish wrongdoers."[10] Indeed, one could use these spirits and other forces against enemies, by resorting to what we think of today as magical practices. Antiquity has left us thousands of curses and magic spells, intended to avenge private wrongs, trip up opponents in upcoming court sessions, and punish thieves. Jewish and Christian elements crept into some of these texts in late antiquity, which shows the durability and adaptability of magical lore.[11]

We must take these magical sources seriously; the ancients surely did. There were scores of countercurses, defensive spells, and protective amulets. In fact, the *bullae* ornaments that Roman children wore around their necks were supposed to ward off the evil eye.[12] In a harsh world where people were desperate to have some control over their lives, depositing a lead curse tablet into a well or a grave provided psychological comfort. Casting a spell against whoever stole your cloak or plow might not work, but then again it might, and at least it was doing *something*. We even have a handful of so-called confessional inscriptions, in which criminals make public restitution for their crimes, believing that a deity was justly persecuting them in response to a victim's curse.[13] Magical practitioners can be found in all socioeconomic classes, but magic may have particularly appealed to the lower classes, for whom institutional help was least available. In other words, curse tablets and other magical texts provide rare written evidence for self-help.

---

10. Maximus of Tyre, *Dissertationes* 9.6. He apparently delivered his forty-one philosophical lectures in Rome at the court of Commodus. Cf. Plotinus *Enn.* 4.7.20.

11. The best introductory treatments are Gager, *Curse Tablets*;Faraone and Obbink, *Magika Hiera*; Tomlin, "The Curse Tablets" (from Sulis Minerva's cult at Bath); and Betz, *Greek Magical Papyri*.

12. Protective spells and antidotes: *Pap.Graec.Mag.* 5.70–95, 8.32–35, 36.178–87, 211–30, and 256–64, 70.1–4 and 26–51, 71.1–8; Kotansky, *Greek Magical Amulets*. A demotic antidote to poison and potions: PDM 14.563–74 (Betz, *Greek Magical Papyri*); Coptic examples abound in Meyer and Smith, *Ancient Christian Magic*. Cf. Pliny *HN* 28.3.10–18.65 and similar magical practices throughout other texts and corpora, such as the *Cyranides*, the "Damigeron-Evax" text about magic stones (in Halleux and Schamp, *Les lapidaires grecs*), and various magic bowls that come predominantly from late ancient Mesopotamia (see BeDuhn, "Magical Bowls," and Levene, *A Corpus of Magic Bowls*). Belief in the evil eye was widespread: Verg. *Ecl.* 3.103, Publilius Syrus 216, Persius 2.31–34, Aelian *VH* 1.14; in Jewish culture, *Avot* 2.11 (2.16 in some editions); cf. *Life of Aesop* 16.

13. On the efficacy of cursing, see Tomlin, "The Curse Tablets," 101–5; and on confessional inscriptions (mostly from second- and third-century Lydia or Phrygia), see Versnel, "Beyond Cursing," and Chaniotis, "Ritual Performances."

One can sympathize with humble bath-goers enlisting a deity's help against cloak snatchers, but the state was clearly uncomfortable with the crime and subversion that magic might provoke. As early as the fifth century BC, the Twelve Tables forbade casting malicious spells and cursing crops. In the first century BC, the Roman republic established a standing court *de veneficiis* that handled black magic. After Germanicus's death in AD 19, an official examination of his quarters revealed every sort of dark curse object: human bodies, spells, lead tablets. The emperors and other state agents sporadically and inconsistently repressed certain forms of magic and unsanctioned religious practices, especially when deemed potentially subversive. Varied wonder workers and holy men became figures of special knowledge and power, but they often came into conflict with mainstream society and secular authority. Astrologers were expelled from Rome at least ten times from 33 BC to AD 93 (sometimes philosophers received the same treatment). At the end of the second century, a governor of Egypt outlawed divination in his province, and the state became even more intolerant of unsanctioned magic in later centuries.[14] So here, too, self-help had its limits.

Self-help and Private Security

By "self-help," I mean addressing problems without recourse to state institutions. It was vital in every era of Roman civilization and evident in every phase of Rome's legal history. The right to repel force by force (*vim vi repellere*) was recognized by Roman law since the Twelve Tables, which permitted killing a burglar at night, during the day if the intruder was armed.[15] There were other

---

14. XII Tab. 8.1, 4. Germanicus: Tac. *Ann.* 2.69, 4.52; Dio 57.18. See further Phillips, "*Nullum crimen sine lege.*" On wonder workers etc., see Brown, "The Rise and Function of the Holy Man" (with 1998 retrospective), and *The Making of Late Antiquity*, 12 and passim; Anderson, *Sage, Saint and Sophist*; Francis, *Subversive Virtue*; for emperors' use of such figures to further their own ends, see Potter, *Prophets and Emperors*. See chapter 5 below on expulsions from Rome. Egypt: Rea, "A New Version of P. Yale inv. 299" (*SB* 14.12144; cf. Frankfurter, "Fetus Magic" on *P. Mich.* 6.423)." Late antiquity: *Collatio* 15 (cf. Exodus 22.18, Deut. 18:9–14); Amm. Marc. 19.12.14 and 29.1–2; *CTh* 9.16.4 (AD 357), 9.16.12 (AD 409), and 16.10.9 (AD 385).

15. XII Tab. 8.12–13; *Dig.* 4.2 passim; Ulp. *Dig.* 43.16.1.27; Paulus *Dig.* 9.2.45.4: "All laws and all conceptions of legal rights allow fending off violence with violence"; *Pauli sententiae* 5.23.8–9 (= *Collatio* 7.2). Cf. Cic. *Mil.* 4.9–11, [Luc.] *Asin.* 18, Apul. *Met.* 9.27, and Alfenus *Dig.* 9.2.52.1. On catching a thief in the act (*furtum manifestum*), see XII Tab. 8.14, with Drummond, *Law*, app. II. On self-help in general, note Nippel, *Aufruhr und "Polizei"* and *Public Order*, esp. 35–46; Bagnall, "Official and Private Violence"; Lintott, *Violence in Republican Rome*; Riess, *Apuleius und die Räuber*, 192–99; Krause, *Kriminalgeschichte*, 60–67; Rivière, "Pouvoir impérial," 27–35; Brélaz, "Lutter contre la violence"; cf. Hunter, *Policing Athens*, esp. 120–51.

cases in which a man might exact punishment on the spot (for adultery, perhaps). The family was a key locus of power, traditionally dominated by the
head of the household (*paterfamilias*). He routinely punished his slaves—
some households may have had specialized slave torturers for the task—and
even his adult children.[16] Numerous stories illustrate antique morality with a
paterfamilias executing children for grave public offenses.[17]

Romans considered the home a sacred space. The Twelve Tables allowed
an aggrieved citizen to summon defendants or witnesses to court (plaintively
shouting outside their target's door if necessary), but legal opinion condemned
invasive, forceful extraction.[18] All members of the household, including slaves,
were expected to defend their residence and storage facilities from illegal intruders. One essential and natural tactic was to call out for help, in order to
alert others to trouble, get assistance, or scare away the burglar or attacker.
This pure form of self-help is copiously attested in novels, papyri, and Rome's
earliest legal traditions. It also reminds us that the state's legal processes loom
in the background, since screaming for help would enable one's neighbors to
provide useful testimony in a later trial.[19] Here, institutional and noninstitutional methods intersect; prosecutions depended on private initiative to get

---

16. XII Tab. 4.2a; Livy 39.18.6; cf. Tac. *Ann.* 2.50; Dio Chrys. *Or.* 15.20; Porph. *Plot.* 11; Drummond, *CAH* VII, 147–48; Lintott, *Violence in Republican Rome*, 26; Nippel, *Public Order*,
31–32. Our fullest sources on specialized slave torturers are creative censures of excess:
Petron. *Sat.* 49.6; Juv. 14.15–24, cf. Apul. *Met.* 6.9. Slave owners at Puteoli could contract
torture services from a firm of professional undertakers: *AE* 1971, 88. Saller, "Corporal Punishment," 157–65, argues against equating parental discipline with treatment of slaves, who
were physically punished much more frequently.

17. Harris, "The Roman Father's Power," notes the dubious historicity of most cases.

18. XII Tab. 1.1, 2.3; Cic. *Cat.* 4.2, *Vat.* 22, *Dom.* 108–9; Gaius *Dig.* 2.4.18; Paulus *Dig.*
2.4.21 and 47.10.23; Daube, "Some Comparative Law"; Saller, *Patriarchy*, 89–90; Treggiari, *Roman Social History*, 74–108; cf. Augustus's 6 BC letter to Cnidos, *Syll.*³ 780
(= *IGRR* 4.1031; Abbott & Johnson 36; Ehrenberg-Jones, 312; *ARS* 147; Sherk, *RDGE* 67;
Oliver, *Greek Constitutions*, 6).

19. On protecting property and defending against housebreaking, *ILS* 8393 (the *Laudatio
Turiae*) 9a (cf. Dio 40.49); Vitruvius 6.5.2; Matt. 12:29; Luke 11:21; Matt. 24:43 (= Luke 12:39);
Apul. *Met.* 4.19 (cf. 3.6, 4.27); Paulus *Dig.* 1.15.3.2, citing a letter from Antoninus Pius; Alciphron 2.16 (3.19, Loeb, pp. 108–11; ca. AD 200); Aelian *Ep.* 14; cf. Tac. *Ann.* 14.43.3. On
shouting for help, see Lintott, *Violence in Republican Rome*, 11–15; Nippel, *Public Order*, 105;
XII Tab. 8.13; Ulp. *Dig.* 29.5.1.28 (citing Hadrian); Suet. *Nero* 45.2; Petron. *Sat.* 9, 21, and 78;
Apul. *Met.* 1.14, 3.27, 4.10, 7.7, 8.29; cf. 3.29 (= [Luc.] *Asin.* 16), invoking the emperor. Similar
behavior is attested throughout the ancient Mediterranean (see Lintott, *Violence, Civil Strife
and Revolution*, 18–23), including classical Athens (Aristoph. *Clouds*, lines 1297 and 1321–25;
Lysias 3.11–19; Hunter, *Policing Athens*, 137–39) and Hellenistic Egypt (*P.Tebt.* 3.804, 112 BC).
Ideally, bystanders would take up the "hue and cry" and pursue the offender, alert others,
and, it was hoped, seize him: e.g., Ulp. *Dig.* 47.2.7.2–3.

the case, defendants, and witnesses to court.[20] Prosecutions were sometimes brought by third parties, private citizens called *quadruplatores, accusatores,* or *delatores*. They are often maligned in the sources but were instrumental in enforcing the law.[21]

Grander households and gardens might have specialized guards, patrollers (*circatores*), watchtowers, and a doorman or gatekeeper to control entry. On large agricultural estates, the chief slave overseer (*vilicus*) was charged with the overall care of the entire estate, including security. On some private estates, a few *saltuarii* served as specialized guards working under the overseer. These highly placed slaves may have been most concerned with guarding their fellow slaves, many of whom worked in chain gangs and slept, chained, in secured barracks (*ergastula*).[22] Landlords enforced payment of rent by seizing the goods, crops, or even the family members of deadbeat tenants, placing them under embargo with their own private guards.[23] Dogs, "animals easily stirred up by nocturnal rustlings," in Livy's words, were crucial in protecting all kinds of property from would-be intruders. Literary sources frequently show apprehensive inhabitants unleashing ferocious guard dogs against suspect strangers.[24]

Outside the home, violence was a real threat, especially for the lower classes.[25] Travelers on long trips carried weapons for self-defense and kept

---

20. Hobson, "The Impact of Law," argues that the rural poor found little protection in the law and the courts.

21. For thorough (and less hostile) assessments, see Rutledge, *Imperial Inquisitions,* esp. chaps. 1 and 3; Rivière's *Les délateurs* and "Encouragement" cover the late empire also.

22. Doormen (*ianitores* or *ostiarii*; Greek *thurôroi*): Sen. *Constant.* 14.1, 15.5; Columella, *Rust., praef.* 10; Apul. *Met.* 4.18 (cf. Apul. *Met.* 1.15; Mark 13:34; John 10:3; *Acts of Peter* 9; Lucian *Salaried Posts* 10; Paulus *Dig.* 1.15.3.2; guards within a house: Juv. 6.031–34; Achilles Tatius *Leucippe,* 5.25, 6.2). Vilici: Columella *Rust.* 1.8.10, 1.8.16–17, 11.1.22–23. See further Rostovtzeff, "Die Domänenpolizei"; Magie, *Roman Rule* 2, 1548; Bradley, *Slavery and Society,* 70, 101; Nippel, *Public Order,* 102; Carlsen, "*Saltuarius*"; and Riess, *Apuleius und die Räuber,* 181. *Saltuarii* are best attested in Italy; they and their eastern counterparts, the *oreophylakes,* also worked on imperial estates (Brélaz, *La sécurité publique,* 165–67).

23. E.g., *P.Vindob.Sijpest.* 27 (third or fourth century); see also my commentary on the recently published *P.Oxy.* 75.5054 (second century).

24. Livy: 5.47 (cf. Ovid *Met.* 8.687). Also note Diod. Sic. 1.87.2, Columella *Rust.* 7.12.1–9, and Schwartz, "Dogs." Literary sources: see esp. Apul. *Met.* 8.17 and 2.4.4–5, 4.3, 4.19–20, 9.36–37; Verg. *Geor.* 3.404–8; Phaedrus 1.23 (= Perry 403, "The Faithful House-dog"); Petron. *Sat.* 29 (the ecphrasis of the "Beware of dog" painting inside the entrance of Trimalchio's home; cf. 65, 72) and 95; Longus *Daphnis and Chloe* 1.21; and Chariton *Callirhoe* 4.2, where barking dogs foil a prison escape. On Pompeii's mosaics, note Veyne, "*Cave canem*," 59, 66; and Clarke, *Looking at Laughter,* 51–57. Dogs guarded shops, too: Paulus *Dig.* 9.1.2.1.

25. On the level of violence in Roman society, see Fagan's excellent paper, "Violence."

watch when they stopped for the night.[26] In town, going about armed was less common and might alarm others. In republican Rome, armed retinues and bodyguards presaged political turmoil or tyrannical aspirations.[27] But there was safety in numbers, and rarely would a respectable citizen leave home without at least one attendant in tow. The lowly had to make way for the grand entourages of local Big Men, whose friends, clients, and slaves could serve as scufflers in case of trouble.[28] The fact that hangers-on insulated elites from everyday crime perhaps retarded the development of public-security measures. Nonetheless, in public fora, tumultuous crowds might get away with demands for popular justice by rioting or harassing—sometimes even lynching—their targets.[29] At the more mundane level, bathers raised a hullabaloo when thieves were caught on the premises, and a shopkeeper posted a monetary reward for returning a stolen pot (with more for handing over the thief, too).[30]

Unofficial Search Parties, Posses, and Closed Societies

It is natural for people to band together in response to crises and threats, so it is no surprise that the sources attest unofficial posses and search parties. One famous example is Pliny's letter about a son's search for his father, a Roman knight who had disappeared in northern Italy with his entire traveling party. Fictional sources sketch further descriptions of civilians working together to find missing persons, recover stolen livestock, and carry out citizens' arrests of manifest rogues.[31]

---

26. Hor. *Sat.* 2.1.39–46; Petron. *Sat.* 62; Jos. *BJ* 2.125 (on the Essenes); Apul. *Met.* 2.18; *Philogelos* 56; cf. Celsus *Med., pr.* 43. Carrying arms for self-defense on a journey was legal: Marcianus *Dig.* 48.6.1; Brunt, "Did Imperial Rome Disarm Her Subjects?" (*pace* MacMullen, *Roman Social Relations*, 35). For guards on ships, see Ulp. *Dig.* 4.9.1.3 and Casson, *Ships and Seamanship*, 140, 309, 320.

27. E.g., Quintil. *Inst.* 5.11.8 and 7.2.54, Plut. *Marius* 35.2, Dio 6.20 (Zonaras 7.20 = Loeb vol. 1, p. 184); cf. Cic. *Off.* 2.25, Diod. Sic. 19.9.7.

28. Note Juv. 3.239–48, 268–308; cf. McGinn, *Prostitution*, 334.

29. Sen. *Constant.* 15.1; Lintott, *Violence in Republican Rome*, esp. 6–34; Nippel, *Public Order*, 22–24, 39–46; Riggsby, *Crime and Community*, 170; Barry, "Exposure"; Kelly, "Riot Control"; cf. Apul. *Met.* 2.27, Philostrat. *VA* 1.15.

30. Sen. *Ep.* 56.2 (see further Catull. 33; Fagan, *Bathing in Public*, 36–39); *CIL* 4.64 (Pompeii; cf. *CIL* 4.6701). Compare the posted descriptions for recovering fugitive slaves (chapter 2 above), a process that began with private initiative.

31. Pliny *Ep.* 6.25. Pliny was not optimistic about the search. The disappearance happened somewhere beyond Ocriculum, an Umbrian town on the Via Flaminia. Pliny, mentioning

Posses may have been towns' main instruments for fighting problematic bandits in the surrounding countryside. Appian incidentally mentioned the citizens of Minturnae sweeping a nearby marsh for bandits in 43 BC. Juvenal suggested that wild places in second-century Italy continued to be swept for troublemakers, complaining that "however often the Pomptine marsh and Gallinaria woodland are made safe again by armed guard (*armatus custos*), all these highway robbers stream from there to here (Rome), like beasts to a feeding ground." A letter from the emperor Commodus to the Lycians of Boubon in AD 190 praised them for bravely defeating local brigands, killing some, capturing others.[32] The sources are not generous with details of policing operations. In the cases cited above, we do not know if the bandit hunters were state-sanctioned or vigilante, a standing organization or an ad hoc rabble. We will turn soon to official security arrangements, but we should be mindful that irregular posses probably did much of the bandit fighting. Jesus's rebuke against his arresters in Gethsemane, "Have you come out with swords and clubs to arrest me as though I were a bandit?" may originally have been a barbed comment largely lost on us nowadays: the chief priest's men look like a ragtag gang about to go on a bandit sweep.[33]

Fighting bandits with informal civilian posses might verge on being illegal, as military command and the killing that went with it properly belonged to governors and other authorized Roman officials. But within reasonable limits, the right of an individual to defend himself from violence with violence could apply to communities facing an emergency. One example was the Jewish diaspora revolt late in Trajan's reign, when civilian magistrates had to

---

a parallel case he knew of, suspected foul play by the victim's slaves. In the *Laudatio Turiae*, after the young wife's parents were apparently murdered in the countryside, she and her sister seem to have successfully punished the murderers; the text is fragmentary and vague, so it is unclear if they used legal means to do so: *ILS* 8393.1.3–9. Fictional sources: [Luc.] *Asin.* 41; Apul. *Met.* 7.25–26, 8.29; Alciphron (ca. AD 200) *Ep.* 2.16 (3.19; Loeb, pp. 108–11).

32. App. *BCiv.* 4.28.120; Juv. 3.306–8 (on which, see Braund, *Juvenal Satires*, 226; *BAtlas* 44 C2–3 and D3; *BAtlas* 44 F4; the satirist may have had military, not civilian, patrols in mind). Boubon (*BAtlas* 65 B4): *AE* 1979, 624 (*IB* 5); cf. Jones, *The Greek City*, 212, and *The Criminal Courts*, 116.

33. This saying originated in the earliest gospel, Mark 14:48, which the other synoptics follow: Matt. 26:47–55; Luke 22:47–52. In the first two gospels, the arrest party is described as an armed crowd or rabble (*ochlos*, Mark 14:43, Matt 26:47). Then, in Luke (22:52), the posse becomes more official, for the temple authorities themselves appear, with the captains of the temple guard (*stratêgoi hierou*, on which, see Brown, *The Death of the Messiah*, app. 5). By the time John (18:3, 18:12) reached final form in the late first century, the arresting posse has swelled to a military unit (*speira* or cohort, hundreds of men if taken literally) accompanied by civilian Jewish police attendants (*hupêretai*). The growth of institutional and military policing, in other words, is reflected in the gradual evolution of Christian literature.

worry about procuring weapons, hastily forming civilian militias, protecting property, and reassuring their own terrified family members. The whole conflict is murky, but before the army finally restored order, the fighting was between Jewish and gentile civilians, each side apparently fearing annihilation at the hands of the other.[34] Moreover, with banditry endemic in many areas, emperors and governors were often glad to take whatever help they could get, it seems (note Commodus's letter above). Furthermore, Roman authorities normally did not proactively investigate whether communities' operations stayed within the limits of Roman law. (Instead, they largely responded to complaints filed by people with the means and opportunity to do so. Some of the "bandits" repressed in local civilian operations could just have been marginal, uncooperative outsiders whose only "crime" was getting in the town's way and lacking any standing to appeal to Roman authorities.) What mattered for communities at the local level is that their policing measures worked effectively enough, without generating complaints to the Romans.

This avoidance of Roman interference allowed for the existence of various closed societies, truly autonomous cliques within the empire. We do not usually think of the Dead Sea Scrolls as documents about the Roman Empire, but the sectarians at Qumran lived in the Roman province of Judaea. Their own laws (which they never submitted to Rome for approval, as far as we know) included the death penalty for religious crimes. Maybe they never carried it out.[35] But there was no Roman legal inspector visiting these men (who, after all, voluntarily joined the sect), and even if there were such inquiries, how could any outsider penetrate the sect's esoteric complexities?[36] Indeed, the Qumran sect was purposefully set up in such a way as to be closed to outsiders. New initiates swore intimidating oaths of loyalty. The Temple Scroll mandates crucifixion for any sect members who go to gentile authorities against their brethren. Christians and later Jewish communities also banned taking

34. I have in mind evidence from the Egyptian theater of the revolt, particularly the experiences of the *stratêgos* Apollonios. See Pucci Ben Zeev's fine study, *Diaspora Judaism*, esp. 18–50, 153–54, 168–75 (citing *CPJ* 2.436–38); also note Kortus, *Briefe des Apollonius-Archives*, esp. 89–146.

35. Damascus Document 9–10, 12 (lines 2–3, with Leviticus 20:27), 16; 4Q159 fr. 224.10–11; Temple Scroll 64.6–13. Vermès conjectures that these laws probably reflected a theoretical future age: *The Complete Dead Sea Scrolls*, 38. Later rabbinic communities may have executed criminals; see Origen's letter to Julius Africanus, §14; and Berkowitz, *Execution and Invention*, esp. 12–17.

36. Compare Pilate's frustration in the gospel accounts and Gallio's disinterest in Acts 18 (chapter 7 below). Even greater cultural and linguistic barriers would exist between Qumran sectarians and an elite Roman.

their problems to gentile authorities. Such groups were able to practice their own laws and customs with minimal state interference, as long as no one appealed to outside authorities.[37]

State-sanctioned Occasional Militias and Watches

Evidence for permanent, standing local police arrangements in the western provinces is very thin. Judging from legal inscriptions found in Roman Spain, the organs of municipal government in some places could initiate a militia or citizen guard if needed. Chapter 103 of the charter for the Colonia Genetiva Julia (Urso), founded in Baetica by Caesar in 45/44 BC, states that by a simple majority vote, the town councilors can permit the chief magistrates to lead the colony's inhabitants out "under arms for the purpose of defending the territories of the colony." Such a military levy probably reflects the instability of the late republic (indeed, the enormous Battle of Munda was fought nearby in 45). We do not know if the colonists ever took advantage of the clause, which may have become a dead letter as soon as the civil wars ended.[38]

A clearer policing provision comes in a municipal charter (the fullest we have) from a town not far from Urso, the *Lex Irnitana* of AD 91: "The aediles...are to have the right and power of managing the food supply, temples, sacred places, town, roads, districts, drains, baths, market, of checking weights and measures, and of managing watches when occasion arises" (*vigilias cum res desiderabit*). The potential watch at Irni is one of the only specialized civilian policing arrangements we can be sure was in effect west of Rome during the later principate. We do not know if circumstances ever demanded that the municipal aediles called up a watch. (Aediles performed important routine police functions in their own right, without the backing of a citizen watch; see below.) Nor does the charter's vague language clarify what sort of

---

37. Oaths: Jos. *BJ* 2.139–46 (assuming the Qumran sect was part of the Essene movement described in Greek and Latin sources, as most experts believe). Death penalty for going to gentile authorities: TS 64.6–13; Schiffman, *Sectarian Law*, 77, 85 n. 48 (Byzantine-era Ein Gedi synagogue inscription). Christians: 1 Cor. 6:1–10; cf. Matt. 18:15–17. According to Livy 39.8–19, the senate and magistrates repressed Bacchic cults in 186 BC after informants revealed their debaucheries.

38. Crawford's trans., *RS* 25 (*CIL* 2²/5.1022 c. 103). Tablet c, col. V, lines 2–4; Hardy, *Roman Laws and Charters*, 47 n. 110; cf. *ILS* 6882. Our copy of the *Lex Ursonensis* dates from the late first century AD, so the security measure in chap. 103 remained on the books into the imperial era, despite ample time to change it. See Frederiksen, "Republican Municipal Laws," esp. 192; Crawford, *Roman Statutes* 1, 395–98; Talbert, "The Decurions," 58–59; and Mackie, *Local Administration*, 223. On the military context in 45 BC, see Gelzer, *Caesar*, 292–98. Most of the Pompeian troops at Munda were Spanish natives.

problems might call for a watch. Other towns likely had comparable provisions for a watch, since other charter fragments from Flavian-era Spain exactly parallel different parts of the *Lex Irnitana.*[39]

Some scholars have interpreted Greek and Roman youth groups as militias at the ready for town defense. In their late teens and early twenties, young men of the propertied classes often practiced rudimentary military skills and agonistic sports. In an emergency, the town could call on them to safeguard the city or patrol its territory. During the late third century, when communities in once-peaceful areas faced aggressive invaders and civil strife, youths helped repel an attack on the walls of Saldae in Mauretania, and "select young men" in Pisidia helped suppress "bandits." But these were occasional emergencies that did not define their intended role in the imperial era.[40]

We do have certain epigraphic references, not to fully describable institutions but at least to a municipal official called the *praefectus vigilum* ("prefect of the watches")[41] This official seems to have been a specialized police officer, if Apuleius's novel can be trusted when it gives an idealized portrait of a "prefect of the night watch" (*praefectus nocturnae custodiae*): "For I am in charge of nocturnal security and to this day, I think no one can find fault in the diligence of my vigilance." This character claimed he spied a crime the night before as he "was going around inspecting the whole town, house by house, with scrupulous care." Considering that this is all part of an elaborate joke on the narrator, one might hesitate to trust Apuleius here. Indeed, some assume that "*vigiles*" and "prefects of *vigiles*" were actually firemen more than police, following the model of firefighting in early imperial Rome.[42] (See chapter 4

---

39. Adapted from Crawford's translation from González's 1986 *JRS* edition, *Lex Irnitana* Tab. IIIA, 19, lines 5–7, 12–13, adopting the emendation of *mensas* ("tables, counters") to *mens<ur>as* ("measures"). Cf. 79 on safeguarding sacred buildings and monuments, which may have been guarded by public slaves, *pace* Galsterer, "Municipium Flavium Irnitanum," 84. See also Talbert, "Decurions," 58 (on Pliny *NH* 3.3.30).

40. *AE* 1928, 38; Ballance and Roueché, "Three Inscriptions," 105, fragment I.A.1.7–13. Youths of Apollonia in Caria helped patrol its mountainous territory: *BCH* 32 (1908), 499–513 = Robert, *Carie* 162. See Kleijwegt, *Ancient Youth*, 94–97, 106–9; and Brélaz, *La sécurité publique*, 183–203. On the traditional security duties of ephebes in classical Athens, see Hunter, *Policing Athens*, 151–53.

41. The evidence is heavily Gallic: *CIL* 12.3166: *praefecto vigi[lum]* at Nemausus (Nîmes), where a *praefectus vigilum et armorum* ("prefect of the watch and of arms," probably the same office) is attested nine times: *CIL* 12.3002, 3210, 3213, 3223, 3232, 3247, 3259, 3274, 3296; also, two examples just outside of Nîmes: *AE* 1895, 35 (= *ILGN* 516); and *AE* 1969/70, 376 (= *AE* 1992, 1216). A *praefectus vigilum* is attested at Lyon: *CIL* 13.1745 (second century). Cf. *AE* 1912, 20; and *AE* 1967, 478 (= *AE* 1973, 525; Ephesus, fourth century).

42. Apul. *Met.* 3.3 (set in Hypata); cf. Petron. *Sat.* 78, for *vigiles* as firemen.

below, where I resist drawing too stark a line between firefighting and polic-ing.) Western "prefects of the watches" probably performed routine police duties, and indeed, the title of at least one magistrate from an inscription in Switzerland leaves no doubt: *praefectus arcendis latrociniis* ("prefect for defend-ing against bandit attacks").[43]

Regarding methodology, provincial *vigiles* (or their Greek equivalents, *nykto-phylakes*, "night guards") could wield weapons if the magistrates so desired. Even if they were armed, they might not enjoy any significant technological advantage over the people they were guarding against. Thieves and night prowlers, how-ever, were vulnerable in that they needed to avoid detection and attention.[44] So the most powerful tool in some night watchmen's arsenals may have been bells. Cassius Dio mentioned that in his own time (late second and early third cen-tury), guards carried bells at night to help raise an alarm in case of trouble.[45]

References to provincial *praefecti vigilum* in Latin fiction and inscriptions provide further evidence for night watches outside of Rome, relative to the more abundant evidence in the east.[46] While only in Irni do we find explicit provision for creating and supervising an ad hoc *vigilia* or watch, there was probably nothing in other local charters to *prohibit* raising an emergency watch, patrol, or posse. "Elastic" clauses common in many town charters seem to allow it.[47] The western legal inscriptions, at any rate, suggest that there was

---

43. *CIL* 13.5010 = *ILS* 7007; *AE* 1978, 567 (Noviodunum, modern Nyon on Lake Geneva); cf. the rather fragmentary *AE* 1978, 501 = 1982, 716, from Bois l'Abbé (northern France). Some aspects of this magistracy remain obscure; see Riess's overview in *Apuleius und die Räuber*, 204; I have not seen Lamoine's *Le pouvoir local*. The *praefectus Bingiensium* (Bingium = modern Bingen am Rhein in Germania Superior) may be a similar office; see *CIL* 13.6211 and Ott, *Die Beneficiarier*, 120.

44. Sometimes elite writers tried to imagine the viewpoints of criminals, especially vivid in the novels' low-life settings. Note Tertullian's resentful contrast (*Apol.* 1.11) between Chris-tians and "real" criminals: "Evil-doers long to remain concealed and avoid detection; when caught, they are afraid." The second-century *Life of Secundus the Philosopher* (*Sententiae* 6) calls the moon "an object of hatred for evil-doers" hoping to conceal their deeds in darkness.

45. Dio 54.4.4: "For those who guard communities (*sunoikiai*, perhaps "apartment blocks" of Rome; Millar, *A Study*, 212) at night carry bells, so that they can signal to one another when-ever they need to do so." Dio's chosen verb *kôdônophorein* ("to carry bells") itself has a rich security pedigree: Aristophanes (*Birds* 842, 1160) also used it in relation to guard-duty praxis.

46. Hirschfeld long ago noted the similarity of this prefecture to the eastern eirenarchs (discussed below), about whom we know more: "Gallische Studien III," 97.

47. E.g., on the enumeration of magisterial powers, *Lex Irnitana* 19.17–22, granting the ae-diles the right and power (*ius potestasque*) to act, as long as they do nothing contrary to exist-ing laws; 20.32–37 repeats the formula for the quaestors, and chap. 18 would have had a

normally no standing corps of police but at most only provision for occasional ad hoc musters when needed. True, we have some scattered references to "commanders of the watch" (*praefecti vigilum*), but we cannot assume that they commanded an organized, standing police force.

Local Magistrates and Market Police

The nearest equivalents to a standing local police force in most western communities were the town magistrates themselves and their attendants (*apparitores*). Magistrates were doubly powerful, first by virtue of their office but also because they were by definition members of the local elite, whose importance to imperial society is hard to exaggerate. By "local elite," I mean the decurions or members of the curial class who served as magistrates and members of town councils, where they usually sat for life. They oversaw collection of taxes for Rome and represented the community's interests to higher Roman authorities, who typically allowed a great deal of local autonomy. Competition for local honor impelled members of the curial class to provide valuable services and benefactions to their communities. This sort of public service could be rancorous or financially stressful, and by the second century, some were resisting magistracies and council membership. Despite these difficulties, it was the duty of magistrates and the council to keep order at the local level.[48]

In the west and in Roman colonies throughout the empire, magisterial offices were modeled on the traditional magistracies that developed in the city of Rome during the republic. In the context of Italian and provincial communities, everything was on a smaller scale than at Rome, not surprisingly, and local magistracies took various forms. The chief magistrates of many communities were shadows of Roman consuls, "two men" (*duoviri* or *duumviri*) serving as co-mayors for one year, assisted by the same types of attendants as consuls in Rome. Of course, they lacked *imperium*, so they could not put anyone to death or command troops (routine duties of the Roman provincial governor; see chapter 7 below). Many eastern communities had already fully developed their own civil institutions in the Hellenistic age, and Roman rule

---

similar clause for the *duoviri*. Per the oaths of the magistrates, *Lex Irnitana* 26.43–46, each must swear "that he will do whatever he deems proper by this charter and by the common welfare" of Irni's citizens. Cf. the magistrates' oaths in *Lex Salpensana* 26.45.5–7 and *Lex Malacitana* 59.

48. See Slootjes, "Local *Potentes*," with references, for complexities in the concept of local elites. On their public-order role, note Apul. *Met.* 10.6. On dodging service, see Millar, "Empire and City."

did not radically alter their forms or titles. They lost their old military functions, but eastern town councils and chief magistrates (usually called archons or *stratêgoi*) otherwise retained local autonomy. Policing powers of western and eastern magistrates were similar, although we will see that many eastern communities also had specialized guards or police officers.

It was obviously dangerous to run afoul of a town's magistrates, especially when one's status was low. According to the author of Acts, the leading magistrates of Philippi had Paul and his companions stripped, severely beaten, and thrown in jail, not realizing that they were Roman citizens. The novelist Chariton has a top magistrate (*stratêgos*) in Caria search, interrogate, and arrest a band of suspicious slaves. We also have an urgent private letter on papyrus that highlights a local Egyptian magistrate's violent prerogative: "To Proutas, greetings. Whenever you get this note come up, as the *stratêgos* has beaten me because of you, since up to this day you have (still) not come, whereas all the others have come. So by all means do come up, lest I'm beaten another time. I bid you good health." The jurist Paulus mentioned the possibility of a magistrate looking around town to catch whomever he was after. A third-century collection of pithy sayings falsely attributed to Cato the Elder includes the admonition *Magistratum metue* ("Fear the magistrate").[49]

Lower officials performed important police work, too. In republican Rome, the aediles were mid-level magistrates who oversaw public shows, the upkeep of roads and buildings, and regulating markets. Aediles in Italian and provincial communities typically shared the functions of their grander counterparts at Rome, implementing standards set by the duovirs or council. They were assisted by a small staff, mainly slaves. In the Greek east, *agoranomoi* and *logistai* executed similar functions, also with a servile staff. Specifically, they were supposed to prevent fraud, ensure honest weights and measures, determine where and when markets could operate, and make sure applicable taxes and fees were paid. On this last point, an ancient joke book tells us, "A misogynist standing in the market proclaimed, 'I'm selling my wife tax-free!' When they asked him why, he said, 'So she'll be confiscated.'"[50]

---

49. Acts 16:22–24; Chariton *Callirhoe* 4.5; *P. Ups. Frid* 9 (second or third century, provenance unknown); Paulus *Dig.* 9.1.2.1; *Disticha Catonis* 18 or *Sententiola* 11; cf. Petron. *Sat.* 65.

50. Persius 1.129–30; *Lex Irnitana* 19; Juv. 10.100–102; Apul. *Met.* 1.24–25; the joke is *Philogelos* 246, third or fourth century (cf. *Life of Aesop* 27); *IGRR* 4.146 (Cyzicus); *ILS* 5602–16, passim. Also note the lavish tomb of the Pompeian aedile G. Vestorius Priscus, apparently depicting his official duties before he died at the age of twenty-two: *AE* 1912, 70; Clarke, *Art in the Lives of Ordinary Romans*, 187–203; cf. *CIL* 4.1096 and 10.8067.1–2. See further Magie, *Roman Rule*, 60–61; Jones, *The Greek City*, 215–17, 230, 234; Shaw, "Rural

There are two further points to stress. First, despite the encroachment of soldiers in policing that we will see in subsequent chapters, market regulation remained in the civilian sphere. Second, it is no surprise that market regulators are well attested in the Roman Empire, for this was a common feature in numerous other premodern civilizations, from classical Athens to the early Islamic Middle East and Aztec Mexico.[51] This deep-seated need for market fairness is evident in Christian literature and was already important to the writer(s) of Deuteronomy, who warned, "You shall not have in your house two kinds of measures, large and small. You shall have only a full and honest weight; you shall have only a full and honest measure." A first- or second-century AD Tannaitic commentator glossed on this same passage: "Appoint an *agoranomos* for this."[52]

Indeed, Jewish sources provide some of our best information on policing markets in the Roman Empire, attesting price and quality controls, sometimes enforced by threats and violence. These texts also reveal the fear that gentile inspectors would contaminate ritually pure foodstuffs; in at least one case, a guard was posted lest a shipment of kosher fish sauce be contaminated by "libated" wine.[53] We also see evasion, corruption, and abuse, as when an

---

Periodic Markets," 92; Nippel, *Public Order*, 18; Jakab, *Praedicere und cavere*, 70–85, 110–22; Alston, *The City*, 190–91; Brélaz, *La sécurité publique*, 72–73. On eastern magistracies, see Dmitriev, *City Government*. On equating *agoranomoi* and *logistai*, see the scholium to Aristoph. *Acharn.* 720: "*agoranomoi*, whom we now call *logistai*." The duties of *astynomoi* in some cities are comparable: Papinian *Dig.* 43.10; cf. *OGIS* 483 (= *SEG* 13.521), a lengthy Hellenistic law from Pergamum, reinscribed under Hadrian, with Cox, "The *Astynomoi*"; and Saba, *The Astynomoi Law*. On office titles connoting similar duties, see Sperber, "*Calculo-Logistes-Hashban*," and *The City in Roman Palestine*, chap. 3. In the papyri of Roman Egypt, *agoranomoi* were notaries for private contracts rather than market police: Benaissa, "Sixteen Letters to Agoranomi."

51. *Athênaiôn Politeia* 51 specifies sixty-five *agoranomoi*, *metronomoi* (enforcing weights and measures), *sitophylakes* (ensuring grain at fair price), and trade-exchange supervisors (*emporiou epimelêtai*) for classical Athens and the Piraeus. On *hashban* and *muhtasib* (both mean, roughly, "calculator") of the Islamic Mediterranean, Crone argues that this institution evolved from *agoranomoi* and entered Arabic from Jewish terminology (*Roman, Provincial and Islamic Law*, 107–9); Foster stresses that the *muhtasib* was primarily a religious authority ("Agoranomos and Muhtasib," 140–41). Cf. Qur'an, Sirah 17.35: "And give full measure when you measure, and weigh with a balance that is straight" (Muhsin Khan and Taqi-ud-Din Al-Hilali's translation). The Aztecs policed their markets against counterfeiters and cheaters: Berdan, "Crime and Crime Control," 264.

52. Sifrei Deuteronomy, sec. 294 on Deut. 25:14–15, trans. Sperber, *The City*, 32. Christian literature: Mark 4:24, Matt. 7:2, cf. Cyprian *Ad Demetr.* 3.

53. B. Avoda Zara 34B, describing late-third-century Akko (Acre), translated and discussed at length by Sperber, "On Social and Economic Conditions"; see further Sperber, *The City*, 34–39.

agoranomos "went out to inspect the measures, and found the shopkeepers locking up [their shops] (in order to avoid his inspection). He seized the first one and beat him, and the others, on hearing this, opened [their shops] of their own accord."[54] A text of unknown date mentions a butcher displaying his goods in the market. A passing *logistês* started eyeing the meat. "Master," the butcher told him, "I have already sent you a present." One midrashic text brings up a market manager confronting a fraudulent banker. "He said to him: 'You are cheating on your measures.' [The banker] replied to him: 'I have already sent a present to your house.'"[55]

Magisterial Attendants and Public Slaves

We have mentioned the importance of an entourage in private life; the same is certainly true for the public sphere. There is no better opportunity for spectators to "read power" than in a procession. One second- or third-century papyrus preserves a list of guards for local magistrates in a procession connected to the town's gymnasium. Some officials are allotted four guards, others are given one or two, depending on (and reinforcing) the magistrate's relative importance.[56]

Most important, though, are the regular attendants of magistrates, known collectively as *apparitores*. The four main positions were criers (*praecones*), lictors, "waymen" (*viatores*, who ran errands and delivered messages and summonses), and professional clerks (*scribae*). They all seem to have developed at an early date along with the offices themselves (indeed, the fasces-bearing lictors who accompanied magistrates with *imperium* were Etruscan in origin). In Rome, these men formed corporations of rotating panels (*decuriae*), divided by office and magisterial rank, from which magistrates drew appointees. With the growth of empire, the system branched out into provinces and lasted into Byzantine times, although it grew ever more ceremonial. Meanwhile, Christian bishops gradually took on functions and trappings that once belonged exclusively to civil magistrates. During the time period we are most concerned with, *apparitores* were a phenomenon of the western empire. (Outside of east-

---

54. Yalkut Shimoni Numbers (Hukkat) section 763; cf. Pesikta de-Rav Kahana, Aser Te'aser 2, which also mentions shopkeepers hiding from *agoranomoi* (Sperber, *The City*, 33, 41). These midrashic texts are very difficult to date; Sperber conjectures third or fourth century).

55. Tanhuma Leviticus, Zav *ad init.*; Numbers Rabba 20.18 (fourth century?); Sperber, *The City*, 33–34, 42–43.

56. *P.Amh.* 2.124, from the Hermopolite nome.

ern colonies that followed the Roman model, the staffs of most eastern magistrates consisted of public slaves; see below). Italian and provincial *apparitores*
operated similarly to the Roman system but on a smaller scale and with less
specialization in offices.[57]

A further difference is that in Rome, *apparitores'* status rested in part on
the robust system of *decuriae*, in which they were continuously employed,
upwardly mobile professionals, not attached to any one boss. The very paucity of inscriptions from non-Roman *apparitores* suggests that their status
was lower and their service more casual. Magistrates probably handpicked
them, and they probably only served as long as the magistrates who chose
them (one year in most cases). This style of apparitorial service may well have
benefited the magistrates. An ambitious duovir would value the power of
selecting his own strong-arm attendants and having them completely responsible and indebted to himself. Thus, he could best wield *lixas et virgas*
("subordinates and rods of authority"), as Apuleius put it, to exercise power.
At least in republican Rome, there had been several counterbalancing magistrates; then the principate focused power at the top. But in relatively autonomous provincial communities, if there were no major divisions among the
elite, the smaller-scale apparitorial system and the overall local power scheme
would foster the growth of narrow little oligarchies. This situation suited
Rome, as long as it brought stability.[58]

Some *apparitores* performed important police duties and probably played a
considerable security role in towns with no other police. Specifics are hazy.
Three orders of *apparitores*—scribes, *viatores*, and heralds—have left little evi-

---

57. *Apparitores* in Rome: *Lex Cornelia de XX Quaestoribus* (= Crawford *RS* 14 = *ARS* 67–68 =
Bruns 12 = *FIRA* 10); Jones, "The Roman Civil Service," 38–42; Badian, "The *Scribae*"; and
esp. Purcell, "The *Apparitores*." I describe the system more fully in Fuhrmann, "Keeping the
Imperial Peace," 48–53. Mommsen, *Römisches Staatsrecht* I, 332–71, remains valuable and
may be the best treatment of *apparitores* outside of Rome; also note *Lex Ursonensis* 62–63
(*CIL* 2²/5;1022 = Crawford *RS* 25), *Lex Irnitana* 73 (cf. *decuriae* in F, 86); and Fear, "La *Lex
Ursonensis*." Details on provincial apparitorial arrangements are obscure, in part because the
scant sources increasingly use the catch-all phrase *decurialis* (or βουλευτικός; qv. in Mason,
Greek Terms) for all grades. Etruscans: e.g., Livy 1.8. Bishops: e.g., Euseb. *Hist. eccl.* 7.30.6–9
(with Millar, "Paul of Samosata," 11–13; and Norris, "Paul of Samosata," esp. 59–68); Optatus
De Schism. Donatist. 3.4; and Shaw, "Rural Periodic Markets," 111–14. Public slaves (*dēmo-
sioi*): Jones, "The Roman Civil Service," 38. Smaller scale: note that at Narbo, there was one
decuria of *viatores*, and it was combined with the lictors' *decuria*: *CIL* 12.4447–48 = *ILS* 6973;
cf. *CIL* 3.6759. The same combination of *decuriae* may have been in effect at Ostia: *CIL*
14.409 = *ILS* 6146 (cf. Meiggs, *Roman Ostia*, 181–82).

58. Mommsen, *Römisches Staatsrecht* I, 334; Fear, "La *Lex Ursonensis*," 72; Apul. *Met.* 1.24 (a
provincial aedile). We will see in chapter 7 below that the local elites were frequently *not*
united.

dence of direct involvement in policing. The only specific mention of non-lictor *apparitores* doing police work outside of Rome are two fictional episodes that we have already encountered (chapter 2 above): Petronius's scene (*Sat.* 97–99) in which a herald and a *viator* enter private lodgings searching for a missing slave and the herald Mercury's search for the runaway Psyche in Apuleius's *Golden Ass* (6.7–8). The dearth of information on municipal *viatores* is somewhat surprising, as they have a rich pedigree as figures of public (dis)order in republican Rome; since grasping tribunes of the plebs had no lictors, they often tried to exercise power through their *viatores*.[59] Moreover, any time a town magistrate needed to send a message or summon someone, he would notionally employ a *viator*. Lictors loom larger in the sources, apparently overshadowing and gradually subsuming *viatores*. Their duties overlapped somewhat, and in fact, in Narbo, we find an inscription that mentions a *lictor viator* of the community, suggesting that the offices themselves were merging.[60]

Lictors' strong impact in our sources partly derives from their visibility. They carried the symbols of the high magistrates' power to coerce and punish: the fasces. These were five-foot-long bundles of rods (*virgae*) bound with a red cord, sometimes including an axe. A lictor carried this imposing instrument on his left shoulder, preceding his magistrate wherever he went, announcing his approach and clearing his way. *Fasces* became a metonym for the lictors themselves in Latin and Greek sources. Livy and other antiquarians invented chilling scenes of Roman magistrates commanding their lictors to unbind their fasces, to deliver corporal or (given the axe) capital punishment. Frequent references to flogging entered the language. "Why, I was nearly flogged at the bath for going around and trying my verse on the people sitting there," Petronius's glib poet protested. By the time of the principate, the fasces had become ceremonial but remained powerful symbols. Anthony Marshall noted that fasces were never "merely decorative or symbolic devices carried before magistrates in a parade of idle formalism. Rather, they constituted a portable kit for flogging and decapitation.... Their punitive associations never became as historically 'distanced' for the average citizen as have those of ceremonial maces and swords in modern societies."[61]

---

59. Livy's history is particularly rich in tribunes' misuse of *viatores*; see Habicht *RE* "Viator," esp. coll. 1929–32, for full citations, and cf. Gell. *NA* 13.12.

60. *CIL* 12.4447 (Narbo); Mommsen, *Römisches Staatsrecht* 1, 361–62.

61. Mason, *Greek Terms*, 82–83, and q.v. *lictor* in Index IV; Petron. *Sat.* 92; Marshall, "Symbols and Showmanship," 130; cf. Nippel, *Aufruhr und "Polizei,"* 161–69.

The number of lictors attending a magistrate was the measure of the man, an obvious fact for sensitive observers to note. Augustus's privilege "to have twelve fasces at all times and everywhere" was significant and had to be treated with finesse; Dio censured Domitian's taking *twenty-four* lictors—even into the senate house—as another example of his impolitic excess.[62] In Italian and provincial communities, only chief magistrates normally had lictors proper, two in number. Each of the duovir's lictors carried a fasces (also called *bacilla* in a municipal context), though smaller than Roman ones and necessarily without the axe, since municipal authorities lacked the power of capital punishment. These municipal lictors performed some general police duties and provided "administrative support" as necessary. In the Acts of the Apostles, for instance, lictors deliver messages for the magistrates of Philippi to the jailer holding Paul and his party. In Apuleius's novel, they arrest Lucius and act as forceful bailiffs in his (mock) trial; later, town magistrates order lictors and public slaves to search the house of a man accused of theft.[63]

Another significant character who appears with *apparitores* in relevant episodes from Roman novels is the *servus publicus*, a slave owned by the city he served. *Servi publici* performed important routine tasks in municipal administration and acted as general support staff for upkeep of their city.[64] Public slaves seem to have especially helped town aediles (burdened as they were with so many duties) maintain buildings and public works. They took on incidental security roles as temple wardens (*aeditui*), and as caretaker guards (*custodes*) and doormen (*ianitores*) of public buildings. Public slaves may have served as a night watch and fire guard in some places, as they once did in Rome.[65] These slaves could also accompany magistrates, help them make arrests, and otherwise impose their will; when acting as such enforcers, public

62. Dio 54.10.5 (Augustus) and 67.4.3 (Domitian); compare Livy 3.36.4–5; Tac. *Agr.* 45.

63. *Bacilla*: Cic. *Leg. agr.* 2.34.92; the funeral monument of Poplicola in Ostia offers a good illustration: *Scavi di Ostia* 3.1, plate 30. Acts 16:35–38. Apul. *Met.* 3.2, 3.9, 9.41; cf. 11.8. The Greek version of the story by (pseudo?) Lucian retains the use of magisterial *apparitores* (*hupêretai*, a general term for assistants or attendants, which can mean lictors) in the latter search episode (45). Cf. Chariton *Callirhoe* 3.4 and 4.5.

64. Mommsen, *Römisches Staatsrecht* 1, 320–32; Halkin, *Les esclaves publics*; Eder, *Servitus Publica*; Weiss, *Sklave der Stadt*; Lenski, "*Servi Publici*."

65. Aediles' duties: *Lex Irnitana* 19. *Lex Ursonensis* 62 grants the aediles four public slaves. Fire guard: Paulus *Dig.* 1.15.1; Mommsen, *Römisches Staatsrecht* 1, 328–29; and Eder, *Servitus Publica*, 37–56, 69–71, 88–91.

slaves were often called *ministri*.[66] They played as important a role in the empire's Greek cities (where they were typically called *dêmosioi*) and had a long security pedigree: classical Athens had famously used enslaved Scythian archers to keep order at public meetings. Later, public slaves of imperial-era Greek cities covered many of the duties not only of their servile counterparts in the western empire but also of *apparitores*, since most Greek cities lacked *apparitores*.[67]

Some scholars have argued that, in contrast to the Scythian slaves of ancient Athens, Roman *servi publici* would ordinarily not be employed in direct coercion against citizens.[68] Nonetheless, even an eminent citizen might be put under the hands of public slaves, should he or she (considering Perpetua and other female martyrs) be accused of something nefarious, and thus lose customary rights and privileges. Novels and Christian texts feature *servi publici* in arrests and trials, and they were often the penal staff of provincial communities, serving as torturers and executioners.[69] We have noted (chapter 2 above) their involvement in holding recaptured fugitive slaves. They were also commonly prison guards, the best-known case being Pliny's inquiry to Trajan regarding Bithynian prisons. Concerned that the slaves might not be trustworthy, he reinforced them with soldiers. Trajan disliked this use of soldiers

---

66. For public slaves called *ministri* or *ministeria*, see, e.g., Pliny, *Ep.* 10.31–32; on police functions of such *ministri*, e.g., Ulpian *Dig.* 11.4.1.6, which concerns public slaves taking arrested runaway slaves into custody (cf. Petron. *Sat.* 97–98; see chapter 2 above). On this function and the official property search of accused burglars, see Eder, *Servitus Publica*, 77–79. *Ministri* of magistrates were not always servile. Apuleius's use of *ministri* is somewhat ambiguous but usually seems to indicate public slaves: *Met.* 3.2, 9.41, 10.10. Applied to a man, *publicus* often stands by itself as a substantive for *servus publicus*, as in numerous inscriptions.

67. Nippel, *Public Order*, 13; Plato, *Protagoras* 319c. Citizen bailiffs replaced the Scythians in the fourth century BC: Hunter, *Policing Athens*, 145–49. On *dêmosioi* as equivalents to *apparitores*, see Jones, "The Roman Civil Service," 38, but note that *dêmosioi* in general could denote free persons serving public liturgies, and in Egypt, the term can refer to a class of free police officers.

68. Mommsen, *Römisches Staatsrecht* 1, 326; Nippel, *Public Order*, 12–13; cf. Gell. *NA* 13.13.4. One must wonder to what extent this civil distinction, which was not always heeded in Rome, was observed in the provinces, where our sources are not as good.

69. E.g., Petron. *Sat.* 97–8; Apul. *Met.* 3.2, 9.41, 10.10; cf. the arrest of Jesus, in which a slave of the chief priest is among the arrest party in all four gospels (Mark 14:47, Matt. 26:51, Luke 22:50, John 18:10). On public slaves as torturers and executioners, see Halkin, *Les esclaves publics*, 97–98, 166–67, 171–72; Eder, *Servitus Publica*, 84–85, 98; and Chariton *Callirhoe* 3.4, where *dêmosioi* act as bailiffs and torturers in the same public trial. For the persistence of this role, note Lenski, "*Servi Publici*," 344–45; and the executioner in *Martyrium Agapae* 6.1 (Thessalonica, AD 303).

and had Pliny revert to the original practice.[70] It is one of the first substantial issues that Pliny queried, and not apparently as an arrangement in a single city but general praxis "of the cities" (*civitatium*). Subsequent history would overturn Trajan's decision, for in the second century, soldiers became increasingly involved with penal detention and punishment,[71] as they would in several other aspects of provincial security.

Civil Police Forces in Asia Minor

Heretofore our discussion has been rather western in focus, but we turn now to two eastern regions whose police institutions were the most full and systematic: Asia Minor and Egypt. The various provinces of the former were marked by bold contrasts between the Greek cities' vibrant urbanism and the traditionally rural societies of the Anatolian plateau. As the *duoviri* and other magistrates held sway over Roman towns, in Greek cities, executive boards of *prytaneis*, *stratêgoi*, or *archontes* led administration of civil affairs. In addition, the traditional council (*boulê*) retained much of its importance under Roman rule, supervising the overall maintenance of public order. The council also provided the magistrates who had the greatest impact on public order, including the top magistracies, and lesser ones, such as the *agoranomoi* and *sitones* (see above on aediles), the *astynomos* ("town guardian"), and also the *grammateus* ("clerk," literally "scribe"). Depending on the circumstances, any of these magistrates might be called on to try to reassert public order, as when, for example, the *grammateus* of Ephesus finally dispersed the "riot of the silversmiths" in Acts.[72]

---

70. Pliny *Ep.* 10.19–20; cf. *Dig.* 4.6.10 and Weiss, *Sklave der Stadt*, 110–16. Prison guards regularly doubled as executioners. Prison maintenance was generally under the care of a magistrate or assigned to a prominent citizen as a liturgy. We do not have space here for a full treatment of imprisonment and punishment in the Roman Empire, which has been covered well by others: Millar, "Condemnation to Hard Labour"; Gustafson, "Condemnation to the Mines" and "*Inscripta in Fronte*"; Lovato, *Il carcere*; Rivière, "*Carcer et uincula*"; Krause, *Gefängnisse* (esp. 24–42); Torallas Tovar and Pérez Martín, eds., *Castigo y reclusión*; Bertrand-Dagenbach et al., *Carcer* and *Carcer* II. Contextualizing St. Paul's prison experiences: Rapske, *The Book of Acts*; Tajra, *The Martyrdom of St. Paul*; Wansink, *Chained in Christ* (esp. chap. 1); and Cassidy, *Paul in Chains*, chap. 4. I have not seen Rivière, "Captivité et retour de captivité." Cf. Hunter, "The Prison of Athens" and "Plato's Prisons"; Bauschatz, "Ptolemaic Prisons"; and Peters, "Prison before the Prison." Soldiers' penal duties are discussed below.

71. Eder, *Servitus Publica*, 87; Rapske, *The Book of Acts*, 252; Krause, *Gefängnisse*, 249–56, 307–8; Hauken and Malay, "A New Edict of Hadrian"; cf. *O. Krok.* 65 and 100, and see below, esp. chapters 7 and 8.

72. Acts 19:35–41; Schulte, *Die Grammateis*. On the following sketch, see, above all, Brélaz's excellent 2005 *La sécurité publique*, 69–230. On the council, see Magie, *Roman Rule* 1, 642–55; on regional differences, Mitchell, *Anatolia*.

Yet, unlike some other areas, cities in Asia Minor instituted a variety of specialized police offices, most of which emerged as compulsory liturgies in the early second century. A handful of cities had night *stratêgoi*, implying a night watch. There was a great amount of local variation within Asia Minor. For example, in Lycia, the provincial council (*koinon*) appointed an *archiphylax* ("chief of the guard") and a *hypophylax* ("subchief of the guard") to supervise regional security and tax collection. This arrangement was unique.[73] In the rest of Asia Minor's western regions, the most common specialized policemen were the *eirênarchai* ("officers of the peace"), attested more than a hundred times in Asia Minor.[74] The *Digest* describes eiren-archs (or "irenarchs," following the Latin spelling) as those "who are in charge of public discipline and correcting behavior" and lists the irenar-chate among civic duties taken up by the local elite. The irenarchate clearly required a great outlay of money to support the armed force that eirenarchs commanded. Indeed, wealth was probably the real qualification of an eire-narch: the fact that children sometimes held the office suggests that their families paid for security services actually performed by others. Sponsoring this office would have been a good way for a rich father to boost his son's entry into public life, as many eirenarchs went on to attain the highest magistracies.[75]

Ordinarily, however, the post was not a sinecure but involved exertion and sometimes hazard. The notable orator and hypochondriac Aelius Aristides desperately sought to evade nomination in an area where bandits had earlier killed a local official. It was eirenarchs' job to secure outlying city territories against such brigandage, which was a common problem in Asia Minor. In Xenophon of Ephesus's novel, after the "damsel in distress" is shipwrecked

---

73. Night *stratêgoi* are attested in Laodicea ad Lycum (*BAtlas* 65 B2) and in three Carian communities: Sebastopolis (*BAtlas* 65 B3), Tabae (*BAtlas* 65 A3), and Tralles (Brélaz, *La sécurité publique*, 79–84; cf. Dio Chrys. *Or.* 20.2); information on them is scant. Lycia (in southwest Turkey today): Brélaz, *La sécurité publique*, 213–25, 407–16.

74. See Hirschfeld, "Die Sicherheitspolizei," 602–9; Jones, *The Greek City*, 212–13; Magie, *Roman Rule* 1, 647, and 2, 1514–15; Mitchell, *Anatolia* 1, 165–66, 195–97, 234; Riess, *Apuleius und die Räuber*, 204–12; Rife, "Officials"; Wolff, *Les brigands*, 177–82; Sänger, "Die Eirenar-chen"; and esp. Brélaz, *La sécurité publique*, 90–122, 338–41, 349–81. The post is also attested (meagerly) in the European Greek provinces: Jones, *The Greek City*, 349; Brélaz, *La sécurité publique*, 378–81. In Egypt, eirenarchs appeared later and differed from the institution in Asia Minor (Brélaz, *La sécurité publique*, 335–37; and see below).

75. Arcadius *Dig.* 50.4.18.7, which enumerates the irenarchate among personal *munera*, civil services taken on by an eminent citizen "which are performed by mental activity or the exertion of bodily labor, without any [financial] loss to the man undertaking them" (*Dig.* 50.4.18.1; note also 50.4.1). Nevertheless, the irenarchate could cost a great deal of money. On children serving, see Mitchell, *Anatolia* 1, 196; Magie, *Roman Rule* 1, 647, 650.

and captured by brigands (leitmotifs of the genre), a hero appears to save her from imminent human sacrifice:

> There was heard a noise from the forest and the trampling of men's feet. It was the chief of peace in Cilicia, Perilaos by name, a man from the top ranks of Cilicia's elite. This Perilaos came suddenly upon the bandits with a large force and killed them all, but for a few he took alive.... When they came to Tarsus, he put the bandits in jail.[76]

Eirenarchs did command police subordinates but usually only a small hand-ful, rather than the large squad that Xenophon mentioned. These underlings were called *diôgmitai* ("pursuers" or "chasers") and were probably drawn from the humbler strata of the eirenarch's town.[77] Their joint operations seem to have been mostly in the hinterlands and are best illustrated by early martyr texts, in which police hunt down prominent Christian leaders. In the *Martyr-dom of Polycarp*, the aged bishop of Smyrna flees to various country estates, until "*diôgmitai* and horsemen," led by the eirenarch Herod—a scion of an important local family—find a slave from whom they extract information under torture. The eirenarch's name is almost certainly an invented scriptural parallel, but once he finds Polycarp, his actions are plausible, despite the mar-tyrological tropes. He was eager to arrest the man and convey him to the am-phitheater but initially treated him with the respect due to an elderly member of the elite. The eirenarch tried to persuade the bishop to cooperate and avoid execution, but by the time they reached the amphitheater, the eirenarch had lost patience with the old man and brusquely threw him out of the carriage they had shared. He then handed Polycarp over to the provincial governor, who tried him and executed him before the bloodthirsty mob.[78]

---

76. Aristides: *Or.* 50 (= *Sacred Tales* 4).63–94, esp. section 72; *I. Hadr.* 84, with Robert, *Études anatoliennes*, 97; Mitchell, *Anatolia* 1, 166. Xenophon: *Ephesiaca* 2.13 (cf. 3.95); ὁ τῆς εἰρήνης τῆς ἐν Κιλικίᾳ προεστώς is a transparent circumlocution for *eirênarchês* (Rife, "Offi-cials"), as is Aristides' φύλαξ and προστῆναι τῆς εἰρήνης (*Or.* 50.72–73; Brélaz, *La sécurité publique*, 95–96). As classicizing litterateurs, both authors would eschew Roman-era neolo-gism. Xenophon's consensus date (for which this passage is crucial) is second century, but Rife ("Officials") lowers the *terminus post quem* to the mid-first century AD and does not rule out a third-century date. The irenarchate was a municipal, not province-wide, office; there was no "eirenarch of Cilicia."

77. See Brélaz, *La sécurité publique*, 145–57. On problems with the lexicography of *diôgmitai*, see Baldwin, "Leopards," with C. P. Jones's important corrections in "A Note on *Diogmitae*."

78. *Mart. Pol.*, 6–8 on his arrest, 9–16 on his trial before the governor of Asia and execution. The eirenarch is last mentioned in 17, when his father persuades the governor to have Poly-carp's body burned to prevent relic taking. This is one of our earliest martyr accounts;

FIGURE 3.1. *I.Prusa ad Olympum* 23: Gravestone of a mounted *paraphylax* with three subordinates (*diôgmitai?*) on foot, mid second century. From *Die Inschfriften von Prusa ad Olympum* I, no. 23 (Bursa Museum Inv. 6726), courtesy of Dr. Rudolf Habelt GMBH.

Diôgmitai may have also been commanded by police officials called *para-phylakes*, who patrolled their city's territory. A tombstone from Prusa in Bithynia depicts a *paraphylax* on a horse, accompanied by three men on foot, who are armed with a sword and large shields (see figure 3.1). Another funer-ary relief from near Ephesus depicts a mounted *paraphylax* next to three men on foot, each dressed in a tunic and girded with a short sword, a curved club, and a small round shield, the light armament that seems to have been common to antibrigand operations (see figure 3.2, the best extant depiction of civilian police). While no ancient text specifically states that *diôgmitai* worked under *paraphylakes*, the two trios of footmen portrayed with each *paraphylax* are likely *diôgmitai* or similar figures under their charge.[79]

---

conjectural dates range from 155 to 177 (Musurillo, xiii). Cf. the eirenarch in the 251 martyr-dom of St. Nestor (*Acta Sanctorum* (Boll.) Feb. III p. 634). In *The Martyrdom of Conon* 2, an eirenarch's squadron (*taxis*) helps an auxiliary soldier search for Christians; medieval tradi-tion dates this *passio* to Decius's reign, but Musurillo (xxxiii) suggests that it was written in the fourth century and is largely ahistorical.

79. *I.Prusa ad Olympum* 23 (figure 3.1, mid-second century); *I.Ephesos* 7.1.3222 (figure 3.2, first or second century). Robert first identified the three men in the second relief as

FIGURE 3.2. *I.Ephesos* 7.1.3222: Second- or third-century relief found near Ephesus, depicting a mounted *paraphylax* with three associates, possibly *diôgmitai*. From T. Drew-Bear, "Three Inscriptions from Asia Minor," courtesy of *Greek, Roman, and Byzantine Studies*, Duke University.

The *paraphylax* magistracy is the second-best-attested civilian police officer in Asia Minor (after the eirenarch), appearing in inscriptions throughout the first through third centuries. They are possibly connected to Hellenistic-

diôgmitai: Études anatoliennes, 103; note also his statements in *BCH* 1928, 108–9. See further Drew-Bear, "Three Inscriptions," 61–69, and M. P. Speidel, "The Police Officer." Before this relief came to light, Hirschfeld ("Die Sicherheitspolizei," 607) could only infer antibandit weapons from Christian sources, e.g., Luke 22:52: "Have you come out with short swords (*machairai*) and wooden clubs (*xyla*), as if I were a bandit?" (my translation).

era officers with a similar title (*paraphylakitai*). Eminent local citizens served as *paraphylakes* in pairs, assuming duties parallel to those of the irenarchate. In cities where both posts existed, the *paraphylakes* served in their own right, not as subordinates to eirenarchs. Eirenarchs were more involved in targeted arrests and judicial process; *paraphylakes* seem to have been occupied with routine patrols of outlying areas.[80] If so, their regular surveillance probably deterred more crime than eirenarchs' flashier forays into the bush. Nonetheless, the latter office, with its ties to the Roman governor, held greater social cachet.

Eirenarchs indeed worked closely with provincial governors, who selected eirenarchs from a list of nominees the city submitted to them.[81] They served for one year, sometimes with a colleague, and repeat tenure was common. The modus operandi of the eirenarch and his deputies was to search their city's rural territory for brigands and wanted outlaws, arrest and interrogate them, then draw up a report (*elogium*) of the interrogation, which he delivered, along with the outlaw, under guard, to the governor or magistrates for trial. Eirenarchs were expected to testify at the trial of the people they apprehended, as attested in legal evidence and by the presence of arresting officers in martyr trials. Some historians have inferred a Roman emperor's involvement in the creation of the irenarchate, since its operations were rather large-scale and reflected the imperial desire for peace and stability throughout the several provinces where eirenarchs are attested.[82] If so, Trajan is a likely possibility, since the earliest firmly dated epigraphic evidence for the office is 116/117, the

---

80. Mitchell, *Anatolia* 1, 196; Dmitriev, *City Government*, 209–12; Brélaz, *La sécurité publique*, 123–45 and 381–401, collecting sixty epigraphic references to *paraphylakes*. Another official, the meagerly attested *(h)orophylax*, seems to have policed mountainous border zones of some cities; Brélaz, *La sécurité publique*, 157–71. An early second-century BC treaty between Miletus and Heraclea ad Latmum (*BAtlas* 61 F2) has *(h)orophylakes* arresting and returning runaway slaves from either city: *Milet* 1(3), 150 (= *Syll.*³ 633).96–99.

81. In AD 153, Aelius Aristides was on a ten-man list: *Or.* 50 (= *Sacred Tales* 4).72–74. Brélaz (*La sécurité publique*, 108–11) argues that Aristides' case has been misinterpreted as a universal model and that eirenarchs were probably chosen by the council as if they were magistrates. But it seems that the governors' role persisted through the fourth century, since *CJ* 10.77 (Honorius and Theodosius II) attests it again in 409: "Suitable eirenarchs, who ensure concord by safeguarding the provinces' peace and security throughout their individual territories, are to be named by the decurions, at the discretion of the provincial governors." The third-century Ovacık inscription quoted below further evidences gubernatorial involvement in appointing eirenarchs. This is not to say that governors directly supervised eirenarchs' routine activities. See now Brélaz, "Aelius Aristide".

82. Magie, *Roman Rule* 1, 647; Jones, *The Greek City*, 212–13; Jones, *The Criminal Courts*, 116; *Dig.* 48.3.6, cited further below. Brélaz argues that the irenarchate was not imposed from above: *La sécurité publique*, 114.

last year of his reign.[83] However, recent studies lean toward a first-century date.[84] All in all, we simply do not know the story of the eirenarch's origin.

Some eirenarchs won esteem for their effectiveness. A recently published set of inscriptions from the Turkish village of Ovacık praises the antibandit activity of an eirenarch, whom they also call "brigand chaser" (*lêistodeioktês*). The fascinating contents of the lines in question are, in fact, a series of popular acclamations:

> Let him who (acts) on behalf of the city remain (with us)!
> Let him who (acts) on behalf of peace remain (with us)!
> This is of benefit to the city! A decree for the brigand chaser!
> Let the well-born brigand chaser guard the city!
> Let him who has killed the brigands guard the city!
> Let him who has acted as the city's advocate (*ekdikos*) guard the city!
> Let him who has often acted as advocate for the city remain (with us)!
> Let him who has…sent grain (*annôna*) remain (with us)!
> Let him who (acts) on behalf of peace remain (with us)!
> Let Hermaios remain (with us)! Let the son of Askoureus remain
>   (with us)!
> Hermaios, son of Askoureus, as brigand chaser as long as we live!
> Let him remain (with us) so that we can live!
> Let him remain (with us) according to the order of the governor!
> Let him who has often saved the city remain (with us)!
> Let him who sent supplies to the city remain (with us)!

Taking such pains to preserve popular chants prefigures the later, fully developed use of acclamations as political tools—and sometimes weapons.[85] At

---

83. Hirschfeld, "Die Sicherheitspolizei," 602; Riess, *Apuleius und die Räuber*, 205, citing the Carian inscription published in *BCH* 9, p. 346–47 (#30, = Robert *La Carie* #168).

84. Rife, "Officials," 103–4; Brélaz, *La sécurité publique*, 116; Dmitriev, *City Government*, 206–7. The irenarchate in Egypt followed a different pattern of development, absent from the papyri until 196; qv. in Lewis, *The Compulsory Public Services*; see further Nelson's introduction to *P.Turner* 42. Gagos and Sijpesteijn argue that Egyptian eirenarchs did not take a dominant role in civil policing until the fourth century: "Towards an Explanation," 80.

85. Ballance and Roueché, "Three Inscriptions," 87–112. I have slightly modified their translation. Ovacık lies in what was the territory of Termessos in northern Lycia (*BAtlas* 65 D4); we do not know its ancient name. The inscriptions, dated circa 278–84, are also discussed in Zimmermann, "Probus"; and Mitchell, "Native Rebellion." On acclamations, see further Ballance and Roueché, "Three Inscriptions," 109–12, with literature cited, esp. Roueché, "Acclamations," and *CTh* 1.16.6 (= *CJ* 1.40.3), Constantine's 331 order that acclamations for (or denunciations against) provincial governors should be sent directly to the emperor.

issue here is pressure on the governor to reappoint Hermaios as eirenarch. In a cynical view, Hermaios may well have orchestrated the acclamations; alternatively, Hermaios may have been *resisting* reappointment, against pressure from the people and the governor. Either scenario would nevertheless offer us a powerful testament to the needs and hopes that would resonate through a cross-section of society, from ordinary commoner to provincial governor. And we need not be too snide; the overall context of the inscriptions points to difficult security tasks well executed by father and son. Ovacık inscriptions II and III honor Hermaios's son Kiliortês for suppressing brigands. All three Ovacık inscriptions are set in the heightened military instability of the late third century. In fragment I.A.1.7–13, Hermaios is described as leading "selected young men" (*neaniskous epilektous*) to Cremna, which was probably connected to the great and lengthy siege operations against an uprising there in 278.[86]

The power of the irenarchate could tempt its holders to commit abuses of justice. Hadrian tried to restore proper process to trials, demanding that governors quit using solely the eirenarchs' reports (*elogia*) to condemn a captive without a full trial. Eirenarchs were singled out in this rescript "because it has been found that not all of their *elogia* are written in good faith." The future emperor Antoninus Pius dealt directly with eirenarchs when he served as proconsul of Asia; he seconded Hadrian's concern to reform provincial trials, insisting that eirenarchs attend the trials and go through their own reports for the evaluation of the judge. Here, the persecutor could become the persecuted, for if the eirenarch was found to have acted maliciously or spuriously added to his account, Antoninus Pius urged "that he be punished as an example," lest anyone ever attempt to perpetrate that miscarriage of justice again.[87]

Left to their own devices, the eirenarch's underlings could also get out of hand. In the account describing the martyrdom of Pionius in Smyrna during the Decian persecution, *diôgmitai* pulled Pionius and other arrested Christians from jail, manhandled them, and tried to make them eat sacrificial meat, despite Pio-

86. The theme of Ovacık II, a letter from a higher official, is reminiscent of Commodus's commendation of Boubon for the same feat (*AE* 1979, 624). Ovacık III is a resolution by the council and the people, probably of Termessos: Ballance and Roueché, "Three Inscriptions," 105; Mitchell, *Cremna*, 208–10; Mitchell, *Anatolia* 1, 234–35; and Mitchell, "Native Rebellion"; cf. Davies, "Cremna" on the archaeology of the Cremna siege works.

87. *Dig.* 48.3.6, pr. The future emperor Antoninus Pius served under Hadrian as governor of Asia, probably in 135–36; see *Dig.* 48.3.6.1 for his measures. All of 48.3.6, drawn from Aelius Marcianus, may have ultimately originated from Antoninus's experiences as proconsul of Asia. Eirenarchs were later the target of a damning imperial rescript dated AD 409: *CTh.* 12.14.1, on which see Brélaz, *La sécurité publique*, 118–21.

nius's complaints about the illegal denial of a proper hearing before the governor. Having failed in their misdeed, they forced the Christians back into jail, but not before one of the *diôgmitai* struck Pionius's head, probably with the club that constituted part of their customary armament. Even if these events are largely fictional, they still suggest the general ill will between Christians and civil police in times of persecution. After all, Christians themselves called state persecution *diôgmos*, perhaps reflecting their bad experiences with the *diôgmitai*.[88]

One further negative example helps reveal a darker aspect of policing in the Roman Empire. An inscription from a village in the territory of Hierapolis in Phrygia states that visiting *paraphylakes* must not take anything from the villagers besides firewood, fodder for their horses, and lodging. It further specifies that they are not to extort money from the village leaders.[89] Louis Robert thought that this text revealed police oppression of helpless villagers. Stephen Mitchell, noting that Roman policing is almost always discussed in relation to brigandage, goes even further:

> Police activity extended beyond the repression of banditry to cover many other aspects of keeping order in rural areas. In particular eirenarchs, *paraphylakes*, and their small forces of armed men were in the last analysis the only means available to compel the peasant inhabitants of city territories to make their material contribution to the administration and prosperity of the community, and to the taxes and other demands imposed by Rome.... The gendarmerie brought the law of the city to bear on the side of urban dwellers and landowners against villagers whose main interest lay in avoiding their attentions as far as possible. The old euphemism that a police force exists to maintain law and order rarely appears more hollow than in the communities of Roman Asia Minor.[90]

---

88. *Martyrdom of Pionius* 15, 18; Mitchell, *Anatolia* I, 196; here, the *diôgmitai*'s commanding officer is called a hipparch, which Brélaz thinks we should understand as an eirenarch (*La sécurité publique*, 150). Euseb. *Hist. eccl.* 4.15.46–47 mistakenly dates Pionius's martyrdom to Marcus Aurelius's reign. While the *Passio Pionii* is explicitly set in 250, Musurillo (xxx-viii–xxxix) suggested a fourth-century date for its actual composition. Robert authoritatively argued for a mid-third-century date: *Le martyre*, 2–3 (on chronology) and 91 (on *hipparchoi*, with Jones, *The Greek City*, 213).

89. *OGIS* 527, discussed by Robert, *Études anatoliennes*, 103–4, and Mitchell, *Anatolia* I, 195. *Paraphylakes* seem to have been very active in this area; note esp. *MAMA* 4.297, which ordains that negligent shepherd slaves be denounced to the *paraphylakes* and flogged if they allow their flocks to damage vineyards.

90. Robert, *Études anatoliennes*, 104; Mitchell, *Anatolia* I, 197; cf. Hopwood, "Policing the Hinterland," 174–76. Mitchell proceeds to parallel Rome's large-scale exploitation of the provinces to cities' microcosmic exploitation of villages in their territories.

Mitchell may overstate his case somewhat—after all, we usually know about police brutality and corruption from government efforts to correct it—but he is right to remind us that police are used not only to encourage public order but also to impose state control. We will see the same elements at work in military policing.

Civil Police Forces in Egypt

No province of the empire was more fully policed than Roman Egypt. This is the impression we get from the papyri, which evidence a daunting variety of guards and village policemen, in addition to military police. (One can reasonably question whether the nature of this ample papyrological documentation distorts our view, but the actual level of policing in Egypt probably was higher than in other provinces. Anyone wishing to argue otherwise must try to do so without explicit evidence.) The main reason Egyptian policing was so highly developed is simple: unlike what occurred with any other region of their empire, when the Romans took Ptolemaic Egypt in 30 BC, they absorbed a country with its own deep tradition of institutional policing, perhaps stretching all the way back to the Old Kingdom (ca. 2600–2150 BC). The idea of steady police development from pharaohs to emperors is alluring, but continuity cannot be clearly traced. Instead, documents illustrate ongoing experimentation in Egyptian policing throughout antiquity.

The most important police officials in Ptolemaic Egypt had been the *phylakitai*, career professionals possibly influenced by a New Kingdom model, the Medjay. There is also limited evidence for peasants in Ptolemaic Egypt being impressed to guard crops and dikes.[91] Roman Egypt saw the proliferation of new types of civilian and military police. The Romans also heavily expanded compulsory services, with the result that by the second century, numerous types of liturgies and corvées involving guard and police duties cropped up. Institutional policing was growing in the empire as a whole, but we can specifically query why policing (civilian and military) expanded in Egypt at this time. Numerous classical authors maligned Egypt as innately

---

91. Kool (*De Phylakieten,* 100) and Bagnall ("Army and Police," 67–8) suggest continuity between Medjay and Ptolemaic police; Bauschatz ("Policing the *Chôra,*" 19, 245–48) is rightly skeptical, citing dearth of evidence. Bauschatz's recent detailed studies (e.g., "The Strong Arm of the Law?" and "Archiphylakitai") compliment the fairness and effectiveness of Ptolemaic policing.

disordered, but there must be a more direct reason than this hackneyed prejudice.[92]

We can proffer one clear possibility: the Jewish diaspora revolt of 116–17. The obscurity of the sources on this widespread, alarming crisis prevents us from determining the background and chronology of the conflict, despite its massive impact. But several documented events witness this conflict's lawlessness and carnage. In Cyrene, for example, temples, public buildings, baths, and roads were destroyed. In Cyprus, Jews massacred thousands of people in Salamis but then were themselves extirpated. The Alexandrian populace fell into devastating clashes between Greeks and Jews, leading to destruction of religious properties on both sides. Vicious battles raged in the rest of Egypt, damaging many buildings and farms. Egyptian Jewry never recovered, and years later, the province was still reeling from the destruction.[93] When fighting first erupted, sufficient military forces were not available to counter Jewish attacks, and, as noted above, civilians seem to have supplemented an inadequate Roman force. In at least one case, they were soundly defeated.[94] Despite their military title, the nome-chief *stratêgoi* ("generals") were purely civilian by this time, but one Apollonios, *stratêgos* of the Apollonopolis-Heptakomia nome, went into battle, probably with an irregular militia raised from his district. Those closest to him had no faith in his military capabilities. In fact, we have two rather humiliating letters, one from his terrified wife, who begged him to foist any dangerous tasks onto subordinates, and another from his superstitious mother, who seemed to fear that the Jews would roast (and eat?) him.[95]

We should not underestimate the potential impact of such a wide-scale collapse of basic security. The experience may have prompted emperors and governors to allow more soldiers to be posted as police.[96] At the same time,

---

92. E.g., Polyb. 34.14, Strabo 17.1.12, Juv. XV (passim), and esp. Tac. *Hist.* 1.11; on Alexandria, see chapter 6 below. On the balance between military and civilian policing in late Roman Egypt, see Bagnall, *Egypt in Late Antiquity*, 173; and Aubert, "Policing the Countryside."

93. Fuks, "The Jewish Revolt," and "Aspects"; and Pucci Ben Zeev's excellent *Diaspora Judaism in Turmoil.* She argues in her fifth chapter that large-scale fighting occurred solely in 116–17, with only preliminary and obscure conflicts in 115.

94. *C.Pap.Jud.* 2.438 (= Smallwood *Docs…Nerva* 57) and 2.450 (= *P.Oxy.* 4.705); cf. Amm. Marc. 27.9.6.

95. Pucci Ben Zeev, *Diaspora Judaism in Turmoil*, chaps. 2 and 7; *C.Pap.Jud.* 2.436–37 (= *P. Giss.* 19 and 24). In the latter, the first two letters of the verb *optaô* ("roast," cf. Dio 68.32.1) are very uncertain; some editors read *êttaô* ("defeat"). See Pucci Ben Zeev, 171–73.

96. Contrast Trajan's reluctance in Pliny *Ep.* 10.77f., cited in this chapter's opening; this theme will be developed in the following chapters.

the Jewish revolts may have reinforced the impression that provincial communities could not rely on Roman arms and authority for security. This realization might help explain the continuation, and in some places (such as Egypt) the strengthening, of civilian policing. I doubt that it is by mere chance that one of our fullest descriptions of Egyptian guard organization, *P.Brem.* 23 regarding Heptakomia in November 116, was created just as the Jewish revolt was menacing this part of Egypt. Indeed, this document was found among papyri connected to the *stratêgos* Apollonios.[97] It preserves a meticulous *diataxis paraphylakês* ("arrangement of the watch") throughout the various streets and alleys of Heptakomia, topographically defined from one specific house to another. Ten guards in all were allotted a roughly equal number of houses—127 or so each—as their beat.

The town watch was an important part of Egyptian civilian policing, but we are only scratching the surface of Egyptian guards' variety and functions. The great variety of *-phylax* compounds denoting specialized guards illustrates the diverse security tasks that the authorities of Roman Egypt deemed important. We hear of field guards, guards of the threshing floor, sluice guards (as irrigation was so vital to Egypt), crop guards, prison guards, day guards and night guards, watchtower guards and lookouts, harbor guards, estate guards, river guards, guardians of the peace and eirenarchs, bandit catchers, and just plain "guards." Not many of these are attested before the second century. Altogether, more than a fifth of all known liturgies and corvées involved security duties.[98]

At this point, we should say more on the duties of night watchmen and other guards. Like most liturgical police offices, *nyktophylakes* served for one year, and the available figures suggest that a village that had this institution might employ from one to twenty night watchmen. Some night guards may

---

97. Pucci Ben Zeev does not mention *P.Brem.* 23 in her book on the revolt (*Diaspora Judaism in Turmoil*). Hennig, "Nyktophylakes," 281–82, argues that the revolt and the papyrus were not connected. I think that the date, subject matter, and source (Apollonios's archive) of *P.Brem.* 23 clinch its connection to the Jewish conflict in Egypt. There are some parallels to this document, but none predates it: e.g., *P.Oslo* 3.111 (Oxyrhynchus, AD 235); *P.Oxy.* 1.43v (AD 295, contemporaneous with the revolt of Domitius Domitianus). Because *P.Brem.* 23 was found in Hermopolis Magna, scholars sometimes erroneously use it as a description of that city, rather than of Heptakomia (also known as Apollonopolites Heptakomias).

98. This list is largely drawn from Lewis, *The Compulsory Public Services*, q.v. ἀγροφύλαξ, ἀλωνοφύλαξ, ἀφεσιοφύλαξ, γενηματοφύλαξ, δεσμοφύλαξ, ἐπιτηρητὴς δεσμίων, πρὸς θύραις, ἡμεροφύλαξ, μαγδωλοφύλαξ (cf. *burgarii* and *skopelarioi*), νομοφύλαξ, νυκτοφύλαξ, νυκτοστράτηγος, ὀρεοφύλαξ, ὁρμοφύλαξ, πεδιοφύλαξ, ποταμοφύλαξ, ἀρχινυκτοφύλαξ, ἀρχιφύλαξ, εἰρηνοφύλαξ, λῃστοπιαστής, παραφύλαξ, and φύλαξ. See also Bagnall, "Army and Police"; Drecoll, *Die Liturgien*, esp. 79–216; and Homoth-Kuhs, *Phylakes und Phylakonsteuer*.

actually have also worked in the daytime: a fragmentary third-century oath attests that the swearer will attend to the city watch "through both night and day."[99] There was no simple division between "night guards" and guards specifically called "day guards," who actually appear only in some regions of far southern Egypt (the "Thebaid," after the Pharaonic center of Thebes). One detects much regional variation here from the rest of the Nile Valley. Whereas most of the police duties listed above were one-year liturgies requiring a decent minimum income, most guard and police work in the Thebaid was performed by Egyptian peasants as a sort of imposed corvée. Perhaps this was because the Thebaid was less Hellenized and poorer than the rest of Egypt. There, guards served for just a single month, organized into small groups under the charge of a *dekanos*, a native who served as an intermediary between his fellow Egyptians and the Roman authorities—usually soldiers—to whom they were ultimately responsible. We also see this sort of combination of military and civilian policing in the staffing of watchtowers, in Egypt and beyond.[100]

The importance of guards lay primarily in the provision of basic security and the deterrence of crimes. But there is another important aspect of policing in Egypt, with ample parallels elsewhere: arresting individuals and summoning them before the magistrates. In many Roman cities, we have seen this task performed by general attendants of the magistrates who implemented the will of their superiors. In Egypt, this duty was performed by specialized liturgical policemen such as the *archephodos* ("head inspector," roughly), the *kômarchos* ("village chief"), or the eirenarch.[101] Police called *dêmosioi* played a subordinate role to higher police authorities. One reason Roman Egypt may have developed a wide variety of police offices is that until AD 200, most Egyptian communities lacked civic structures that were common elsewhere, such as a council and their related magistracies—the institutions most concerned with local civilian policing elsewhere. Instead, the *stratêgos* performed much of this policing

---

99. *P.Harr.* 2.204; cf. Hennig, "*Nyktophylakes*," 284–85 and passim.

100. Bagnall, *The Florida Ostraka*, 25–27, and "Army and Police."

101. This is roughly the chronological order in which the offices predominated in rural Egypt: the *archephodos* was the dominant village policeman in the earlier centuries of Roman Egypt, eclipsed by the *kômarchos*, under Philip the Arab (r. 244–249) near the end of the period we are examining. Although eirenarchs existed in earlier centuries, they did not come to dominate rural policing in Egypt until the time of Diocletian (294–305): Gagos and Sijpesteijn, "Towards an Explanation," 77–78. What complicates the matter is that several types of Egyptian police offices coexisted in the second through fourth centuries, and their relationships to one another and functional distinctions are elusive; see Bagnall, *Egypt in Late Antiquity*, 134–35.

role.[102] The policing duties of the *archephodoi* and others under their command could certainly overlap with those of guards, but largely surveillance duty was kept separate from the function of summoning and arresting. In fact, after Oxyrhynchus's police staff had been cut in the late fourth century, night guards vehemently complained about having both to serve summonses and to perform the watch with no assistance.[103]

When Grenfell and Hunt published the first volume of *Oxyrhynchus Papyri* in 1898, they included two documents that they called "Orders to Arrest," a name that caught on in future editions of similar texts. A closer look at this class of police documents illumines some facets of policing in Egypt and also offers a rare glimpse into ancient criminological paperwork.[104] They are concise directives, normally lacking much detail or explanation. "To the *archephodos* of the village Karanis. Send up immediately Aphrodisios..., accused by Dêmetrios." Another reads, "To the *archephodos* of Nemera. Send Dionysios son of Valerius and Taaphunchis daughter of Mieus, on the petition of Hatrês son of Pausiris. Phaôphi 2."[105] The usual pattern includes an address to a police authority of a specified village, an aorist imperative verb (ordinarily *pempô*, "send," or one of its compounds), the names of the accused and their accuser, a date (using traditional Egyptian months), and sometimes a request for urgent compliance.[106] Until the third century, the identity and office of the sender are usually not mentioned, suggesting that it was the nome *stratêgos*. Thereafter, various officials issued such orders, including military officers. Later orders more frequently included the occupations of the accuser and the accused and the cause of the action (often failure to pay taxes), and from the third century onward, the issuer often sent a guard, policeman, or soldier to ensure that the summons was served and enforced. Sometimes civilian policemen themselves

---

102. While *stratêgoi* held the fullest police powers, Gagos and Sijpesteijn go too far in asserting ("Towards an Explanation," 80) that they "monopolized" police functions in early Roman Egypt.

103. *P.Oxy.* 7.1033 (= *Sel.Pap.* 2.296), quoted below.

104. See Browne's introduction to *P.Mich.* 10.589–91; Hagedorn, "Das Formular"; Bülow-Jacobsen, "Orders to Arrest"; Gagos and Sijpesteijn, "Towards an Explanation," updating Bülow-Jacobsen's list; and now *P.Oxy.* 74.5001–12 with Gonis's update of Gagos and Sijpesteijn's list.

105. *P.Mich.* 10.589, Karanis, second or third century; *P.Oxy.* 61.4115, ca. 200–250; here, after the date, the rest of the line is marked out with XXXXXXXXX.

106. A related class of text is a complaint to the *stratêgos* or other official, requesting that he issue such an order. Such petitions are common; see, e.g., the third-century Oxyrhynchite papyrus in Eitrem and Amundsen, "Complaint of an Assault" (=*SB* 6.9421).

were told to appear before the summoning authority, should they fail to find their targets. A recently published papyrus preserves an oath sworn by an *archephodos* and an *eirênophylax*, threatening punishment if they do not search out and find three individuals.[107]

Properly speaking, these are not necessarily arrest warrants but are summonses for hearings, lacking specific language of police arrest. More careful terminology is gaining circulation.[108] But we should be wary of obscuring de facto realities with de jure distinctions. Summonses are weighty matters. At the very least, they show the beginning phase of a legal process enforced by state police power, by which an individual may lose his or her freedom. And they convey a clear sense of immediacy, an expectation of prompt compliance that one would be unwise to ignore. We have already noted a *stratêgos* who had someone beaten because his associate had failed to appear when summoned. "So by all means do come up, lest I'm beaten again!" the poor man begged.[109] Some modern scholars have found it hard to believe that, contrary to Greco-Roman law, one could essentially be arrested before being formally charged and tried.[110] But the practical mechanics of law and order depended much on the status of the accused, and on other considerations.[111] For many Egyptian peasants who had the misfortune of being the subject of a summons, their experiences often would have amounted to an arrest, especially when the order itself was delivered by a police official.

A further curiosity is the way these texts are written. When the reed pith of the papyrus plant is mashed together to form a writing surface, the fibers of the plant form lines, which scribes used as a handy writing guide. Because the strips were laid out perpendicularly, only on one side could a scribe write "along the fibers," and doing so was the norm. Yet most of these summonses

---

107. *P.Oxy.* 74.5004 (third century) instructs an *archephodos*: "Immediately send Aquila son of Apolegius, or his father who is his guarantor, or else you yourself come up" (my translation; *P.Oxy.*'s is faulty); cf. *P.Oxy.* 74.5011. A military officer (*decurio*) issued *P.Oxy.* 74.5005 (third or fourth century) to civilian *dêmosioi*, ordering them, "Immediately come with the soldier sent by me"; cf. *P.Oxy.* 5006. Other examples of soldiers enforcing summonses include *P.Wisc.* 24, *P.Oxy.* 1.64 and 74.5010; these texts are generally dated "third or fourth century." Oath: *P.Oxy.* 74.5000 (AD 166–169); cf. *P.Giss.* 84.

108. See esp. Gagos and Sijpesteijn, "Towards an Explanation," 77–79, noting that Grenfell and Hunt's ties to the British army may have colored their interpretation of the processes involved in these summonses.

109. *P.Ups.Frid* 9 (second or third century, provenance unknown).

110. Gagos and Sijpesteijn, "Towards an Explanation," 78.

111. See *Dig.* 48.19; Garnsey, *Social Status*; and Bagnall, "Official and Private Violence." For late antiquity, note *P.Oxy.* 9.1186 and MacMullen, "Judicial Savagery."

are written "across the fibers" on rather narrow strips of papyrus.[112] Because papyrus, though plentiful, was not altogether cheap, it seems that frugal government offices used leftover strips of papyrus for summonses, the meager contents of which could easily fit if the scrap of papyrus was rotated 90 degrees. Some have inferred a certain casualness in this process, and there are some suggestions of mass production. Private invitations were sometimes similarly produced; multiple copies of pithy invitations have been found on the same papyrus strip, suggesting that they were written all at once and then cut off like tickets. Summonses differ in that they were necessarily individual affairs, but these, too, have been found in small groups on the same strip. Some were probably never sent—they were probably archival "carbon copies," so to speak—but there is enough evidence to suggest that summonses were sometimes written and issued in batches.[113]

At first glance, Roman Egypt may appear to be a tightly run police state, but the papyri can be somewhat misleading. Numerous petitions seeking redress for a crime (usually theft) do not necessarily signify proactive policing. Many of these complaints were likely filed to create a legal paper trail in mere hope, not assurance, of eventual redress.[114] Nevertheless, this documentary behavior shows some faith in the administrators, civil police, and outposted soldiers who regularly received petitions from civilians. So-called orders to arrest also attest official follow-up on complaints of crime and help illustrate Egypt's comparatively large civil and military police apparatus. Moreover, they suggest state effort to work across local boundaries. "Orders to arrest," in fact, probably emerged in the first century as an institutional means to facilitate addressing intervillage disputes and crimes. In one complex case, a police-led search party hastened to follow thieves to another village in hot pursuit, but when they arrived, they were themselves beaten and imprisoned. Matters would not have gone so badly had

112. Gagos and Sijpesteijn ("Towards an Explanation," 81–82) noted that in the eighty published orders for which the direction of the writing is noted by the editor, "64 or 80% are written across the fibers." Most of the thirty summonses in Gonis's updated list (*P.Oxy.* 74, pp. 134–45) are written across the fibers, or along them on reused pieces of papyrus.

113. *P.Harr.* 2.196A and 196B (second or third century) are on the same strip and were probably never issued. *P.Cair.Preis.* 6A and 6B are likewise on the same papyrus. Gagos and Sijpesteijn ("Towards an Explanation," 82–85) suggest that they were sent and that an additional fourth-century summons (*P.Cair.* inv. 10,539) was originally conjoined to them; they offer the same theory for *BGU* 11.2081 and 2082 and credit P. J. Parsons as the prime mover behind their "mass production" theory.

114. As is explicit in some documents, e.g., *P.Mich.* 9.527 (Karanis, AD 186–188). Unfortunately, I have not seen Kelly's 2011 *Petitions, Litigation, and Social Control in Roman Egypt*.

the victim first been able to obtain a proper summons from a higher authority.[115] This important class of police document surely helped avoid disputes concerning police jurisdiction. Moreover, Egypt's centralized structure allowed the Roman provincial governor to cross local jurisdictional lines more easily, distributing lists of wanted outlaws to all of the nome *stratêgoi*.[116]

The Limits of Self-help and Civilian Policing

We have noted in passing the difficulty that civil police and the magistrates who commanded them might face in trying to keep public order and impose their will. To appreciate whatever measure of stability they succeeded in maintaining, let us look more closely now at the factors that could limit the ability of town magistrates to keep order. One possibility is divisions among the elite. There are many attestations of local political rivalries, but we must remark on the overall lack of political violence of the sort that plagued Greece and Rome before the establishment of the *pax Romana*—imperial court intrigues and a few civil wars aside.[117]

Still, class stasis and local politics could pose problems for local magistrates trying to keep order. As a guest speaker before the citizens of Tarsus, Dio Chrysostom criticized the political deadlock between common citizens and their inflexible superiors in the council (*boulê*). In Dio's own city of Prusa, civil strife had been bad enough that a governor revoked the right of assembly; later, Dio begged his assembled fellow citizens not to riot in the presence of the governor, who had just restored their privileges. Plutarch's advice to local politicians of his day further highlights the difficulties that leaders had in preventing mayhem.[118]

---

115. *P.Mich.* 6.421, discussed again below at the end of this chapter. Cf., e.g., *P.Mich.* 9.523 (Karanis, AD 66).

116. *P.Oxy.* 60.4060, a collation of documents from the office of the *stratêgos* of the Oxyrhynchite nome in the year 161, contains lists of wanted men (mostly native Egyptians who were evading liturgical service as guards but also some burglars) whom the prefect wanted all *stratêgoi* to search for.

117. Political rivalries: Plut. *Prae. ger. reip.* 814–15; Dio Chrys. *Or.* 40, 45, 47; Pliny *Ep.* 10.81f; Bekker-Nielsen, *Urban Life*. Overall lack of political violence during the principate: Aelius Aristid. *Or.* 26 ("To Rome"), e.g., sections 29 and 76.

118. Dio Chrys. *Or.* 34.16 (Tarsus); 48.1–3 (Prusa, where abuse of public resources was the issue of the day; cf. *Or.* 40, 45, 47; on fear of punishment for rioting, note Acts 19:40 and Suet. *Tib.* 37.2–3 on punishing Pollentia and Cyzicus for outbreaks of disorder); Plut. *Prae. ger. reip.*, esp. 815b–d; Meyer-Zwiffelhoffer, Πολιτικῶς ἄρχειν, 307–15.

Provincial towns, furthermore, lacked riot police. An army garrison was present in some locales during the early empire, but this was not the norm. Especially in late antiquity, urban rioting became a problem that the public security forces could scarcely control. If Greek sources such as Acts of the Apostles, Plutarch, Lucian, Dio Chrysostom, and Philostratus can be believed, hortatory rhetoric or a philosopher's terse rejoinder could defuse tense situations that might otherwise have led to violence. In any case, it is clear that local leaders did not always succeed in controlling the masses. Famine in particular destabilized social restraints in provincial communities.[119] Amid such troubles, local leaders probably often behaved as Dio Chrysostom did after an angry mob marched on his house with torches. Suspected of hoarding grain amid fear of famine, he eloquently remonstrated with them, reminding them of his past benefactions. But to give his words point, he threatened to complain to Roman authorities. In the absence of an effective local police force, fear of imperial retributions could be a controlling factor.[120] Epigraphic evidence, incidentally, shows that Dio's hometown may well have had *paraphylakes* and *diogmitai* at the time, but neither Dio nor any other writer ever cited them as a stabilizing force in the city.[121]

A further challenge to provincial magistrates' ability to keep order was intercity competition. Tacitus relates the story of a deadly melee that broke out at a gladiatorial show between partisans of Pompeii and Nuceria—somewhat reminiscent of violent clashes among modern European football hooligans. Tacitus wrote that the trouble began with an exchange of taunts—characteristic of "small-town insolence"—and escalated into stone throwing and then swordplay. Nero allowed the senate to settle on a penalty; as a result, illegal associations (*collegia*) were dissolved, and the sponsor of the show was exiled along with those who were thought to have been behind the disorder. The populace was punished by the banning of such games for ten years. In fact, the ruins of Pompeii have yielded a wall painting that probably depicts the tumult, with figures fighting inside and

119. Riots: Bagnall, *Egypt*, 164; Gregory, "Urban Violence." Greek rhetoric: Lucian *Demon.* 11 and 64; Philostr. *VS* 526 (= 39.2–8 K, on Lollianus of Athens), *VA* 1.15, and 4.8, inter alia; cf. Suet. *Jul.* 70 and *Epitome de Caes.* 15.9. The fact that people in Nicomedia did nothing to stop a major fire (Pliny *Ep.* 10.33) might suggest class conflict in that city. Famine and disorder: Rostovtzeff, *SEHRE*, 146–47, 599–600; Duncan-Jones, *Structure and Scale*, 252–53.

120. Dio Chrys. *Or.* 46, esp. section 14. We will see below that Dio often threatened to bank on his Roman connections amid disputes with fellow Prusans: e.g., Dio *Or.* 45.8; cf. Plut. *Prae. ger. reip.* 814.

121. *I.Prusa ad Olymp.* 23 (= figure 3.1), conjecturally dated to the mid second century. Dio's *Oratio* 46 probably dates from the 70s AD.

outside of the amphitheater.¹²² Then, for what it is worth, there is Juvenal's strange tale in Satire XV of a battle between two neighboring Egyptian towns that worshipped competing gods. He claimed that the battle was started by the *primores ac duces* ("eminent citizens and leaders") of each town and sub-sequently devolved into wanton cannibalism.¹²³ More realistically, Tacitus described quarrels between Lepcis Magna and Oea erupting into open combat, while Dio Chrysostom alluded to a boundary dispute between Tarsus and a smaller neighbor, which may have compelled the latter to seize the tract forcibly.¹²⁴

Some measure of local pride and neighborly resentment is to be expected, but our evidence suggests that lack of cooperation between cities and towns could impede the magistrates' ability to control basic crime. Dio Chrysostom made just this point while criticizing the discord between Nicomedia and Nicaea, pointing out one advantage of concord between the cities:

> And if some malefactor is found who deserves to be brought to justice, no longer would he evade punishment by fleeing from here to there, or from there to here. As it is now, your cities offer secret safe-harbor, so to speak, against one another, and those who have wronged one city have a refuge in the other city. But if we establish harmony [between

---

122. Tac. *Ann.* 14.17 (AD 59): "The people of Pompeii, where the show was held, came off better." The fresco is NM inv. 112,222 from house I.iii.23 (see the cover of this book). Pompeii's graffiti reflect local rivalries, e.g., *ILS* 6443a–6444. Cf. Dio Chrys. *Or.* 40.28–29 on rivalry between Prusa and Apamea (in Bithynia) expressed by insults at entertainments.

123. Juv. 15.40 and passim. Once discounted on geographical grounds, Petrie's 1895 excavations proved the proximity of the two towns, Ombos and Tentyra (*BAtlas* 80B1) and bolstered the background of the dispute. See Calderini and Daris, *Dizionario* III, 387, and IV, 391. Courtney (*A Commentary*, 590–91) swallows the story whole—even the cannibalism. The polymath Jack Lindsay, who devoted chap. 9 of his *Daily Life in Roman Egypt* to Juvenal XV, interpreted the story as a confused account of a fertility rite (115). Egyptians were supposedly notorious for religious conflicts leading to bloodshed: e.g., Plut. *De Is. et Os.* 72, 380b–c for an old dispute between Oxyrhynchus and Cynopolis which broke into violence until the Roman authorities interceded.

124. Tac. *Hist.* 4.50 (early in Vespasian's reign); discord between the two African neighbors led to bloodshed through armed conflict (*per arma atque acies*). The involvement of Gara-mantes nomads necessitated an auxiliary force to restore order; see further *Hist.* 2.21, 3.57, and 4.3; as MacMullen points out (*Enemies*, 339), local rivalries in Campania proved as divisive as the political strife of AD 68–69. Tarsus: Dio Chrys. *Or.* 34.10–14, 43–48; cf. Tac. *Hist.* 1.65 for discord between Lugdunum and Vienne, and Herodian 3.2.7–9 and 3.3 on ill will between various eastern communities. On boundary disputes, see Elliott, "Epigraphic Evidence." Heller (*Les bêtises des grecs*) provides a detailed study of intercity rivalries in Roman Asia and Bithynia.

Nicomedia and Nicaea], men will have to be good and law-abiding, or else get out of Bithynia.[125]

Countering crime and reinforcing public order were difficult tasks, and local security forces were not always up to the challenge. A late papyrus (AD 392), preserving the appeal of two Oxyrhynchite night guards to their superiors, offers the clearest indication of the sorts of problems that ancient guards of any period might have faced:

> Being appointed to the care of the peace we execute public orders irreproachably, while also attending to the city watch; but being constantly under the necessity of producing various persons in accordance with the command of our lords the superior magistrates and having no assistance either of public employees (*dêmosioi*; likely subordinate policemen but perhaps public slaves) or inspectors (*ephodeutai*) we often run the risk, one would almost say, of our lives, because these assistants have been taken from us and we go about keeping the watch all alone.

They closed their petition by requesting that either their auxiliary staff be reinstated or their duties be suspended, "lest we be held responsible at our peril."[126]

More than reinforcing the simple difficulty of police work, this revealing text also reminds us that the public-security apparatus of towns was subject to the vicissitudes of budgetary and liturgical constraints, with the natural result that (then as now) some communities had to make do with insufficient resources. The night guards' complaint also makes an important differentiation between two facets of policing: "producing various persons"—arresting and summoning suspects, reminiscent of the role of *apparitores* and other magisterial attendants—and patrolling and keeping watch over the city, which is reminiscent of *vigiles* and *nyktophylakes*. These are two distinct tasks. To

---

125. Dio Chrys. *Or.* 38.41–42, addressing the Nicomedians; note also 38.32 on smugglers benefiting from Nicaea and Nicomedia's discord (cf. *P.Oxy.* 1.36) and 38.33–40 on other problems therefrom. The two cities were disputing the title *prôtê* ("first [city]"); see Robert, "La titulature de Nicée"; Jones, *The Roman World*, 87; Meyer-Zwiffelhoffer, Πολιτικῶς ἄρχειν, 307–15; and now Heller, *Les bêtises des Grecs*, 283–341, with tableau 4.

126. *P.Oxy.* 7.1033 (= *W.Chr.* 476; translation adapted from *Sel.Pap.* 2.296), from the *nyktostratêgoi* (intermediary police officials) to the *riparii* of the Oxyrhynchite nome. *Riparii* were important civil police officials in late Roman Egypt: Bagnall, *Egypt in Late Antiquity*, 165; Alston, *The City*, 280; and Torallas Tovar, "The Police in Byzantine Egypt," and "Los *riparii*."

cover them both, police officials ideally should have had the assistance of a larger support staff or other types of guards or police, lest the security apparatus be stretched too thin. As usual with papyri, we do not know how this petition was answered. It is as likely as not that the supplicants had to continue doing more with less (which was still more police than many cities in the empire had). We cannot discern whether their plea had real merit, but it is hard to imagine that the situation they described made for more effective policing.

Occasionally, simple ineffectiveness was the problem. We should not dwell unduly on the point, for even today, for a variety of reasons, our highly professional police do not succeed in preventing many routine crimes or in solving them and arresting guilty criminals. But rarely do criminals show such brazen disdain for public authority as the highway robbers who stole a pig and a tunic from two swineherds, then beat and bound not just them but also the outnumbered watchtower guard (*magdôlophylax*).[127] Even if the authorities were conscientious about enforcing the law, serious criminals could still find room to operate by finding weak spots within the thin security patchwork of various officials, guards, and soldiers, outmaneuvering and outnumbering the forces of public order.

Then there was the classic problem of jurisdiction boundaries. Aside from "orders to arrest," there is little explicit evidence that civilian police forces of different cities actually cooperated with one another.[128] The papyri attest to criminals leaving their own towns and villages to commit thefts; local officials had more trouble rectifying wrongs in such cases. One case went remarkably awry, suggesting not only problems of jurisdiction but criminal collusion to boot. According to an inhabitant of Karanis who had two donkeys stolen from him, he and his local police officer (an *archephodos*) went together and tracked the donkeys to the territory of another village, Bacchias. Just as they were about to arrest the culprits, the police officials of Bacchias arrested, robbed, and beat them. They were released three days later, well after the thieves had a chance to abscond.[129]

---

127. *P.Fayûm* 108, Arsinoite nome, ca. AD 171. *Magdôlophylakes* were sometimes very young; in *O.Florida* 2, a military officer requests a civilian young man (*neaniskos*) to replace a *magdôlophylax* who was just a small boy (*mikros*). Cf. *P.Tebt.* 3.733. (143 BC), in which a thief stole some clothing by force in the presence of a guard. See further Baldwin, "Crime and Criminals," 258–59.

128. Sherwin-White, *Roman Society and Roman Law in the New Testament*, 98; cf. Dio Chrysostom's probably vain pleas that Nicomedia and Nicaea start cooperating against smugglers and other criminals: *Or.* 38.32–42.

129. *P.Mich.* 6.421 (Karanis, reign of Claudius). The beginning is lost, so we do not know the addressee; it was likely the prefect of Egypt or the nome *stratêgos*. Compare *P.Goth.* 13,

At times, then, keeping order depended on the existence of a superior authority. This was Rome, of course. But imperial authority was not always the friend of local magistrates, especially those who failed to control their citizens. Magisterial police duties could be subject to imperial oversight, particularly when an accused malefactor possessed eminence and social privilege, or, as with Saint Paul the Roman citizen, other grounds for appeal and protection. One might compare an early-third-century military policeman who was taken to task by the governor of Egypt for seizing and torturing an innocent man without the presence of witnesses.[130]

These limitations of local policing may constitute one explanation for emperors' and governors' involvement in public order and the concomitant growth of military policing, to which we will now turn.

P.Brem 26, and *BGU* 1.46. For later parallels, cf. *P.Oxy.* 19.2233 (AD 350), on the assault of the Tychinphagians against the settlers of Ptolema, with a *riparios* policeman demanding that the authorities of Tychinphagi send the guilty parties to Ptolema; and *P.Oxy.* 16.1832 (fifth or sixth century), where a village chief gives refuge to a female thief. See further Baldwin, "Crime and Criminals," 258. On the intersection of intervillage disputes and police corruption, which is most attested in Byzantine Egypt, see further Baldwin, "Crime and Criminals," 262, and Lindsay, *Daily Life*, 119–21. On the general theme of corruption, see Schuller, "Grenzen," 9–21, and *Korruption*; and MacMullen, *Corruption* (with Talbert's review in *Phoenix* 1991).

130. *P.Berol.* inv. 7347, from AD 200–207; Rea, "Proceedings before Q. Maecius Laetus." (*SB* 16.12949.)

4

"I brought peace to the provinces": Augustus and the Rhetoric of Imperial Peace

WE MOVE NOW to the emperor's role in creating peaceful and stable conditions within the empire, starting here with a particular focus on Augustus, then on Rome and Italy under his successors (chapter 5), and finally on the provinces (chapter 6). Emperors' involvement in public order was real and direct; they routinely became involved in all sorts of problems and conflicts and used soldiers as police to enforce their will. Before immersing ourselves in the numerous details of policing and public order, we must first acknowledge the importance of rhetoric and symbolism. Diverse voices produced a rhetoric of imperial peace, and anyone who handled a coin stamped *pax* or *concordia* was exposed to it.[1] Many invested their hope and faith in the emperor's just power and revered his image throughout every province.[2] Note, for example, the address of an unknown orator to an unknown emperor:

> Now every continent is at peace, both land and sea crown their ruler, Greeks and barbarians alike now extol him! Your rule, just like some ship or protective wall, has been restored and fortified, and has firmly reaped its benefits; what could surpass this valor? Or what condition could be better and more advantageous than this? Is there not complete security for anyone to travel wherever he wishes? Are not all the harbors everywhere bustling; the mountains just as safe for wayfarers

---

1. On *concordia* and *pax*, see Weinstock, *Divus Julius*, 260–69; Levick, "*Concordia*"; Osgood, *Caesar's Legacy*, 189–91 (with fig. 4.8 of *RRC* 529.4b; cf. 480.24). Also note Roberts, "A Study of *Concordia*," 8–43; and Lobur, *Consensus*, esp. 38–58.

2. On the emperor as symbol, note Lendon, *Empire of Honour*, 174–75. On images of the emperor, Ando, *Imperial Ideology*, 206–316; Revell, *Roman Imperialism*, 80–109; and Boatwright, "Antonine Rome."

as the cities are for those who inhabit them? For goodwill holds sway over the plains, and all fear has been eradicated from everywhere.[3]

This trite oration could well derive from a generic rhetorical exercise, with no particular ruler in mind; the author certainly included many of the topoi common in royal encomia.[4] Despite the patent exaggerations, praise for safety and stability reveals the real desires of the empire's inhabitants. Otherwise, it would not resonate rhetorically with the audience or the reader.

Aelius Aristides, in his *Roman Oration* delivered to the court of Antoninus Pius, praised the empire for securing a safe, orderly world. He cited the empire's good order (*akribeia*) and the lack of barbarian incursions, revolts, or governors ("satraps") at arms against one another. When he claims that cities are not garrisoned or divided against one another, he especially diverges from reality. But his purpose is to extol the stability of the empire, where "the whole world sings as one in celebration with tighter harmony than a chorus, praying together that this empire shall survive through eternity, so wonderfully is it directed by its chorus-leader ruler!"[5] To this we might compare Pliny's panegyric to Trajan, in which the fawning Pliny praised the kindness (*benignitas*) of the *princeps* and exclaimed "so great is the security of our times!"[6] The power relationships are obvious, but statements like these may have also served as a tactful way of trying to guide the *princeps* to let his behavior live up to the flattery he received.[7]

Naturally, Pliny was praising Trajan in contrast to Domitian, who had created an atmosphere of fear in Rome. Consequently, senatorial historians and

---

3. Pseudo-Aristides 35 (*Eis Basilea*), 36–37; cf. Epict. *Diss.* 3.13.9.

4. Many different addressees have been proposed, from Trajan to a ninth-century Byzantine ruler. Stertz, "Pseudo-Aristides," comes closest to my own view, stated with full bibliography in Fuhrmann, "Keeping the Imperial Peace," 95–97. Topoi: Menander Rhetor 2.373 and 375–77, as well as *Eis Basilea* 9, and cf. pseudo-Dionysius of Halicarnassus *On Epideictic Speeches*, 1.259 (probably second or third century).

5. Aristid. *Or.* 26.29 (Keil's edition; Oliver's ignores a likely lacuna); cf. 26.104 (with heavy religious overtones) and 26.100–101 on the safety of travel. Behr, *Aelius Aristides and the Sacred Tales*, 88–90, and *P. Aelius Aristides: The Complete Works*, 373, favors AD 155 or 156 for the delivery of Aristides' most famous speech.

6. Pliny *Paneg.* 50.7: *Tanta benignitas principis, tanta securitas temporum est...*; cf. 42.1 and 49.1–4, and Tac. *Agr.* 3, 44, vs. 41.

7. In this case, Trajan may have lived up to this rhetoric, when he showed no interest in punishing Dio Chrysostom for placing a statue of the emperor near some graves (Pliny *Ep.* 10.82) and when he would not tolerate compulsory loans (*Ep.* 10.55) or anonymous denunciations of Christians (*Ep.* 10.97).

philosophers depicted him as the quintessential tyrant.[8] The shaping of an emperor's historical legacy was a complex process, of course, but many emperors clearly stooped to gross excesses. There had been cruel emperors before Domitian, and others would follow. This brings up a further complexity in evaluating the emperor and public order, namely that public order sometimes meant one thing to the emperor and something else to various groups of his subjects. Balanced with the hopeful rhetoric of stability and justice was the emperor's desire to maintain his own power and use it effectively to impose his will against problem groups. We see this most clearly in senatorial hostility to denigrated emperors such as Tiberius and Domitian and later in the anti-Christian measures of Decius and Valerian. We should not approach the emperors' security measures with the assumption that they were primarily trying to help ordinary people. Sometimes this may have been the case, but overall the emperors' efforts seem aimed at maintaining power. General stability was conducive to this end, but benefits to the populace were nevertheless largely incidental.

Furthermore, just as we cannot overly trust the positive rhetoric of the good king providing just order to his people, we must likewise be suspicious of negative rhetoric. The inept author of the *Historia Augusta*, for instance, squarely blamed provincial disorders on Gallienus's character flaws.[9] Credit for provincial conditions—good or bad—tended to accrue to the emperor, even when he had little to do directly with creating those conditions. This phenomenon reflects the ancient mentality that the ruler's character had great impact on the condition of his realm. The religious logic of most Romans added divine implications: if the empire prospered under a certain ruler, divinity was on his side. Setbacks, and especially military defeats, revealed divine wrath.[10] Also active here are the forces of executive periodization; papyri and inscriptions from the principate are usually dated by the year of the emperor's reign. Only a small, illogical jump leads to the implication that events dated by an emperor's reign occurred *because* of the emperor.

---

8. Notably Tacitus, Dio, and Epictetus (the equestrian Suetonius was more evenhanded). Starr ("Epictetus") and Long (*Epictetus*, 35 and 194) argue that Domitian is the direct target of Epictetus's frequent remarks on tyranny. It was a mark of "good" emperors that they did not take great interest in charges of treason (*maiestas*), e.g., SHA *Hadr.* 18.4.

9. SHA *Duo Gallieni* 5.1.

10. See Fears, *Princeps*; on the republic, cf. Rosenstein, *Imperatores Victi*; and on the later empire, Olster, *Roman Defeat*, 30–45. Amit ("Propagande") stresses the people's view of the emperor's *felicitas* as a force that determines conditions in the empire. More work on Roman "triumphalism" in the principate is needed. Cf. the "Mandate of Heaven" concept in traditional China.

Moreover, our sources often give the emperor credit for conflict negotiation or security measures that were mostly the work of subordinates.[11] This misappropriation extends to correspondence. We have noted, for instance, Commodus's letter to the Boubonians, celebrating their suppression of bandits (chapter 3 above); the distracted emperor's secretarial staff likely wrote the letter.[12]

At the same time, the emperor may have existed more as an idea than as a real individual in the minds of his subjects. Many provincials probably did not even know who was emperor. When Jesus asked whose head was on the coin, his interlocutor vaguely replied, "Caesar's."[13] It seems that most people at least did know that there *was* an emperor—knowledge that should not be taken for granted in a realm encompassing so many remote places. He could be a powerful symbol of protection, as when people in need of help clung to his statue or invoked his name, as if he were a god.[14]

But as a real historical individual, what real impact on public order did any emperor have? Considering the multiple difficulties and complexities of our sources, the influence of bias and rhetoric, and the emperor's currency as a mere symbol, the question is not easily answered. Nevertheless, over the next three chapters, I will show that emperors did affect security and imperial order in Rome, Italy, and the provinces. I will do so by describing the emperors' approach to and involvement in several cases of disorder and the use of soldiers under their command as police. The story begins with the Republican civil wars and Augustus's rise to power.

---

11. E.g., see below on Tiberius's investigations of slave prisons in Italy before he became *princeps* (Suet. *Aug.* 32 and *Tib.* 8).

12. *AE* 1979, 624. Millar's *The Emperor in the Roman World* probably overstates the extent to which the average emperor typically labored over his correspondence. In his uncharitable review of Millar ("Rules of Evidence"), Hopkins is right to point out (183–85) that not all emperors were equally responsible. Millar replied to his critics in an afterword in the 1992 reprint of the book; note esp. 640 and 648–50.

13. The exchange is found in all of the synoptic gospels: Matt. 22:21; Mark 12.16; Luke 20:24, specifying that Jesus's opponents were trying to trick him into making a treasonous remark, on which they would be able to denounce him to the Roman authorities. The lackadaisical attitude of the ass in Phaedrus 1.15 suggests a lack of popular interest in exactly who the current emperor was. Around the year 400, Synesius (*Ep.* 148) claimed that everyone knew there was a ruler because of yearly taxes but that some of the yokels around Cyrenaica still supposed that Agamemnon was king.

14. E.g., Philostrat. *VA* 1.15, Pliny *Ep.* 10.74, Gaius *Institutes* 1.53, and *Dig* 21.1.17.12, all on seeking the religious inviolability of a supplicant (ἀσυλία) by clinging to the emperors' statues (see Rigsby, *Asylia*, 586; Gamauf, *Ad statuam licet confugere*; and Naiden, *Ancient Supplication*, 38, 250–56). Also note Apul. *Met.* 3.29 and section 16 of the corresponding Greek short story. On the emperor's symbolic importance among elite provincials, see Stertz, "Aelius Aristides' Political Ideas," 1254–62.

Octavian Augustus's reign as undisputed leader of the Roman world from 31 BC to AD 14 established lasting trends in imperial law, administration, and oversight of public order. He set the pattern for how later emperors approached the numerous problems brought to their attention and their stance toward provincial governors and other subordinates. While the growth of military policing outside of Rome is most discernible in the second and third centuries, here, too, Augustus was a groundbreaker. It was he who started the trend of using soldiers for regular policing purposes. More symbolically, Augustus created a durable precedent by depicting himself as the guarantor of domestic peace and stability. The public's overall receptiveness to this image of stability and order continued under Augustus's successors, who themselves perpetuated Augustan-style propaganda (for lack of a better word). By both his direct involvement in challenges to order and the symbolic role he fashioned for himself, Augustus's principate was foundational for the history of Roman imperial policing and public order. His principate concretely molded the way his successors exercised power. In addition, the security measures that the first *princeps* laid down in Rome and Italy continued growing, eventually becoming part of a fuller-fledged military police apparatus that reached into every province of the empire.

Before Augustus: Republican Precedents

Recent scholarship has thoroughly investigated public order in the Roman republic, stressing the absence of a modern-style police force.[15] One should not imagine, however, that republican Rome was entirely without police or that the republic's approach to public order was consistently laissez-faire. Censors oversaw public morals, praetors issued legal injunctions, aediles policed markets and other public spaces, and tribunes of the plebs could arrest anyone who was abusing a citizen. A trio of minor magistrates, the *triumviri* or *tresviri capitales*, were specialized police officials who administered Rome's jail and executions therein, supervised a modest nocturnal patrol (hence their alias *nocturni*), and seem to have exercised jurisdiction over minor crimes, arresting and dispensing summary justice to slaves and low-class citizens in the Forum, near the jail.[16] Also near the jail and the Forum was the Tarpeian

---

15. Nippel, "Policing Rome," *Aufruhr und "Polizei,"* and *Public Order*; Lintott, *Violence in Republican Rome*; Riggsby, *Crime and Community*.

16. See further Robinson, *Ancient Rome: City Planning and Administration*, 150–82; Nippel, *Public Order*, 4–27. For the *tresviri capitales'* survival into the imperial era, see Dio 54.26.6 and Hillebrand, "Der Vigintivirat," 13–15, 49–52, 116–20. On the jail (*carcer Tullianum*; the

Rock, a cliff whence some criminals were thrown, and the Gemonian Steps, where bodies of the executed were sometimes exposed for further humiliation.[17] State punishment was built into the central topography of the city and culturally strengthened by durable traditions: Romulus himself was said to have ordered several bandits to be hurled from the rock. It is noteworthy that Augustan-era writers depicted Augustus's putative ancestor as a repressor of banditry.[18]

As the republic's chief executives, the consuls would ordinarily hope to be outside of Rome, winning military glory against foreign enemies. But sometimes consuls and other important officials were assigned to law-and-order problems. According to Livy, both consuls were tasked with investigating and punishing Bacchic devotees throughout Italy in 186 BC. Aediles arrested Bacchic priests and kept watch to prevent worship services, and the *tresviri capitales* set extra watches especially to guard against arson, with lower neighborhood officials reporting to them.[19] In response to Catiline's conspiracy in 63 BC (the year of Augustus's birth), Cicero as consul posted guards in Rome and in some Italian towns.[20] Rome reluctantly employed large armies against slave revolts in Sicily and Italy, which required difficult policing operations afterward.[21] We have already noted (chapter 2 above) one such special command, that of Augustus's biological father in southern Italy in 60 BC.

---

appellation "Mamertine" is postclassical), see Richardson, *A New Topographical Dictionary*, 71; cf. Sall. *Cat.* 55.3–4 and Cic. *De legibus* 3.2–11.

17. See Cadoux, "The Roman *Carcer*." We are not sure where the *rupes Tarpeia* was; Richardson (*A New Topographical Dictionary*, 378) favors the southwest end of the Capitolium, while Coarelli (*Rome and Environs*, 31–32) places it on the Arx, between the temple of Juno Moneta and the Forum. Exposure of bodies on the *scalae Gemoniae* is first attested under Tiberius; see Barry, "Exposure, Mutilation and Riot."

18. Dion. Hal. 2.56.3, actually censuring Romulus for excessive cruelty. Livy's description (1.4) of the twins' youthful attacks on brigands is wholly positive.

19. Livy 39.14–18; cf. *ILS* 18.

20. Cic. *Cat.* 1.1–11, 2.26–27; Sall. *Cat.* 30.7, 32.1, 36.3, 50.3, 55.2.

21. The first two great slave revolts were based in Sicily in the late second century, followed by Spartacus's great Italian uprising in the late 70s BC, on which see Shaw, *Spartacus*, and Urbainczyk, *Slave Revolts*. Following the first revolt, the governor of Sicily in 132 BC recaptured 917 fugitive slaves: *ILLRP* 454 = *ILS* 23. Following the second revolt in 100 BC, slaves were banned from carrying weapons on the island, an extraordinary and hard-to-enforce measure, as servile herdsmen's duties normally called for arms. The otherwise infamous governor of Sicily, Verres, helped secure the island from involvement in Spartacus's revolt: Sallust *Hist.* 4.32 M; Brennan, *The Praetorship*, 489, cf. 431–34 and 477–80; Plut. *Crassus* 10.3; and Cic. *Ver.* 2.5.7.

Rampant piracy drove the Romans to extraordinary maritime policing. As early as 102 BC, Mark Antony's grandfather fought pirates as praetor in Cilicia (southeastern Asia Minor). In 74, Mark Antony's father likewise served (less successfully) a special praetorian command in the eastern Mediterranean. Around the same time, a young Julius Caesar (b. 100 BC) was kidnapped and ransomed by pirates in the Aegean; once free, he hunted them down and punished them as a private citizen. Pirates grew so bold that they raided Ostia, Rome's port, and, in a separate incident, captured two praetors, their lictors, and their entire entourage in southern Italy. Soon thereafter, in 67, despite heavy political opposition, Pompey was given unprecedented power to eradicate piracy: a three-year command over the whole Mediterranean, with several subordinates. The disruptive civil wars allowed piracy to crop up again, until Augustus consolidated his power.[22] Augustus, in fact, claimed to be the culmination of this tradition, proclaiming not only "I brought peace to the provinces" but also "I freed the sea of pirates."[23]

Rebel slaves, pirates, and other persistent law-and-order problems pushed the Roman republic to extend the policing role of the state, the power of certain leaders, and the role of the military in enforcing the state's will. It is significant to compare the deaths of the Gracchi, whose tribunates ushered in an age of political violence that brought down the republic. The elder brother, Tiberius, was killed in 133 BC by a makeshift lynch mob of prominent citizens and their retainers, wielding improvised weapons. Gaius's destruction was more professionally and officially effected: when violence broke out after Gaius assumed a bodyguard in 121, the senate gave the consul Opimius special authority to suppress Gracchus and his supporters; his main instrument in so doing was a body of Cretan archers he had at hand. Use of mercenary

---

22. Qv. "piracy" in OCD[2] (Badian) and OCD[3] (de Souza, with his *Piracy in the Graeco-Roman World*, 42–199). There were earlier actions against pirates, e.g., in the Balearic islands in 121: de Souza, *Piracy*, 92–96. On the rise of Cilician piracy, note Strabo 14.5.2. On M. Antonius's command in 102, cf. the law of 100 BC, the so-called *lex de piratis*: *FIRA* I[2] 9; Crawford *RS* n. 12, with Geelhaar, "Some Remarks on the *lex de provinciis praetoriis*." On Mark Antony's father (all three Antonii mentioned above shared the same name), Linderski clears up confusion in "The Surname of M. Antonius Creticus." On the background to the *lex Gabinia*, which ultimately granted Pompey extraordinary powers, note App. *Mith.* 92–95; Dio 36.17–24, 36.37. See also Brennan, *The Praetorship*, 357–58, 406–7, 426, 434 (noting other Roman setbacks and counterpirate efforts). On piracy amid the transition from republic to empire, see Braund, "Piracy under the Principate."

23. Augustus's line about pirates (*mare pacavi a praedonibus*, *RGDA* 25.1) alludes to his rival Sextus Pompey (cf. Livy *Per.* 123, 127–28). The claim of provincial pacification (*RGDA* 26.2–3) specifies territories in Spain, Gaul, Germany, and the Alps gained through honorable wars of expansion; cf. Vell. Pat. 2.90–91.1.

soldiers to restore order was exceptional, but the controversial so-called final decree of the senate (*senatus consultum ultimum*, or *SCU*) reappeared throughout various first-century BC crises, to bolster magistrates' policing powers. This provision recognized a state of emergency and called on the magistrates (usually but not always the consuls) to restore order, "lest the state suffer any harm."[24] In the summary of his achievements published in AD 14, Augustus himself reminded his fellow citizens that the senate had empowered him with an *SCU* very early in his career, in January 43 BC.[25]

Another extension of magisterial power in the late republic were the proscriptions, first under Sulla in the late 80s BC and again in 43–39 BC under the Second Triumvirate of Lepidus, Mark Antony, and Octavian. These began with a series of lists issued by Sulla, first with 80 names, then up to a probable total of 520 (some sources claim thousands). The triumvirs proscribed at least 300 people, maybe many more.[26] Anyone could kill someone on the list for a reward, and by opening the process to the populace, the state seems to have devolved policing authority to private initiative. In fact, the whole process was aberrant, dictatorial, and in clear contravention of republican traditions. The executions of the proscribed were rather military in style, and especially during the second proscription, it was mainly soldiers who did the hunting and killing.[27]

---

24. App. *BCiv.* 1.16, 1.25–26; Plut. *Ti. Gracch.* 19 and *C. Gracch.* 13–14, 16. On the Cretan archers, note Stockton, *The Gracchi*, 195–97. On the *SCU*, see Cic. *Cat.* 1.4 (*ne quid res publica detrimenti caperet*; cf. *Cat.* 4.13, *Phil.* 5.34 and 8.14; and Asconius 34C) and Sall. *Cat.* 29, with Mitchell, "Cicero and the *Senatus Consultum Ultimum*"; Drummond, *Law, Politics and Power*, 79–113; and Lintott, *Violence in Republican Rome*, 149–74, 183–84.

25. *RGDA* 1.3; cf. Dio 46.29–31 and 48.33.3 (40 BC). Here, Augustus did specify that the consuls shared in the *SCU* "lest the state suffer any harm"; otherwise, he obfuscated the conflict with Antony and Decimus Brutus at Mutina.

26. On the number of those proscribed, see Hinard, *Les proscriptions* 116–20, 264–69. The sources clash: under Sulla, Appian (*BCiv.* 1.95) claimed more than 1640; Val. Max. 9.2.1 has 4700 victims; Hinard (*Les proscriptions*, 119) follows Plutarch for a total of 520. Some were senators; most were equestrians. Hinard thinks that the Second Triumvirate proscribed a total of 300 by 39 BC; Osgood (*Caesar's Legacy*, 63) thinks that the number "probably reached several thousand." Again, the sources are vexed and contradictory; Appian (*BCiv* 4.5–7) says 300 senators and 2000 equestrians were killed or had their wealth confiscated during the second proscription, but Hinard suggests that not all of these were officially proscribed. In any case, during both proscriptions, the lists were liquid, and many were able to evade execution.

27. In fact, as soon as the proscription list was posted, according to Appian (*BCiv.* 4.12), "the gates and all other avenues of escape from the city were secured, along with the harbor facilities, marshes and pools, and any other place suspected of being a clandestine refuge. The countryside was entrusted to centurions roving everywhere to find people." See further 4.17–20, 22, 25–28, 30; cf. Hinard, *Les proscriptions*, 43, 241–42, 322–23, 511–12. Cicero was the most famous victim, killed by a centurion in charge of a squad of soldiers: App. *BCiv.* 4.19.

In other words, soldiers increasingly executed the will of a state that was becoming more autocratic as the republic disintegrated.

The Augustan principate echoed precedents from other leaders. There was Pompey's extensive *imperium* and multiple provinces that he ruled through legates, for example. Pompey also used legionaries to establish order in Rome in the late 50s.[28]

But the key figure is Octavian's adopted father, Julius Caesar. Because Caesar was usually focused on pressing military challenges, evaluating his approach to domestic law and order is difficult, and the vast amount of modern ink spilled in his honor rarely clarifies this issue.[29] One extraordinary policing initiative (albeit a short-lived one) was the strict enforcement of a sumptuary law in 46 BC, probably to stem aristocratic competition. According to Suetonius, Caesar posted guards (*custodes*) at markets to enforce measures against extravagant consumption and invasively used his soldiers and lictors to snatch luxury foods from people's dining rooms. Here, Suetonius also mentioned that Caesar annulled an ex-praetor's marriage which was not to his liking, presaging a certain invasiveness into private life continued by Augustus and his successors.[30] In his thorough study of imperial-era informants and prosecutors, Steven Rutledge reminds us that "the apex of legislation enabling delation came from not a Gaius or a Nero, but Augustus."[31]

Both Caesar and Augustus sponsored legal remedies for provincials who had suffered from rapacious Roman governors.[32] They were even more concerned to improve life in Rome and Italy. Caesar made a law requiring that at least one-third of the shepherds employed by ranchers in Italy must be freeborn (Suet. *Jul.* 42.1); he was probably aiming to make rural areas safer and prevent slave insurrections. He also seems to have banned certain clubs. In the last decades of the republic, these *collegia* had undermined stability by operating as factions and street gangs. Augustus later made a law that repeated this ban, and future emperors would keep restricting the privilege of

---

28. Cic. *Mil.* 37.101; Caes. *BCiv.* 3.1; Dio 40.50–54.

29. A notable exception is Yavetz's careful reading of the ancient evidence and modern historiography in *Julius Caesar and His Public Image*, which I have largely followed below.

30. Suet. *Jul.* 43; cf. Dio 43.25. Caesar's sumptuary measures apparently fell apart when he himself left Rome: Cic. *Att.* 13.7 (45 BC).

31. Rutledge, *Imperial Inquisitions*, 178; cf. Rivière, "Encouragement," 331.

32. Caesar's *lex Julia repetundarum* was passed in 59, during his first consulship, the last in the line of republican anticorruption laws that started in 149; see Cic. *Fam.* 8.8; *Dig.* 48.11. It remained in force throughout the imperial era. Caesar himself terribly mistreated provincials: e.g., Suet. *Jul.* 54. For Augustus's measures, see below on the Cyrene edicts.

free assembly when they deemed it necessary.[33] It is unclear if Caesar restricted clubs by sponsoring a formal law (*lex*) or by just decreeing what he wanted by fiat, from an unrivaled position of power (this was within the scope of his untraditional dictatorship). Augustus preferred more traditional legal mechanisms but could certainly obtain legal sanction for anything he wanted. He had as much power as Caesar but sought a more palatable style in using it. In Tacitus's view, Augustus gradually arrogated to himself the former power of the senate, magistrates, and laws. By the early third century, it seems that no one questioned that the word of the emperor was law.[34]

Let us end with further examples Augustus wished to avoid. In hindsight, he saw the opposition that Caesar's flirtation with monarchy created. Then, for whatever reason, Caesar facilitated his own assassination by dismissing his bodyguard of Spanish soldiers.[35] We will see that Augustus and later "Caesars" were less willing to chance that fate; military bodyguards became the norm. Octavian also differed from his great-uncle in the latter's policy of clemency (*clementia*) toward opponents.[36] Even after laying down triumviral powers and establishing the principate, Augustus never lacked the ability to eliminate potential rivals (or allies to do so on his behalf; see below on Egnatius Rufus). The principate was a decent compromise after so much civil war, and Augustus's mere longevity helped him live down his tainted youth. But the fact that one of the proscribing triumvirs rose to a

---

33. Caesar's restrictions on *collegia* (probably in 46 BC) are only attested in Josephus *AJ* 14.213–15 (noting that synagogues were excepted) and Suet. *Jul.* 42.3: *cuncta collegia praeter antiquitus constituta distraxit* ("he dissolved all clubs except those which were long established"). Some scholars have wondered if Suetonius confused Caesar's measures with Augustus's more firmly attested ones (*CIL* 6.2193 = *ILS* 4966; cf. Dio 54.2), which he describes in nearly identical terms (32.1): *collegia praeter antiqua et legitima dissolvit*; see literature cited in Yavetz, *Julius Caesar*, 85–96. Restrictions of this sort often impinged on dubious religious sects: Dio 52.36; Pliny *Ep.* 10.96.7 (cf. 10.33–34); see above on the repression of Bacchic cults.

34. Caesar: note Dio 42.20. Augustus: Tac. *Ann.* 1.2 (*insurgere paulatim, munia senatus magistratuum legum in se trahere*). Third century: Ulpian *Dig.* 1.4.1; Peachin, *Iudex vice Caesaris*, 14–28.

35. Nic. Dam. 101.22.12–13 (*FGrH* 90, F 130); Vell. Pat. 2.57.1; App. *BCiv.* 2.107–9, 2.118; Plut. *Caes.* 57.7–8; Suet. *Jul.* 86; for background and possible explanations for Caesar's dismissal of the Spanish guard, see Weinstock, *Divus Julius*, 163–74, 217–21; Yavetz, *Julius Caesar*, 41–42, 64, 206–7; and Canfora, *Julius Caesar*, 322–24. Imperial bodyguards are treated further below. Caesar or Augustus could cite the precedent of Rome's founder: Livy (1.15.8) claimed that Romulus had 300 armed bodyguards, even in peacetime. Ver Eecke (*La République et le roi*, 234–39) notes that ancient Romans could remember Romulus's *Celeres* guards positively as an elite corps of the founder-king or negatively as an element of tyranny.

36. Yavetz, *Julius Caesar*, 174–75; Dowling, *Clemency and Cruelty*, esp. 20–28.

long, sole rule was not forgotten (Asinius Pollio's half-jest about Octavian, "It's not easy to write against one who can proscribe you," was remembered for centuries).[37] Moreover, he knew that he won the civil war by means of the soldiery, and he never lost the power to use the troops to solidify his position.

Augustus's Impact on Public Order: Italy and the Pax Romana

The writers and artists who worked under Augustus praised the first *princeps* for ending war and insecurity, offering the world the blessings of peace and justice. Much of their sentiments matched Augustus's own propagandistic reflections on his career.[38] Therein lay more exaggeration and rhetoric, of course, but considering the usual state of the world, we should not undervalue the real achievement of Augustus and his successors and their loyal subordinates. For the first two centuries of the empire, they provided some measure of political stability and communal security, which was by no means perfect but remains unprecedented in the history of western Europe and the Mediterranean basin. One could justifiably credit this success to lucky advantages: the natural relief felt when Octavian's victories ended a generation's civil war or the chance cooperation of foreign peoples whose hostility did not really begin to threaten the empire until the late second century.[39] Even so, keeping the peace required much energy from the emperor and his allies.

Greg Woolf has described the so-called *pax Romana* as a near state of continued war. "The Roman peace did not mean that provincials had no experience of violence," Woolf notes, citing the squalid insecurity so many people experienced at the time and the afflictions of poverty, brigandage, requisitions, and corruption. "What *pax Romana* did claim," Woolf maintains, "was

---

37. Macrobius *Sat.* 2.4.21; cf. SHA *Hadr.* 15.13.

38. On pro-Augustan literature and art (e.g., Hor. *Epist.* 2.1.1–4 and *Carm.* 1.2.21–52), note Syme, *The Roman Revolution*, 459–75; Zanker, *The Power of Images*; Galinsky, *Augustan Culture*; and Osgood, *Caesar's Legacy*, offer rewarding surveys. In *Bread and Circuses,* Veyne rejects the label of "propaganda" for the pro-imperial discourse of the time. On Augustus's autobiographical *Res Gestae Divi Augusti* (*RGDA*), promulgated at the end of his life in AD 14, see new editions and commentaries by Scheid (2007) and Cooley (2009). On Augustus's earlier autobiography, now lost, see Yavetz, "The *Res Gestae* and Augustus' Public Image."

39. Note Tacitus's perceptive remark (*Germ.* 33): "If the barbarians have no love for us, at least let there remain and persist among them, I pray, hatred for each other; for as our imperial destiny drives us forward, then there can be no greater fortune than discord among our enemies."

an end to civil war."⁴⁰ Indeed, foreign wars of expansion were deemed good, and Augustus initiated many such campaigns. But we should not focus solely on the lack of civil war in delineating the blessings of peace. The empire's inhabitants hoped that the emperor, as the chief wielder of state authority, would establish overall domestic security. While this expectation is perhaps naïve, we will see that it is detectable from both the top and the bottom echelons of society.

We must start with Augustus, because it is to his early, tentative attempts at curbing brigandage and other elements of disorder that we can trace the modest beginnings of more widespread policing evident in later centuries. Besides policing the capital itself, Augustus's placement of security stations in Italy started the trend of expanding military policing throughout the empire. By the early third century, one African writer claimed that "throughout all the provinces military stations are assigned to the hunting-out of brigands," with hundreds of documents showing soldiers working as police among civilians by the second and third centuries.⁴¹ Augustus's early measures were born in response to pressing security needs and furthered by the general and lasting hope that Rome would provide some modicum of public order—an expectation that also has roots in Augustus's early career.

When the young Gaius Octavius became Julius Caesar's heir in March 44, the city of Rome had already seen several bouts of political violence, Italy had suffered through military campaigns and forced land reallotment to warlords' soldiers, and the provinces had endured invasions, requisitions, billeting, and wholesale theft at the hands of Roman potentates and corrupt officials. The next fourteen years would bring much of the same terror, often at the hands of Octavian himself, until he eliminated his last rival in 30 BC. In his own words, "By universal consent I had power over all things." Thereafter, the broken republic gave way to a political compromise known as the principate, an arrangement by which Octavian, henceforth *Augustus* ("revered," post-27 BC), shared power and showed respect for republican traditions and was yet

40. Woolf, "Roman Peace," 185–86, writing in the context of Foucault's remark (*Power/Knowledge*, 123) quoted on page 171: "Isn't power simply a form of warlike domination? Shouldn't one therefore conceive all problems of power in terms of relations of war? Isn't power a sort of generalized war which assumes at particular moments the forms of peace and the State? Peace would then be a form of war, and the State a means of waging it."

41. Suet. *Aug.* 32.1 and *Tib.* 37.1; Tertull. *Apol.* 2.8: *Latronibus vestigandis per universas provincias militaris statio.* Cf. Aelius Aristid. 26.101, on roads and security stations (*stathmoi* = Latin *stationes*) in remote regions, which supposedly make travel safe. All will be discussed in detail below, esp. in chapter 8.

recognized as *princeps* ("leading citizen") with unrivaled power (*RGDA* 34.1). Of course, he retained control of the army.

Nothing is perfect, but the new system brought greater military and political stability, which fostered social and economic improvements in formerly war-torn provinces.[42] Roman provincial administration remained flawed and rather minimal, but some of the worst excesses of republican maladministration were improved, now that the careers of Roman officials depended on the will of one man. Looking back on the monstrous upheavals of the late republic, writers who lived under the principate recognized that the new regime generally improved life in the provinces. Even Tacitus, so fervently republican in sentiment, had to admit, "The provinces did not disapprove of this new state of affairs, since rule by the Senate and people had always been mistrusted on account of the potentates' conflicts and the magistrates' greed. There was no viable legal protection, for the laws were thrown into disorder by violence, corruption and, worst of all, money."[43]

But late-republican disorder lingered. In addition to the legacy of political violence and civil unrest in the capital, troubles elsewhere demanded that Augustus take measures to impose law and order. Instability created an atmosphere in which lawlessness thrived in Italy itself, the seat of empire, where its embarrassing political ramifications could not be ignored. Appian noted:

At this time (36/35 BC) Italy and Rome itself were openly infested with bands of robbers, whose doings were more like barefaced plunder than secret theft. Sabinus was chosen by Octavian to correct this disorder. He executed many of the captured brigands, and within one year brought about a condition of absolute security. At that time, they say, originated the custom and system of cohorts of night watchmen (*nyktophylakes*) still in force. Octavian excited astonishment by having put an end to this evil with such rapidity.[44]

---

42. See Scheidel et al., *The Cambridge Economic History*, esp. Kehoe's contribution, "The Early Roman Empire: Production," for scholarly consensus on economic growth in this period (which matches contemporaries' impressions: de Souza, *Piracy*, 195–204). Not all agree: Millar doubts that the civil wars disrupted local economies throughout the empire ("The Mediterranean and the Roman Revolution").

43. Tac. *Ann.* 1.2: *Neque provinciae illum rerum statum abnuebant, suspecto senatus populique imperio ob certamina potentium et avaritiam magistratuum, invalido legum auxilio quae vi ambitu postremo pecunia turbabantur.*

44. App. *BCiv.* 5.132.547: ληστευμένης δὲ κατὰ συστάσεις τῆς τε Ῥώμης αὐτῆς καὶ τῆς Ἰταλίας περιφανῶς καὶ τῶν γιγνομένων ἁρπαγῇ μετὰ τόλμης ἢ ληστείᾳ λανθανούσῃ μᾶλλον ἐοικότων, Σαβῖνος (=Calvisius Sabinus, *RE* 13) ὑπὸ Καίσαρος αἱρεθεὶς εἰς διόρθωσιν πολὺν μὲν

Appian may have confused these early measures with the establishment of the *vigiles* watchmen in AD 6, although he might have been referring to a previous, experimental guard. Whatever the case, it is notable that Appian drew a connection between late-republican disorders and the police apparatus of his own time, a century and a half later.

Suetonius also remarked on Octavian's attempts to control disorder in Italy, describing problems left over from the civil wars that the first *princeps* had to address:

> Very many terribly ruinous problems which were harmful to the public good had endured because of the customary lawlessness of civil wars, or had even arisen in peace-time. For huge numbers of violent vagabonds were about, openly girded with swords, as if for the sake of protecting themselves. And travelers in the countryside were seized—freeman and slave alike—and impressed into forced labor in owners' private prison-houses (*ergastula*). Also, behind the legal title of new clubs (*collegia*), many factional groups with a political slant were meeting in order to conspire every sort of crime. Therefore he countered bandit activity (*grassaturae*) by distributing stations (of soldiers) in the fitting locations, he inspected the penitentiaries, and he dissolved all the *collegia* except the long-standing and legitimate ones.[45]

εἰργάσατο φθόρον τῶν ἁλισκομένων, ἐνιαυτῷ δ' ὅμως εἰς εἰρήνην ἀφύλακτον ἅπαντα περιήγαγε. καὶ ἐξ ἐκείνου φασὶ παραμεῖναι τὸ τῆς στρατιᾶς τῶν νυκτοφυλάκων ἔθος τε καὶ εἶδος. θαυμαζόμενος δὲ ὁ Καῖσαρ ἐπὶ τῷδε ὀξέως οὕτως ἐξ ἀδοκήτου διωρθωμένῳ πολλά. Loeb trans. Appian preceded these remarks by noting that many cities were placing Octavian among their tutelary gods. Cf. Tac. *Ann.* 6.11 and Dio 54.19, discussed by Davies, "Augustus Caesar," 17–18.

45. Suet. *Aug.* 32.1: *Pleraque pessimi exempli in perniciem publicam aut ex consuetudine licentiaque bellorum civilium duraverant aut per pacem etiam exstiterant. Nam et grassatorum plurimi palam se ferebant succincti ferro, quasi tuendo sui causa, et rapti per agros viatores sine discrimine liberi servique ergastulis possessorum supprimebantur, et plurimae factiones titulo collegi novi ad nullius non facinoris societatem coibant.* (It is unclear whether the roving *grassatores* are the ones kidnapping workers for *ergastula*; I lean toward taking the sentence as a tricolon of three distinct problems: highway violence, illegal enslavement, and shady clubs. On *ergastula*, see chapter 3 above.) *Igitur grassaturas* [some manuscripts have *grassatores*, the violent footpads themselves] *dispositis per opportuna loca stationibus inhibuit, ergastula recognovit, collegia prater antiqua et legitima dissolvit.* On this passage, Shaw ("The Bandit," 315–16) highlights landowners' role in supporting banditry, pointing also to an amnesty that Octavian issued in 33 BC for senators who may have taken part in banditry or piracy: Dio 49.43.5. The *Historia Augusta* states that Hadrian (18.10) likewise "suppressed the *ergastula* of slaves and freedmen."

Two important points need to be made here regarding Suetonius's methodology. First, the biographer's method of composition highlights an emperor's involvement in public-order matters as one factor in his overall evaluation. Many of Suetonius's vitae contain a chapter on measures the emperor took to establish order and stability when problems arose.[46] Second, just as emperors largely monopolized military triumphs for the achievements of subcommanders, they often monopolized credit for public order, even when subordinates deserved a great share of the praise. While Suetonius credited Augustus with ending kidnapping into illegal slave prisons in Italy, in his biography of Tiberius, Suetonius revealed that this was actually a job given to Augustus's stepson and future successor early in his career.[47] Augustus was responsible indirectly, as a delegator of authority, and we only know that young Tiberius deserves more credit because he eventually became emperor.

Comparing Suetonius's biographies of Augustus and Tiberius reveals another important fact. One could literally translate his brief remark at *Augustus* §32, *grassaturas dispositis per opportuna loca stationibus inhibuit*, as "Augustus countered bandit attacks by (means of) distributing stations throughout the fitting locations." These security stations were manned by soldiers. We know this from a section of Suetonius's biography of Tiberius, which directly resumes discussion of the security measure first mentioned in *Augustus* §32: "He (Tiberius) took utmost care in keeping the peace from ambushes and incidents of banditry and the lawlessness of insurrections. Throughout Italy he placed stations *of soldiers* at closer intervals than before."[48] Not only did Augustus's innovation stick, but his successor even increased the number of these military stations. As noted above, these *stationes* seem to be an early creation of the first emperor which gradually expanded. The two quotations of Suetonius cited here likely refer only to Italy, but many Roman soldiers were performing police functions among civilians in the provinces by the early second century, and thereafter military policing continued to expand.[49]

---

46. E.g., *Jul.* 42, *Aug.* 32, *Tib.* 37, *Claud.* 25, *Nero* 16, *Vesp.* 8; compare a related criterion, emperors as judges: *Claud.* 15, *Nero* 15, *Vesp.* 10, *Dom.* 8. While Suetonius clearly thought that some *principes* were better than others, he came as close as any ancient author to writing evenhandedly.

47. Suet. *Tib.* 8; cf. *Aug.* 32.

48. Suet. *Tib.* 37.1: *In primis tuendae pacis a grassaturis ac latronibus seditionumque licentia curam habuit. Stationes militum per Italiam solito frequentiores disposuit.*

49. I do not mean to imply that a direct imperial command created every military policing station in the empire; their origins are typically murky. The spread of military policing in the provinces is discussed primarily in chapter 8 below. We will see that some terms having to do with military policing (e.g., *stationarius*, seemingly related to the *stationes*),

Augustus's Impact on Public Order: The Provinces

While Augustus clearly used soldiers under his command to implement new policing arrangements, these measures were mostly applied to Rome and Italy. On the grand scale, the army as a whole could be seen as a police force against major domestic and foreign threats, and he distributed the legions accordingly. For instance, the geographer Strabo noted that Augustus guarded the newly acquired province of Egypt with three legions and an additional twelve cohorts, three of them cavalry, at critical points throughout the land. Three cohorts, normally about five hundred men each, guarded the southern frontier. As for the splendid metropolis Alexandria, a whole legion (about five thousand men) plus three additional cohorts warily guarded the populace that Strabo and others considered so factious and fractious.[50] Augustus may well have shared Strabo's low opinion; in any case, he knew that a city with its own proud and recent imperial legacy could not be left to its own devices. Nor would he risk having a rival use Alexandria as a base from which to mount a challenge. Senators were barred from entering Egypt, which was the only major province whose governor was from the equestrian rather than the senatorial order. At least some Alexandrians did not begrudge their new ruler's leadership: Suetonius's biography (98.2) offers a striking scene near the end of Augustus's life, in which some Alexandrian sailors, clad in white with religious paraphernalia, sing out to him, "Through you we can live! Through you we can sail! Through you we can enjoy freedom and good fortune!" The peace and prosperity that those sailors celebrated were secured by the legions.

Of all of the changes and reforms of Augustus's principate, one of the most important was the gradual institution of a standing professional army. In the early republic, legions had been filled by landowning citizens mustered for occasional, usually short campaigns. They provided their own arms and received little pay from the state. The late republic saw frequent crises of recruitment, loyalty, and discipline. Sometimes, penniless soldiers expected land upon discharge and were willing to lend a violent hand in politics to help their commander help them. Octavian unscrupulously thrived against his

---

are first attested under Trajan. Pliny's correspondence with Trajan mentions military *stationes* and the pressure to create more of them, despite that particular emperor's reluctance to detach soldiers from the legions: Pliny *Ep.* 10.20, 10.22, 10.26–27, 10.74, 10.77–78 (quoted at the beginning of chapter 3 above); all will be discussed in detail.

50. Strabo 17.1.12. Strabo visited Egypt soon after Octavian absorbed it into the Roman Empire.

rivals in this atmosphere. In firm control as Augustus, he set about regular-izing pay and service, with the result that by the end of his reign, Rome had a professional standing army. The legions now mainly consisted of citizen vol-unteers who served twenty-five years and were regularly paid by the state, with a large discharge bounty if they survived to honorable discharge. Suetonius (*Aug.* 49.2) thought that these payments were meant to prevent the soldiers from stirring up trouble after they left the service. Augustus made efforts to segregate civilians and soldiers; most of the latter he stationed on distant fron-tiers, he forbade them to marry, and he even assigned them separate seats at shows.[51] This artificial alienation between soldiering and civilian life was a real change from lengthy periods of war in the republican era, during which most free, propertied, and able-bodied Italian men probably served stints as soldiers.[52] The legions were supplemented by a nearly equal number of auxil-iary soldiers (*auxilia*) whose pay and other service conditions were inferior to those of legionaries; they were typically provincials rewarded with citizenship after their service as infantry, cavalry, light-armed troops, or marines. We will see that both legionaries and auxiliaries were regularly involved in policing.

The army that Augustus created was about three hundred thousand strong, and it was by far the most expensive burden on the treasury—indeed, it must have consumed more than half of the budget.[53] Looking ahead, after Augustus's wars of expansion, most soldiers probably never saw combat; that is, for most of the decades we are focusing on, the Roman army was a peacetime force.[54] Em-perors and other commanders worried that idleness would make the men soft and mutinous.[55] They would also be wasting tax revenue if they did not employ the troops for *some* purpose—the importance of this point would be hard to ex-aggerate. Thus, there was a tendency to use soldiers for many nonmilitary pur-poses. Soldiers were dispatched as surveyors, engineers, even judges. They built roads, supervised mines, and collected supplies. We see this pattern already in the reign of Augustus, who had his troops dredge Egypt's irrigation canals (Suet. *Aug.* 18.2). Much of the police work that soldiers performed in the provinces

---

51. For recent overviews, see Eck, *The Age of Augustus*, 114–22, and Gilliver, "The Augustan Reform." On the marriage ban (which lasted until 197), see Campbell, "The Marriage of Soldiers," and Phang, *The Marriage of Roman Soldiers*. Shows: Suet. *Aug.* 44.1: *Militem secre-vit a populo*; cf. 14 and 40.1.

52. See Brunt's classic *Italian Manpower* and, more recently, Rosenstein, *Rome at War*.

53. On estimates for the state's budget and the army's cost, see Hopkins, "Taxes and Trade"; Campbell, *War and Society*, 84–85; and Herz, "Finances and Costs."

54. Dobson, "The Roman Army: Wartime or Peacetime Army?"

55. Phang, *Roman Military Service*, 221–25, 246–47.

under Augustus's successors was on this model: special, temporary tasks assigned to groups or individuals. But too much of this kind of work was deemed a bad thing. As did others, Augustus seemed aware that nonmilitary activity could jeopardize discipline and battle-readiness.[56]

Augustus does not seem to have instituted new units of military police in the provinces, with one possible exception. Tacitus mentioned a military cohort guarding Lugdunum (modern Lyon) in AD 21, just seven years after Augustus's death. If this unit was a special garrison, Augustus may have installed it sometime after 15 BC, when an important imperial mint began operating there. We should also note that economically and politically, Lugdunum became a major capital city of the Gallic and German provinces, hence a potential center for regional separatism or political usurpation. These are logical reasons for stationing a permanent force there, but we lack proof of Augustus's involvement.[57] His successors, we will see, favored having military police units in Lugdunum and many other places.

Augustus's involvement with public-order challenges in the provinces was normally more indirect and performed through intermediaries, responding to problems brought to his attention via letters, petitions, or embassies. This relatively passive approach to government was the main theme of Fergus Millar's 1977 book *The Emperor in the Roman World*, which stresses the pervasive and well-documented pattern of "petition-and-response." Early Augustan examples of this style of Roman imperial government appear even before the establishment of the principate in 27 BC, and examples abound thereafter (chapter 6 below).[58]

---

56. See Suet. *Aug.* 24–25 (cf. 49.2); *SC de Pisone* 52–53; Lobur, *Consensus*, 18. In *Dig.* 49.16.12.1, the jurist Macer quotes a work called the *Disciplina Augusti*, telling commanders not to assign their soldiers to private tasks such as hunting and fishing. We cannot know if Augustus wrote this text; Phang is inclined to think that he did: *Roman Military Service*, 211; also note Albertini, "Addendum aux fragments."

57. Tac. *Ann.* 3.41.1, in which a Roman legate suppressed a tribal uprising with the cohort on guard in Lyon (*cohorte quae Lugduni praesidium*); cf. the revolt of Julius Vindex in 68 as a later regional challenge to Rome and on the mint, *ILS* 2130. Bérard, noting the lack of epigraphic evidence, is probably right to dismiss the common view that this cohort was a *cohors urbana* on the model of Rome's urban cohorts (see below): "La garnison de Lyon," *pace*, e.g., Freis, *RE* 1965, *Urbanae cohortes*, col. 1129. It was likely Claudius or Nero who installed an urban cohort there later in the first century (chapter 6 below).

58. For a wide selection of examples of Augustus's attempts to settle various provincial problems, see references in Millar, *The Emperor in the Roman World*, 6–7, 230–31, 257, 318, 321, 343–44, 376, 386, 431–38 passim, 443, 448, 454, 465, 479, 410–11, 530 (at times, the author may trust Josephus too uncritically); also, Oliver, *Greek Constitutions*, documents 1–12. The senate in some cases received embassies and, at the discretion of the *princeps*, could assist in adjudicating conflicts.

Looking at the provincial issues that caught Augustus's attention and the way he reacted to them, one sees a rather balanced and moderate leader who prioritized harmony, good order (or obedience), and basic religious and human decency. He does not seem to have been overly beholden to any one provincial community or social class. In 27 BC, Augustus and his consular colleague Agrippa tried to prevent misappropriation of public and sacred property in the province of Asia.[59] We learn from an inscribed stone obtained in Nazareth that Augustus may have issued an edict threatening the death penalty for violating tombs.[60] In response to an embassy, he even had private slaves from Cnidos tortured in Rome and used information therefrom to over-turn a local decision regarding an assailant killed while attacking a house.[61]

None of this is to say that he treated all people equally. He certainly was keen to protect Roman citizens in the provinces; according to Cassius Dio, Augustus "subjected the people of Cyzicus to slavery, since they had flogged and killed Roman citizens amid some disorder (*stasis*), as he did to the Tyrians and Sidonians, on account of discord in Syria."[62]

One inscription worth discussing in some detail contains five edicts of Augustus and a *senatus consultum* ("decree of the senate") that he sponsored, all in response to problems in Cyrene.[63] The first edict was a reaction to pro-

---

59. *SEG* 18.555 (= Sherk, *RDGE* 61; *IKyme* 17; Sherk, *Augustus* 95; Sherk, *Hadrian* 2).

60. *SEG* 8.13 = *Collectio Froehner* 70 (Robert, ed.); Ehrenberg-Jones 322; *ARS* 133; Sherk, *Hadrian* 27. Headed simply ΔΙΑΤΑΓΜΑ ΚΑΙΣΑΡΟΣ, "Decree of Caesar," the inscription cannot be dated. I agree with Robert and many others that Augustus is the most likely issuer. The association with Nazareth, where the stone was purchased (but not necessarily found) in 1878, has led some to connect it (dubiously) to the disappearance of Jesus's body. The decree seems to be a local measure, as violation of sepulture was not a capital crime in Roman law at the time. See Zulueta, "Violation of Sepulture"; Giovannini and Hirt, "L'inscription de Nazareth"; Chancey, *Greco-Roman Culture and the Galilee of Jesus*, 56–58.

61. *Syll.*³ 780 (6 BC; = *IGRR* 4.1031; Abbott & Johnson 36; Ehrenberg-Jones 312; *ARS* 147; Oliver, *Greek Constitutions*, 6.) It seems that the killed assailant belonged to a prominent family, whose influence ensured an unfair verdict against the defenders of the house; see Sherk's commentary in *RDGE* 67. Cnidos's status as a "free city" makes Augustus's interfer-ence all the more striking.

62. Dio 54.7.6: τούς τε Κυζικηνούς, ὅτι Ῥωμαίους τινὰς ἐν στάσει μαστιγώσαντες ἀπέκτειναν, ἐδουλώσατο. καὶ τοῦτο καὶ τοὺς Τυρίους τούς τε Σιδωνίους διὰ τὰς στάσεις ἐποίησεν, ἐν τῇ Συρίᾳ γενόμενος. Cf. 57.24; Tac. *Ann.* 4.36.2, Suet. *Aug.* 47, *Tib.* 37.3. According to late Chris-tian sources (e.g., Orosius 6.22.2), Augustus had to suppress an Athenian revolt around AD 13; see Bowersock, *Augustus and the Greek World*, 103–8, and "The Mechanics of Subversion," 292, 298.

63. *SEG* 9.8 (= Ehrenberg-Jones 311; Oliver, *Greek Constitutions* 8–12; Sherk, *Augustus* 102; Sherk, *Hadrian* 13). The first four edicts date from 7/6 BC, the last edict and the *senatus consultum* from 4 BC.

vincial complaints of unjust treatment of Greeks at the hands of Roman jurors in capital court cases. In response to "embassies from the cities of the province (Crete-Cyrenaica),"[64] Augustus established a system whereby a Greek could be tried by a mixed jury that included Greeks, preferably with a Greek acting as prosecutor. In the second edict, Augustus remarked on two investigations of possible treasonous activity, the first of which turned out to be bogus. But in the second case, he ordered that one Aulus Stlaccius Maximus be held until he could further investigate the accusation that Stlaccius had "taken statues from public places, including one under which the city had inscribed my name."[65] The third edict ordained that citizens of Cyrene who had attained Roman citizenship were still liable, in most cases, to local liturgies. The fourth edict allowed Greeks in noncapital judicial cases to be tried by Greek jurors. In the final edict, Augustus thus introduced the *senatus consultum* appended to it: "From this (decree of the senate, which applied to all the provinces) it will be clear to all inhabitants of the province how concerned the senate and I are that none of our subjects improperly suffer harm or exaction."[66] The attached *senatus consultum* created a new senatorial process for the restitution of money extorted from provincials by Roman officials, streamlining and expediting the judicial process of these *de repetundis* trials.

So, the Cyrene edicts are significant in showing Augustus responding carefully and responsibly to a number of provincial issues and conflicts that came to his attention. More than that, though, they bring up the Augustan roots of many of the mainstays of provincial administration and imperial rule that would shape the empire for centuries. Here we have the origins of the format for the anticorruption *de repetundis* trials in Rome and the use of the senate as a court for many such cases, which we see most clearly in Pliny's letters.[67] Augustus's interest in the case of his vanished statue evokes the emperors' concern with possible treason against them, ranging from slights to their majesty to conspiracies toward assassinations and coups d'état. In their bleak portraits first of Tiberius's late reign and then of other paranoid *princi-*

64. *SEG* 9.8.i, line 8: αἱ πρεσβῆαι τῶν ἐκ τῆς ἐπαρχήας πόλεων…

65. Envoys from Cyrene alerted Augustus to this crime; *SEG* 9.8.ii, lines 51–53: Αὖλον δὲ Στλάκκιον Μάξιμον, ὃν Κυρηναίων οἱ πρέσβεις αἰτιῶνται ἀνδριάντας ἐκ τῶν δημοσίων τόπων ἠρκέναι, ἐν οἷς καὶ τὸν ὧι ἡ πόλεις τὸ ἐμὸν ὄνομα ὑπέγραψεν.

66. *SEG* 9.8.v, lines 79–82: ἐξ οὗ δῆλον ἔσται πᾶσιν τοῖς τὰς ἐπαρχήας κατοικοῦσιν ὅσην φροντίδα ποιούμεθα ἐγώ τε καὶ ἡ σύνκλητος τοῦ μηδένα τῶν ἡμῖν ὑποτασ<σ>ομένων παρὰ τὸ προσῆκόν τι πάσχιν ἢ εἰσπράτ<τ>εσθαι.

67. See overall Talbert, *The Senate of Imperial Rome*, chap. 16.

pes, Tacitus and Dio depicted excessive *maiestas* prosecutions as instruments of terror by which the emperors cowed their opposition, real or imagined. Nominally, these charges aimed to punish infringements on the majesty of the Roman people, but already in the late republic, the definition of *maiestas* was becoming hazy. Under the emperors, its penalties grew harsher, and its scope broadened to cover a wide variety of offenses, not least of which was disloyalty to the supreme representative of the Roman state.[68]

After all, every emperor, even the more balanced ones, had all civilians and soldiers swear loyalty to himself and his family every year (another Augustan precedent), in addition to yearly communal prayers for his safety and celebrations of his accession and birthday.[69] These religious celebrations increasingly recognized the emperor's superhuman nature. Among numerous acknowledgments of the divine nature of the emperors, we may single out the decree of the *koinon* of Asia, which declared that their calendar should start with Augustus's nativity, ἡ γενέθλιος ἡμέρα τοῦ θεοῦ ("the birthday of the God"), for it was the divine blessing of Augustus "which divinely ordered our lives (and) created with zeal and munificence the most perfect good of our lives by producing Augustus and filling him with virtue for the benefaction of mankind, blessing us and those after us with a savior who put an end to war and established peace."[70]

---

68. Regarding Augustus and *maiestas*, note Tacitus *Ann.* 4.34 on Augustus's relative tolerance of dissent, compared with Tiberius; Tacitus may be retrojecting his view of Domitian onto Tiberius, however. For the expansion of the scope of *maiestas*, see *Dig.* 48.4 and Bauman, *The Crimen Maiestatis* and *Impietas in Principem*.

69. The annual oath of allegiance had its roots in Augustus's requesting such an oath of all Italians in 32, in preparation for Octavian's clash with Antony and Cleopatra. The early emperors were most assiduous in administering the oath to the military, but there are numerous indications that provincial civilians also vowed their loyalty and officially beseeched the gods on the emperor's behalf. Note *AE* 1988, 723, for a 6/5 BC oath of loyalty to Augustus from Conobaria in Baetica, and *ILS* 112 (a decree thanking the *princeps* for settling a local dispute) for Narbo's celebration of his birthday; cf. *OGIS* 532 (= *ILS* 8781) and *Dig.* 48.19.6. See also Pliny *Ep.* 10.35f, 10.52f, 10.88f, 10.100f; and Herrmann, *Der römische Kaisereid*.

70. *OGIS* 458 (= Ehrenberg-Jones 98; Sherk, *Augustus* 65), probably from 9 BC. ἐπειδὴ ἡ θείως διατάξασα τὸν βίον ἡμῶν πρόνοια σπουδὴν εἰσενενκαμένη καὶ φιλοτιμίαν τὸ τελεότατον τῶι βίωι διεκόσμησεν ἀγαθὸν ἐνενκαμένη τὸν Σεβαστόν, ὃν εἰς εὐεργεσίαν ἀνθρώπων ἐπλήρωσεν ἀρετῆς, <ὥ>σπερ ἡμεῖν καὶ τοῖς μεθ᾽ ἡμᾶς σωτῆρα χαρισαμένη τὸν παύσαντα μὲν πόλεμον, κοσμήσοντα δὲ εἰρῆνην. Trans. from L&R I, 624. Political considerations were the driving force. The *koinon* (Latin *concilium*) was the yearly province-wide council. Augustus encouraged these meetings, which came to focus on the civic worship of the emperor himself in the Greek east (where king worship was a Hellenistic tradition) and his *genius* (tutelary spirit) in the west, where *principes* themselves were normally only worshipped as gods if the senate deified them after their deaths. Syme noted, "The different forms the worship of Augustus took in Rome, Italy and the provinces illustrate the different aspects of his rule—he

Augustus's involvement in the affairs of Cyrene is all the more striking because Crete-Cyrenaica was not an "imperial" province under one of the emperor's directly appointed legates but a so-called "senatorial" province whose direct administration was notionally retained by a senior ex-magistrate appointed by the senate. Thus, we have an illustration here of Augustus's full powers—*maius imperium*—which allowed him to intercede in the affairs of any province in the empire. This privilege was officially recognized by the senate in 23 BC,[71] and the senate confirmed this and other broad powers for later emperors. The *Lex de imperio Vespasiani*, in which the senate officially acknowledged the authority of Vespasian in AD 69 or 70, decreed that "whatever measures, human and divine, private and public, he deems to be advantageous for the majesty of the state (*respublica*), he shall have the right and power to enact them, just as the deified Augustus (held this right and power)."[72]

We have seen how the emperor's sweeping powers were felt in the provinces, as when embassies and petitions came to Rome requesting settlement of various problems. Although our evidence is fragmentary, Augustus was likely involved in another important element of Roman public order: the settlement of boundary disputes. An incomplete inscription from modern-day Portugal names the emperor and a legate and later mentions a legal dispute (*causa*), just as the text breaks off completely.[73] The legate surely played a larger

---

is Princeps to the Senate, Imperator to army and people, King and God to the subject peoples of the Empire" (*The Roman Revolution*, 475). Later, the sources malign first-century emperors who encouraged divine flattery, e.g., Barrett, *Caligula*, chap. 9; on Domitian, see *AE* 1973, 137; and Suet. *Dom.* 13.2. By the late third century, the emperors had few qualms about being considered gods on earth.

71. It is no surprise that Augustus exercised full power even before the "second settlement" of 23; note *SEG* 18.555 (= Sherk, *RDGE* 61 = *Augustus* 95, 27 BC, on public and sacred property in Asia) and Dio 54.3 (the awkward M. Primus affair, which Dio probably dates too late). Cf. above on *Syll.*³ 780 (= *IGRR* 4.1031; Abbott & Johnson 36; Ehrenberg-Jones 312; *ARS* 147; Oliver, *Greek Constitutions*, 6), in which he interfered with a local decision by the free city Cnidos.

72. *Lex de imperio Vespasiani* (= *ILS* 244; Ehrenberg-Jones 364; McCrum-Woodhead 1), lines 17–19: *utique quaecunque ex usu reipublicae maiestate divinarum huma na rum publicarum privatarumque rerum esse {e} censebit, ei agere facere ius potestasque sit, ita uti divo Aug.* The document also acknowledges that Tiberius and Claudius held these powers; it omits the names of usurpers and emperors who suffered posthumous condemnation. Cf. Tac. *Hist.* 4.3, suggesting that the senate conferred on Vespasian the usual powers of the principate.

73. 1.1 in Elliott, "Epigraphic Evidence," 59–60: *Imp(erator) Caesar Div[i f(ilius) Augustus co(n)s(ul)]/XIII trib(unicia) potest[ate—terminos]/August(ales) inter [—et—]/ie(n)ses Q(uinto) Artic(u)le[io Regulo leg(ato)—]/causa cognit[a—].* Elliott notes the superiority of Scheithauer's reading (EDH 017,849) over earlier editions (e.g., *AE* 1954, 88). This inscription is probably related to the determination of *termines* ("boundaries") *Augustales* in the Iberian peninsula known from other texts.

role than Augustus himself; the emperors frequently delegated authority, and it was considered preferable to settle land disputes at the local or, failing that, provincial level. Indeed, emperors were rarely eager to get involved in messy local affairs. Provincial communities enjoyed relative autonomy but in turn were expected to handle local difficulties themselves. Provincials sometimes appealed directly to Rome for help, although their governor usually acted as an intercessor and buffer, filtering out, so to speak, many issues that an emperor would otherwise have to take on himself.

While Augustus was largely content to rely on his deputies and on "petition-and-response" governance, this does not imply indifference toward what was happening in the provinces. In fact, he was ambitious enough to initiate the empire's message-bearing system of requisitioned transport, generally (but inaccurately) referred to today as the "public post" or *cursus publicus*. It was not a postal or transit service available to all but a system of road stations (*stationes*) and other transport infrastructure, which was supposed to be restricted to official, specially authorized travelers. This transport system developed in stages and depended on local communities contributing essentials such as boats, wagons, beasts of burden, and fodder.[74] Augustus's motive, according to Suetonius, was "so that what was going on in each of the provinces might be announced to him and known more quickly."[75]

---

74. Kolb's *Transport und Nachrichtentransfer* supersedes previous treatments. The term *cursus publicus* is not attested before the early 300s (*Paneg. Lat.* 6.7.5; *CTh* 8.5.1; cf. *P. Panop. Beatty* 2.275), so it should be reserved for the late-antique system. It would be more accurate to call the more modest system of the early principate *vehicula, vehiculatio,* or *angareia*. Kolb stresses the durability of Augustus's measures: *Transport und Nachrichtentransfer,* 54, 71; Kolb, "Transport and Communication," 95–97. On the Augustan background of the system, see further Eck, *Die staatliche Organisation Italiens,* 88–94. Eck raises the possibility that Augustus initiated the *praefectus vehiculorum* office in Italy, though direct evidence is lacking. These "prefects of vehicles" are better known in the second and third centuries, when they are attested in the provinces as well. The praetorian prefects also helped administer the *vehicula*. See further Holmberg, *Zur Geschichte des* cursus publicus, 90–94; Pflaum, *Essai,* 250–64, 272, 351–54, 376–79; and Kolb, *Transport und Nachrichtentransfer,* 152–71.

75. Suet. *Aug.* 49.3: *Et quo celerius ac sub manum adnuntiari cognoscique posset, quid in provincia quaque gereretur.* The biographer noted that at first he used stations manned by young men (*iuvenes*), apparently as relays, but switched to having the stations equipped with vehicles to allow the same messenger to make the whole journey back and forth. This change "seemed better, since whoever carried the letters from place to place could also be questioned, if necessary" (*commodius id visum est, ut qui a loco idem perferunt litteras, interrogari quoque, si quid res exigant, possint*). The following section of the biography (50) pertains to the great care that Augustus took in sending documents and letters, including the official *diplomata* that entitled their bearers to use of the vehicle service. Only holders of valid *diplomata* were allowed to use the system to requisition supplies or animals from local communities, but we will see that abuses were very common.

Moreover, although the expansion of the empire's road network would have been a blessing in many ways to provincial communities, Augustus's activity as overseer of road building and administration was primarily aimed at strengthening Roman control of Italy and the provinces.[76] As Stephen Mitchell has noted, "this gigantic network of highways, which was not to be equalled or surpassed before the present [i.e., twentieth] century, is one of the most telling symbols of the control which Rome exercised throughout her empire, and of the organization which was imposed on it.... The roads of the empire had been designed and built to suit the state's needs, above all those of its armies."[77]

Many ancient sources, however, exaggerate Augustus's involvement in the provinces and his impact on provincial peace. We have noted how Augustus declared, "I cleared the sea of pirates," with some justification, one-sided though it is.[78] In the pages of Velleius Paterculus's fawning history, the simplistic author claimed that after so many glorious victories in Dalmatia and the Alps, and especially in Spain, where the Romans had faced a century and a half of stiff resistance, "these provinces, so diffuse, so populous, so feral, Caesar Augustus reduced to peace nearly fifty years ago," and he accomplished it so well that "thereafter they were free even from brigandage."[79] Of course, Augustus and his generals did end large-scale resistance in Spain but not to the extent that banditry disappeared; there and elsewhere, bereaved families

---

76. On Augustus and roads, see Suet. *Aug.* 30.1 and 37.1, and the numerous milestones bearing his name (e.g. Ehrenberg-Jones 288–94, involving some roads built near military camps or linking colonies in still-unsettled areas); roads were a significant means by which Augustus united Italy under his sway: Laurence, *The Roads of Roman Italy*, chaps. 4 and (focusing on repression of banditry) 13. Mitchell, discussing an inscription dating to Tiberius's early reign, points out ("Requisitioned Transport," 113) that the initial prohibition against unauthorized use of the *vehiculatio* would have been from Augustus's instructions (*mandata*—the earliest documentary use of this term, discussed below) to the governor who commissioned the inscription.

77. Mitchell, "Requisitioned Transport," 106.

78. *RGDA* 25.1; see above for background. Small-scale, opportunistic piracy persisted (Braund, "Piracy"; de Souza, *Piracy* 205–13), but the boast is not without some merit: Piracy declined to a minimal level after Augustus stabilized the empire and would not become a serious problem again until the third century.

79. Vell. Pat. 2.90: *Has igitur provincias tam diffusas, tam frequentis, tam feras ad eam pacem abhinc annos ferme quinquagenta perduxit Caesar Augustus, ut quae maximis bellis numquam vacaverant, eae...etiam latrociniis vacarent.* Velleius wrote under Tiberius and published his history late in his reign. (Cf. Livy 28.12 and Florus 2.25–34 for similar glorifications of Augustus's pacification of Spain and other provinces, with Strabo 4.6.6 on the Alps.) Note that Augustus used this Cantabrian War as the endpoint of his lost autobiography (Suet. *Aug.* 85.1), although it was Agrippa who mopped up tough resistance by 19 BC, incurring heavy losses.

continued to inscribe "killed by brigands" on funerary monuments of their loved ones.[80] In fact, Cassius Dio claimed that Augustus was so enraged at the bandit activity of one Caracotta in Spain that he went to the extreme measure of offering a reward of one million sesterces for his capture.[81] Amid the many factors in imperial propaganda and expectations, the rhetoric of public order held great importance for Augustus and for his successors.

Augustus and Military Police in the City of Rome

While some of Augustus's antibandit efforts in the provinces may have been exaggerated, his security reforms in Rome itself—made in response to late-republican disorder—left a clearer mark.[82]

First, some formalities. To cement his position, in 23, Augustus assumed tribunician power, which was renewed annually. His manifest advertising of this power aimed, at least in part, to reassure ordinary Romans that he would protect them. After all, that was the raison d'être of the tribunes of the old republic. Augustus and his successors also extended the tribunician power to denote heirs to the principate; furthermore, the powers of a tribune served as a constitutional expedient by which to manage the senate.[83]

In addition, we must note that, like other magistrates holding *imperium*, Augustus had the privilege of being attended by lictors. It was a point of

80. Syme sniffed, "Not even brigandage in Spain after 25, that is a tall story" ("The Conquest of North-West Spain," 103; = *RP* 2, 848). Note *AE* 1982, 512 (Baetica): *[a]b latronib(us) oc(c) isus est*; *ILS* 8509, an undated funerary inscription from Baetica, notes that its twenty-one-year-old dedicatee "was killed here" (*hic interfectus est*); cf. *AE* 1989, 480, from Hispania Citerior. On inscriptions that specify "killed by brigands" or some variant, see, e.g., *ILS* 8504–8 (from Italy and the Balkans); *AE* 1934, 209; *AE* 1901, 19; *ILJug.* 1434 (all from Moesia Superior); and *AE* 1903, 203 (Aquileia), with Riess, *Apuleius und die Räuber*, 17–18.

81. Dio 56.43.3. When Caracotta supposedly came to Augustus of his own accord, Augustus gave him the reward. The event is undatable, as Dio (fl. early third century) related it as an anecdote illustrating the dead *princeps'* disposition. The whole episode may well be fictional; see the comments on Bulla Felix below (chapter 5).

82. On the following sketch of policing in Rome during the early principate, see further Keppie in *CAH* X, 384–87; Nippel, *Public Order*, 85–98; Campbell, *The Roman Army*, 38–45; Brélaz, "Lutter contre la violence," 229–34; Kelly's excellent "Riot Control" and "Policing and Security"; Ménard, *Maintenir l'ordre*.

83. According to Appian (*BC* 5.132.548), the people first acclaimed Octavian as perpetual tribune in 36 BC. On Augustus's *tribunicia potestas* down to the "Second Settlement" of 23 BC, whereby the *TRIB. POT.* became the most acknowledged legal vehicle of the first *princeps'* authority, see *Res Gestae* 10.1; Dio 49.15.5–6, 51.19, 53.32.5–6; Oros. 6.18.34; Yavetz, *Plebs and Princeps*, 88–102; and Rowe, *Princes*, chap. 1, with Talbert, "Germanicus and Piso," 182.

special distinction that Augustus was permitted twelve such attendants. While municipal lictors outside of the capital routinely handled important police duties (chapter 3 above), in Rome, lictors and fasces were largely ceremonial at this time. Ceremonial guards are not necessarily useless in an emergency; by way of modern comparison, the pope's Swiss Guards, for instance, are highly trained for contingencies. Yet there is no evidence that any emperor would expect such help from lictors. As Nero's fortunes were closing in on him in 68, he made himself sole consul, although in his last hours, his lictors vanished. Lictors seem to have been likewise absent from other violent impe- rial death scenes; when the end came for Pertinax, for example, the emperor was defended by a single chamberlain (*cubicularius*), who stabbed two of the praetorian murderers. Emperors had more specialized guards for protection, who were obviously not always effective.[84] Augustus was wary of Caesar's fate: at one particularly tense meeting of the senate, he may have worn chain mail and a sword under his tunic and had ten stout friends standing by as any ap- proaching senator was searched for weapons.[85]

One of the original purposes of lictors was to clear the path of the magis- trates they served, using their imposing rods of authority to get people out of the way.[86] A special element of Augustus's military guard, the *speculatores*, served this purpose for him and his first-century successors, using long, knobbed lances to protect the *princeps*.[87] But the guardians Augustus might have relied on most in a real emergency were the almost mercenary *Germani corporis custodes*—"German bodyguards," recruited from un-Romanized areas.[88] Tacitus suggested that Nero especially trusted them because they were

84. Suet. *Nero* 43.2; SHA *Pert.* 11. At best, Rome-based lictors might accompany messengers and deputations, e.g., Dio 54.10.2. See also Millar, *The Emperor in the Roman World*, 616.

85. Suet. *Aug.* 35.1–2. Suetonius did not seem wholly convinced, saying "it was thought" (*existimatur*) that Augustus wore sword and mail and citing Cordus Cremutius for senators having to approach singly after being searched. The context is Augustus's second review of the senate in 18 BC, when he removed about two hundred senators. Cf. SHA *M. Ant. Car.* 2.9, Caracalla in the senate after eliminating his brother Geta.

86. We do catch a glimpse of this traditional role in Pliny *Paneg.* 23, where Trajan's lictors help him make his way through friendly crowds.

87. Claudius never dared to go to a banquet unless he was surrounded by *speculatores cum lanceis* (Suet. *Claud.* 35). See also Suet. *Aug.* 74 and *Galba* 18 (where the emperor is almost wounded by his own *speculator's* lance when a crowd presses toward him); Hirschfeld, "Die Sicherheitspolizei," 586–88; and M. P. Speidel, *Riding for Caesar*, 33–35

88. See Bellen, *Die germanische Leibwache*, and M. P. Speidel, "*Germani corporis custodes.*" Often overlooked in modern histories, these "Germans" were recruited mainly from the

foreigners or outsiders (*externi*), and Suetonius questioned Galba's decision to disband this guard, for "they had been extremely faithful to previous emperors amid many trying experiences."[89]

Members of the praetorian cohorts were also considered personal guards of the emperor. It was within the scope of republican tradition for a general to have a commander's cohort (*cohors praetoria*), a guard stationed at the general's headquarters (*praetorium*). Under the triumvirs in the late first century BC, this became a small bodyguard drawn from the commander's troops. Augustus expanded this institution into a permanent garrison of privileged troops stationed in and around the capital. By 23 BC, there were nine praetorian cohorts, of either five hundred or one thousand men each, drawn mostly from Italy, whose members enjoyed higher pay, bigger donatives, and shorter terms of service in comparison with ordinary legionaries. The praetorian soldiers donned their fine regalia for ceremonial occasions, but their day-to-day purpose was to reinforce the emperor's control of the gargantuan capital city. After all, Rome's population at this point was around one million. No other European city would match this size until London in the eighteenth century. Active-duty soldiers had never been regularly stationed in the city during the republican era. Augustus's modification of this deeply ensconced republican tradition necessitated some finesse; ordinarily, most praetorians were not in the city but scattered around its environs, armed with swords but wearing civilian clothing.[90]

Batavians, and different groups of them were attached to various members of the imperial family or to other favored individuals (e.g., Augustus's great general, Statilius Taurus). Augustus dismissed his German guard after the Varian disaster in AD 9: Suet. *Aug.* 49.1. According to Josephus (*AJ* 19.114–26, 19.138–53), they were the first to detect Caligula's murder and were eager to avenge it, slaying the guilty and the innocent alike as they came upon them. Suetonius (*Calig.* 58.3) adds that his litter bearers also tried to come to his defense.

89. Tac. *Ann.* 15.58; Suet. *Galba* 12.2: *Item Germanorum cohortem a Caesaribus olim ad custodiam corporis institutam multisque experimentis fidelissimam dissolvit.* Galba thought they were sympathetic to Gnaeus Dolabella, so he sent them home without pay.

90. Suet. *Aug.* 49.1; Tac. *Hist.* 1.38.2, *Ann.* 4.2.1. There is some ambiguity regarding whether their swords were normally displayed openly; at Tac. *Ann.* 16.27.1, when Nero wished to intimidate the senate, a throng of praetorians is described as "wearing togas, but swords unconcealed" (*globus togatorum…non occultis gladiis*). More work on the praetorians is sorely needed. Durry's *Les cohortes prétoriennes*, published in 1938, is still considered the leading treatment, followed in 1939 by Passerini's *Le coorti pretorie*. The former remains valuable but is not without problems (note Syme's review); the latter is less thorough and concentrates more on the prefects of the guard (where there is less dearth of modern work: e.g., Howe, *The Pretorian Prefect*, and Absil, *Préfets du prétoire*). Stöver's *Die Prätorianer* (1994) is weak on epigraphic evidence. We look forward to Bingham's forthcoming book; her 1997 dissertation, "The Praetorian Guard," only treats the Julio-Claudians (see 9–36 on origins of the guard, with Kennedy, "Some Observations").

In addition to the nine praetorian cohorts, Augustus also created three *cohortes urbanae* ("urban cohorts"). Their exact relation vis-à-vis the praetorians in Rome's security scheme being unclear to us, it is this group that scholars most often assume worked as a day-to-day police force.[91] The urban cohorts may well have been created just to provide more policing support, especially when the emperor was out of town. Some praetorians always accompanied him outside of Rome, but the soldiers of the urban cohorts were more homebound.[92] They were not as favored as the praetorians (for example, soldiers of the urban cohorts had to serve twenty years before discharge, the praetorians only sixteen), but they were similar enough that ancient observers often did not bother differentiating between the two in their accounts of the period. Moreover, Augustus's urban cohorts were given unit numbers X, XI, XII, running serially from the praetorian cohorts I through IX.[93]

Augustus was also eager to prevent the negligence and arson that had given rise to destructive conflagrations in Rome. There had been some previous attempts at fire control on the part of aediles or by the board of *tresviri nocturni* (*capitales*) commanding state slaves (*servi publici*) and even with the slave gangs of private individuals. These measures were not satisfactory; so, then, in the words of the jurist Paulus, "The deified Augustus resolved to take the matter into his own hands. For it was agreed that there was no one who better guarded the safety of the *res publica* than Caesar, and that no one else would suffice."[94] In 22 BC, the *princeps* put a specialized corps of six hundred state slaves under the aediles for the prevention of fires. Persistent problems of both the combustible and the political variety continued to plague the city, however. Following a major fire in 7 BC, the city was reorganized into fourteen regions, and the slave fire brigade was put under the supervision of neighborhood leaders (*vicomagistri*) of Rome's 265 wards (*vici*). After so much trial and error, finally, in AD 6, Augustus hit upon an experiment that would

---

91. E.g., Keppie, *CAH* X, 385: "These urban cohorts served as a police force for the city." This is not an unreasonable conjecture, but details are largely lacking. See further below.

92. See Millar, *ERW*, 33, 61; and Ricci, *Soldati delle milizie urbane*, esp. 17–18. We do not know exactly when the *cohortes urbanae* were created; see Freis, *Die cohortes urbanae*, 4–5; and Sablayrolles, "La rue, le soldat et le pouvoir," 133–34. They did some campaigning outside of Italy: Bérard, "Le rôle militaire des cohortes urbaines."

93. Cohort numbering gradually became jumbled, as various cohorts were deleted and added. Freis's *Die cohortes urbanae* remains the leading discussion. Note also his *RE* article (in Suppl. 10) "*urbanae cohortes*."

94. *Dig.* 1.15.1–3: *deinde Divus Augustus maluit per se huic rei consuli. . . . Nam salutem rei publicae tueri nulli magis credidit convenire nec alium sufficere ei rei, quam Caesarem.* Cf. Suet. *Aug.* 30.

become permanent. Out of the freedmen class, he appointed nearly four thousand *vigiles*—seven cohorts of night watchmen—as a military fire brigade. If a fire did break out, the best they could do normally was to demolish buildings in the path of the blaze. Limitations of technology impeded their remedial abilities as fighters of fire, so their nightly patrols (each cohort covering two city *regiones*) were largely preventive. Their firefighting activities crossed over into the policing sphere in various ways, such as guarding against negligence and arson and deterring petty crime.[95]

As for issues of command, Augustus himself initially directed the praetorian guard, but in 2 BC, he created two equestrian prefects as intermediaries—coveted posts, which steadily grew in importance.[96] An equestrian also commanded the *vigiles*, the *praefectus vigilum*. But the urban cohorts were commanded by an ex-consul, the *praefectus urbi* ("urban prefect"). Ostensibly a revival of an ancient office, this post was a weighty one from the start, and it accrued even more power over the next centuries.[97] Augustus's first choice for the post, the redoubtable M. Valerius Messalla Corvinus, gave it up after just six days, claiming that he did not know how to exercise official power that was *incivilis*—contrary to traditional citizen spirit.[98] Future holders of this power had no such qualms, as the urban prefecture became one of the top posts of a senatorial career. As subcommanders over individual cohorts, career soldiers who had served as senior centurions (*primi pili*) were installed as military tribunes. This arrangement was common to the praetorian guards, urban cohorts, and *vigiles*. But their primary loyalty was to the *princeps*.

Estimating conservatively, by AD 6, Augustus had nearly ten thousand security personnel policing Rome, approximately one per hundred inhabitants of the city. Comparing this ratio to recent data shows how exceptional

---

95. The *Digesta* material on the duties of the prefect of the *vigiles* (1.15, written by Paul and Ulpian in the early third century) covers several sorts of burglaries and thefts, but all of these responsibilities were not necessarily in force in Augustus's day. Baillie Reynolds's brief 1926 monograph *The Vigiles of Imperial Rome* is still cited but has been wholly superseded by Sablayrolles's magisterial 1996 tome *Libertinus miles: Les cohortes de vigiles*. Sablayrolles discusses all of the evidence of the *vigiles* acting both in a police capacity and as firefighters but clearly lays stress on the latter as their raison d'être.

96. See Arcadius Charisius *Dig.* 1.11.1 and Bauman, *Crime and Punishment*, 106–14.

97. On the background of this office, see Tac. *Ann.* 6.11; Vitucci, *Ricerche sulla* praefectura urbi; and Yavetz, *Julius Caesar*, 124–25. Growth in power: Bauman, *Crime and Punishment*, 100–106. (I have been unable to see Ruciński's 2009 book, *Praefectus urbi*.)

98. Tac. *Ann.* 6.11.4; Jerome *Chron.* 164H (probably drawn from a lost portion of Suetonius's *De viris illustribus*); Valvo, "M. Valerio Messalla Corvino," 1673–74; Syme, *The Augustan Aristocracy*, 211–12; and Ando, *Imperial Ideology*, 140.

imperial Rome was. For example, if we look at major European cities in the 1890s, nothing comes close to ancient Rome's per capita situation: Paris had 285 inhabitants per policeman, Berlin had 313, London and Vienna about 435.[99] Imperial Rome's level of police coverage exceeded that of major city-states such as Singapore and Hong Kong in the late 1980s and may have surpassed national levels in all countries except for Nicaragua under the Sandinistas.[100] In 1998, New York City's Independent Budget Office collected data for the twenty-five largest cities in the United States. Washington, D.C., had about 150 inhabitants for every police officer; New York City was second with 190. The average was 345 per police officer. Indianapolis's ratio was 1:768.[101] According to data published in 2006, policing grew in every country of the world during the preceding twenty years, for a global average of 860 people per police officer (down from 1:1300 in 1988). Despite this recent growth, Augustan Rome's police presence was still twice as concentrated as Singapore's in the twenty-first century.[102] And Roman policing would thicken under Augustus's successors.

Conclusion

"On the whole," Ramsay MacMullen noted, "we hear little of people attacked or houses broken into in the accounts of the time. This is the more surprising because the swollen garrisons in Rome were rather meant to prevent any challenge with political overtones, such as had shaken the Republic."[103] Strictly

---

99. These are the figures cited by Hirschfeld, "Die Sicherheitspolizei," 579–80.

100. Kurian, *World Encyclopedia of Police Forces* (1989), app. IV, "Population per Police Officer." Some sample data: Andorra 1125, Egypt 446.7, France 632, Italy 285.7, Luxembourg 434.6, Malta 276.9, Nicaragua 93, Saudi Arabia 280, U.S.S.R. 1045.4, U.K. 400, U.S.A. 458.5. Countries that range from 106.2 to 193.3 civilians per police officer include the Bahamas, Bahrain, Brunei, Cuba, Cyprus, Iraq, Israel, Mali, Mongolia, Nauru, Oman, Seychelles, and Uruguay. Kurian lists no figures for North Korea.

101. Independent Budget Office, "Police Staffing Levels," figure 2.

102. Kurian, ed., *World Encyclopedia of Police Forces* (2006 revised edition), viii and 822. Sample data: Antigua and Barbuda 120, Australia 438, Austria: 267, Bahamas 125, Bahrain 180, Bosnia 171, Egypt 3605, Greece 209, Israel 228, Italy 167, Monaco 64, Nicaragua 88, Qatar 73, St. Kitts and Nevis 97, Singapore 242. Chapter 5 below will show that Rome's Severan-era police contingents exceeded the modern figures listed here.

103. MacMullen, *Enemies of the Roman Order*, 164, on conditions in Rome. I believe that his time frame is Augustus to Constantine. He goes on to say that the Rome-based military units "were adapted only partly and gradually to the punishment (very rarely the detection or prevention) of ordinary crime"; he must have in mind the law codes preserving the opinions of the Severan and later Roman jurists.

speaking, MacMullen's reflection on the political nature of military policing in Rome is true: much of Roman policing was carried out in the interests of those in power, not to protect the weak. Indeed, Rome remained a dangerous place for the ordinary civilian, especially should he venture out alone at night.[104] Petty thefts continued to plague lower-class neighborhoods; Pliny the Elder referred to "innumerable incidents of terrible burglary," which compelled the *plebs urbana* to secure their windows with shutters.[105] Nevertheless, despite imperfect law enforcement and the preeminence of political motives, Rome's lower orders would have still enjoyed some incidental benefit of the emperor's security measures. We can cite examples for both tendencies. When news from Germany of the Varian disaster hit Rome in AD 9, Augustus strengthened patrols to head off any kind of tumult.[106] Augustus felt that his power was at stake; this is the kind of critical situation that was probably the most significant prompt for new police measures. But once a new police institution is in place, it can be used for more generous purposes. Suetonius (*Aug.* 43.1) tells us that Augustus posted guards around Rome on days when major spectacles were held, lest thieves take advantage of so many absent householders. Of course, the general state of law and order was inextricably linked to political stability. Any emperor would want to provide the urban *plebs* with some elements of security—or at least appear to do so—just as he provided them with grain and entertainments.[107] Disorder in the capital threatened the imperial regime, and moreover, deficiencies in citizen security could give rise to political threats.

The career of Egnatius Rufus provides the best example. As a young, ambitious aedile in 22 or 21 BC, he courted great popularity in Rome by effec-

---

104. See, e.g., Juvenal's Third Satire, esp. lines 278–308.

105. Pliny the Elder, *HN* 19.19.59: *iam in fenestris suis plebs urbana imagine hortorum cotidiana oculis rura praebebant, antequam praefigi prospectus omnes coegit multitudinis innumerae saeva latrocinatio.* "The urban populace once gave onlookers everyday rustic scenery by imitating gardens in their windows, before the savage incidence of burglary of an innumerable multitude compelled all views to be blocked." On this tricky passage, see Boatwright, "Luxuriant Gardens," 72, and Linderski, "*Imago hortorum.*" The imitation (*imago*) may refer to paintings of gardens; Linderski argues for miniature gardens in baskets or pots affixed to windows. It is uncertain whether this *latrocinatio* refers to a specific outbreak of crime that Pliny witnessed in the first century AD. Linderski suggests (307) that "it may well be only an example of Pliny's moralizing, his praise of old customs versus the creeping corruption of the present."

106. Suet. *Aug.* 23.1: *hac nuntiata excubias per urbem indixit, ne quis tumultus existeret.* In AD 9, Quinctilius Varus lost three legions plus auxiliaries in the great ambush in Germany's Teutoburg Forest (probably near modern Kalkriese).

107. See Yavetz, *Plebs and Princeps*, esp. 123–28; cf. Yavetz, "The Urban Plebs."

tively organizing his own private slaves into a firefighting force. This charitable initiative must have embarrassed the *princeps*, as it highlighted Augustus's failure to safeguard the city from fire. In all likelihood, it was Egnatius's troublesome example that directly spurred Augustus to begin developing better firefighting squads under his aegis, first with six hundred specialized state slaves in 22 BC but culminating, of course, in his experimental establishment of the *vigiles*. The competition from Egnatius was unwelcome, and matters would become worse. Despite Augustus's own fire-prevention efforts, Egnatius's aedileship left a mark. He quickly succeeded to the praetorship, probably in 20 BC, and thereafter tried to use his popularity with the plebs to win an immediate (and probably illegal) consulship. A tense crisis ensued. After his supporters rioted when his candidacy was blocked, Egnatius had to be arrested, charged with conspiracy, and executed.[108]

The awkwardness and tension of the Egnatius Rufus affair remind us that Augustus's reign was not always smooth. Overall, though, what we see is a legacy of success, in which Augustus set the state's pattern of using soldiers to enhance security among civilians. This period also saw the development of crucial state infrastructure (military roads and the *vehiculatio* transport system) and long-lasting patterns in the way Rome handled conflicts (boundary disputes, "petition-and-response" governance). Art, literature, and religion gave expression to the blessings of peace, touted imperial virtues, and made the emperor a potent symbol of stability and justice. Not all of this was without precedent. For example, under Augustus, Egyptian religious rites were suppressed in and around Rome.[109] One might compare Roman repression of Bacchic rites, banning philosophers and rhetoricians from Rome, expulsion of "Chaldeans" (astrologers) and Jews, all in the second century BC.[110] Monitoring

---

108. See Dio 53.24.4–6; Vell. Pat. 2.91–92; Sablayrolles, *Libertinus miles*, 9. Egnatius Rufus's career (PIR² 3.32) is difficult to date precisely; he may have been aedile in 26 BC, although most scholars favor a later date—22, 21, or 20, i.e., in the same year that Augustus established the fire brigade of six hundred *servi publici*, or soon thereafter. Phillips, "The Conspiracy of Egnatius Rufus," 109–11, argues that he was aedile in 21 and praetor in 20. If that is the case, then not only was his candidacy for consul probably illegal, but his quick succession to praetorship was likewise contrary to the customs of the *cursus honorum*. See also A. Birley, "Q. Lucretius Vespillo," 716–23, and Dettenhofer, *Herrschaft und Widerstand*, 121–23, 193. Augustus was not present in Rome when Egnatius was arrested and executed.

109. Dio 54.6.4–6, crediting Augustus's associate Agrippa. Cf. Suet. *Aug.* 42.3.

110. *ARS* 28–28a (= Livy 39.17.3, 186 BC) and 34 (161 BC); Val. Max. 1.3.2 (139 BC). On this last passage, see Lane, "Sabazius," and Gruen, *Diaspora*, 15–19. The *praetor peregrinus* of 139, C. Cornelius Hispallus, expelled the astrologers not only from Rome but from all of Italy. In 92 BC, the censors reprimanded rhetoricians: *ARS* 59.

Rome's populace and expelling problem groups became a regular occurrence under Augustus's successors (chapter 5 below). One can only guess how popular such measures were. What is clear as we turn from Augustus to his successors is that people in the Roman Empire expected officials to use their power for the stability and good order of the community. Sometimes military police were applied to that purpose. In Rome and Italy, emperors more often used military police to safeguard their own power. Augustus's central importance to the history of Roman policing will be even more apparent after we study how the following centuries unfolded.

5

"*To squelch the discord of the rabble*": Military Policing in Rome and Italy under Augustus's Successors

IT TOOK AUGUSTUS more than fifty years to remold his reputation, from war-lord to symbol of domestic peace and stability. The success of his efforts can be measured by his successor's desire to associate himself with Augustus's perceived achievements.[1] Tiberius's subordinates played along. In fact, obedience to Tiberius was linked to the honor owed to Augustus, to such an extent that an offense against one registered as a slight to the other. Note, for example, the recently discovered senatorial decree condemning the memory of Gnaeus Piso, who was not only accused of directly violating the cult of *divus Augustus* but was also charged with trying "to stir up civil war, all the evils of which have long since been banished by the divine guidance of the deified Augustus and by the virtues of Tiberius Caesar Augustus."[2]

The police apparatus that Augustus established in Rome helped Tiberius secure his rule. In Tacitus's account of the transfer of power, soldiers keenly guarded the ailing Augustus and his wife as they waited for Tiberius to arrive. As soon as Augustus died, an officer was specially instructed to kill Augustus's exiled grandson, Tiberius's potential rival. Tiberius quickly made sure that he had the loyalty of the soldiers, above all the praetorians; he

---

1. See, e.g., Tac. *Ann.* 1.77. Lyasse, *Le Principat*, appreciates the individual complexities of this emulation for each of Augustus's first-century successors. Cf. de Blois, *The Policy of the Emperor Gallienus*, 120–49; Cooley, "Septimius Severus"; and Barnes, "Aspects of the Severan Empire."

2. On Piso's supposed violations of Augustus's religious rites, see *SC de Pisone* 68–70. Quoted are lines 45–47: *bellum etiam civile excitare conatus sit, iam pridem numine Divi Aug(usti) virtutibusq(ue) Ti. Caesaris Aug(usti) omnibus civilis belli sepultis malis.* Gnaeus Piso the Elder was accused of murdering Germanicus and challenging imperial authority early in Tiberius's reign (AD 20). This text was first published in 1996 by Eck et al. in *Das Senatus consultum*; also see the 1999 special issue of the *American Journal of Philology*, vol. 120, no. 1; Rowe, *Princes*; and Flower, *The Art of Forgetting*, 132–38. For other links between loyalty to Tiberius and devotion to Augustus's memory, see Tac. *Ann.* 3.66 and the opening of the Pisidian inscription (*JRS* 66, 107–9) in Mitchell, "Requisitioned Transport" (discussed further below).

communicated his grasp on power by appearing everywhere with a military guard. Tiberius paid out three hundred sesterces to each ordinary soldier in accordance with Augustus's will, five hundred to the soldiers of the urban cohorts. Praetorians received a thousand.[3]

Despite these efforts, Tiberius's accession was not entirely smooth. Knowing the vicissitudes of power and the potential challenges facing him, he compared ruling the empire to holding a wolf by its ears (Suet. *Tib.* 25.1). For good reasons: The legions in Germany and Pannonia mutinied for better conditions, and theater factions starkly divided the populace of Rome. In AD 15, a number of soldiers, including a centurion, died in a fracas in the theater, "while trying to prevent insults against the magistrates and to squelch the discord of the rabble."[4] (Although service in the city was more commodious than marching around a frost-bitten frontier, it could still be challenging and risky.) Throughout his reign, Tiberius continued to rely on military police in Rome and Italy. Suetonius claimed that "above all he was concerned to keep the peace from street violence, banditry, and lawless dissension.... He took zealous precautions lest popular uprisings arise, and severely repressed them once they started."[5]

Early Emperors' Use of Soldiers as Police in Rome and Italy

Soldiers helped impose order in the capital under Tiberius's successors, but we know little about the actual day-to-day policing routines of the various soldiers stationed in Rome. Part of the problem is that writers such as Tacitus rarely differentiated among praetorians, soldiers of the urban cohorts, and other military men, preferring the catch-all word for soldiers, *milites*.[6] It is clear, however, that they arrested would-be political opponents and could be called out for a show of force when needed, as in the aftermath of the Varian disaster and the Pisonian conspiracy in Nero's reign. After Nero learned of

---

3. Tac. *Ann.* 1.5–8; Suet. *Aug.* 101.2, *Tib.* 22–24.

4. Tac. *Ann.* 1.77 (cf. 1.16, 1.54, Suet. *Tib.* 25). A praetorian tribune was injured in the same incident. Such lawlessness had started the previous year, the year of Augustus's death, and was getting worse. Upper-class fans were a large part of the problem. This particular outbreak led the senate to enact many measures to curb the insolence of the fans, which Tacitus does not specify, focusing instead on restrictions against the actors. See Dio 57.14.10 and Suet. *Tib.* 37.2, on the ineffectiveness of these measures, which ultimately led Tiberius to exile the pantomimes (Dio 57.21.3), a step that would be repeated by other emperors.

5. Suet. *Tib.* 37.1–2; cf. Vell. Pat. 2.126.2.

6. Nippel, *Public Order*, 93; Ménard, *Maintenir l'ordre*, 26–27.

this plot in 65, he "became increasingly afraid and protected himself with a bolstered guard. Indeed, with the buildings occupied by soldiers and the sea and river likewise besieged, it was as if he had arrested the whole city, for there were infantry and cavalrymen hovering over the public squares, private homes—even the countryside and territories of neighboring towns."[7] Having used his soldier-police to liquidate whomever he wished to be out of the way, Nero rewarded them handsomely.[8]

Augustus's successors also used praetorians for these sorts of elimination missions outside of the capital in Italy. Claudius's wife, Messalina, for example, seems to have persuaded him to get rid of Valerius Asiaticus, a former consul. Claudius sent out the praetorian prefect Rufrius Crispinus "with enough troops to put down a rebellion" to hunt down their victim, whom they found and arrested at Baiae near Puteoli.[9] This ugly business of destroying personal enemies highlights the praetorians' main purpose of safeguarding the emperor and his family. It behooved them to advance the emperor's interests, no matter how heinous. The emperor did not pay the praetorians hundreds of thousands of sesterces in salary and bonuses to chase cat burglars and muggers, making the streets safe for the ordinary citizen. That said, the new military police gave the regime greater stability, and the *vigiles* at least were manifestly concerned with making life in the city safer.

Emperors used military units as a disciplinary reaction force to impose order and inflict exemplary punishment on problematic Italian communities. After a scandalous incident in Pollentia, Tiberius sent "a cohort from the city"

---

7. Suet. *Aug.* 23.1 (AD 9, see chapter 4 below); Tac. *Ann.* 15.58 (quoted). One might compare the anxiety around the prosecution of Gnaeus Piso the Elder in AD 20. The *S. C. de Pisone patre* inscription reveals concern (cast as praise) for the loyalty of the soldiers and mandates the display of the decree in legionary bases (lines 159–72).

8. See Tac. *Ann.* 15.60–72. Two praetorian tribunes saw to the deaths of Lateranus and Seneca, although a centurion of the guard delivered the final death sentence to the latter. (Cf. Juv. 10.17–18: "a whole cohort besieges the fine mansion of the Laterani," making the point that soldiers rarely storm humble upstairs apartments.) Attendant soldiers actually intervened to avert the suicide of Seneca's wife, Paulina. The double-dealing praetorian prefect Faenius Rufus was seized by a soldier whom Nero kept with him on account of his bodily strength. Subrius Flavus, a tribune of the guard, was executed at the hands of one of his colleagues. Nero sent another guard and cohort into a dinner party of the consul M. Julius Vestinus Atticus; his guests were held under arms well after their host had committed suicide. For their loyalty, Nero gave two thousand sesterces and free grain to each of the soldiers (*manipulares*; Tacitus is imprecise, but it was probably the praetorians alone who received this donative). Cf. Suet. *Calig.* 23, *Vesp.* 5.3, *Titus* 6, *Dom.* 8.5.

9. Tac. *Ann.* 11.1 (AD 47): *cum militibus tamquam opprimendo bello.* Rufrius: *PIR*[2] 7.1.169. Valerius Asiaticus: *RE* VII A[2] 106 (coll. 2341–45); he committed suicide back in Rome during his trial (*Ann.* 11.2–3).

and another from the Alpine client kingdom of Cottius against the Pollentians. The soldiers surrounded the city, infiltrated it from all sides, and imprisoned most of its people and leaders (decurions) for life.[10] After a small
naval crew detected an incipient slave revolt in southern Italy in AD 24, the
same emperor hastily dispatched a strong force commanded by a praetorian
tribune (Tac. *Ann.* 4.27). Later, under Nero in 58, a praetorian cohort was stationed in Puteoli to establish order there amid violent riots and charges of official corruption, instilling fear through the "punishment of a few."[11] Military
police were a key tool the emperors used to encourage a stable atmosphere in
Italy as well as in Rome.

They had other forces at their disposal for sensitive missions besides praetorians. Most notoriously, a naval commander loyally served Nero by assassinating his mother, Agrippina the Younger. Tacitus imagined that the
dynastically minded praetorians would be unwilling to cooperate in killing
Germanicus's daughter.[12] Often, we cannot be sure if certain military agents
were praetorians or some other kind of soldier. Otho, for example, dispatched
a reservist (*evocatus*) to kill Galba's former praetorian prefect.[13] Emperors
would use whatever trustworthy soldiers were at their disposal for such grim
tasks.

---

10. Suet. *Tib.* 37.3 A crowd of Pollentians had held the body of a *primipilaris* centurion
hostage, in order to force his family to pay for a gladiatorial show. While this cohort dispatched from the city (*cohors ab urbe*) was conceivably an urban cohort, the praetorians were
most often used for policing missions in Italy. Rivière argues that the punishment, *vincula
perpetua*, could have been a life of hard labor, such as in a stone quarry or other *opus* (cf. Pliny
Ep. 10.31–32): *Le cachot*, 91–95, 130–33. Also note the punishment of Sena (modern Siena) for
outrages committed against the senate: Tac. *Hist.* 4.45.

11. Tac. *Ann.* 13.48: *paucorum supplicio*. In Tacitus's account, action was precipitated by op-
posing delegations *to the senate* from rival factions in Puteoli; he made no mention of imperial involvement. The senate obviously still had some capacity to hear problems from Italian
communities, but Nero or one of his praetorian prefects must have been involved in the
punishment and garrisoning of the cohort.

12. Tac. *Ann.* 14.3–8. Anicetus was commander of the fleet at Misenum, an imperial freedman, and Nero's former tutor. He contrived to have Agrippina drown in the wreck of a sabo-
taged ship. When this complicated plan fell through, he and a few other naval officers killed
her the old-fashioned way. A deputy of Tiberius used private agents or soldiers (Tacitus was
unsure which) to arrest the false Agrippa Postumus (actually a former slave of Augustus's
disowned grandson) in AD 16: Tac. *Ann.* 2.40.

13. Tac. *Hist.* 1.46; the victim was Cornelius Laco. *Evocati* were soldiers who had served long
enough for discharge but could be drawn back into limited service as a reserve force. The
one mentioned here may have been a praetorian or could have even performed the task in
hopes of joining the guard, for the disorders of 69 allowed (or compelled) many soldiers to
switch the type of service they were enrolled in: Tac. *Hist.* 2.94.

More mundane duties in Rome included policing the audience of games and entertainments, which could become rowdy. One might assume that gladiator shows, with their inherent violence, sparked the most disturbances among fans in Rome. In fact, theatrical mime competitions were much more problematic, as were chariot races, especially in later years. In both cases, crazed fans of certain performers formed theater claques or circus factions that would occasionally brawl.[14] It is notable that even though Nero tried to curry popularity by removing military guards from the shows, he eventually reinstalled them.[15] Unstable *principes* who were themselves overinvolved devotees of particular spectacle competitors, such as Caligula, Nero (naturally), Vitellius, Domitian, Commodus, and Caracalla, supposedly used their guards to threaten and even execute spectators who did not seem to support the "right" side.[16]

There were many occasions on which the security reforms instituted by Augustus backfired for his successors. Instead of providing stability, the Rome-based military units sometimes created problems themselves or did not respond to threats against their emperor. Amid various emergencies, the *vigiles* almost never interceded on behalf of their paymaster. One exception was in 31, when Tiberius used the *vigiles* as agents of Sejanus's downfall; this act amounted to pitting one type of Roman police against another, the night watchmen against the praetorians—much to the latter's chagrin, since they were still loyal to their prefect Sejanus.[17] According to Dio, in the great fire of

---

14. Note above, on Tac. *Ann.* 1.77, the theater brawl in which soldiers and civilians died. See MacMullen, *Enemies of the Roman Order*, 168–73; Alan Cameron, *Circus Factions*, esp. 157–97; and Fagan, *Lure of the Arena*, 148–54.

15. On Nero, see Tac. *Ann.* 13.24 (mentioning a *statio cohortis adsidere ludis solita*: "the accustomed stationing of a cohort to watch over the games") and 14.15 (on Burrus and a *cohors militum*—"cohort of soldiers" and their officers at Nero's theatrical debut); cf. Suet. *Nero* 26 and Dio 61.8.1–3, which also highlight Nero's own misbehavior. Both praetorians and urban cohorts guarded entertainments (note *Dig.* 1.12.1.12 below on the *cohortes urbanae*, and Bingham, "Security at the Games"). With the focus on the praetorian prefect Burrus in Tac. *Ann.* 14.15, it seems that here, as in *Ann.* 1.77, the soldiers in question were praetorians.

16. Suet. *Calig.* 30.2, *Vit.* 14.3, and *Dom.* 10.1; Tac. *Ann.* 16.5.3; Pliny *Pan.* 33.3–4; Dio 73.20–21; Herodian 4.6.4–5. Commodus's biographer claims that he ordered the marines (*milites classiarii*) who spread the arena's awnings to slaughter the audience, because he thought his adoring spectators were actually mocking him: SHA *Comm.* 15.6.

17. Dio 58.9 and 58.12. Sablayrolles cites this episode as evidence that the *vigiles* could be quite military in nature: *Libertinus miles*, 42–43. The urban cohorts and praetorians seemed poised against each other in 41, just after Caligula's assassination: Suet. *Claud.* 10.3. In the disorders of AD 69, the *vigiles* and urban cohorts fought for Vespasian's brother, Flavius Sabinus (the urban prefect), against Vitellius's praetorians and German bodyguards: Josephus *BJ* 4.645; Tac. *Hist.* 3.64, 3.69–70. Dio (74.9) claimed that

64, the soldiers in Rome, eager for more plunder, actually started new fires, and even the *vigiles* were guilty of this treachery.[18] Most notorious was the praetorian guard's interference with imperial succession, reaching a low point with the greedy "auctioning of the empire" that brought Didius Julianus to power in 193.[19] After Septimius Severus marched on Italy to oust the highest bidder, he completely replaced the disgraced guard with legionaries who had supported him.[20] The praetorians' ability to interfere politically came to an end in 312, when Constantine dissolved the praetorian guard upon taking Rome from his rival Maxentius.

Despite this shaky legacy, Augustus's successors maintained and even bolstered the military police stationed in the capital during the principate. Continuing disorder in Rome made this necessary. Especially when there was a food shortage, the urban populace might physically assault the emperor himself. This seems to have happened to both Claudius and Antoninus Pius.[21] So various emperors revived semimercenary personal bodyguards similar to the *Germani corporis custodes*. After Galba disbanded the original German bodyguards, emperors may have relied more on their *speculatores* as special military guards (chapter 4 above).[22] Later, Trajan, or possibly one of the Flavians, created a special horse guard, the *equites singulares Augusti*. When Septimius Severus came to power, he doubled their number to two thousand. They were drawn mostly from the German and Danubian provinces (Raetia, Noricum, Pannonia). The *equites singulares Augusti* were apparently so similar to the Julio-Claudians' earlier German bodyguards that

---

Pertinax could have killed a band of two hundred praetorians, who invaded his palace to assassinate him, with "the night guard and cavalrymen" (τῇ ... νυκτερινῇ φυλακῇ καὶ τοῖς ἱππεῦσιν), which probably means *vigiles* and *equites singulares Augusti* at his disposal. Herodian (1.12.9) claimed that the urban cohorts hated the "cavalrymen" (here, probably the *equites singulares Augusti*) and protected people against them in a riot under Commodus (see Whittaker, "The Revolt of Papirius," for background). Also note Sablayrolles, "La rue," 147.

18. Dio 62.17.1: "The soldiers, and among them also the night watchmen (*vigiles*), looking out for plunder, not only did not put out the fire, but even set new ones." Cf. Tac. *Ann.* 15.38.7 and, on the aftermath of Caligula's assassination, Josephus *AJ* 19.160.

19. According to his biographer, Didius Julianus promised each praetorian twenty-five thousand sesterces and actually paid out thirty thousand to each; SHA *Did. Jul.* 3.2. See also Dio 74.11 (all Cassius Dio references are to the Loeb edition).

20. Dio 75.1; Herodian 2.13. Curran gives an excellent sketch of the next several decades: *Pagan City*, 26–35.

21. Suet. *Claud.* 18.2; *Epitome de Caes.* 15.9.

22. E.g., Tac. *Hist.* 1.35, where a *speculator* (chapter 4 above) acts as if he has killed Otho to protect Galba.

they shared the same nickname: *Batavi*.[23] As a full-fledged cavalry unit, they were naturally of more use outside of the city, which was just as well, since many later emperors spent more time campaigning and less time amusing themselves in Rome. Of course, we are not to imagine these *equites* always atop their horses when doing guard duty in Rome. We know, for example, that they served as foot guards in the emperor's palace.[24]

It was not until Tiberius's reign that the praetorian guards were stationed together in Rome itself, based from a permanent, unified camp.[25] The number of praetorians fluctuated in the first century, until Domitian fixed the number of praetorian cohorts at ten, and at this point, we can be certain that they were each one thousand strong. It was also in Flavian times that the urban cohorts in Rome underwent a significant expansion, growing to four cohorts of one thousand each. By 205, there were 7840 *vigiles* serving in Rome, with detachments in Ostia and Puteoli also. It was Claudius who "stationed individual cohorts [of *vigiles*] at Puteoli and Ostia to prevent outbreaks of fire," a measure that was likely related to his concern over the capital's grain supply.[26] In fact, marines (*classiarii*) regularly patrolled the roads from Ostia and Puteoli to Rome.[27] The Roman navy had major fleets based at Misenum (near Naples) and at Ravenna; not only did they police Italy's coasts, but each of these fleets also had a detachment permanently stationed in Rome. There they helped administer bloody spectacles—mainly by manning the massive awnings (*vela*, literally "sails") to shade the crowd, but

---

23. See M. P. Speidel, *Die Equites Singulares Augusti* and *Riding for Caesar*, 10–11, 29–76 and passim. Speidel notes that the *cohortes praetoriae* had their own cavalry units and points out that despite changes in name, emperors always had some sort of mounted soldiers among their guard. He sometimes might go too far in equating general German bodyguards with specialized cavalry, however. Herodian 4.7.3 states that Caracalla selected his personal guard from especially well-built German auxiliaries.

24. E.g., Dio 74.9.

25. Suet. *Tib.* 37.1 mentions the establishment of a unified praetorian barracks in the context of Tiberius's efforts against lawlessness. According to Tacitus (*Ann.* 4.2), this was at the instigation of the prefect Sejanus, in order to increase their power and ability to intimidate. On the *Castra Praetoria* (located at the northeastern edge of the city) and other camps, see Coulston, "Armed and Belted Men," esp. 82–86; Lissi Caronna, "Castra praetoria; and Busch, "*Militia in urbe*" (I have not seen her *Militär in Rom*)."

26. Suet. *Claud.* 25, cf. 18; on the context, see Osgood, *Claudius Caesar*, 182–87. Much of the wheat imported from Africa and Egypt entered Italy through these two port cities. Epigraphic evidence for the Ostian detachment (which also came to cover nearby Portus) stretches into the late fourth century. Comparatively little is known of the cohort of *vigiles* at Puteoli, which may not have remained nearly so long.

27. Suet. *Vesp.* 8.3.

Commodus once supposedly called on them to punish spectators. They also may have served as harbor police.[28]

Notionally, this amounts to more than 23,840 military police in Rome, not counting seamen or *frumentarii* (chapter 6 below). We remarked in chapter 4 that Augustan Rome's 1:100 police-to-civilian ratio compares very favorably with the police presence in most modern urban environments. It more than doubled in strength by the early third century, and there was now roughly one military policeman for every forty-two residents of Rome. Another way to express this extraordinary level of coverage is that any male randomly chosen off the street would have a 1-in-21 chance of being a soldier.[29]

Septimius Severus and the Bandit King Bulla

Septimius Severus's triumphal entry into Rome in 193 marked a change in the ethos of military policing in both Rome and Italy. The new praetorian guard he installed was no longer of the traditional "pure Roman stock" (that is, drawn from Italy and historic Roman provincial communities), although he may have compensated for this change by increasing the number of *vigiles* and urban cohorts drawn from local recruits.[30] Thereby he also tightened his grip on the capital. In one case, he even called on civilians to help his soldiers police the capital. In a letter addressed to the board of fifteen men preparing for the Secular Games of 204, he and his sons "instruct[ed] urban property-owning civilians and renters to ensure with diligence the safety of the city districts, along with our soldiers on patrol, during these

---

28. See Coulston, "Armed and Belted Men," 78, and Coarelli, *Rome and Environs*, 171, 337. We do not know the size of these detachments. The *Castra Misenatium* was near the Colosseum, so the Misenum marines may have been chiefly responsible for its *vela*. The Ravenna fleet's camp was probably in Trastevere, near the large Naumachia complex where Augustus (*RGDA* 23) and later emperors staged mock sea battles. They may well have helped put on these shows. We lack explicit evidence of either unit acting as river police in Rome, but the Ravenna camp's probable proximity to the Tiber raises the reasonable possibility that they guarded the bustling depots around the Aventine Hill. Known cases of seamen policing Italy and Rome (discussed in broader context below): Tac. *Ann.* 4.27; SHA *Commodus* 15.6; *CIL* 11.6107 = *ILS* 509, lines 14–15 (AD 246).

29. Of course, these figures rest on many assumptions: accuracy of sources, the presence of the emperor in Rome, population of one million, equal numbers of men and women, and military units at full strength. Military units often operated below full strength, as Goldsworthy points out in *The Roman Army at War* (passim).

30. E. Birley, "Septimius Severus." For the guard in the later third century, see Potter, *The Roman Empire at Bay*, 257.

nocturnal festivities."³¹ While the *vigiles* were not fully military in nature at their conception, they were clearly considered soldiers by the early third century.³²

The legal enumeration of the urban prefect's duties, as we have it in Justinian's *Digesta*, reflects an increase in that official's policing capacity, the growth of which may have been largely thanks to Septimius Severus himself. Indeed, citing a letter of Severus, Ulpian noted that "the prefecture of the city has arrogated to itself all criminal cases whatsoever, and not only those which are committed within the city, but also those which are committed beyond the city in Italy."³³ Ulpian also charged this official with keeping order at the shows and to use the soldiers of the four urban cohorts under his command to do so: "And indeed he should also have posted soldiers (*stationarii*) placed in different places to protect the peace of the commoners' seats (*popularia*) and to report to him what is happening and where."³⁴ Thus, in Severan times, the urban prefect had absorbed much of the public-order maintenance and legal jurisdiction traditionally associated with the praetors, aediles, and other traditional republican magistracies.³⁵

By this point, the competence of the prefect of the *vigiles* had likewise crossed into criminal jurisdiction, but he could only hear cases over petty thefts, burglaries, and robberies; serious cases (such as intentional and malicious

31. *CIL* 6.32327 (p. 3824; cf. *ILS* 5050a), lines 20–22: *admonemus Quirit[es d]ominos urbano[s ... et eos quo]que qui mercede habitant in noctib[us feriarum illarum ut una cum mili]tibus nostris circumeuntibus reg[ionum] tutelam [diligenter administrent].* The activity of nocturnal patrolling and care for the safety of Rome's *regiones* suggests that these *milites* (soldiers) were *vigiles*.

32. Sablayrolles, *Libertinus miles*, 51–54 (stressing the Severan emperors' close ties with the *vigiles*).

33. Ulp. *Dig.* 1.12.1.pr.: *Omnia omnino crimina praefectura urbis sibi vindicavit, nec tantum ea quae intra urbem admittuntur, verum ea quoque quae extra urbem intra Italiam.* But the urban prefect's exact jurisdiction is not altogether clear: a separate citation of this same letter (*Dig.* 1.12.1.4) specifies a one-hundred-mile radius for the prefect's power. Ulpian *Dig.* 1.12.3 states that he could appoint judges outside of Rome, although he himself could exercise his authority only while inside the city. See Vitucci, *Ricerche*, 52–81, with Cadoux's critical review, 156–60. Note also Juvenal 4.77–78, comparing an urban prefect to a *vilicus* (chief slave manager of an estate; chapter 3 above) and 13.157–58, on a conscientious *praefectus urbi* who hears criminal cases all day.

34. *Dig.* 1.12.1.12: *Quies quoque popularium et disciplina spectaculorum ad praefecti urbi curam pertinere videtur: et sane debet etiam dispositos milites stationarios habere ad tuendam popularium quietem et ad referendum sibi quid ubi agatur.* Watson's translation of this passage is inaccurate; *ad tuendam popularium quietem* here refers not to monitoring the populace (*populares*) in general but to the surveillance of the *popularia* (neuter plural), the physical area where the lower orders sat at games; cf. Suet. *Claud.* 25.4 and *Dom.* 4.5 for parallel usages of the term. On *milites stationarii* (roughly, "posted soldiers," or "soldiers on guard duty"), see chapter 8 below; this is the only attested usage of the phrase in Rome itself.

35. Nippel, *Public Order*, 94–96. Some manuscripts of the *Liber Pontificalis* (22.5) have the urban prefect conducting the trial of Pope Cornelius (AD 251–253) with the emperor.

arson) were to be remitted to the superior urban prefect. Both could order summary punishments, such as flogging, for misdemeanors (Ulp. *Dig.* 1.15.4). In
fact, as real imperial power in later centuries moved to other centers, leaving the
urbs Roma with only symbolic importance, the urban prefecture evolved into a
sort of de facto mayor cum chief of police over the still-large and sometimes
unruly population of Rome. All three military police branches (praetorians,
urban cohorts, *vigiles*) were disbanded in the fourth century, making it difficult
for the urban prefect to keep order in late antiquity. In a letter to Theodosius,
Bishop Ambrose asked: "Do you not remember, emperor, how many homes of
the prefects at Rome were torched, and no one avenged them?"[36]

The disorders of AD 193 in Rome also highlight the growing political importance of the urban prefect. Unlike the praetorian prefect and the prefect of the
vigiles, both equestrian posts, the *praefectus urbi* was a consular-level senatorial appointee and thus a potential *princeps*. Holding this post and its command of the
urban cohorts gave Pertinax leverage in his ascent to the throne after Commodus's death. Didius Julianus's rival bidder, Sulpicianus, was also the urban prefect.
Thus, later emperors were keen to ensure the loyalty of the man holding this
office; Didius Julianus, in fact, installed his own son-in-law.[37] Tacitus famously
remarked that Nero's fall and the ensuing usurpations in AD 68–69 "revealed the
secret of empire, that an emperor could be made elsewhere than at Rome."[38] Later
emperors, however, likewise realized that despite the political and military changes
since the early principate, an emperor still might be made *in* Rome.

Accordingly, safeguarding the loyalty of Rome, in an era when the emperor was often absent on campaign, was one motive that prompted Septimius Severus to break with custom and station a legion, the *II Parthica*, in
Italy itself. It was posted at *castra Albana*, just thirteen miles southeast of
Rome. As under previous emperors, some soldiers from the praetorian guard
and urban cohorts continued to be detached from their units in the city and
outposted as *stationarii* in Italy and the provinces;[39] but now the emperors and

---

36. Ambrose *Ep.* 40.13; on disorder in fourth-century Rome: Amm. Marc. 14.6, 28.4.

37. SHA *Did. Jul.* 3.6; cf. *Hadr.* 5.5.

38. *Hist.* 1.4. As *praefectus urbi*, Vespasian's brother Flavius Sabinus was an influential player
in the civil strife of AD 69: note esp. Tac. *Hist.* 3.64–75.

39. Praetorians as outposted *stationarii*: *I. Ephesos* 6.2319 (= *ILS* 2052, *CIL* 3.7136, Ephesus); *I.
Smyrna* 382 (third century); *AE* 1991, 1668 (= *ILS* 9072, *stationarius ripae Uticensis*); *AE* 1981,
344 (=*AE* 1957, 218, Heba, northwest of Rome, second or third century); cf. *AE* 1937, 250 (a
dedication found in Bithynia from a cavalryman of the *equites singulares Augusti*). The Saepinum inscription (*CIL* 9.2438, *JRS* 73, pp. 126–27; ca. 170, quoted at the end of chapter 2 above)
may allude to praetorian *stationarii* in rural Italy. Soldiers from the urban cohorts as *stationarii*:
AE 1954, 53 (Thuburbo Maius, south of Carthage, post-AD 177).

their administrators had another large body of troops to draw from for nearby policing tasks and for ensuring their authority in the capital. This sort of change also reveals a growing decline in Italy's status. Initially, Italy was differentiated from the provinces by special treatment and institutional arrangements: it had no governor, its inhabitants were free from many taxes and liturgies, and there was normally no military draft. As the third century played out, though, Italy lost these benefits and indeed became just another group of provinces in Diocletian's reorganization at century's end.[40]

The usurpations of 193, the reign of Severus, and the problematic succession of emperors of his dynasty all reveal that the state had become thoroughly militarized. To be sure, military prowess was a fundamental Roman virtue, and any perspicacious observer knew that Augustus's power ultimately rested on the soldiers. But imperial militarism was made palatable by the traditional Republican façade of the principate, and Suetonius noted that Augustus, "*after* the civil wars, never called his men 'comrades' either in assemblies or edicts, but 'soldiers.'"[41] Such pretenses grew ever thinner throughout the second century, as *principes* often called their men *commilitones* ("fellow soldiers").[42] When friends of the rhetorician Favorinus criticized him for bogusly conceding a trivial academic point to Hadrian, he retorted that a man who commands thirty legions may safely be considered the most learned of all.[43] Civilians still appreciated gestures of republican modesty, even in the late fourth century, when generals such as Stilicho acted as the effective head of the empire.[44]

But the reality under Severus and his successors was unmistakable: a legion was stationed in Italy, and Rome was swarming with more than twenty thousand military police. In more stable times, this military presence did not seem to cause widespread disruption for civilian life in Rome and Italy (as did the military irregularity amid the disorders of A.D. 68–69), although Juvenal colorfully illustrated the unpleasantness of individual encounters with

---

40. See Ausbüttel, *Die Verwaltung*, 85–103; Lo Cascio, "The Emperor," 165–69, 180–81. *Correctores* served as governors of the Italian provinces: Slootjes, *The Governor*, 19.

41. Suet. *Aug.* 25.1. Nor did Augustus allow his family members to use the term *commilitones*.

42. On the emperors' use of the word *commilitones*, see, e.g., Pliny *Ep.* 10.20 (Trajan) and Dio 72.24.1 (*sustratiôtai*, Marcus Aurelius); and esp. Campbell, *The Emperor and the Roman Army*, 32–39.

43. SHA *Hadr.* 15.12–13.

44. See, e.g., Claudian *De Quarto Consulatu Honorii Augusti*, lines 1–17 (AD 398).

soldiers, even under the "Good Emperors" of the second century.[45] But the third century brought real military changes in Rome, Italy, and beyond. We will see that wandering soldiers caused disturbances in the provinces. Amid growing third-century military and political instability, commanders desperately sought to buy their soldiers' loyalty, economically squeezing the provinces more harshly than at any time since the late Republic.

Traditionalists were not pleased. As a witness to Septimius Severus's entry into Rome, Cassius Dio offered this reaction:

> And he did many things not to our liking, and he was blamed for making the city turbulent through the presence of so many soldiers and by burdening the state by his excessive expenditures of money, and most of all, for placing his hope of safety not in the good will of his associates [in government], but in the strength of his army. Some found fault with him most of all because he abolished the practice of drawing his praetorian guardsmen exclusively from Italy, Spain, Macedonia and Noricum, whereby men of more respectable appearance and milder habits were selected, but instead ordered that any vacancies should be filled from all legions alike. Now he did this with the idea that that he should thus have guards with a better knowledge of the soldier's duties, and should also be offering a prize to those who proved brave in war; but in fact it became only too apparent that he had incidentally ruined the youth of Italy, who turned to brigandage and gladiatorial fighting in place of their former service in the military, at the same time filling the city with a throng of motley soldiers most savage to behold, most terrifying to hear, and most boorish to converse with.[46]

Considering Dio's status as an elite Greek senator, we cannot necessarily put too much stock in his appraisal of the soldiery; as a moralizing historian in the traditional literary genre, Dio in his views on banditry is not necessarily trustworthy. It is significant, however, that he put soldiers and bandits on the same continuum (chapter 8 below).

Dio's most notable theme on banditry is his discussion of the bandit chief Bulla Felix, who pestered Italy itself circa 206–7. Recent research in ancient

---

45. On civilian suffering amid military disorder in 68–69, see esp. Tac. *Hist.* 2.56 and 2.87–88 (Italy); 1.8–9, 1.31–46, 2.88–89, 2.93–96 and 4.1 (Rome). Collapse of military discipline is a major theme in our sources; see Ash, "Severed Heads" and *Ordering Anarchy*; and de Blois, "Soldiers and Leaders." On violent encounters between civilians and soldiers, see Juvenal's fragmentary Satire XVI. Durry ("Juvénal et les prétoriens") identified the soldiers criticized here as praetorian guardsmen.

46. Dio 75.2.2–6. Loeb trans., adapted.

banditry has shown that most brigandage was not on the "social bandit" model of Robin Hood and his merry band of rogues but instead was normally carried out on a small scale by ordinary people who occasionally engaged in criminal misbehavior.[47] Across the board, brigandage seems to have been on the rise in the third century, including some examples that seem to fit the Robin Hood model of a charismatic bandit chief, evading and undermining state authority. In the account found in the epitome of Dio's history, the wily Bulla led six hundred men on acts of limited theft and kidnapping, moderated by a sort of justice toward ordinary people. He cleverly evaded the forces Severus sent against him, largely by imitating forms of legitimate Roman authority. Having outmaneuvered a centurion in charge of his pursuit, Bulla was next countered by a large cavalry force under a praetorian tribune, whom the outraged Severus motivated with dire threats should he fail. In the end, the tribune only succeeded with the help of a man whose wife Bulla had bedded.[48]

The whole story of Bulla is rightly seen as a meditation on the nature of power, with the tenuous and revealing interaction between forces legitimate and illegitimate, so called. When Bulla appeared before Severus's right-hand man, the praetorian prefect Papinian, the latter supposedly asked him, "Why are you a brigand?" To which Bulla replied, "Why are you a prefect?"[49] This exchange is suspiciously polished, as is the whole Bulla story, thus raising doubts about the veracity of the episode. Bulla and other robbers extraordinaires may be more literary construction than fact. Perhaps Dio took Bulla as a catch-all type, representing all bandits who challenged the imperial order and this controversial emperor in particular.[50] Following the old rhetoric of imperial peace and stability, Septimius Severus reportedly bolstered his own legitimacy by seeking to be known as "an enemy to bandits everywhere."[51]

---

47. See esp. McGing, "Bandits, Real and Imagined"; Riess, *Apuleius und die Räuber*; and Grünewald, *Bandits*.

48. Dio 77.10 (= Boissevain 76.10). The cavalry force involved may have been the *equites singulares Augusti*; see M. P. Speidel, *Riding for Caesar*, 63.

49. Dio 77.10.7; cf. Cic. *Rep.* 3.24 Tac. *Ann.* 2.40, and August. *De civ dei* 4.4 for similar rhetorical exchanges. Aemilius Papinianus's (*RE* 105, *PIR²* 1.388) legal work is often cited in Justinian's *Digest*.

50. On the literary construction of Bulla and Maternus as bandit antikings, see Grünewald, *Räuber*, 157–95 (= *Bandits* 110–36); Shaw, "The Bandit," 334–38; and Riess, *Apuleius und die Räuber*, 168–71. The bandit Maternus will be discussed below. Riess (170) calls Maternus and Bulla "den literarisierten Räubern par excellence," more literary symbol than reality. Also consider Dio 75.2.4 (Loeb p. 198), in which a major eastern bandit named Claudius rode up to Severus as if he were an officer, saluted and kissed the emperor, and then rode off safely, without Severus knowing who he was.

51. SHA *Sev.* 18.6: *Latronum ubique hostis.*

In their actual opposition to bandits, we must note that imperial administrators relied heavily on Roman soldiers. As noted in chapter 3 above, there were elements of civilian policing in Italy, but our sources do not detail civilian police operations in Italy during the second and third centuries. In this era of the late principate, soldiers were increasingly dispatched to counter security problems in Italy and beyond, a process that started in the earliest years of the empire, as we have observed. For instance, in the later third century, the emperor Probus dispatched a force of soldiers to crush a band of runaway gladiators and the followers they collected amid their plundering.[52] As brigandage was markedly increasing in third-century Italy, emperors commissioned special commanders (*praepositi*) to lead military forces to resecure parts of central and southern Italy. The town of Canusium (modern Canosa) celebrated a local equestrian's service as *praepositus* "on account of his exceptional work in guarding the security of the region at the behest of the people."[53] The service of a local leader in the Canusium case is atypical, because in the other five known instances of this sort of position, elite *outsiders* were appointed for this security task, including two *primipilares* centurions, an equestrian with ample high-level administrative experience, and a senator who attained the consulship.[54] The inscription that most clearly specifies the nature of this military command mentions a "praetorian agent, deputized against banditry, with soldiers" at his disposal, including a twenty-man detachment of marines from the Ravenna fleet, and his own praetorian cohort.[55] Although the other five inscriptions do not specify, most of the soldiers posted to antibandit *praepositi* were probably praetorians, as we have seen them often used in policing missions in Italy; but units from the navy, urban cohorts, or regular legions were also pos-

---

52. Zosimus *Historia Nova* 1.71.

53. *CIL* 9.334 = *ILS* 2768: *ob ... singularem industriam ad quietem regionis servandam postulatu populi*. This M. Antonius Vitellianus (*PIR*² A 881) had been appointed *praepositus* over the *tractus* of Apulia, Calabria, Lucania, and Bruttium. *Tractus* may refer to his general region of responsibility or may carry the specific meaning of transhumant shepherd trails, by analogy to the modern Italian derivative "tratturo." See above on shepherds and banditry, and Riess, "Hunting Down Robbers," 209 et passim.

54. *AE* 1911, 128 (= *ILS* 9201); *CIL* 11.6336 (= *ILS* 2769); *CIL* 8.26582 (= *ILS* 9018); and *AE* 1968, 109, respectively. Cf. *CIL* 5.1057 (= *CIL* 5. Suppl. Ital. 3 [Pais] 83). A *primipilaris* or *primus pilus* was the chief centurion of a legion, a very high distinction that brought equestrian status upon retirement.

55. *CIL* 11.6107 (= *ILS* 509), lines 10–16, Umbria, AD 246. *Aurelius Munatianus, evocatus ex cohorte VI pr(a)etoria p(ia) v(indice) Philippiana agens at latrunculum cum militibus n(umero) XX clas(sis) pprr (sic) Ravenatis p(iae) v(indicis) Filipporum*. See Flam-Zuckermann, "À propos d'une inscription," and on the possible context of this inscription, see Peachin, "Which Philip?" Note that according to Tacitus (*Ann.* 4.27), marines from the Ravenna fleet had been instrumental in revealing an incipient slave revolt in southern Italy in AD 24.

sible. It is clear that when security challenges exceeded the competency of civilian officials and their limited policing capacity, higher officials looked to employ soldiers as police. We will further see that this increasing militarization of policing was a very mixed blessing. By the third century, the strong sway of the soldiers in policing and other matters of state is clear, reflected in Septimius Severus's alleged deathbed advice to his sons: "Enrich the soldiers, but disdain all the rest."[56]

The Bulla episode and the six Italian *praepositi* inscriptions illustrate two further facets of imperial policing in Italy: the growing policing power of the praetorian prefect and the use of centurions as special agents.[57] Naturally, command over the emperor's elite guard brought the praetorian prefects influence, and the prefects of the early empire arrested and interrogated suspected enemies of the state.[58] Characters such as Sejanus and Nymphidius Sabinus are early examples of power-mongering prefects in Rome, and Macro was clearly the power behind the throne early in Gaius Caligula's reign. Early emperors also used their praetorian prefects to process arrested individuals from the provinces: in 92, Casperius Aelianus supposedly arrested and interrogated Apollonius of Tyana, and Trajan later asked Pliny to send a man to his praetorian prefects in chains (*vinctus*) because he was found in Bithynia despite a previous sentence of banishment from the province.[59] The apostle Paul may have also been handed over to the prefect after his arrival in Rome, where he was guarded by a soldier.[60]

---

56. Dio 77.15.2: τοὺς στρατιώτας πλουτίζετε, τῶν ἄλλων πάντων καταφρονεῖτε. The verbatim text suggests that Dio was eager to stress his accuracy here: τάδε λέγεται τοῖς παισὶν εἰπεῖν (ἐρῶ γὰρ αὐτὰ τὰ λεχθέντα, μηδὲν ὅ τι καλλωπίσας). "He is said to have spoken these words to his sons (for I relate his words just as they were spoken, with nothing embellished)." Cf. Dio 78.10. Both Septimius and Caracalla substantially raised soldiers' pay.

57. Caracalla tried using centurions to orchestrate the praetorian prefect Plautianus's ouster in 205: Dio 77.3.2–4. To be sure, centurions assassinating state enemies in Italy predates the principate: e.g., App. *BCiv.* 4.28.

58. On the following discussion of the evolution of the praetorian prefect's criminal jurisdiction and policing powers, see, above all, Absil, *Préfets du prétoire*, 67–76. Also note Jones, *The Criminal Courts*, 98; Millar, *The Emperor*, 122–32; Sablayrolles, "*Fastigium equestre*"; Honoré, *Ulpian*, 4, 28–36; and Salway, "Equestrian Prefects." By the early third century, emperors were referring criminal cases from all over the empire to be tried by them.

59. See Absil, *Préfets du prétoire*, 127 and 156. Casperius Aelianus (ca. AD 93): *PIR²* 2.462. On Apollonius, see Philostr. *VA* 7.16–28 (material from this fantastic biography must be taken with the proverbial grain of salt). Trajan: Pliny *Ep.* 10.57. See also Dio 69.18 on Q. Marcius Turbo's (*RE* 14.2, coll. 1597–600) conscientiousness in performing his duties under Hadrian.

60. Phil. 1:13 and Acts 28:16; cf. 1 Clement §5 (late first century). Sherwin-White conjectured (*Roman Society*, 108–10) that Paul was probably handed over to an administrative subordinate to the praetorian prefect, the *princeps castrorum* of the praetorian cohorts. (Although *principes castrorum* ["heads of camp"] are well attested in the legions, explicit documentary evidence for *praetorian* heads of camp starts only under Trajan: *ILS* 9189.) See further Tajra's somewhat speculative *The Martyrdom of St. Paul*, esp. 40–45.

While Seneca mentions the prefect Burrus working with Nero in the punishment of two bandits (*Clem.* 2.1.2), it was in later centuries that the praetorian prefects' administrative, judicial, and military roles had grown to such an extent that they essentially became assistant emperors. The Saepinum inscription (chapter 2 above), from early in Marcus Aurelius's reign, offers the first hard evidence for the prefects' independent and ample police authority in Italy (where, again, there was no provincial governor). It preserves shepherds' complaints of mistreatment at the hands of local officials and *stationarii* and a menacing letter from the praetorian prefects to the magistrates of Saepinum, urging that abuses be stopped, especially since some of the affected flocks belonged to the emperor.[61]

Tigidius Perennis can be seen as a prefect of a new, ambitious stamp. Having orchestrated the downfall of his colleague Taruttienus Paternus in 180, Perennis held the office under Commodus until 185. The aloof emperor left him to his own devices, and accordingly, Perennis became heavily involved in administrative and legal matters, asserting his authority even in the face of senators. It was only when he encroached too far into military matters that Commodus got rid of him.[62] The power of Septimius Severus's ambitious praetorian prefect Plautianus is said to have rivaled—even surpassed—the emperor's. (Plautianus's military entourage included domestic spies and centurions for special missions, as when he sent some to the eastern frontier to steal zebras.)[63] It was his successor, Papinian, who supposedly presided at Bulla's trial and condemned him to the beasts.[64] By the 290s, the jurist Arcadius Charisius wrote that "the authority of the prefects has deservedly grown, to such an extent that there can be no legal appeal from the praetorian prefects.... For the emperors trusted that they, who are summoned to the splendor of this duty on account of their singular initiative and by their verified faith and earnestness, would not render judgment differently than he himself would render judgment."[65]

---

61. *CIL* 9.2438 = Abbott & Johnson 109, with Corbier, "Fiscus and Patrimonium" (whence *AE* 1983, 331). Dated to the years 169–172, it is partially quoted in chapter 2 above.

62. P. Taruttienus (or Tarruntenus or Tarrutenius) Paternus: *PIR²* T 35; *RE* 4 A2, coll. 2405–7. On Commodus and Tigidius Perennis (*RE* 6 A1, coll. 952–56), see SHA *Commodus* 4.7, 5.1–6, 6.1–2, *Pertinax* 3.3–6; Dio 72.9.1–2; Euseb. *Hist. eccl.* 5.21; and Howe, *The Pretorian Prefect*, 11–14.

63. Dio 76.14–15. C. Fulvius Plautianus (*PIR²* 3.554) served from ca. 197 until Caracalla orchestrated his death in 205 (Dio 77.3.2–4). See Salway, "Equestrian Prefects," 120–24.

64. Aemilius Papinianus (*RE* 105, *PIR²* 1.388, the jurist cited in the *Dig.*) was prefect from 205 to 211 or 212.

65. *Dig.* 1.11.1.1: *praefectorum auctoritas...in tantum meruit augeri, ut appellari a praefectis praetorio non possit.... credidit enim princeps eos, qui ob singularem industriam explorata*

In the Presence of the Emperor

Emperors and their subjects feared each other. Domitian used to complain that no one believed that a conspiracy against an emperor had really been discovered unless it succeeded in killing him.[66] The conspiracy against Domitian succeeded because he was betrayed by his own chamberlains. The trustworthiness of personal servants was essential. Emperors were vulnerable to the disloyalty of their doormen, who carefully controlled entry to their bedchamber. In public settings, emperors varied in their attitudes toward searching callers for weapons. Claudius, for example, was a proponent of the practice; Vespasian dispensed with it, despite the tension of the civil war that brought him to power. There were situations in which emperors could not be surrounded by a throng of military guards. Meetings of the senate could be especially problematic, where emperors had to strike a balance between civility and personal safety.[67]

Ordinarily, though, armed guards accompanied the emperor wherever he went, and people were well aware that the emperor had the effective power of life and death over anyone in his presence. By the Severan age, when the principate's republican façade had faded, this element of the imperial entourage might intimidate even the most nonthreatening innocents. Such was the case with the orator Heracleides of Lycia, who apparently broke down in the middle of an extemporaneous speech "fearing the emperor's guard."[68] Many later emperors spent little time in Italy, but the cruelty of earlier emperors who resided there remained long in the popular memory. Suetonius related an anecdote in which Caligula blackly joked to the consuls that he could have both of their throats cut by merely nodding his head.[69] It is no wonder that Seneca took pains to advise young Nero to limit strictly his power to inflict violence—a

---

eorum fide et gravitate ad huius officii magnitudinem adhibentur, non aliter iudicaturos esse ... quam ipse foret iudicaturos. Arcadius's period of activity cannot be securely dated, but Honoré (*Emperors and Lawyers*, 115–19) conjectures that he was Diocletian's *magister libellorum* ("master of petitions") in 290–91. Honoré's method of stylistic and statistical analysis is not without controversy (see, e.g., Millar, "A New Approach," 272), but he may be on safe ground with Arcadius's particularly ornate style.

66. Suet. *Dom.* 21.1; cf. Cic. *Off.* 2.25, Dio Chrys. 6.35–39. On detection of conspiracies, see Sheldon, *Intelligence Activities*, 150–53, 279–80.

67. Suet. *Aug.* 19.2 and 35.1–2, *Tib.* 25.3, *Claud.* 35, *Galba* 10.3, *Vesp.* 12, *Dom.* 16–17; Tac. *Ann.* 4.21, 11.22.1; Dio 58.17–18; cf. Dionysius of Halicarnassus 2.13.

68. Philostr. *VS* 2.26.614: δορυφόρους δείσαντα. See also Millar, *ERW*, 64, on the later imperial body guard. Constantine's appearance without bodyguard at the Council of Nicaea in 325 was a symbol of trust and good faith in the assembled clergy.

69. Suet. *Calig.* 32, one of many Suetonian anecdotes of Caligula's ill-tempered character.

power that, the philosopher acknowledged, was limited by little else than the ruler's temperance.[70] (Of course, Seneca would eventually fall victim to his former pupil's wrath.) While most second-century emperors cultivated an air of tolerance, restraint, and clemency worthy of Seneca, one never knew when a Hadrian or a Marcus Aurelius might suddenly degenerate into a Caligula or a Nero.

In fact, the emergence of imperial autocracy gave rise to a vibrant literary topos in second- and third-century literature: audacious denunciations of emperors on the part of heroic men who would rather die than live dishonestly under tyranny. This appealing "speaking truth to power" theme has deep roots in Stoic and Cynic philosophy, which would eventually be paralleled in some facets of Christian martyrology. Examples include Tacitus's guarded admiration of Helvidius Priscus and other senators of the "Stoic opposition" or Plutarch's account of the interaction between Alexander the Great and Diogenes the Cynic.[71] Herodes Atticus vehemently berated Marcus Aurelius so much that the praetorian prefect Bassaeus Rufus remarked on his apparent desire for execution. But, as Alexander did before him, the virtuous philosopher-emperor chose not to play the tyrant.[72] In other accounts, though, the emperor ordered summary execution for provincials who insulted him during trials or hearings.[73]

The most striking specimen of the genre is the series of semiliterary papyrological fragments known as the *Acta Alexandrinorum* ("*Acts of the Alexandrians*," or, much less correctly, "*Acts of the Pagan Martyrs*," by analogy to Christian *acta*).[74] These texts preserve bits of polished narrative and dialogue between

70. Sen. *Clem.* 12.1–4, 13.1–5, 19.5–8 and passim. See Roller's discussion, *Constructing Autocracy*, 239–43.

71. Tac. *Agr.* 2, *Ann.* 13.49, 14.12, 14.48–49, 15.23, 16.21–35 (the manuscript breaks off in the midst of Thrasea's death scene). Diogenes the Cynic's outspokenness earned Alexander's admiration: Arrian *Anabasis Alex.* 7.2; Plut. *Alex.* 14 (cf. 13 on his admiration for a defiant Theban woman; contrast 50–51, the murder of Cleitus).

72. Philostr. *VS* 2.1.561 (cf. the encounter between Apollonius and Domitian in *VA* 7.33ff). Bassaeus Rufus (*PIR*² 1.69) is one of the actors involved in the Saepinum-Bovianum inscription (quoted at the end of chapter 2 above) relating to the theft of imperial livestock. On suicidal rudeness to emperors, cf. the *Acta Alexandrinorum* corpus discussed below, esp. the remark of "Trajan" in *Acta Alex.* 8 (= *CPJ* 2.157), col. 3, lines 40–41.

73. E.g., the fictional second-century *Life of Secundus the Philosopher* depicts Hadrian ordering a *speculator* (chapter 4 above) to take the stubborn, mute philosopher from Athens to the port for execution (Perry, ed., *Secundus*, 72–74); cf. *Paradosis Pilati* (fourth century?) 8–10 (Ehrman and Pleše, *The Apocryphal Gospels*, 506–8).

74. The first pieces were published at the end of the nineteenth century. The most convenient editions are Musurillo's *The Acts of the Pagan Martyrs* and his 1961 Teubner edition

haughty members of Alexandria's Greek elite and various Roman emperors from Caligula to Commodus. Pointedly anti-Roman, virulently anti-Semitic, and scornful toward native Egyptians, the *Acta Alexandrinorum* are written from a Greek perspective and represent the triple ethnic division that so troubled the empire's second-largest city. These Alexandrian patriots are depicted bravely facing death so that they can defiantly look Claudius in the eye and call him "a reject son of the Jewess Salomê" and then (against the *princeps'* explicit warning) mock his friend Herod Agrippa as "a two-bit Jew." A most arresting exchange occurs between an Alexandrian gymnasiarch and Commodus, in which the former charges the latter with "tyranny, ignorance of the good, and lack of education," dismissing Commodus as a "bandit chief" as he is led off to execution.[75]

This is stirring stuff, no doubt, and the earliest editors assumed that the *Acta Alexandrinorum* were official documents. Some of the Alexandrian characters can be identified with individuals in other historical records; but later scholars, noting novelistic and rhetorical elements in the *Acta*, have formed a consensus that the texts derive from expansions of real events, drawn from embassy reports or oral accounts from witnesses. Even this limited assessment probably overestimates the *Acta Alexandrinorum*'s historicity.[76] In any

---

(*Acta Alexandrinorum*) and *Corpus Papyrorum Judaicarum* II, 55–107 (i.e., *C. Pap. Jud.* or *CPJ* 2.154–59, eds. Tcherikover and Fuks, whom I generally find more trustworthy than Musurillo). Note also a new fragment of *CPJ* 2.155 published by Musurillo and Parássoglou ("A New Fragment"), with a full reedition in Kuhlmann, *Die giessener literarischen Papyri*, 4.7. Most of the copies we have are second- or third-century. Harker's fine recent study *Loyalty and Dissidence* supersedes previous treatments.

75. Claudius: *Acta Alex.* 4a col. 3 (= *CPJ* 2.156d col. 3), lines 11–12; and *Acta Alex.* 4b col. 1 (= *CPJ* 2.156b col. 1), lines 17–18: τί/[μέλει σοι ὑπὲρ Ἀγρίπ]που Ἰουδαίου τριωβολείου. ("What do you care for a three-obol Jew like Agrippa?" On the meaning of τριωβολεῖος, see Harker, *Loyalty and Dissidence*, 43–44.) We are not sure which descendant of Herod the Great this is supposed to be. It is probably Agrippa I in AD 41 (Tcherikover, *CPJ* 2.156, intro.; Smallwood, *The Jews under Roman Rule*, 253; Harker, *Loyalty and Dissidence*, 23–24); others think Agrippa II in 53 is more likely (Musurillo, *Acts of the Pagan Martyrs*, 126–28; Barrett, *Caligula*, 79). The Salomê in question is probably the sister of Herod the Great (see Musurillo, 128–29). Commodus: *Acta Alex.* 11b, col. 2 (=*CPJ* 2.159b), lines 12–13; and 11b, col. 4, line 8: σὺ ὁ λῄσταρχος.

76. E.g., Musurillo, *Acts of the Pagan Martyrs*; Crook, *Consilium Principis*, 84, 134; MacMullen, *Enemies*, 84–88; Barrett, *Caligula*, 79; and Griffin in *OCD³* ("basically historical," 11) are rather trusting of the *Acta*'s historicity, although Crook aptly points out that emperors might tolerate frankness—even limited hostility—from people appearing before them, thus expressing their virtue of *patientia*. See esp. Crook's app. 4 on παρρησία, "free speech." More guarded assessments of the *Acta*'s historicity are offered by Smallwood, *The Jews under Roman Rule*, 250–53; Bowman, *Egypt after the Pharaohs*, 43 ("probably largely fictional"); Kuhlmann, *Die giessener literarischen Papyri*, 117–18; Fuhrmann, "Keeping the Imperial Peace," 144; and Harker, *Loyalty and Dissidence*, 174–78.

case, the very circulation of such material is striking.[77] And especially if they *are* fictitious, the *Acta Alexandrinorum* reveal a vivid provincial perception of what it was like to appear before the chief representative of a resented hegemony, in which the courageous speakers of truth to power were dragged off to the executioner. In a key passage, Gaius Caligula apparently ordered one disputant to be burned alive.[78]

Conclusion: Monitoring the Populace

A major irony in the *Acta Alexandrinorum* is the Greeks' perception that the emperors were biased in favor of Jews. While there are certainly many instances of cooperation between Roman officials and particular Jewish leaders, Jews were often on the receiving end of Roman hostility.[79] Indeed, a common way in which the emperors monitored and policed Rome was by expelling or repressing scorned groups such as Jews, Christians, certain philosophers, astrologers, and soothsayers.[80]

Emperors targeted these groups for varied reasons. They feared people asking astrologers about their own deaths, potentially destabilizing their rule.

---

77. MacMullen (*Enemies*, 87) assumes that writing and circulating such texts was criminally dissident. Harker (*Loyalty and Dissidence*, 35–36, 175–76) points out that the *Acta*'s depiction of Caligula is no worse than our mainstream sources, nor is their hostility toward Claudius any more treasonous than Seneca's *Apocolocyntosis*. For provincial hostility toward the Roman emperor in the third century, cf. the opening lines (1–6) of the *Thirteenth Sibylline Oracle*.

78. The reading of the phrase in question is secure: *Acta Alex.* 3, col. 3 (*CPJ* 2.155), lines 24–25: Γάιος Καῖσαρ ἐκ[έ]λευσεν τὸ[ν] κα-/-τήγορον καῆναι. "Caesar Gaius ordered the accuser (who may be a native Egyptian) to be burned." Perhaps this refers to nonlethal torture. Bell ("Acts of the Alexandrines," 30) thought Caligula was inflicting the archaic (and rare) Roman punishment for calumny: branding with the letter *K*. But most editors assume immolation (Musurillo, Tcherikover in *CPJ* 2.155, Kuhlmann in *Die giessener literarischen Papyri*, 4.7). Compare Nero's treatment of Rome's Christians: Tac. *Ann.* 15.44.

79. In fact, the showdown between a Jewish sage and a tyrannical king in the apocryphal 4 Maccabees can be seen as a loose Jewish parallel to the *Acta Alexandrinorum*. 4 Macc. was written some time in the first century AD, although it is set two centuries earlier. See MacMullen's discussion in *Enemies of the Roman Order*, 83–84.

80. The earliest imperial "cleansing" of unsavory groups from Rome occurred under Augustus, when Agrippa expelled astrologers and charlatans from the city: Dio 49.43.5; cf. 54.6.4–6 and Suet. *Aug.* 42.3; see chapter 4 above for republican precedents. Other cases include Joseph. *AJ* 18.65–80 and Tac. *Ann.* 2.85.5 (Tiberius, Jews, and followers of Egyptian rites); Suet. *Tib.* 36 (Jews and astrologers, cf. Dio 57.18); *Tib.* 37 (theater faction leaders and actors); Acts 18:2 and *Claud.* 25 (Jews, but cf. Dio 60.6.6); Tac. *Hist.* 2.62 (Vitellius vs. astrologers); Dio 65.9.2 (Vespasian vs. astrologers; cf. Suet. *Vitell.* 14); Suet. *Dom.* 10.3 (philosophers); *CTh.*9.16.12 (AD 409, against astrologers). Christians: Tac. *Ann.* 15.44, Suet. *Nero* 16; cf. *Liber pontificalis* 18/19 (Duchesne ed., I, 54, 154, expulsion of leaders in 235).

Philosophers were notoriously outspoken. Jews and Christians were simply marginal and unpopular. Traditionally minded Romans had an almost eugenic disdain for the former slaves, strange easterners, and charlatans whom they saw infiltrating the populace. But ordering these people to leave Rome or Italy was mostly about public posturing on the part of the *princeps*; there were no door-to-door searches. Tacitus described one expulsion of astrologers from Italy as *atrox et inritum*—severely worded but empty and wholly ineffectual. In another work, Tacitus wrote that astrologers were "a class of men who were faithless to the powerful and treacherous to those hoping for power; in our city they will always be banned but always retained."[81]

Emperors did use troops to monitor Rome's inhabitants. We have noted above soldiers posted at the games and *vigiles* patrolling to catch arsonists and burglars. They could also target individuals and perhaps even root out dissent. The Stoic philosopher Epictetus mentioned that "in this fashion the rash are ensnared by the soldiers in Rome. A soldier, dressed like a civilian, sits down by your side and begins to speak ill of Caesar, and then you, too, just as though you have received from him some guarantee of good faith in the fact that he began the abuse, tell likewise everything you think, and the next thing is—you are led off to prison in chains."[82] I know of no other evidence for soldiers in Rome acting as *agents provocateurs*, laying this sort of *random* trap in Rome. In AD 89, Domitian expelled philosophers, including Epictetus; if this anecdote has any truth to it, perhaps it reflects the particularly autocratic aspects of Domitian's reign. Much depended on the temperament of the *princeps*. Cassius Dio complained that the emperor Caracalla "was informed of everything from everywhere, even the most insignificant things; and he accordingly ordered that the soldiers who kept their ears and eyes open for these details should not be punished by anyone but himself. Nothing good came of this order, but rather another set of tyrants to terrorize us—even these soldiers."[83]

---

81. Tac. *Ann.* 12.52; *Hist.* 1.22. Phillips, "*Nullum crimen*," 264, notes ten expulsions of astrologers. Hatred and distrust of astrologers was not limited to rulers: Cato *Agr.* 5.1–5, Juv. 6.553–91, and Artemidorus *Oneirocritica*, preface; Columella wrote a lost treatise *Against the Astrologers* (ca. AD 60). On eugenic anxiety, see Gowers, "The Anatomy of the City," 30. See further MacMullen, *Enemies of the Roman Order*; Rutgers, "Roman Policy toward the Jews"; and Gruen, *Diaspora*, 8, 15–19; cf. Harris, *Dreams and Experience*, 189, 220–21.

82. Epict. *Diss.* 4.13.5: Οὕτως καὶ ὑπὸ τῶν στρατιωτῶν ἐν Ῥώμῃ οἱ προπετεῖς λαμβάνονται. Παρακεκάθικέ σοι στρατιώτης ἐν σχήματι ἰδιωτικῷ καὶ ἀρξάμενος κακῶς λέγει τὸν Καίσαρα, εἶτα σὺ ὥσπερ ἐνέχυρον παρ' αὐτοῦ λαβὼν τῆς πίστεως τὸ αὐτὸν τῆς λοιδορίας κατῆρχθαι λέγεις καὶ αὐτὸς ὅσα φρονεῖς, εἶτα δεθεὶς ἀπάγῃ. Loeb trans.

83. Dio 78.17, Loeb trans., adapted. Dio seems to be speaking on behalf of the senatorial order.

Even well-regarded emperors employed soldier-police to gather damaging information from unsuspecting people. Hadrian's biographer found fault with the emperor for using *frumentarii* soldiers (chapter 6 below) to snoop into not only the affairs of his own household but even the private lives of his friends.[84] (Unlike the soldiers in Epictetus's anecdote above, these soldiers' invasions of privacy and violations of trust are carefully targeted.) Many emperors were more eager than Hadrian to control citizens through fear; Suetonius claimed that Caligula often repeated the proto-Machiavellian dictum, *Oderint, dum metuant*: "Let them hate me, so long as they fear me."[85] At times, emperors would inflict fear and threats not only in Rome but in any province of the empire; we will now see that the emperor's ability (and inclination) to use soldier-police to enforce public order and imperial control extended outside of Rome.

Before turning to the provinces, let us briefly review and evaluate the situation in Rome and Italy under the emperors. The former had an enormous contingent of military police, which often operated outside the city in Italy. These troops protected the emperor and his family, and the praetorian guard in particular often performed the unpleasant task of liquidating the emperor's rivals and personal enemies. *Vigiles*, urban cohorts, and other institutions made the streets safer, safeguarded grain delivery, and helped make mass entertainments possible. Surrounded by strong deputies, emperors could kill whomever they wanted.

All that said, the growth of policing and security personnel in Rome and Italy created new problems, not least of which was the fact that many emperors died at the hands of their own guards. Cassius Dio described praetorians and other soldiers he witnessed in the late 220s as a surly lot—menacing, disobedient, and murderous. At one point, praetorians and civilians became embroiled in a bloody three-day battle; the soldiers could only get the upper hand by starting fires in the city. Later, they killed their prefect, the jurist Ulpian, even though he had taken refuge in the palace with the emperor Alexander Severus and his mother (who themselves were later murdered by recalcitrant soldiers, as were most third-century rulers).[86] Edicts of expulsion and thousands of soldier-police were no panacea for imperial disorder, if there was a collapse of consensus and social order. That is essentially what happened

---

84. SHA *Hadr.* 11; cf. Tac. *Ann.* 4.67–69.

85. Suet. *Calig.* 30, citing a line from Accius's (ca. 160–90 BC) lost tragedy *Atreus* (fragment 203). How the English language lacks Latin's ominous concision!

86. Dio 80.2–5; cf. Herodian 6.9; SHA *Alex. Sev.* 51.4, 59.6–60.2. On Ulpian's death and service as praetorian prefect: Honoré, *Ulpian*, 27–36, arguing that he died in 223 or 224.

again in the year 238: an unpopular emperor (Maximin Thrax), provincial officials, provincial armies, senators, urban plebs, and praetorians variously aligned against one another, and five emperors died in five months. Civilians in northern Italy apparently starved Maximin's army into submission. In Rome, there was chaos, as civilians and gladiators battled praetorian guardsmen, dropping roof tiles from above and ultimately besieging their well-fortified camp. It seems that the praetorians surrendered only after the civilians successfully cut their water supply.[87]

Policing, in itself, was not enough.

---

87. The main source for the civil war of 238 is Herodian, books 7–8, with relevant SHA biographies; note also Ando, *Imperial Ideology*, 196, 243–45 (throughout, Ando stresses consensus as a necessary element in making the empire work); Potter, *The Roman Empire at Bay*, 168–72; Ménard, *Maintenir l'ordre*, 77–89; and Drinkwater, "Maximinus to Diocletian," 30–33.

6

"Let there be no violence contrary to my wish": Emperors and Provincial Order

The Ethos of Imperial Administration: Petition and Response, Trajan and Pliny

No emperor wanted to suffer Nero's fate. The last Julio-Claudian seems to have been aloof from administration, allowing his underlings to mismanage affairs. He failed to handle intensified problems in the provinces, such as the ruinous state of affairs in Judaea before the First Jewish Revolt. Forced to suicide in 68 as power slipped out of his hands, he also failed to forestall potential rivals outside of Rome. Dynastic propaganda may distort the record and exaggerate a previous emperor's flaws, but even so, it is hard to make the case that Nero was an effective administrator.[1]

Many later emperors were more responsible, but others were just as bad. How much did the emperor's attitude toward administration matter in the lives of his subjects? We will keep that an open question for now, but from the second century on, the general trend is toward greater imperial involvement with the provinces: many emperors and senators now had provincial roots, and the empire became less politically and culturally centered on Italy and Rome; moreover, earlier habits of negotiation and politicking—petitions, embassies, official speeches—became more regular and widespread;[2] finally, innovation in institutional policing helped keep the periphery connected to the center.

---

1. On Neronian maladministration, see, e.g., Jos. *BJ* 2.250–308, Plut. *Galba* 4.1, Suet. *Nero* 32; and de Blois, "Soldiers and Leaders." Cf. Tac. *Hist.* 4.48 on the effect of Gaius's reign on Africa. Less credibly, this theme is a leitmotif of the *Historia Augusta*'s biography of Gallienus.

2. Speeches on official occasions played into the "Second Sophistic" revival of Greek oratory, as the writings of Philostratus, Menander Rhetor, and others attest. Also note Harrison, *Apuleius: A Latin Sophist*, and Sandy, *The Greek World of Apuleius*.

Not all conscientious administrators were deemed good emperors. Neither Domitian nor his successor found a meet balance between firmness and politesse. As Cassius Dio commented (68.1.3), it was one thing to have an emperor under whom no one was allowed to do anything (Domitian), but it was even worse to live in a reign where anyone was allowed to do anything (Nerva). One reason many senators may have detested Domitian is that, unlike some of them, this emperor actually cared about provincial justice and was brash about it. Suetonius, writing under Hadrian, acknowledged Domitian's scrupulosity in administering justice, noting, "He took so much care in pressuring city magistrates and provincial governors that these officials were never more moderate or just. Thereafter we have seen very many of these officials accused of every sort of crime." Hadrian, too, was active in this realm of provincial oversight, if we can trust his biographer: "Indeed, as he traveled around the provinces he punished procurators and governors in accordance to their misdeeds, so seriously that it was believed that he himself had instigated the accusers through his own agency."[3] While emperors usually were not proactive in seeking out provincial problems to solve, we have a mass of evidence that proves that they sought to redress elements of disorder and maladministration when they came to their attention, on issues ranging from cattle rustling and calumny to runaway slaves.[4] They were central to the judicial system and regularly played a very direct role in legal affairs.[5]

A responsible (or paranoid) emperor could gain some knowledge of what was going on in the provinces by sending and receiving letters; hearing embassies; questioning traveling friends, officials, or soldiers (especially *frumentarii*, as we will see); or taking to the road or the seas himself. A typical way of learning about problems in the provinces was by receiving a petition (*libellus*) from an aggrieved party; the emperor could reply with a *subscriptio*, a decision "written under" the petition. There are only a handful of extant verbatim

---

3. Suet. *Dom.* 8.2 (and note 3.2 on the alleged decline of his administration); SHA *Hadr.* 13.10.

4. Cattle rustling (*abigeatus*) in Baetica: *Dig.* 47.14 (Trajan and Hadrian). *Calumniae* (including illegal attempts to enrich prosecutors): e.g., Suet. *Dom.* 9.3; cf. 8.1–2 (but in Suetonius's simplistic scheme, this is before Domitian turned to cruelty, §10–11); Justin, *Apol.* 1.68 (= Euseb. *Hist. eccl.* 4.9) and 1.70; in *Epitome de Caes.* 42.21 (a late source), Trajan's wife spurs him to end the calumnious denunciations of greedy procurators in the provinces. (Against treason informers, cf. Dio 68.1.2 and *Acta proc. S.Cypr.* 1.5.) On imperial determination to curb slave flight, see chapter 2 above.

5. On the emperor's general involvement in the judicial and legal system, see Millar, *The Emperor in the Roman World* (henceforth *ERW*), 3–11, 228–40, 516–37; and Peachin, *Iudex vice Caesaris*, 10–91. Peachin goes on to collect and analyze evidence for judges specially appointed by the emperor as "judges in the place of Caesar" in the late principate.

petitions from civilians; we will see that abuse by soldiers and officials is a common leitmotif in these texts. In response to these and other problems (such as boundary disputes), the emperor often referred the matter back down to provincial governors or procurators, in many cases reiterating standards of law and order already expressed in imperial mandates.[6]

Emperors also relied on correspondence with subordinate officials. The letters exchanged between Trajan and Pliny the Younger constitute our fullest source of information on the official relationship between a *princeps* and a provincial governor. Pliny's appointment, circa 110–112, as "legate *pro praetore* of the emperor with consular power" over the province of Bithynia and Pontus was extraordinary, in that he was a special appointee of Trajan commissioned "to set proper bounds by shaping the habits of the province, and to establish guidelines which would be useful to its stability in perpetuity."[7] Fergus Millar has stated that "letters carried by messenger between governors and emperors were in fact the essential mechanism which allowed a centralized, if passive, government to be carried on."[8] Millar sees emperors responding to problems but not seeking them out, noting, for example, "that the correspondence of

---

6. On the *libellus-subscriptio* "petition-and-response" procedure, see Millar, *ERW* (the fullest exposition of this model of governance), 240–52, 537–49 and Connolly, *Lives behind the Laws*. On passing the buck, see Hauken, *Petition and Response*, part 1, where he also usefully collects the seven extant *libelli*, discussed further below. They are (with the chronological numbering used by Hauken in part 1.1 and henceforth) **no. 1**, *CIL* 8.10570 and 14,464 (from the imperial estate Saltus Burunitanus in Africa Proconsularis, to Commodus in 181); **no. 2**, *CIL* 8.14428 (from an imperial estate near Gasr Mezuar in Africa Proconsularis, also to Commodus in 181); **no. 3**, Keil and Premerstein *Dritte Reise* no. 55 (from an imperial estate near Aga Bey Köyü in Lydia, to the Severans ca. 197–211); **no. 4**, Keil and Premerstein *Dritte Reise* no. 28 (from a village near Kemaliye in Lydia, probably also to the Severans, ca. 197–211); **no. 5**, *IGBulg* 4.2236, with a reedition by K. Hallof in *Chiron* 24 (1994) (from the village Skaptopara in Thrace, to Gordian III in 238); **no. 6**, *MAMA* 10.114 (and appended to the edition of no. 5 in *IGBulg* 4.2236) (from the imperial estate Aragua in Phrygia, to Philip the Arab ca. 244–47); **no. 7**, *TAM* 5:1.419 (from a village near Kavacik in Lydia, to Philip the Arab in 247/48). Compare Septimius Severus's assurance that his procurator and the governor will keep farmers on an imperial estate safe from illegal exactions: Hauken et al., "A New Inscription from Phrygia," and Tabbernee and Lampe, *Pepouza and Tymion*, chap. 4. Finally, in the few extant inscriptions that cite direct imperial involvement in boundary disputes, the *princeps* delegated authority to a subordinate stationed in the provinces: Elliott, "Epigraphic Evidence," 19–20 (on *CIL* 10.8038 and Oliver, *Greek Constitutions*, nos. 108–18).

7. The title is from the posthumous inscription that preserves Pliny's *cursus honorum* most fully: *CIL* 5.5262 = *ILS* 2927, lines 2–4: *Legat. pro pr. provinciae Pon[ti et Bithyniae] consulari potesta[t.] in eam provinciam e[x s.c. missus ab] imp. Caesar. Nerva Traiano Aug.*; also quoted, Pliny *Ep.* 117 (Trajan): *Sed ego ideo prudentiam tuam elegi, ut formandis istius provinciae moribus ipse moderareris et ea constitueres, quae ad perpetuam eius provinciae quietem essent profutura.*

8. Millar, "The World of the *Golden Ass*," 66 (319 in the 2004 reprint); cf. Philo *In Flacc.* 12.100.

Pliny and Trajan contains not a single example of a letter sent spontaneously by the emperor."[9] One may object that Roman officials were not wholly passive, that Book X of Pliny's letters is purposefully edited, and that Trajan showed interest and initiative in assigning Pliny's governorship. Reservations aside, Millar's "petition-and-response" model of Roman imperial governance remains very useful, as the sources usually indicate an administrative ethos that was more reactive than proactive.[10]

Upon the assumption of their duties, most governors received an official set of administrative guidelines (*mandata*) from the emperor. Millar is right to suggest that for many governors, the *mandata* "might represent the only positive communication from the emperor to an office-holder in the entire course of his functions."[11] Trajan and Pliny expressly referred to the emperor's *mandata* in five exchanges of letters, regarding limits on the number of soldiers an equestrian officer could have at his disposal (*Ep.* 10.22), slaves discovered among army recruits (10.30), the legal restoration of men banished from the province (10.56), the suspension of potentially disruptive associations or clubs (*hetaeriae*, 10.96, the well-known letter concerning Christians), and banning the distribution of public funds to private individuals (10.110–11). Amid various legal and criminal regulations, the emperor's basic concern for public order in the provinces is evident.

About a hundred years after Trajan's reign, the jurist Ulpian advised that "a good and serious governor should see to it that the province he rules remains pacified and quiet" by "earnestly searching out evil men and clearing them from his province." (How governors attempted to do this is treated in chapter 7 below.) This passage describes a fundamental priority of Roman rule, and Ulpian's contemporary Paulus reiterated the importance of this pub-

---

9. Millar, *ERW*, 317. Cf. Mitchell, "Requisitioned Transport," 114.

10. Ando, in his thorough and wide-ranging *Imperial Ideology and Provincial Loyalty in the Roman Empire*, lays more stress on the emperor broadcasting his charisma, actively reaching into the provinces, seeking consensus and legitimization. Regarding the latter, Lendon's paper "The Legitimacy of the Roman Emperor: Against Weberian Legitimacy and Imperial 'Strategies of Legitimation'" is not to be missed. Connolly's *Lives behind the Laws* further refines our understanding of petitions."

11. Millar, *ERW*, 317; on the development of *mandata* (Greek *entolai*), 313–17, 323–24 and 328, although Millar may overstate the extent to which their contents became ossified into standardized "boiler plate" text. Nothing prevented emperors from altering or adding to the regular instructions in particular *mandata*, and with so little direct evidence available to us, firm conclusions are elusive. See further Potter, "Emperors, Their Borders and Their Neighbors"; and Meyer-Zwiffelhoffer, Πολιτικῶς ἄρχειν, 279–84. On the *mandata* under which Pliny operated, see Sherwin-White, *The Letters of Pliny*, 543–44, 547. On promulgation of *mandata*, see Ando, *Imperial Ideology*, 113–16. Senate-appointed proconsuls did not routinely receive *mandata* from the emperor during the early principate.

lic-order function and specified their inclusion in *mandata* that emperors issued to provincial governors: "The emperors' *mandata* state that he who commands the province must take care to purge the province of evil men."[12]

The Expansion of Military Policing in the Provinces: Frumentarii

Emperors' reach into provincial order did not depend wholly on governors as intermediaries; they also used soldiers as direct agents. According to Eusebius of Caesarea, when young Alexander Severus's powerful mother, Julia Mamaea, wished to see the renowned Christian philosopher Origen of Alexandria, she dispatched a "military escort" to fetch him to Antioch, where she was staying. In this case, her intentions were friendly; after discoursing for a while, she let him return home.[13] Other holders of imperial authority would not be so benign to Christian leaders, and Mamaea could have used the same means to summon Origen for hostile questioning or execution if she were so inclined. Indeed, we have seen above (chapter 5) how paranoid emperors used soldiers at their disposal to locate and eliminate opponents.

The emperors never established a formal, specialized secret service or quick-reaction force to root out treason, arrest internal enemies, or assassinate individuals in the provinces. Private denunciation (*delatio*) in the provinces played a part in suppressing opposition.[14] So did ad hoc strikes assigned to underlings—usually soldiers of various kinds. For example, Caligula sent a centurion with a squad of soldiers on a fast ship from Italy to Alexandria to arrest the governor of Egypt, an impressive operation, which included slipping unnoticed into the huge city at night, infiltrating a dinner party with a soldier disguised as a servant, securing the exits of a house, and taking their quarry by surprise.[15] According to Tacitus, a centurion was dispatched from Rome in 70 to trump up charges and then execute Lucius Piso, proconsul of

---

12. Ulp. *Dig.* 1.18.13.pr.: *Congruit bono et gravi praesidi curare, ut pacata atque quieta provincia sit quam regit*; Paulus *Dig.* 1.18.3: *in mandatis principum est, ut curet is, qui provinciae praeest, malis hominibus provinciam purgare*; see also Marcian *Dig.* 48.13.4.2, Callistratus *Dig.* 48.19.27, and Bowman, "Provincial Administration," 352.

13. Euseb. *Hist. eccl.* 6.21: μετὰ στρατιωτικῆς δορυφορίας αὐτὸν ἀνακαλεῖται. Cf. *Paradosis Pilati* (*The Handing Over of Pilate*) 1 (Ehrman and Pleše, *The Apocryphal Gospels*, 504).

14. On provincial *delatores*, see Rutledge, *Imperial Inquisitions*, 71–78, discussing Judas Iscariot as a notable example. Pliny's letters show delation at work in his province, e.g., *Ep.* 10.81, 10.96. See also Rivière, *Les délateurs*, esp. 274–85.

15. Philo *In Flacc.* 13.109–15; cf. Herodian 7.3.

Africa. Perhaps he was specialized in this sort of work, for this centurion was found to have been one of the killers of a previous troublesome enemy in Africa, Clodius Macer.[16] The usurper Avidius Cassius was killed in Syria by a centurion and a military decurion in 175.[17]

Emperors continued using different types of soldiers for occasional missions, but a new military institution of the later principate started performing many of these special policing tasks, such as execution, arrest, and domestic espionage: the *frumentarii*. They may have been instituted by Domitian, although they enter our records in full force a little later, in the early second century.[18] *Frumentarii* had a headquarters on the Caelian Hill in Rome, and a number of sources attest that second- and third-century emperors used them, sometimes nefariously, for critical ad hoc tasks in Rome and abroad.[19] For this reason, the imperial *frumentarii* constitute the closest thing to a military quick-reaction force in the service of the emperor; they have even been called "the Roman Secret Service."[20] While we should avoid such anachronism and exaggeration, *frumentarii* sometimes were a heavy-handed instrument of imperial power.[21]

Their name suggests that their original task was provisioning grain (*frumentum*) for the army.[22] If so, the *frumentarii*'s early role as grain procurers

---

16. Tac. *Hist.* 4.49. Clodius Macer was a legionary commander (*legatus*) who cut grain shipments to Rome in 68; see further Tac. *Hist.* 1.7 and 1.73. Vespasian's ally Mucianus sent the centurion against L. Piso.

17. Dio 72.27.2–3; this was supposedly ordered without the emperor's approval.

18. Sinnigen ("The Roman Secret Service") tentatively assigns their use as imperial agents to Domitian. Austin and Rankov (*Exploratio*, 136) apparently take the existence of this force for granted throughout the first century. Dating the origin of their police function is complicated by continued use of the adjective for grain supply, whereas their policing role is not strongly attested until the early second century. See Paschoud, "*Frumentarii*," 215–32, and Clauss, *Untersuchungen zu den* principales.

19. On the *frumentarii*'s Roman headquarters, see Baillie Reynolds, "The Troops Quartered in the *Castra Peregrinorum*"; Rankov, "*Frumentarii*, the *Castra Peregrina*, and the Provincial *Officia*"; Richardson, *A New Topographical Dictionary*, 77–78; Lissi Caronna, "Castra peregrina"; Claridge, *Rome*, 311; and Coarelli, *Rome and Environs*, 215–16. Today, the church of S. Stefano Rotondo partially covers the *castra peregrina*; the *mithraeum* discovered under that site was part of this camp.

20. Anachronisms in Sinnigen's article of that name are not limited to its title, unfortunately. Baillie Reynolds, "The Troops Quartered in the *Castra Peregrinorum*," 170, also calls the *frumentarii* an "Imperial secret service."

21. "Special units such as the *frumentarii*," Nippel usefully cautions, "were not the gigantic surveillance apparatus terrorizing the population that has sometimes been inferred from the alleged analogy with modern systems of state police and secret services." *Public Order*, 100–101. Schuller makes a similar point about the later *agentes in rebus*, "Grenzen," 3–8.

22. Rankov, "The Origins of the *Frumentarii*," dissents (perhaps correctly) from the standard view, arguing that their name comes from an award of extra grain rations, on the model of *beneficiarii* and *cornicularii*. There is not enough evidence for firm conclusions.

would have created links between the provincial population and the military administration, which was ultimately responsible to the governors and the emperor. Consequently, as police agents, their functions crossed boundaries between periphery and center. Because no single ancient source elucidates their organization and functions from top to bottom, it will be useful to draw certain distinctions and study their operations on two levels, the provincial and the imperial. At the provincial level, they were sometimes attached to the governor or else operating semi-independently, perhaps in conjunction with military requisition officials or civilian tax collectors.[23] (Much of what we know about them comes from civilian complaints about their excessive exactions.) We will return to provincial *frumentarii* in the next two chapters; here, we will focus on *frumentarii* who worked closely with the emperors.

We have already noted Hadrian's surveillance of his friends via *frumentarii*; to this we might add a similar case, a letter (fictitious, no doubt) of the emperor Gallienus quoted in the *Historia Augusta*'s glowing biography of his successor, Claudius II (r. 268–270). Gallienus had supposedly learned through his *frumentarii* that the future emperor held a low opinion of him. In another incident, Macrinus is said to have used a *frumentarius* to investigate sexual misconduct of some soldiers. Under Commodus, the praetorian prefect Paternus apparently ordered *frumentarii* to murder Saoterus, one of Commodus's debauchers. If true, this incident shows that the praetorian prefects shared in the command of the *frumentarii*, a reasonable likelihood considering the prefects' growing power around this time. In 193, Didius Julianus may have sent a centurion of the *frumentarii* "well known for killing senators" to assassinate Septimius Severus. The *Historia Augusta* also suggests that the *frumentarii* were employed as special imperial messengers, as in the civil war of 238, when Pupienus Maximus circulated *frumentarii* "to every province to order that anyone who helped Maximinus (Thrax) would be considered an enemy."[24]

---

23. The actions of *frumentarii* in the provinces are covered further in the following two chapters; chapter 7 examines *frumentarii* who were clearly attached to the governor, while chapter 8 discusses those who seem to be acting independently on detached service from their military units. It is this latter variety that generated the most complaints from provincials. Q.v. φρουμεντάριος in index 6 of Hauken's *Petition and Response* (citing five instances), and see further Herrmann, *Hilferufe*. Mann ("The Organization of *Frumentarii*") incorrectly allots all *frumentarii* activity to direct imperial supervision; see Rankov's correction, "*Frumentarii*, the *Castra Peregrina* and the Provincial *Officia*."

24. All of these anecdotes, alas, are from the *Historia Augusta*: *Claud.* 17.1 (likely extrapolated from *Hadr.* 11); *Macrin.* 12.4 (a *frumentarius* reveals that some soldiers had bedded the maidservant of their host, and the emperor cruelly punished them); *Comm.* 4.5 (Paternus = P. Taruttienus Paternus: *PIR²* T 35; *RE* 4 A2, coll. 2405–7); *Maximus et Balb.*, 10.3. The SHA name Didius Julianus's centurion Aquilius (5.8: *notus caedibus senatoriis*); Mommsen and others thought he was M. Aquilius Felix (*PIR²* A 988, Pflaum *Carrières* 225 A), who went

Such imperial messengers faced danger in times of unrest. Tacitus noted that "some soldiers and centurions" carrying messages for Vespasian in AD 69 were caught and sent to Vitellius, who executed them. Cassius Dio's history offers several other cases: When Pertinax succeeded the assassinated Commodus in 193, many provincial governors arrested the messengers who brought the news, fearing a trick on the part of Commodus. Didius Julianus's special messengers failed him in their loyalty, as those sent to kill or beseech Septimius Severus as he marched on Rome went over to his side. In discerning the direction events were taking, shrewdness trumped obedience. Or competing messengers could create chaos. As Macrinus was losing his grip on power, he and the Severans similarly sent messengers to the provinces and the legions, with the result that many on both sides were killed as contradictory messages caused turmoil and confusion.[25] The text of Dio, as we have it (patchy later summaries for these books), does not call these letter-carrying soldiers *frumentarii*, although this function is attested enough that some scholars equate soldiers denoted as *angeliaphoroi* ("message bearers") or *grammataphoroi* ("letter carriers") with *frumentarii*.[26]

Our literary and epigraphic evidence suggests that *frumentarii* linked various facets of imperial power, circulating among soldiers and civilians in the provinces and gathering information for emperors and governors, among other tasks. But they were prone to abuse. Aurelius Victor remarked, "These *frumentarii*, although they seem to have been instituted to search out and report on whatever disturbances were emerging in the provinces, by nefariously inventing false charges and instilling fear everywhere (especially in more remote areas), they shamefully plundered everything."[27]

---

on to have an impressive civil career under the man he was supposed to have killed: *ILS* 1387 lists *(centurio) fr(umentariorum)* among his early offices; this identification is a reasoned conjecture but no more. Soldiers mentioned by Herodian (3.5.4, Severus's scheme to assassinate Albinus) may be *frumentarii*, although they are not specified as such. On growth of the praetorian prefects' powers, see chapter 5 above.

25. Tac. *Hist.* 2.98; Dio (epitome) on Pertinax: 74.2.5 = Loeb vol. 9, 128); on Didius Julianus: 74.16.5–17.1 (cf. SHA *Did. Jul.* 5, *Sev.* 5, *Pesc. Nig.* 2); on Macrinus and the Severans in AD 218: 79.34.6–7. Compare Amm. Marc. 14.1.6–7, on Gallus's use of spies in Antioch.

26. Viz. Rankov, "*Frumentarii*," 180, and Mason, *Greek Terms*, 5 and q.v. "frumentarius" in index IV. (On shortcomings of Mason's lexicon, note Drew-Bear's review, "Latin Terms"). The most careful evaluation of the evidence is by Kolb, *Transport und Nachrichtentransfer*, 281–99. On additional *grammataphoroi* who may be *frumentarii*, see also Dio 79.14.1 and 79.15.1, and 79.39.3 on the *angeliaphoroi* of Macrinus; some of these soldiers may be working in what Kolb identifies as the army's internal communication system, separate from what she calls the *cursus publicus* infrastructure.

27. Aur. Victor, *de Caes.* 39.45.

But one problem with the literary evidence on imperial *frumentarii* is that most of these sources were written well after Diocletian abolished them. This is, in fact, the context of Aurelius Victor's remarks on this "pestilent clan"; Victor also notes their similarity to the blandly labeled *agentes in rebus* ("agents in affairs"), the successors of the *frumentarii*, who served a more centralized and assertive bureaucracy.[28] Neither Victor nor the author of the *Historia Augusta*—lackluster antiquarians at best—had any living memories of the *frumentarii*, and they may have been projecting what they knew of the *agentes in rebus* onto the second and third century. We can only hope that they are trustworthy on this point. The general picture they draw is feasible enough, if we correct for exaggeration. In any case, we will see (chapter 8 below) that *frumentarii* are well attested epigraphically; they are not a fanciful invention of our imperfect literary sources.

If Aurelius Victor was right to say that the *frumentarii* were "instituted to search out and report on whatever disturbances were emerging in the provinces," we have therein positive proof of an obvious fact. No emperor wanted provincial problems to spiral out of control. We have noted Nero's fate. His eventual successor, Vespasian, was supported by the legions under his command in the great Jewish revolt. First-century Jewish writers and the Christian New Testament reveal that Roman Palestine was something of a powder keg, rife with sectarian tensions of all sorts. One grievous symptom of these problems was violence, feuding, and banditry in the province; Book II of Josephus's *Jewish War*, covering Nero's early reign, discusses the suppression of various bandit chiefs and the emergence of hit-and-run political assassins, the *sicarii*. To be sure, Josephus's politics distort his narrative, and recent research on banditry shows that it was normally small-scale.[29] But at times, brigandage

---

28. Aur. Victor, *de Caes.* 39.44, on improved standards of justice under Diocletian: "and the pestilent clan of the *frumentarii*, which are very similar to *agentes rerum* (= *in rebus*) now, was disbanded." Cf. Jerome, *In Abdiam* 1. Diocletian probably created the *agentes in rebus*, although they are first attested in 319 (*CTh* 6.35.3). In the early fourth century, they were most active as couriers and inspectors of the *cursus publicus* but seem to have some expanded police powers and intelligence duties by mid-century. See Sinnigen, "The Roman Secret Service"; Jones's discussion in *LRE* 578–82 is better and more restrained, although it somewhat obscures their policing role in the provinces. This is especially so of *agentes in rebus*, who were also called *curiosi* ("snoops," literally), another military-policing term that first appears in the late principate (chapter 8 below).

29. Note esp. Jos. *BJ* 2.245–81, with Horsley, *Bandits*, 48–87, 190–259; parts of the New Testament independently back up these points, e.g., Acts 21:38. In *The Zealots*, Hengel shows that many of the "bandits" described by Josephus were his own enemies, often politically motivated warlords (some of whom were from an elite background) who opposed Rome and its collaborators. On recent research on banditry, see Riess, *Apuleius und die Räuber*; cf. Krause, *Kriminalgeschichte*, 157–72.

grew bad enough to undermine the authority of the Roman Empire on a large, and embarrassing, scale, just as piracy had undermined Roman hegemony in the late republic. Flare-ups of banditry in less developed areas also made the rhetoric of imperial peace look hollow and threatened the overall integrity of the empire.[30]

Ordinarily, local communities were responsible for checking banditry; this responsibility also rested with the governor, as we will see. The emperor might encourage local efforts from a distance, but there were outbreaks of resistance that evoked a more direct imperial response. We have mentioned Dio's story (dubious, perhaps) of Augustus's anxiety over Caracotta's brigandage in Spain. Tacitus noted Tiberius's and Claudius's concern that conspirators in Rome might stir up rebellion in the provinces. Security measures in the capital could coincide with efforts to stabilize the provinces, as when Tiberius exiled four thousand Rome-based Jews, drafting them as soldiers or paramilitaries to fight bandits in Sardinia.[31] Marcus Aurelius had to counter widespread brigandage in Spain and the Nile Delta.[32] According to Herodian, Commodus failed to check a popular bandit movement led by Maternus, a deserter in Gaul. Like Dio's Bulla story, Herodian's account of Maternus seems to have fictional elements; Commodus sends menacing letters to the governors of the Gallic provinces (Pescennius Niger, Clodius Albinus, Septimius Severus—each would later claim the throne), but ultimately, Maternus is betrayed by his own men after their bandit chief plans to become emperor. Even if Maternus is largely fictional, there probably was some sort of disorder involving deserters at this time.[33] Almost a hundred years later, Probus dispatched troops to fight wide-scale brigandage in Isauria.[34]

---

30. Shaw ("The Bandit") describes rough mountain areas such as Isauria as semiautonomous war zones, which were never truly integrated into the empire (cf. Scott, *The Art of Not Being Governed*). On a smaller scale, this was true of swamps and thickly forested wasteland around cities: see esp. Shaw, "The Bandit," 307–10, citing Antioch as one example. One could cite Rome itself, where the Pontine marshes to the southeast (*BAtlas* 44 C2–3 and D3) were notorious as ruffians' lairs: Juv. 3.306–8, also mentioning the Gallinarian forest (*BAtlas* 44 F4) outside of Cumae.

31. Encouraging from a distance: e.g., *AE* 1979, 624 (Commodus to Boubon; see chapter 3 above); *CJ* 8.40.13. Augustus and Caracotta: Dio, 56.43.3; rebellion in the provinces: Tac. *Ann.* 4.28 and 11.1; Sardinia: Tac. *Ann.* 2.85.5, Jos. *AJ* 18.65–84, Suet. *Tib.* 36, and Dio 57.18.5a.

32. Against Moors in Spain in 171: SHA *Marc.* 21.1. The Egyptian *boukoloi* ("herdsmen"), 172–73; Marcus's main agent was Avidius Cassius, who would later attempt usurpation: SHA *Marc.* 21.2, Dio 72.4, and, on the xenophobic depiction of these marsh dwellers as animalistic cannibals, Shaw, "The Bandit," 312.

33. Herodian 1.10.1–7; cf. SHA *Comm.* 16.2, *Pesc. Nig.* 3.4–5, and *CIL* 11.6053. See Shaw, "The Bandit," 335–36; and Grünewald, *Bandits*, 124–36, *contra* Alföldy, "*Bellum desertorum*."

34. SHA *Probus* 16.4–6; Zosimus 1.69–70.

The emperors' extension of military policing in the provinces was not limited to the creation of the *frumentarii* or occasional reactions against brigandage. Just as Claudius stationed cohorts of *vigiles* in Ostia and Puteoli (Suet. *Claud.* 25), two important provincial centers each received an urban cohort (on the model of those based in Rome) as a permanent garrison. Augustus himself may possibly have posted the one at Lugdunum (Lyon), the head city of the Gallic provinces and the site of an important mint. An epitaph of a soldier from this unit calls it "the cohort of Lugdunum at the mint."[35] Vespasian stationed an urban cohort in Carthage. His reasons for doing so could have included a mix of economic and political motives: monitoring the large city, safeguarding revenue collection, and especially ensuring the capital's grain supply, much of which came from Africa.[36] Food shortages in Rome, or even the fear thereof, often caused unruliness and popular hostility toward the *princeps*. The spread of administrative stations manned by *beneficiarii consularis* in the second and third centuries (chapter 8 below) likely involved imperial endorsement. Moreover, we have various second- and third-century epigraphic indications that soldiers from the praetorian guard and *equites singulares Augusti* were outposted for police duties in the provinces.[37] Because of their close association with the emperor, the outposting of soldiers from these guards may have involved decisions from the emperor or from his "right-hand" men, the praetorian prefects. Judging from Pliny's correspondence with Trajan, the distribution of small numbers of troops in the provinces was not beyond the attention of the emperor.[38]

---

35. On Augustus and Lugdunum, see Tac. *Ann.* 3.41 and chapter 4 above; *CIL* 13.1499 = *ILS* 2130: *L(ucio) Fufio Equestre, mil(iti) coh(ortis) XVII Luguduniensis ad monetam*. Also note *AE* 1993, 1194, and *CIL* 13.11177. If it was not Augustus who posted the unit there, it was one of the other Julio-Claudians, as Tac. *Hist.* 1.64 shows a *cohors XVIII* in place in AD 69. The inscriptions elude precise dating and attest different unit numbers (*XIIII, XVII*). See Bérard, "La garnison de Lyon" and "Une nouvelle inscription."

36. See Echols, "The Provincial Urban Cohorts"; Freis, *RE* supp. 10 "Urbanae cohortes," cols. 1129–31 and *Die Cohortes urbanae*, 31–35, 61–62, 86–87; and Duval, "À propos de la garnison." Bérard argues that it was possibly Domitian, not his father, who posted the unit here: "Aux origines." On Carthage during the disorders of AD 68–70, see Tac. *Hist.* 1.7, 1.11, 1.37, 1.73, 2.97, 4.49, all on Clodius Macer (see above); and *Hist.* 4.38 and 4.48–50 on the Carthaginians who proclaimed L. Calpurnius Piso emperor in 70.

37. E.g., *I.Ephesos* 6.2319 (= *ILS* 2052, *CIL* 3.7136, Ephesus) and *ILS* 9072 (= *CIL* 8.25438, near Hippo Diarrhytus in Africa) on praetorians posted as *stationarii* (see below), and *AE* 1937, 250, on an *eques singularis Augusti stationarius* stationed in Bithynia.

38. Pliny *Ep.* 10.19–22, 10.27–28, 10.77–78, discussed further below.

Imperial Oversight of Provincial Order

The emperors also involved themselves in civil disputes arising from factions that divided various communities. For instance, maltreatment of Roman citizens in Cyzicus moved Tiberius to deprive it of its cherished status as a free city (Suet. *Tib.* 37.3). Following complaints of widespread abuse, that same emperor allowed the senate to review the right of sanctuary offered to criminals in the temples of several Greek cities. The senate scaled back the operation of this traditional right of asylum, warning that religion must not be used as an excuse to allow criminal disorder.[39] Pliny and Trajan discussed a number of intracity conflicts (described below), and when their Bithynian acquaintance Dio Chrysostom's overzealous building plans sparked hostility from his own fellow citizens in Prusa, the orator menacingly advised them that he could appeal all the way up to the emperor if they did not acquiesce to his wishes.[40] Particularly serious was the discord plaguing Alexandria, a city with its own imperial heritage but whose ugly tripartite ethnic division (privileged Greeks, alienated Jews, and lowly Egyptians) the Romans now had to negotiate. An emperor's attitude could have an impact on provincial security. Gaius Caligula's poisonous combination of megalomania and indifference to problems in Alexandria clearly allowed violence there to get out of hand.[41] Indeed, in his letter to the Alexandrians, Gaius's successor, Claudius, claimed that the recent violence between Greeks and Jews should properly be called a war and warned all parties to desist from their mutual enmity, lest "I be constrained to show what a benevolent and kind ruler can be when he is turned to righteous anger."[42]

Here, Claudius cited one of the mainstays of imperial control to the Alexandrians: the unspecified threat of retribution. The vagueness of such admonitions may have lessened their real impact, but it also allowed the ruler's flexibility to determine a future course of action, including a specific penalty

39. Tac. *Ann.* 3.60–63 (cf. Suet. *Tib.* 37.3), on which see Rigsby, *Asylia*, 580–86.

40. Pliny, *Ep.*10.59–60 and 81–82, e.g.; Dio Chrys., *Or.* 45.8. Cf. *Or.* 46.14; Plut. *Prae. ger. reip.* 814–15.

41. For general background, see Smallwood, *The Jews under Roman Rule*, chap. 10; Modrzejewski, *The Jews of Egypt*, chap. 8; and Kasher, *The Jews*, 20–4. On another key source for this Alexandrian disorder, see van der Horst, *Philo's Flaccus: The First Pogrom*.

42. Col. 4, lines 73–74, 79–82. Claudius's letter to the Alexandrians was originally published in 1924 as *P.Lond.* 6.1912 (= Bell, *Jews and Christians*, 1–37; *CPJ* 2.153, Smallwood, *Docs....Gaius* 370). Most of the letter concerns the Greeks' eagerness to enrich the imperial cult, alienating their monotheistic opponents further. On the impact of this document on our assessment of its sender, see Osgood, *Claudius Caesar*.

should one prove necessary. Imperial action against troublesome communities often amounted to reduction of privileges and civil status, but bloodier alternatives were always on the table for extreme cases (or extreme emperors). The Alexandrians knew that there was a legionary force stationed just outside the city; according to Josephus, the prefect of Egypt, Tiberius Julius Alexander, had dispatched two legions and a detachment from Libya against them amid a tumult at the outbreak of the First Jewish War.[43] The Alexandrians, whose factions often ran afoul of the emperors and their delegates, had a thoroughly raucous reputation. In Dio's account, Caracalla even ordered the slaughter of the urban populace during an imperial visit there, supposedly because of its dislike of him.[44]

Often, however, the emperor conveyed even his threats through subordinates, especially provincial governors. Thus, a *legatus pro praetore* governor, administering Galatia early in Tiberius's reign, could warn those who were using the state transport system illegally: "But since the lawlessness of certain men demands immediate punishment," the governor will enforce proper state transport rules "not only by my own power, but also by the divine majesty of the best *princeps*, from whom I received this very thing (i.e., the proper transport regulation) in his official instructions (*mandata*)."[45] Indeed, abuses of the official transport service generated numerous complaints to officials, including the emperor. Imperial reaction to this type of problem illustrates

---

43. Jos. *BJ* 2.494–98; the Roman force supposedly only attacked Jewish participants in the strife. At *BJ* 7.369, Josephus suggests a casualty figure of sixty thousand Jews.

44. Detail on Caracalla's Alexandrian slaughter is elusive, as it rests mainly on two shaky sources, Dio in epitome (77.22–23) and the *Historia Augusta* (*M. Ant.* 6); also note *P.Giss.* 2.40. A full treatment of Alexandrian disorder would fill a large volume. Evidence for the general unruliness of Alexandria's people, hostility among its ethnic divisions, and anti-Roman sentiment is ample, starting quite early in Ptolemaic times (Fraser, *Ptolemaic Alexandria*, 79–81, 90). Note also "Pseudo-Callisthenes," the popular Greek Alexander romance, 1.31 and 3.34; Strabo 17.1.12; Dio Chrysostom's speech before the Alexandrians mentions the use of soldiers (cf. SHA *Tyr. Trig.* 22.1–3) to put down yet another riot, probably in the early 70s (*Or.* 32.72; note also sections 22, 31–32, and 53, with C. P. Jones, *The Roman World of Dio Chrys.*, 36–44, 134; and Barry, "Aristocrats"); Dio 65.8; *Thirteenth Sibylline Oracle*, line 74, with Potter, *Prophecy and History*, 39, 252–53; Euseb. *Hist. eccl.* 6.41 (reign of Decius); Amm. Marc. 28.5.14; Socrates Scholasticus *HE* 5.16–17 (lynching of Bishop George), 7.13 (= *PG* 67, 761–64) and 7.15 (lynching of Hypatia); Sozomen *HE* 7.15. See further Oost, "The Alexandrian Seditions"; Barry, "Popular Violence" (arguing that Alexandria was not particularly unruly); and on later centuries, Gregory, "Urban Violence," 147–51; Haas, *Alexandria*; and Watts, *Riot in Alexandria*.

45. Mitchell, "Requisitioned Transport" (= *AE* 1976, 653; *SEG* 26.1392), lines 4–7, with commentary and Mitchell's later corrections in "The Requisitioning Edict" (adopting the reading *id ipsum in mandatis* in line 7 from Frisch, "Zum Edikt"). The *mandata* must have been from Augustus, recently deceased at the time the governor wrote this warning.

serious determination on the part of emperors to enforce proper adherence to
the law. It is no wonder, then, that in his last extant letter to Trajan, Pliny
seemed apprehensive in asking the emperor (after the fact) to grant a permit
to his wife so that she could rush to her aunt following a death in the family.
Pliny must have known the importance that emperors attached to these documents, which makes an earlier exchange all the more startling. In *Epistula*
10.45, Pliny flatly asked Trajan if out-of-date permits (*diplomata*) could still be
used. As one would expect, Trajan replied firmly in the negative. "That is why,
among my foremost responsibilities, I take it upon myself to send new *diplomata* throughout all the provinces before they (i.e., valid ones) could run out,"
the *princeps* explained. Perhaps Pliny was ignorant of this elementary point of
provincial administration. Alternatively, he may have been seeking to gener-
ate a specific and firm imperial letter to use against people in his area who
wanted to break the rules. In any case, Trajan was not the only emperor who
conscientiously saw to the proper use of *diplomata*. Frustrated by abuse of the
cursus publicus in the fourth century, the emperor Julian even claimed that he
would write out the documents by his own hand.[46]

Repetition of imperial pronouncements regarding *vehiculatio* abuse suggests that in this case, the emperors were fighting a losing battle, but their
continuous involvement proves their determination to try to control this facet
of provincial affairs. Particularly striking is the extract from Domitian's *mandata*, addressed to a procurator, that found its way onto stone in Syria, in
which the emperor minced no words:

> Neither by the renting of beasts of burden nor by the distress of lodging
> should the provinces be burdened....I instruct you to see to it that
> nobody commandeers a beast of burden unless he has a permit from
> me. For it is most unjust that, either by the favor or prestige of certain
> people, requisitions should take place which nobody but myself can
> grant. Therefore, let there be nothing which will break my instructions
> and spoil my intent, which is most advantageous to the cities, for to
> help the weakened provinces is just, provinces which barely have
> enough for the necessities of life.

---

46. Pliny's wife: *Ep.* 120 (*Ep.* 121 is Trajan's kind reply); expired *diplomata*: *Ep.* 46 (I owe the
alternative interpretation to Philip Stadter); Pliny probably received about fifty *diplomata* at
the beginning of the year: Kolb, *Transport und Nachrichtentransfer*, 83–84. Other emperors:
Suet. *Aug.* 50; cf. Suet. *Otho* 7.1 and Plut. *Otho* 3.2; and see now the recently published inscription in Hauken and Malay, "A New Edict of Hadrian," quoted in chapter 8 below. Julian:
CTh. 8.5.12. Regarding who was authorized to use the state transport infrastructure, see
Kolb, *Transport und Nachrichtentransfer*, 71–122; on abuse during the principate, 117–19.

At this point, the autocrat uttered an apt Weberian expression of the state's monopoly on the legitimate use of force: "Let there be no violence used against them [the civilians] contrary to my wish," continuing, "and let no one commandeer a guide unless he has a permit from me, for, when farmers are torn from their homes, the fields will remain without their attention." Domitian bluntly commanded the procurator himself to obey and enforce his rules.[47]

Trajan's rescripts to Pliny reveal his preoccupations with public order in the empire. Pliny felt the need to consult Trajan on a number of individual criminal accusations brought to him (e.g., *Ep.* 10.58, 10.81). On three occasions, Pliny or Trajan mentioned sending arrested individuals to Rome for trial (10.57, *vinctus* "chained", per Trajan's request; 10.74; and certain Christians in 10.96.4, the only case in which the deportees are specified as citizens). Trajan also objected to hosts inviting huge numbers of people to celebrations, especially when guests received cash gifts (10.117). Indeed, Trajan was worried about any sort of gathering, official or unofficial. The province's Christians apparently suspended some of their meetings in response to his *mandata* (10.96.7). Particularly striking is Trajan's refusal to allow an organization of firemen (*collegium fabrorum*) to be created in Nicomedia, and this after fire destroyed a significant part of the city (10.33–34). Pliny earnestly requested one on their behalf, anticipating Trajan's hesitation by stating that its numbers would be limited and that he himself would attend to its creation, ensuring that the force would be engaged in no other activity but fighting fire. "Your notion that it would be possible to institute a fire brigade in Nicomedia would indeed follow the example of many others," Trajan responded, "but let us recall that this province of yours, and especially its cities, have been troubled by just this kind of faction. Whatever name we give them, and from whatever reason, those who group together for a common purpose soon become political factions (*hetaeriae*)."[48] Trajan's attitude might seem paranoid,

---

47. *IGLS* 5.1998 (= McCrum-Woodhead, *Documents* 466), lines 11–12, 17–30: μήτε ὑποζυγίων μισθώσεσιν μείτε ξέ[νων] ὀχλήσεσιν βαρύνεσθαι τὰς ἐπαρχείας....ἐντέλλομαι δὴ καὶ σοὶ φροντί[δα] ποιήσασθαι ὅπως μηδεὶς ὑποζύγιον λάβῃ εἰ [μὴ] ὁ ἐμὸν ἔχων δίπλωμα· ἀδικώτατον <γ>άρ ἐστι[ν], ἢ χάριτί τινων ἢ ἀξι[ώ]<σ>ει τὸ γραφὰς γεινέσθαι, ἃς [μη]δενὶ ἔξεστιν διδόναι ἢ ἐμοί· μηδὲν οὖν γε[νέσ]θω ὃ τὴν ἐμὴν ἐντολὴν καταλύσει καὶ τὴν συμ[φο]ρωτάτην ταῖς πόλεσιν γνώμην φθερεῖ· βοη[θεῖν] γὰρ δίκαιόν ἐστιν ἀτονούσαις ταῖς ἐπαρχε[ίαις] αἳ μόγις τοῖς ἀναγκαίοις ἐξαρκοῦ<σιν>· μηδ[ὲ] βιαζέσθω τις αὐτὰς παρὰ τὴν ἐμὴν βο[ύ]λησιν· ὁδηγόν τε μηδεὶς λαμβανέτω εἰ μ[ὴ] ὁ ἐμὸν ἔχων δίπλωμα· ἐναποσπωμένω[ν] γὰρ τῶν ἀγροίκων, ἀγεώργητοι μενοῦ[σιν] αἱ χῶραι. Trans. adapted from Sherk, *The Roman Empire: Augustus to Hadrian*, no. 95.

48. Pliny *Ep.* 10.34. On disorders caused by political factions in Bithynia, see Dio Chrys. *Or.* 45.8 and C. P. Jones's discussion in *The Roman World of Dio Chrys.*, 100–103. Cf. *I.Ephesos* 215 (a second-century proconsul of Asia's measures against rioting bakers); *Dig.* 47.22; and Tac. *Ann.* 14.17 on disruptive *collegia* at Pompeii.

but he probably knew more than we do about the precarious stability of provincial communities. Indeed, the roughly contemporary picture of Bithynian politics in Dio Chrysostom's orations reveals a fractious climate fraught with rivalries and turmoil. At one point, in fact, one of Pliny's predecessors had suspended Prusa's right of free assembly because of disorder in the Bithynian orator's hometown.[49]

Pliny seems to have been uncomfortable with various provincial policing and security arrangements and often asked Trajan for permission to employ more soldiers in police tasks, for instance, as prison guards (*Ep.* 10.19), escorts for an equestrian official (10.21), escorts for a freedman procurator's mission to acquire grain in Paphlagonia (10.27), and a military police contingent to regulate traffic in Juliopolis (10.77). We will discuss these various security needs from the governor's perspective in chapter 7 below. In Trajan's eyes, however, Pliny's desire to use soldiers on police missions was something to be resisted; he seemed to fear that it would establish precedents that would weaken the manpower of the men's larger units. He rejected all of Pliny's inquiries save one, the additional escort for the grain procurement, and only because it was a limited and temporary change in the regular distribution of soldiers (10.28). Perhaps Trajan's reluctance was because of his imperial military ambitions; he may have had his upcoming eastern campaign on his mind, preparations for which were most likely under way while Pliny was in Bithynia.[50]

In any case, it is probably fallacious to assume from Trajan's opposition to using soldiers as police that "it was the policy of the central government not to employ soldiers as policemen except in unusual circumstances," as Keith Hopwood put it.[51] Even if Trajan's reluctance could be styled as central government policy, then the kind of immediate needs that Pliny was reacting to clearly challenged any governmental hesitation to use soldiers as police. For the real irony here is that just at the time when we have the most explicit imperial opposition to specific expansions of military policing from

---

49. Dio Chrys. *Or.* 48.1, delivered circa AD 102–105.

50. Trajan set out from Rome toward Parthia in the autumn of 113; the main engagements of that infelicitous war were fought in 115 and 116. See Bennett's argument (*Trajan*, 191–93) that Trajan's unprovoked seizure of Armenia and war against Parthia were premeditated as early as 111. (This is not to suggest that Pliny's governorship was in any way related to the upcoming campaign.) Reluctance of emperors to have too many soldiers away from the standards may go back to Augustus himself; see chapter 4 above on the *Disciplina Augusti* cited in *Dig.* 49.16.12.1.

51. Hopwood, "Policing the Hinterland," 173, citing Pliny *Ep.* 10.77.

Trajan, the broader documentary record precisely shows that military policing was manifestly expanding. Although they may have been creations of Domitian, it is around Trajan's time that *frumentarii* are clearly attested doing police work. His reign brings the first firm attestations of *milites stationarii*, outposted soldiers with clear police duties.[52] Appointments of *beneficiarii consularis*, soldiers attached to gubernatorial staffs or posted to administrative stations, were on the rise during the early second century.[53] Whatever the nature of Trajan's hesitation, military policing was growing under Trajan and his second-century successors. They saw the continued growth of these classes of soldiers and the emergence of new terms for soldier-police, such as the *regionarii* centurions who appeared in the later second century, performing police functions already attested for outposted centurions in Trajan's reign.[54] In chapter 8, we will assess the impact of these various types of military police that were spreading throughout the second and third centuries.

One caveat: Contrary to what one might expect, the growth of military policing from the early second century onward did not supplant or reduce the varieties of civilian policing described above in chapter 3. In fact, the eirenarchs of the eastern empire are also first firmly attested under Trajan, and Egyptian papyri preserve ambitious and meticulous distributions of *paraphylakes* and other civilian guards. Trajan, or perhaps Domitian, also seems to have instituted the office of *curator* or *corrector civitatum* ("regulator of the

---

52. The *stationarii* are first attested on twenty-seven *ostraka* pass permits from mines in Egypt's eastern desert, dated AD 108–117, late in Trajan's reign: *O.Claud.* 50–73, 80–82. See below, chapter 8, where I argue that *stationarius* is a rather vague term that ordinarily denotes a low-ranking soldier temporarily outposted for policing or guard duties. Without explicitly using the term, there were clearly soldiers in Pliny's Bithynia behaving much like *stationarii*: *Ep.* 10.77–78, on the centurion posted at Byzantium, who would probably have had legionaries under his command; and *Ep.* 10.74, on a soldier stationed at Nicomedia (*miles qui est in statione Nicomedensi*) who sent Pliny a letter about the complicated case of a man under duress who supplicated Trajan by seeking asylum at the emperor's statue.

53. Nelis-Clément (*Les beneficiarii*, 24–25) notes that the first documentary evidence of outposted *beneficiarii consularis* comes in the mid-first century, with an explosion of extant votive altars dedicated by these troops through the mid-second to mid-third centuries.

54. See esp. Pliny *Ep.* 10.77–78 for the legionary centurion who helped regulate traffic through Byzantium. The evidence of the term *regionarius* (*epi tōn topōn* in Greek papyri, discussed in chapter 8 below) fully emerges soon after Trajan's reign, but even during his years, outposted centurions in Egypt received petitions from victims of crime, as did the later *epi tōn topōn* centurions. See, e.g., *BGU* 1.36 (from Soknopaiou Nesos) and *BGU* 3.908 (from Bacchias), both dated ca. AD 101–103; cf. *P.Ryl.* 2.81, AD 104; Peachin in *P. Sijp.* 15; and Alston, *Soldier and Society*, 86–96.

cities"), an imperial appointment aimed toward reforming mismanagement in local city governments in Italy and the provinces.[55]

Persecutions and Imperial Power

Early emperors were typically hesitant to become entangled in provincial problems that might be handled at the local or provincial level, and were rarely proactive to the point of having direct impact on people's lives with new initiatives. This fact is what makes the "edicts of persecution" of two mid-third-century rulers so surprising. The first, Decius (r. 249–251), ordered every inhabitant of the empire to sacrifice to the gods; hostility to Christianity was not necessarily his main motive. Valerian (r. 253–260) was more ambitious and was explicitly determined to use the means at his disposal to weaken or destroy the Christian church.[56]

From at least as early as Nero's reign, emperors were involved in (or at least aware of) trials and executions of Christians.[57] With the apparent exception of Nero's persecution of Rome's Christians after the fire of 64, early persecutions were "grassroots" affairs that arose as a result of public pressure within a particular locality or province.[58] But soon after Decius came to power, he ordered a universal sacrifice to the gods and required a document (*libellus*) signed by witnesses to certify completion of the requirement.[59] We are not sure exactly when or why, nor do we know the precise contents of the edict (or edicts). Recent scholarship is probably right to situate Decius's measures in the context of traditional Roman religion (perhaps expansions of the typical celebrations offered to a new emperor upon his accession or other ceremo-

---

55. See Pliny *Ep.* 7.15.2 and *Ep.* 8.24.2, with Sherwin-White's commentary (*The Letters of Pliny*, esp. 81 and 478) for further references. Compare the *praepositi* and *evocati* (discussed in chapter 5 above as military officials) chosen by the emperor to fight bandits in third-century Italy.

56. For general overviews of the third-century persecutions, see Frend, *Martyrdom and Persecution*, 389–439; Ste. Croix's classic "Why Were the Early Christians Persecuted?"; Rives, "The Decree of Decius"; Ménard, *Maintenir l'ordre*, 160–67; Potter, *The Roman Empire*, 241–43, 255, 314; and Clarke, "Christianity," 616–47.

57. Nero: Tac. *Ann.* 15.44; Suet. *Nero* 16. Trajan: Pliny *Ep.* 96f. Hadrian and Antoninus: Justin *Apol.* 1.68 (also cited by Euseb. *Hist. eccl.* 4.8.7–9.3). Marcus Aurelius: *Med.* 11.3; Euseb. *Hist. eccl.* 5.1. Possible persecution under Claudius: Suet. *Claud.* 25.4; cf. Acts 18:2.

58. E.g., Tertullian *Apol.* 40.2.

59. For the ancient evidence of the Decian persecution, see Euseb. *Hist. eccl.* 6.39–7.1; Cyprian *De lapsis* and *Epistulae* (passim); *Passio Pionii*; and the various *libelli*, more than forty of which survive on papyrus.

nies) and motivated by a desire to please the gods with a show of religious unity.[60] What is most striking about Decius's orders to sacrifice is the boldness of a mandate that reached so deeply into provincial life. Although the orders may not have been carried out in every part of the empire and arrests of Christians were sporadic, the executions and multiple apostasies resulting from Decius's orders shook the church.[61] It also must have been a bureaucratic bother for polytheists.

Decius's measures set into motion a multifaceted, if unenthused and uncoordinated, police apparatus that had developed since the time of Augustus. According to a document cited by Eusebius, Dionysius, the bishop of Alexandria, was initially pursued by a *frumentarius*, "who went around searching everywhere, the roads, rivers and fields." Eventually, Dionysius was caught by generic "soldiers," along with others. But then some revelers suddenly burst into the house, shouting as if they were bandits, which scared off the soldiers guarding him.[62] During the next persecution under Valerian, this same bishop alluded to a second vigilante rescue, when he and other Christian prisoners were being led off by a joint military-civilian party, including a centurion and other soldiers, plus civilian magistrates (*stratêgoi*) and their attendants (*hupêretai*).[63] If true, these episodes hardly suggest effective policing, but the soldiers involved may have had little interest in dealing with Christians in the first place.

In Smyrna in March 250, civilian policing officials responded first to the emperor's edict, performing the arrest, initial questioning, and jailing of the presbyter Pionius. In chapter 3, we saw that the main police authority in many

---

60. E.g. Ando, *Imperial Ideology*, 207–10; Rives, "The Decree of Decius" (which may go too far in asserting a "religion of empire"). See also Frend, *Martyrdom and Persecution*, 405–7; and Selinger, *Die Religionspolitik des Kaisers Decius* and *The Mid-Third Century Persecutions*. Note Potter, *The Roman Empire at Bay*, 243, on possible influence of Caracalla's *Constitutio Antoniniana*. Eusebius (*Hist. eccl.* 6.34 and 6.39) only tells us that Decius acted out of hostility to his supposedly Christian predecessor, Philip the Arab; see Potter, *Prophecy and History*, 261–68. *Pace* Ando and Potter, I think that Decius must have known that Christians would have trouble obeying his orders; he did not necessarily target them but was perhaps indifferent to the difficulties facing fringe "atheist" Christians. Even garbled second-century invectives grasped Christianity's monotheism, e.g., Apul. *Met.* 9.14.

61. Cyprian (*De lapsis* 8–9) was disgusted that so many Carthaginian Christians were eager to violate their own religion. The bulk of his eighty-one-letter correspondence deals with this crisis and its effects.

62. Euseb. *Hist. eccl.* 6.40. This *frumentarius* was attached to the prefect of Egypt. The revelers were the remnants of a wedding party. Cf. the similar episode in Iamblichus's lost novel *Babyloniaka* (Photios *Bibliotheke* codex 94, 74b24–b31).

63. Euseb. *Hist. eccl.* 7.11.22, an interesting, if opaque, case of military and civilian police cooperating; cf. *Martyrium Cononis* 1–2.

communities was the sitting board of magistrates. In the account of Pionius's martyrdom, however, the main instigator of action against the presbyter is Polemon, a member of an elite family serving as a *neôkoros*, the main steward for a temple of the imperial cult.[64] In his action against Pionius, Polemon had at his disposal a force of *diôgmitai* paramilitaries commanded by a hipparch (see chapter 3), the entire public staff of the city jail, and an official stenographer "to write everything down."[65] So local civilian forces could exercise much sway in enforcing imperial order, yet their authority ultimately was quite limited, and the *Passio Pionii* offers a remarkably conscious acknowledgment of that fact, when Polemon is made to say, "But the fasces do not bear us the power of life and death."[66]

In most cases in the provinces, of course, that full authority could be held only by the governor; all final trials and executions would have involved him (and, indeed, Pionius was not martyred until the governor came to town). We know that some governors seemed eager to hunt out Christians.[67] Others clearly wanted nothing to do with trials of Christians, but they could only go so far in ignoring directives from an emperor whose favor they sought.[68] In chapter 7, we will note that provincial governors were caught between commands from above and popular pressure from below. Such was the case in the 250s, when governors had to deal with both emperors' persecution edicts and local denunciations of Christians that were brought to their attention. Especially during Valerian's later reign, many Christians found that this was a lethal combination.

There are two facts to stress at this point. First, these forces were all set in motion by one thing, namely the emperor's whim. Second, the emperor's will was made concrete by police, especially soldiers on the governor's staff who

---

64. Polemon enters the story early (§3) and remains the driving force in the prosecution of Pionius until he is handed over to the proconsul. Robert thought this Polemon was related to the sophist of the same name (Philostr. *VS* 1.530–544). Smyrna had achieved the great distinction of hosting three temples to the imperial cult, each led by one of three *neôkoroi*. A municipal magistrate called a *stratêgos* enters the narrative at a public assembly in 7.1; he was likely a *stratêgos epi tôn hoplôn* concerned with the mint at Smyrna. See Robert, *Le martyre de Pionios*, 52–53, 67.

65. *Passio Pionii* 9.

66. *Passio Pionii* 10: Ἀλλ' αἱ ῥάβδοι ἡμᾶς οὐ προάγουσιν ἵνα ἐξουσίαν (sc. θανάτου) ἔχωμεν. See Robert's commentary ad locum and cf. John 18:31 and *Acts of Pilate (Gospel of Nicodemus)* A 3.1.

67. E.g., Licinnius Serenianus (*PIR*² L245), governor of Cappadocia, per Cyprian *Ep.* 75.10.1; cf. Tert. *Ad Scap.*

68. Clarke, "Christianity," 641; cf. Tert. *Ad Scap.* 4.2.

acted as arresting agents, bailiffs, secretaries, jailers, torturers, and executioners. Some martyr accounts are rich in this sort of policing detail.[69] According to one story, for example, a governor in Asia Minor sends a herald and then his military guards (*singulares*) in search of Christians; eventually, one of his soldiers, working with a local priest of the imperial cult and a civilian police force (*taxis eirênarchikê*), finds and arrests the humble Christian farmer Conon, whom the governor tortures and executes.[70] Looking at cases in which some details are known (Pionius, Dionysius, Cyprian), it is striking how many different elements of the empire's unsystematic police forces participated in the execution of these individuals, all because of the novel edicts of a distant emperor.

Remote as the emperor was from most of his subjects and despite the fact that the third-century persecutions were implemented unevenly, it seems that the Roman state was now ready for more ambitious intrusion into the lives of provincials. It is further surprising, at first thought, that such a hallmark should occur in the mid-third century, when the Roman state was weakened by so many problems, from serious inflation to foreign invasions. But it was just such challenges that may have spurred Decius and Valerian to take these extraordinary initiatives. Valerian's determination to wield the authority of the state against the Christian church heralds the "dominate," the term that modern scholars have used (in contrast to the principate and its façades) to describe the increasingly militaristic and stringent governmental ethos of the later Roman Empire.

The distribution of soldiers in the provinces helped enable the persecuting emperors to enact anti-Christian measures, testing the limits of state control. Numerous sources attest the spread of military personnel into civilian areas of nonfrontier provinces, a presence that was often unsettling for civilians.[71] These soldiers were certainly active agents of persecution by the time of Diocletian and the Tetrarchs' Great Persecution in the early fourth century, and they were active in the third-century persecutions as well. One martyr account set in Africa during Valerian's persecution in the late 250s describes the soldier-police who were sent to arrest a group of Christians: "It was not a

---

69. E.g., *Passio Pionii* 19–21, *Acta procons. Cypriani* 2 and 5, Cyprian *Ep.* 81.1, *Passio Fructuosi* 1 and 4, *Passio Montani et Lucii* 3, 11, 20–21; cf. *Passio Mariani et Jacobi* 2; see further Lopuszanski, "La police romaine"; and Austin and Rankov, *Exploratio*, 153 (including ample evidence from the Great Persecution).

70. *Martyrium Cononis* 1–4; this martyrdom seems to have occurred under Decius, but the polished narrative contains fictional elements and may have been written much later: Musurillo, xxxiii.

71. Note Lopuszanski, "La police romaine," and Herrmann, *Hilferufe*. Outposted soldier-police and their impact on the provinces is the focus of chapter 8 below.

single *stationarius* soldier here and another there who was hunting us, as in other places, but a violent and relentless bunch of centurions."[72] Around the same time, a Spanish bishop and his deacons were arrested in his home by six *beneficiarii* soldiers, who were also present at his execution.[73]

Although the success of these anti-Christian endeavors was limited, the very attempts were bold, revealing new potential for an emperor's inclination to increase state control and impose his will. The persecutions of Christians from 250 on suggest a world quite different from the generally laissez-faire noninterference of the early empire. Now the state had the potential to be more invasive, and the growth of military policing in the provinces has much to do with that trend.

Conclusion: The Relevance of Augustus

While many aspects of Augustus's principate had faded by the mid-third century, we still see strong echoes of Augustan precedents. Decius's order to sacrifice bore similarities to established rituals, such as the annual oaths of loyalty to the emperors that started with Augustus.[74] The rhetoric of imperial peace, initiated by Augustus and his allies, remained current, whereby "The Good Emperor" symbolized security and justice. Augustus's successors wanted to be associated with these qualities, even (perhaps especially) when stability and order were most lacking. The petition to Gordian III from Skaptopara in Thrace opened with an appeal "to your most fortunate and eternal times"— this in 238, just after a major civil war had taken the lives of Gordian's grandfather and uncle. Or compare the petitioners from Aragua, who depict themselves as the only ones who were suffering in an otherwise utopian realm under Philip the Arab. The empire was at its lowest point under Gallienus, the son of the persecutor Valerian. Sole ruler after 260, when the Persians captured (and eventually skinned) his father, Gallienus nonetheless linked himself to Augustus, advertised his reign as a blessed age, and stressed themes of peace, security, concord, and abundance on his coins.[75] Even at its emptiest,

---

72. *Passio Mariani et Jacobi* 4. The action is set in 259, but the text probably developed throughout the late third century (Musurillo, xxxiv); therefore, post-Valerianic policing might influence this passage.

73. *Passio Fructuosi* 1 and 4.

74. See above, and cf. Herrmann, *Der römische Kaisereid*, and Ando, *Imperial Ideology*, 208, 259–61.

75. Skaptopara: *CIL* 3.12336 = Hauken no. 5 above, lines 11–12. Aragua: *MAMA* 10.144 = Hauken no. 6, lines 9–12. Valerian: Lactant. *De mort. persec.* 5. Gallienus: de Blois, *The Policy*, 120–49.

the rhetoric of imperial peace reflects society's values and people's desire for security.

Augustus's significance is not limited to symbolism. In many ways, he set the pattern for administration. He initiated the imperial post, it is under him that the "petition-and-response" pattern of governance took form, and our earliest reference to gubernatorial *mandata* relates to ones he probably issued.[76] Most important here, he set the precedent for using soldiers to stabilize civilian areas, especially in Rome, where he created new police institutions. *Frumentarii* soldiers were a significant extension of imperial policing. It is usually impossible to assess what role specific emperors played in expanding military policing. Hence the value of Pliny's correspondence with Trajan, which lets us see how one emperor reacted to public-order and policing concerns.

When Augustus used soldiers to provide security in Rome and Italy, he was primarily serving his own political needs but in a way that often benefited the populace. It is hard to see this balance over the centuries in the provinces, where the differences between valid raisons d'état and tyrannical prerogative were seldom clearly delineated. (Decius and Valerian certainly thought their religious policies would help the empire as a whole, although naturally, Christian sources dwell on the distress they caused.) Some *principes* seem benign, and sometimes raison d'état security measures might have the incidental effect of helping ordinary people.

At other times, the emperor himself—that fount of order—became a clear cause of disorder. One might hope that his secretaries and other responsible subordinates could manage the empire's important business while a Caligula debauches himself or while a Nero plays charioteer. But to answer a central question of this chapter, the emperor *did* matter. He was one force in society that could help bring stability; as the most powerful, he also had great power to harm. His character and inclinations could mean the difference between life and death for ordinary provincials, no matter how remote they were from their emperor. If our sources are true at all, Gaius Caligula's dilatoriness, Nero's distractions, Caracalla's anger, and Decius's and Valerian's religious inclinations cost scores of provincial lives; at the other extreme, Domitian's stringent administration earned him the hatred of the senatorial elite but likely helped provincial commoners.

While the actions of emperors certainly affected security and public order in the empire, their subordinate administrators had much more direct involvement with provincial communities. Provincial governors, to whom we now turn, were positioned to have a great impact on local conditions. They were the key figures in security and policing in every province of the empire.

---

76. See Mitchell's comments, "Requisitioned Transport," 116.

7

"*Keep your province pacified and quiet*": *Provincial Governors, Public Order, and Policing*

The Governor's Power and Position

As middlemen between the emperor and provincial masses, governors could face trouble from above and below. Publius Petronius was lucky to survive his governorship of Syria when Caligula ordered him to install a statue of himself in the Jewish temple. Stuck between a mad emperor and an angry populace, Josephus has Petronius say to the latter, "I, too, am bound to obey the law of my master.... I myself, just like you, submit to orders." According to Josephus, both the governor and the locals showed restraint, and Petronius delayed carrying out his orders. As a result, Caligula ordered Petronius's death, but the ship bearing that message supposedly ran into bad weather and finally reached Petronius twenty-seven days after he learned of Caligula's own death.[1]

The position of a Roman governor was paradoxical. On the one hand, the governor was the most powerful person in the province, as the jurist Ulpian noted in the early third century AD: "He has greater authority in the province than all others, except the emperor." This authority ranged from the power to address boundary disputes to the right to inflict the death penalty. The Romans called the latter power the *ius gladii* ("right of the sword"), and he was normally the only one in his province who could wield it. He had the authority to command troops inside the province, and every governor had at least a few hundred of them for policing and other tasks. As judge, a governor could hear any case he wished; however, he was not *compelled* to hear a case, even if the emperor himself had referred disputants to him. In legal terms, within his

1. Jos. *BJ* 2.184–203 (2.195 quoted), *AJ* 18.261–309; Philo *Leg.* 188–348. Smallwood, "Philo and Josephus," trusts Philo over Josephus when the two conflict (including Petronius's "fairy-tale" escape, 120); cf. Mason, "Contradiction or Counterpoint?"

province, he held the power of all of the traditional Rome-based magistracies in his own person.[2]

On the other hand, as Josephus noted, the provincial governor was ultimately answerable to the emperor or the senate. He was usually an outsider and an amateur who lacked special background and training, appointed from Rome to oversee an area that he may have known very little about, to perform functions that he may have had no experience in, for a limited term, which usually did not exceed a few years.[3] Roman provincial governors were supposed to represent Roman rule over societies that had their own complex histories and politics and to keep basic public order with limited means, in places where challenges to security and order were many. At times, the power of the governor seems supreme; at other points, it is clear that he was not in control.

We now turn to some of the key texts and themes that illustrate this paradox and reveal the governor's role in maintaining public order. Our chronological focus ranges from Pliny's correspondence with Trajan (circa 110) to the mid-third century, the time when military policing seems to have been most expansive. We will see both the governors' involvement in this process of expansion and the way various people in the empire viewed them as figures of law and order. We cannot cover every aspect of the governor's position or exhaustively analyze all texts relevant to governors and public order.[4] Looking at selected texts will suffice to show that the governor was the single most important figure in provincial public order, evident in the words of emperors, the actions of governors themselves, and sundry anecdotes that reflect how the governor's subjects viewed him. He was the crucial, powerful link between a distant emperor and subject communities, whose local authority, we have seen, was limited.

First, a note on terminology. There were different types of governor (proconsuls, *legati Augusti pro praetore*, the prefect of Egypt, praesidial procurators),

---

2. Ulp. *Dig.* 1.16.8 is quoted. See also *Dig.* 1.16.6.pr.–1, 1.16.7–11, 1.18.1, 1.18.6.8, 1.18.8–12; Elliott, "Epigraphic Evidence," 20–22, 37–44. Refusal to hear a case: Acts 18:14–17.

3. On the prevalence of amateurishness over specialization in Roman administration, note Brunt, "The Administrators of Roman Egypt," 141–42; and Talbert, "Pliny the Younger as Governor."

4. For recent broad treatments of governors, see Haensch, *Capita provinciarum*; Eck, ed., *Lokale Autonomie* (esp. contributions of Cotton, Nollé, Jördens, Thomas, Galsterer, and Horstkotte); Meyer-Zwiffelhoffer, Πολιτικῶς ἄρχειν; Jördens, *Statthalterliche Verwaltung*; Drogula, "The Office of the Provincial Governor"; and Slootjes, *The Governor and His Subjects*.

but the real powers held by each and provincials' experience of that power are similar enough that I have used the cover-all "provincial governor" throughout this book. I cite the Romans themselves as exemplars, for the Latin word *praeses* is a generic equivalent for any "provincial governor." As one jurist wrote, "The term *praeses* is general, and proconsuls and legates of the emperor and all who govern provinces ... are called *praesides*."[5] Moreover, whether he was a proconsul appointed by the senate or an imperial procurator, a governor's overall position in the world and the shape of his subsequent career largely depended on the will of the emperor.

Governors and Local Politics

Governors had the direct capacity to effect more orderly conditions in their provinces. A major component of this public-order role was their routine assize circuit, judging cases in various provincial communities. Contrary to the administrative systems of many other states in world history, provincial government in the early Roman Empire did not statically rest in one major administrative center but relied instead on what has been called "a peregrinatory system of justice."[6] In the course of Pliny's journey through Bithynia, he had a number of cases brought to him on matters of routine legal problems and the enforcement of fundamental social mores.[7]

Dio Chrysostom's speeches reveal the local pride of towns and cities that had the honor of hosting gubernatorial assizes and the jealousy on the part of communities that were not so fortunate.[8] In some ways, hosting the governor's court was a mixed blessing. The visitors were an economic boon, but some of this traffic was unsavory, for along with jurors, rhetors, and provincial

---

5. On the term *praeses*: Macer *Dig.* 1.18.1. In Greek, *hêgemôn* is a catch-all word for all types of Roman governors (and, indeed, any leader); see Kokkinia, "The Governor's Boot," 181. Cf. Bowman, "Provincial Administration," 351–52: "Governors of all ranks, legates, proconsuls and prefects or procurators, exercised the full range of administrative, military and judicial powers within their provinces which their *imperium* implied; if a proconsul or procurator had only a handful of auxiliary troops in his province, his authority over them was no weaker than that of the legate of Syria over his four legions and auxiliary troops."

6. Burton, "Proconsuls, Assizes, and the Administration of Justice," 92. Note also Marshall, "Governors on the Move"; and Meyer, "The Justice of the Roman Governor"; cf. Haensch, *Capita provinciarum*, esp. 361–89; and Meyer-Zwiffelhoffer, Πολιτικῶς ἄρχειν, 227–37.

7. Among others, see Pliny *Ep.* 10.29–32, 10.65–66, on the legal status of certain slaves; 10.72–73, on family law; 10.49–50, 10.68–71, 10.81–82, 10.96–97, on religious regulations. Pliny probably handled far more cases than his letters alone attest.

8. Dio Chrys. *Or.* 40.33 and 44.11.

notables came slaves, pimps, hustlers, and whores. Moreover, the hospitality due visiting officials could strain local resources.[9] Nevertheless, benefits outweighed disadvantages. Assize centers enjoyed greater dispensation from public duties than ordinary towns.[10] Furthermore, in a system where a neophyte governor might show up in a town and be burdened with a daunting number of petitions all at once, he would have to seek the assistance of local provincials to help sort things out. (One prefect of Egypt received 1,804 petitions in just two and a half days at an assize in Arsinoë.)[11] The governor would probably first consult citizens of the town where the assize was being held, so in intercity disputes, these local assessors could bias him in favor of their own town. There is evidence for this sort of manipulation in an anecdote from Philostratus's *Life of Apollonius*, mentioning a senator sent from Rome to govern Greece, despite his ignorance of Greek culture and language. As a result, "in his mistakes he was as much sinned against as sinner, for his assessors and those who shared with him judicial authority trafficked in justice, treating the governor like a slave taken as booty in war."[12] The governors' de jure authority did not always translate into de facto power.

Provincials treated a visiting governor with ceremonial formalities, which he was expected to endure before getting on to serious business, such as hearing cases.[13] Pliny was also involved in several cities' problems with public works, construction, and dilapidated buildings.[14] This general function is well attested in Justinian's *Digest*, in which Ulpian noted the governor's capacity to force owners to repair neglected eyesores, even offering the overseers of work crews the assistance of his military staff, if necessary.[15]

Gubernatorial inspections naturally raised local anxieties and could bring out the worst aspects of local politics. The speeches Dio Chrysostom delivered in his

---

9. Dio Chrys. *Or.* 35.15. See further Desideri, "City and Country," 96 and 104; C. P. Jones, *The Roman World of Dio Chrys.*, 68, and below, on injustices visiting officials and soldiers inflicted on civilians.

10. Modestinus *Dig.* 27.1.6.2, citing a letter from Antoninus Pius.

11. *P.Yale* 1.61, lines 5–7, early second century; such a large number is not necessarily typical. Ulp. *Dig.* 1.16.9.4 speaks to the necessity of organizing and prioritizing incoming petitions.

12. Philostr. *VA* 5.36; Loeb trans., adapted; C. P. Jones, *The Roman World of Dio Chrys.*, 68. On provincial assessors, see Robert, "Études d'épigraphie grecque," 276–78 (= Robert, *OMS* 2.1175–77).

13. Note Ulp. *Dig.* 1.16.7.pr.; Slootjes, *The Governor and His Subjects*, 105–19; and Meyer-Zwiffelhoffer, Πολιτικῶς ἄρχειν, 238–52.

14. E.g., Pliny *Ep.* 10.17b, 10.23, 10.37, 10.39, 10.70, 10.80, 10.90.

15. Ulp. *Dig.* 1.16.7.1, 1.18.7; cf. Dio Chrys. *Or.* 40.9.

hometown of Prusa in Bithynia provide complex case studies of the difficulties that governors had to negotiate: past cases of disorder, sensitive political issues, charges of corruption, manipulation of public resources. *Oratio 48* is set just before the Prusan assembly was to welcome the governor Varenus. Dio begs the populace to desist from rioting or raising a ruckus but to remain harmonious out of gratitude to Varenus, since he had beneficently allowed them to assemble again. (Apparently, the governor had revoked Prusa's right to assemble because of disturbances there.) Dio urges the people at least to delay barraging Varenus with their problems (*Or.* 48.1–3). The reasons for Dio's determination to keep the people from voicing their problems (and we must remember that it was the governor's duty to hear such complaints) later emerges: misuse of public funds by members of Prusa's elite class, including Dio himself.[16] Appeals for harmony and concord in Greek rhetoric often serve to guard a status quo beneficial to the speaker.[17] Dio certainly wanted to stifle discord; he may have also aimed to keep crooked benefits coming his way by keeping the governor in the dark.

Dio's most controversial initiative was an overambitious building and beautification program, which stirred opposition from every quarter of Prusan society. In the face of this hostility, Dio, who consistently portrayed himself as a man with friends in high places, threatened to appeal to the governor, or even the emperor, in order to receive satisfaction against his opponents.[18] This was probably a bluff, for when Pliny and Trajan discussed Dio in an exchange of letters about ten years later, they did so with no manifest affection, as if he were yet another bothersome little Greek.[19] Pliny's involvements in Prusa show that it was a problem spot in particularly bad shape. It was Pliny's first official destination, and he informed Trajan that he went straight to sorting out Prusa's financial and infrastructural mess. Meanwhile, Dio was embroiled in a dispute with another town notable, Flavius Archippus. Both men emerge as scoundrels; Archippus tried to dodge jury duty and meanwhile faced the

---

16. Dio Chrys. *Or.* 48.9, connected in some way with Dio's beautification plans, discussed below. C. P. Jones dates the speech circa 105 (*The Roman World of Dio Chrys.*, 139). Cf. *Or.* 7.27–28, an elaborate parody of popular resentment against elites who monopolized and misused public resources.

17. Swain, "Reception and Interpretation," 42.

18. E.g., Dio Chrys. *Or.* 40.5–6, 45.8, and 47.19. At *Or.* 44.12 and 45.2, he claimed to have been a friend of Nerva's, and at 41.7 and 47.22, he claimed influence with Trajan and other powerful Romans.

19. See esp. Dio Chrys. *Or.* 40, 45, 47 (ca. 101–3) for the dispute (45.8 for the threat), and Pliny *Ep.* 10.81–82; 10.40 for Trajan's use of the demeaning diminutive *Graeculi* (cf. Dio Chrys. *Or.* 38.38).

charge of illegally breaking out of prison. Later, Archippus brought a suit against Dio before Pliny, accusing Dio of imperial sacrilege for having a statue of Trajan erected near family graves—a potentially lethal charge under some emperors, although Trajan was not interested in pursuing the issue. Dio finally asked to be excused from public works that he had started, and Pliny noted that he was suspected of corruption in the matter. His beautification scheme had failed, and in the end, Dio appears rather small.[20]

We cannot be sure how representative the Bithynian evidence is for the whole empire, but certain elements of it are paralleled in other contemporary sources. Regarding Dio's threat to call in the governor against his opponents, Plutarch saw overreliance on Roman authority as a crisis of his time, lamenting that those who "refer great matters and small alike to the governor make our subject-status a reproach, or rather destroy the whole basis of our political life, reducing us to cowering, frightened impotence," thereby "forcing our rulers to be our masters more than they themselves want."[21] In the course of criticizing Nicomedia for its discord with Nicaea, Dio himself explained how malignant governors might exploit provincial communities that sought his favor:

> Could you not know of the tyrannical power which your discord (*stasis*) gives the governors? For at once whoever wishes to wrong our province comes armed with the knowledge of how to bring it about that he not pay the penalty. For either he allies himself with the Nicaean party and has their group for his support, or else by choosing the Nicomedians he is protected by you. Though it seems he loves one side, in fact he loves neither, and meanwhile he is wronging everybody. But he is protected in his misconduct by those who think they alone are loved by him.[22]

Such ugly plays of power and contention in second-century Bithynia reveal a world where vying groups sought to take advantage of one another, with no party completely innocent. Even appeals for concord had bleak Machiavellian

20. Pliny *Ep.* 10.17a–b, 10.23, 10.58–60, 81–82.

21. Plut. *Prae. ger. reip.* 814–15, Russell's Oxford World's Classics trans. Cf. Salmeri, "Dio," 74. Plutarch further explained that "the primary cause of this evil is the greed and ambition of the local elites" who cannot bear the idea of being bested in domestic struggles by any of their fellow citizens: Plut. *Prae. ger. reip.* 815a.

22. Dio Chrys. *Or.* 38.36. Cf. Robert's "La titulature." According to Dio (*Or.* 38.38), Romans mocked Greek contentiousness as Ἑλληνικὰ ἁμαρτήματα ("Greek failings"). See now Meyer-Zwiffelhoffer, Πολιτικῶς ἄρχειν, 307–15; and Heller, *Les bêtises des Grecs*.

overtones: a further inducement to put aside intercity squabbles that Dio offered to Nicaea and Nicomedia was that if they could only work together, then they would be able to have more muscle over the other cities in Bithynia.[23]

Governors and Corruption

Dio's comments on how a mischievous governor might exploit local rivalries is one of many suggestions we have that provincial governors were often corrupt. The only real institutionalized deterrent to gubernatorial misbehavior was the process by which disgruntled provincials could bring former provincial administrators to trial in Rome; governors of senatorial rank could be tried before the senate, while equestrian procurators and other nonsenators usually appeared before the emperor's court.[24] Prosecutions of governors were very imperfect controls on their behavior. No action could be taken until the governor had left office; emperors and senators in Rome were not usually very interested in provincial happenings; and for the most part, provincials had to use their own resources to send a delegation to Rome to carry out a prosecution, which might not even result in a conviction. In our known cases, however, most prosecuted governors did not go unpunished. The maximum penalty would involve a fine in proportion to the money illegally exacted from the provincials (if that was the issue), the official stigma of *infamia* (institutionalized disgrace), and exile or "relegation" from Italy, all of which could still leave an ex-senator in relative comfort. Juvenal asked the sensible questions, "So what if he (a corrupt governor) is condemned?" and "What's infamy to riches intact?"[25]

Moreover, internal divisions within the province, such as the ones Dio described between Nicaea and Nicomedia, could unravel a prosecution.[26] While many factors limited the potential of official indictment to compel governors to administer their provinces justly, noninstitutional pressures may have been

---

23. Dio Chrys. *Or.* 38.32–34; cf. 38.41–42.

24. Brunt, "Charges of Provincial Maladministration"; Robinson, *Penal Practice,* 78–98; on the senate as court, Talbert, *The Senate,* 460–87 and app. 9. It was Augustus who allowed the senate to try its own members for *repetundae* and other offenses. Only about forty specific cases are known (Bithynia, with seven, generated the highest number), all occurring from the time of Augustus to Trajan, although we have vague suggestions that there were several more (e.g., Dio Chrys. *Or.* 34.9 and 34.38–40). Pliny is our best source: *Ep.* 4.9, 5.20, 6.5, 6.13, 6.29, 7.6, 7.10, cf. 10.56.

25. Juv. 8.94: *Sed quid damnatio confert?* Juv. 1.48–50: *quid enim salvis infamia nummis?*— citing the case of Marius Priscus, on whom see Pliny *Ep.* 2.11 and below.

26. Pliny *Ep.* 7.6 and 7.10. This seems to have happened in the Bithynians' prosecution of Varenus Rufus, the same governor Dio Chrysostom nervously welcomed to Prusa in *Or.* 48.

more effective; most governors would surely not want to get caught doing anything extreme enough to draw the emperor's direct opprobrium, even if the affected provincials were unable to organize an effective prosecution. But the fact remains that post-term prosecutions were among the few tools that provincials could wield against criminal governors. Dio Chrysostom criticized the people of Tarsus for overindulging in gubernatorial prosecutions, thus cheapening their potency. Conversely, he also censured the Ionian League for binding themselves by oath not to prosecute the governor.[27]

Dio himself was accused of colluding with an unnamed "wicked governor." Some Prusans had accused Dio of unjustly inciting the governor to torture or banish certain fellow citizens, after which Dio, according to his accusers, bribed the people so that he would escape retribution for his misdeeds. The wicked governor involved here was probably one of the Bithynian governors accused of corruption whom Pliny defended before the senate.[28] Although our evidence is incomplete, the overall picture suggests that acrimonious local politics and some governors' inclination to take advantage of local conflicts undermined the imperial administration's goal to keep each province pacified and quiet.

These shortcomings, however, are somewhat balanced by clear efforts to administer the provinces uprightly. For instance, the emperor's *mandata* (chapter 6 above) presupposed that the governor would take his duties seriously and rule his province conscientiously. We have noted the routine legal problems brought before Pliny in the course of his judicial circuit, performing a gubernatorial function that was both essential and typical.[29] Gubernatorial measures against crime are discussed below. A further responsibility of the

---

27. Dio Chrys. *Or.* 34.9 and 34.38–40. C. P. Jones suggests that this group was probably the old Ionian league of thirteen cities, not the whole province of Asia (*The Roman World of Dio Chrys.*, 79). Compare John 19:12: "Pilate tried to release him, but the Jews cried out, 'If you release this man, you are no friend of the emperor.'" John is probably the latest and least historical of the canonical gospels, but this exchange (attested only here) is politically astute.

28. Dio Chrys. *Or.* 43.10–12. Von Armin thought that this governor was Bassus, but C. P. Jones makes a good case for Varenus Rufus (*The Roman World of Dio Chrys.*, 102). Brunt cautioned that maybe it was neither: "We have no right to assume that they were the only oppressive proconsuls in Bithynia during Trajan's early years" ("Charges of Provincial Maladministration," 89). On Bassus, see Pliny *Ep.* 4.9, 6.29.10, and cf. 10.56; Varenus: *Ep.* 5.20, 6.5, 6.13, 6.29.11, 7.6, 7.10. Whoever it was, Dio's remarks at *Or.* 43.8 and 43.11 suggest that Dio was going to Rome as a witness for the defense.

29. On the typicality of Pliny's actions in Bithynia, see Talbert, "Pliny the Younger as Governor," esp. 434; Burton, "Proconsuls, Assizes, and the Administration of Justice," esp. 105–6. Also note Burton's comment (92): "That this article is concerned with proconsular governors reflects merely the relatively superior quality of evidence for the 'senatorial' provinces, not any belief in fundamental differences between 'senatorial' and 'imperial' provinces." Cf. Millar, "'Senatorial' Provinces: An Institutionalized Ghost."

governor, well attested by Pliny, is surveillance over the fiscal affairs of provincial communities.[30] On these economic matters, Pliny consistently portrayed himself to Trajan as a fastidiously ethical and responsible agent; Trajan (or his secretarial staff) responded in the same form. Only once did the *optimus princeps* have to urge higher standards than his legate: when Pliny raised the possibility of compelling local elites to take out loans, Trajan rejected the measure as "uncharacteristic of the justice of our times."[31]

Pliny appeared far less saintly, however, in 102, when he led the defense of the former governor Bassus, prosecuted before the senate by the Bithynians for bald-faced theft. The prosecution's evidence was sufficiently strong that the defense had to concede that Bassus had at least accepted gifts, which was illegal in most cases. Despite the effectiveness of the Bithynians' case, general sympathy for Bassus among his fellow senators and the great amount of rhetorical sweat invested by Pliny helped prevent his client from receiving the full penalty.[32]

A major concern of the jurists cited in the *Digest* was to prevent the sort of economic foul play that Bassus committed, reiterating standards against illegal exactions and immoderate gift taking that predated the principate.[33] Ulpian also urged the governors not to allow illegal military exactions.[34] In fact, a consistent effort to protect the meek emerges in these sections of the *Digest*, instructing the governors to protect their innocent subjects from all varieties of vicious abuse, ranging from exploitation by officials and soldiers to overzealous debt collectors and even sexual abuse of slaves.[35] "The governor of the province," for instance, "shall see to it that poor people not be troubled by

---

30. E.g., Pliny *Ep.* 10.17a–b, 10.43–44, 10.54–55, 10.81–84, 10.108–111. We can compare Trajan's creation of *correctores* and *curatores* of cities, as in Pliny *Ep.* 8.24.

31. Pliny *Ep.* 10.55; cf. 10.54 and, for a similar expression by Trajan, 10.97.

32. Pliny *Ep.* 4.9; it later emerges (*Ep.* 10.56) that Bassus's acts as governor were nullified.

33. Ulp. *Dig.* 1.18.6.pr., 1.16.6.3, and Modest. *Dig.* 1.18.18. A court *de pecuniis repetundis* was established in the mid second century BC so that provincials could try to regain money pinched by a governor. G. Gracchus, perhaps Saturninus, Sulla, and Julius Caesar each sponsored laws to make governors more accountable.

34. Ulp. *Dig.* 1.18.6.3 and 1.18.6.6; cf. 1.18.6.5.

35. Most of this material is from Ulpian: *Dig.* 1.16.4.pr., 1.16.9.4–5, 1.18.6.2, 1.18.6.4, and, on collecting fines, 1.18.6.9. Sexual abuse of slaves: Paulus 1.18.21, although this may be more a matter of preventing infamy in the households of slave owners. See Bonfiglio, *Corruptio servi*, esp. 163, 183, 189; cf. the slave girl Photis's sexual escapades in Apul. *Met.* Book II.

injustices, such as being deprived of their only few pieces of furniture, taken for the use of others under the pretext of the arrival of officials or soldiers."[36]

If we had only Pliny's letters to Trajan and the *Digest* to go on, we might almost assume that *all* provincial governors were scrupulously upright. Ulpian's positive encouragements suggest that Roman governors over the centuries needed continuous "reminders" of the proper exercise of their powers. All told, Tacitus was probably still right in claiming that the principate improved the overall lot of the provincials, who during the late republic had suffered more injustice from governors who were freer to abuse them.[37] Corrupt governors under the principate were yielding to temptations that were a tradition of the old republic, and some still thought that provincial fortunes were bleak. Juvenal's Satire VIII, lampooning a pretentious noble and exaggerating as ever, provides a fitting coda:

> So when you at last obtain that provincial governorship you've awaited so long, set some limit on your anger, curb your avarice, feel compassion for the poverty of the locals.... Observe what the laws prescribe, what the curia mandates, what rewards await the good ruler, the thunderbolt of justice with which our senate struck down those governors Capito and Tutor who out-pirated the Cilicians. Yet what came of their condemnation? Hey, Greek provincial, look around for an auctioneer to sell off the threadbare clothes from your back, since (governor) Pansa has grabbed all (his predecessor) Natta left you, then shut up. After all this, you'd be mad to lose your boat-fare.... How big are the rewards you'd snatch from so dire an outrage, seeing that Marius, not long ago, stripped Africa to the bone? But rule number one is this: take care not to victimize men both desperate and courageous. Though you rob them of all their gold and silver, they still possess swords and shields (the plundered keep their weapons).... But if ambition and lust dictate your headlong progress, if you shatter the fasces rods in blood across provincial backs, if blunt axes and an exhausted lictor are your prime delight, then you will find your noble background itself beginning to

---

36. Ulp. *Dig.* 1.18.6.5: *Ne tenuis vitae homines sub praetextu adventus officiorum vel militum, lumine unico vel brevi suppellectili ad aliorum usus translatis, iniuriis vexentur, praeses provinciae providebit.*

37. Tac. *Ann.* 1.2 (see chapter 4 above). Cicero offers ample material from the republic: his Verrine speeches, *Ad Quintum fratrem* 1.1, and the letters usefully collected by Treggiari in *Cicero's Cilician Letters.*

turn against you, to hold a bright torch to your shamelessness. The higher a criminal's standing, the more public the obloquy directed against him for all his moral failings.[38]

The Governor as Crime Fighter

Governors under the republic performed the same sort of mobile judicial functions as their later counterparts. Most would have expended less energy hearing cases, since typical republican governors saw themselves primarily as military commanders. Mundane public order seems to have preoccupied few. The primacy of military glory in the republic's intense political competition encouraged governors to march their troops out in search of a convenient enemy and a quick battle, easy enough to be acclaimed *imperator* without losing many of his own men but generating an enemy body count sufficient for a triumphal entry into Rome—surely the boyhood dream of many Roman men. Even Cicero, one of the republic's most unmilitary figures, fell prey to the urge. While governor of Cilicia in 51–50 BC, one of his greatest anxieties was preparing his inadequate army for a possible engagement with Parthia, which never materialized. Wishing to use his force for some purpose, he attacked a town of the Free Cilicians (Pindenissum; no one in Rome had heard of it, either), which had posed no major threat. He took the town, enslaved its survivors, and sent glowing descriptions of his deeds to Rome.[39]

Under Augustus and his successors, the emperors came to monopolize military triumphs and preferred to save large military commands for themselves, their relatives, or men completely dependent on them. To be sure, the governorship did not entirely lose its military nature under the emperors, especially in frontier provinces that hosted large numbers of troops, provinces whose governors were selected by the *princeps*. Out there, a governor might still win glory, though not a triumphal procession.[40]

---

38. Juv. 8.87–97, 119–24, 135–41: Green's Penguin trans., adapted. Cossutianus Capito was convicted of *repetundae* charges from his governorship of Cilicia (Tac. *Ann.* 13.33, AD 57); Tutor is unknown (perhaps the odd name is a pun); "Pansa" "Natta" may just be typical aristocratic names (see Courtney's *Commentary*). The Marius of line 120 is Marius Priscus, prosecuted by Tacitus and Pliny (*Ep.* 2.11; cf. Juv. 1.59) in 100 and convicted of extortion from his African proconsulship.

39. Cic. *Att.* 5.20 (= SB A.113, no. 11 in Treggiari's collection). We noted in chapter 2 the pretext that the Cilicians were harboring fugitives there.

40. Note, e.g., *Agricola* on the tenure of Tacitus's father-in-law as governor of Britain, or Arrian's governorship of Cappadocia, discussed by Stadter in *Arrian of Nicomedia*, 32–49.

Many internal provinces had no large units of soldiers. Governors used smaller units for what amounted to large-scale police actions amid various crises. According to Josephus, Pontius Pilate twice had his soldiers conceal their weapons, surround groups of querulous Jewish civilians, and then pounce on them.[41] The same author's *Jewish War* describes further disorders throughout the eastern Roman Empire that evoked stark military responses from various governors.[42] I will focus here on the more mundane, but it is worth noting that Josephus largely blamed the outbreak of the Jewish revolt on governors who failed to police and regulate internal problems in their provinces.

Ulpian's description of the governors' duties clearly reveals their important law-and-order functions:

> A good and serious governor should see to it that the province he rules remains pacified and quiet. He will achieve this without difficulty if he earnestly pursues evil men and clears them from his province. For he must hunt out committers of sacrilege, bandits, kidnappers and thieves, punishing each in proportion to the crime he committed. He must also repress their abettors, without whom a bandit cannot lie hidden for long.[43]

The clear element of crime control expressed here likely shaped the way many governors-to-be prepared for their posts. This is the impression we get from a letter to Antoninus Pius from Fronto, in which Fronto explained his preparations before assuming the proconsulate of Asia in 157/158:

---

41. Jos. *AJ* 18.55–62. This part of the text may conceivably have suffered scribal tampering, as the *testimonium Flavianum* on Jesus (which a self-proclaimed Jew such as Josephus could not have written) immediately follows (18.63). Christian medieval copyists may have exaggerated Pilate's cruelty, just as they probably expanded Josephus's mention of Jesus.

42. E.g., Jos. *BJ* 2.494–498 and 7.369 on the prefect of Egypt's military actions against Alexandrian Jews.

43. Ulp. *Dig.* 1.18.13.pr.: *Congruit bono et gravi praesidi curare, ut pacata atque quieta provincia sit quam regit. quod non difficile optinebit, si sollicite agat, ut malis hominibus provincia careat eosque conquirat: nam et sacrilegos latrones plagiarios fures conquirere debet et prout quisque deliquerit, in eum animadvertere, receptoresque eorum coercere, sine quibus latro diutius latere non potest.* Also note Paulus *Dig.* 1.18.3: "He sometimes holds authority even against people from outside his province, if they commit any crime: for the emperors' *mandata* state that he who commands the province must take care to purge the province of evil men (*malis hominibus provinciam purgare*), no matter where they come from." Compare 1 Peter 2:13–14, urging Christians to obey governors (*hêgemones*) since they are sent by God "to punish those who do wrong."

The facts attest, blessed emperor, that I have made every effort and have earnestly desired to perform my upcoming service as proconsul.... I diligently prepared everything pertinent to regulating my province, so that I could apply myself to such weighty business with the help of my friends. I summoned from home the close associates and friends of mine whose trustworthiness and integrity I knew firsthand.... I called to my side from Mauretania my dear friend Julius Senex, not only for his trust and diligence, but also that he might assist with his military excellence in seeking out and repressing bandits.[44]

The ability to keep order seems to have been one of the important traits by which the governor's subjects evaluated him. For instance, in a speech before the proconsul of Africa, Apuleius lauded the governor's "self-control in dealing with the affairs of the inhabitants of this province," adding, "To my knowledge the province of Africa has revered no proconsul more nor feared any less. In no year of office but yours has dishonor had more power than terror in curbing crime (*coercenda peccata*). No one but you has used such power more often for good, more seldom to terrify."[45]

Who knows if any real gubernatorial anticrime measures generated Apuleius's adulation. But it seems that the very proximity of the governor and the soldiers who accompanied him could bring some relief to crime-infested areas. In Apuleius's novel (*Met.* 2.18), one of the characters bemoans the state of affairs in Hypata in Thessaly, where bands of young men (*iuvenes*) roam the streets at night, committing crimes, and alas, "the soldiers of the governor, being so far away, cannot relieve the city of such an outrage." An anecdote from the Stoic philosopher Epictetus also suggests that the governor with his guard was an island of security in a dangerous world: "Here is how the more safety-conscious travelers behave. Having heard that the road is infested with bandits, he doesn't venture to set out alone, but instead waits to journey in

44. Fronto *ad Anton. Pium* 8.1 (= Naber, 169; Haines Loeb I, 236; van den Hout, 166): *militari industria circa quaerendos et continendos latrones adjuvarer*. On the circumstances of the letter, see Champlin, *Fronto and Antonine Rome*, 164. On banditry in Mauretania, see, e.g., *CIL* 8.2615 (= *ILS* 5795).

45. Apul. *Florida* 9.36, trans. Hilton, from Harrison, ed., *Apuleius: Rhetorical Works*. The addressee was Sex. Cocceius Severianus Honorinus, who probably served as proconsul of Africa in 162–63; see Harrison's comments in *Apuleius: A Latin Sophist*, 105–9. Lee puts Apuleius's praise in the context of proconsul Marius Priscus's crimes revealed in AD 100 (Pliny *Ep.* 2.11): *Apuleius' Florida*, 100–101. Cf. Panciera, "Le virtù del governatore."

company with an ambassador, a governor's assistant, or a governor, so that he may travel along safely."[46]

Egypt provides key evidence for the way its governor (the *praefectus Aegypti*) and his secretaries handled paperwork related to crime. Flaccus, as prefect of Egypt, is known to have searched Egyptian households for weapons, both in Alexandria and beyond.[47] Governors could also publicly reiterate their standards and opposition to criminals. Most striking is an official memo from an early third-century governor of Egypt:

> Baebius Juncinus to the *stratêgoi* of the Heptanomia and the Arsinoite nome (district), greeting. I have already ordered you in a previous letter to search out robbers with all care, warning you of the peril of neglect, and now I wish to confirm my resolve by an edict, in order that all inhabitants of Egypt may know that I am not treating this duty as an affair of secondary importance, but offer rewards to those of you who co-operate, and threaten with peril those who choose to disobey. This edict I desire to be publicly displayed in both the capitals and the most conspicuous places of the nomes, penalties and peril awaiting you if in the future any evil-doer is able to use violence without being detected. I wish you good health.[48]

We have noted governors' involvement in appointing eirenarchs in Asia Minor (chapter 3). The governors of Egypt certainly exercised some oversight over local civilian police and sometimes doubted their virtues. A third-century papyrus threatens arrest of the village's "thief catchers" (*lêistopiastai*—their names subscribed below) and trial before the governor, unless they help other village officials (*dêmosioi*) hunt out certain wanted men. It is unclear whether the order came from the governor's office or from the nome *stratêgos*, but there was apparently top-level concern over civil divisions or criminal collusion

---

46. Epict. *Diss.* 4.1.91: Οὕτως ποιοῦσι καὶ τῶν ὁδοιπόρων οἱ ἀσφαλέστεροι. ἀκήκοεν ὅτι ληστεύεται ἡ ὁδός· μόνος οὐ τολμᾷ καθεῖναι, ἀλλὰ περιέμεινεν συνοδίαν ἢ πρεσβευτοῦ ἢ ταμίου ἢ ἀνθυπάτου καὶ προσκατατάξας ἑαυτὸν παρέρχεται ἀσφαλῶς.

47. Philo *In Flacc.* 86–94 (resentfully presented, but Philo must admit that the governor's searches turned up a huge store of arms); cf. *C.Pap.Jud.* 2.158a col. 4 l. 4, and W.*Chr.* 13, containing Flaccus's prohibition against the unregulated carrying of arms. On documents sent by the prefects, see Katzoff, "Sources of Law" and "Prefectural Edicts."

48. *P.Oxy.* 12.1409. Juncinus's prefecture was 210–14. Cf. *BGU* 2.372 = W.*Chr.* 19 (AD 150s), and on the repression of certain magical practices at the end of the second century, Rea, "A New Version of P. Yale inv. 299" (*P.Coll.Youtie* 1.30 = *SB* 14.12144).

in the village.[49] Governors sometimes had to reiterate the proper use of the transport system to soldiers and officials who were using it illegally and abusing civilians. This was true throughout the empire, but some of our most illuminating documents on abuse of the official transport system come from Egyptian papyri, preserving province-wide gubernatorial proclamations against illegal requisitions of boats and animals.[50]

The governor of Egypt took advantage of the province's geographical compactness and long-standing administrative divisions (nomes and further subdivisions). A papyrus from the mid-second century consists of a collation of documents from the office of the *stratêgos* of the Oxyrhynchite nome. It contains long lists of wanted men (mostly native Egyptians dodging liturgical service as guards but also some burglars) forwarded down by the governor, requesting that his subordinate *stratêgoi* look out for the men in their respective nomes. The measure was apparently not successful, as it contains subscriptions from the *stratêgos* to the effect that the men were not found.[51] Besides monitoring the enforcement of civilian guard liturgies, the prefects may have been further involved in the creation or regulation of some. By comparison, an inscription from Thrace refers to the enrollment of civilians as watchtower lookouts and guards that may have involved the governor.[52]

Collectively, the papyrological material from Egypt suggests a level of organization that seems rare in the rest of the empire. Perhaps similar anticrime practices were carried out in other provinces, but evidence for them has simply vanished from the historical record. Or, again, the anticrime measures we see in Egypt may be further proof of that province's peculiar tradition of geographical and administrative coherence. In other provinces, such anticrime paperwork would have to cross over more complex and varied lines of local jurisdiction, involving communities diverse in status and civic organization. Epigraphic evidence suggests parallel efforts in other provinces, with governors ordering their provisos to be widely promulgated or at least posted in prominent, well-frequented places. Furthermore, the province-wide

---

49. *BGU* 1.325, Soknopaiou Nesos.

50. E.g., from Egypt, *PSI* 5.446; cf. Pliny *Ep.* 10.45. Mitchell, "Requisitioned Transport," 111–12, cites further examples; see also Kolb, *Transport und Nachrichtentransfer*, esp. 71–122.

51. *P.Oxy.* 60.4060, AD 166.

52. *IGBulg* 3.1690 (Pizus, AD 202), on which see *SEG* 45.845; Rostovtzeff, "*Synteleia Tironon*"; Bagnall, "Army and Police," 71–72; cf. *SEG* 45.2214 and Kissel, *Untersuchungen zur Logistik*, 75–77.

promulgation of a new governor's edict was a regular occurrence that crossed local boundaries.[53]

Governors, Soldier-Police, and Provincial Resentments

Governors and their entourage must have been imposing figures as they traveled around their respective provinces. A full entourage (*cohors*) would include the governor's quaestor, legates, any informal companions (with their respective servants), and his official staff (*officium*) of civil and military subordinates. There was a certain element of ceremonial pomp involved: as officials who encompassed every power of all of the Rome-based magistracies, senatorial governors were entitled to be accompanied by all of the *apparitores* functionaries discussed in chapter 3 above, including the fasces-wielding lictors.[54] Unlike the pseudo-fasces of municipal magistrates (*bacilla*), gubernatorial fasces could be fully equipped with the axe, a symbol of the *imperium* the governor held as the only person in the province who could impose the death penalty. It is this aspect of governors' law-and-order function that comes through most vividly in provincial sources, especially Christian texts. When the governor arrived in town, death came with him. The public executions he oversaw were free public entertainment and also the stuff of nightmares, as Artemidorus's dream book amply attests.[55]

---

53. E.g., Abbott & Johnson 22, Sherk *RDGE* 52 (first century BC). In *IGRR* 3.119 (= *OGIS* 609, Abbott & Johnson 113, late second century), the governor of Syria, Julius Saturninus, ordered soldiers to stop forcing villagers to billet them, closing with the instructions "Put this letter of mine up in a public place in your village, lest anyone plead ignorance as a defense." Note that the Bithynian Christians ceased some of their meetings in response to Pliny's edict, which, in turn, reflected Trajan's *mandata*: *Ep.* 10.96; cf. *Acta proc. S.Cypr.* 1.7 and Ando, *Imperial Ideology*, 82–86, 109–17.

54. At least in the early empire, gubernatorial procurators would normally not have lictors: Pflaum, *Les procurateurs équestres*, 111, 137. Ulp. *Dig.* 1.16.14 limits proconsuls to six lictors; *legati Augusti pro praetore* would have had five (Sherwin-White, *The Letters of Pliny*, 81–82). Other sources on gubernatorial *apparitores* include Juv. 8.136–37 on lictors (cf. 8.127–28); *Martyrium Cononi* 1 and Apul. *Florida* 9.10–13 for the governor's herald (*praeco*); and on messengers, *RE* "Viator," 2.i, col. 1930; Ulp. *Dig.* 5.1.82; and *AE* 1921, 38–39. On *officia*, see further A. H. M. Jones, "The Roman Civil Service," 44–49; and *LRE*, 592–96; Austin and Rankov, *Exploratio*, 149–55; Rankov, "The Governor's Men"; Palme, "Die *Officia* der Statthalter in der Spätantike"; Meyer-Zwiffelhoffer, Πολιτικῶς ἄρχειν, 64–73, 328–29; Brélaz, *La sécurité publique*, 267–82; and Haensch, "Kontrolle und Verantwortlichkeit"; cf. Eich, "Die Verwaltung der kaiserzeitlichen Armee," esp. 29–31.

55. E.g., Artem. *Oneir.* 1.35, 1.39–40, 1.48, 1.70, 1.77, 2.49–54. See Shaw, "Judicial Nightmares." Meyer-Zwiffelhoffer gives a more positive estimation: Πολιτικῶς ἄρχειν, 143–71. On public executions, see further Coleman, "Fatal Charades"; Potter, "Martyrdom as Spectacle"; and Fagan, *Lure of the Arena*, 252–60.

The element of the governors' entourage that was most essential in carrying out death sentences and other punishments was the governor's military staff. In the course of their travels and public duties, governors would have had a military escort at all times.[56] When governors ordered criminals to be imprisoned, flogged, crucified, burned alive, or thrown to the beasts, their soldiers administered the sentence.[57] They posted a military guard at crucifixions to prevent family and friends from saving the condemned or starting a protest that might lead to a tumult. Worst of all, as Petronius specifies in his "Widow of Ephesus" tale, the military guard sometimes stayed to ensure that the condemned would not receive a proper burial but would stay on display to maximize the supposed deterrent effect. Indeed, when a slave character told Horace that he was not a murderer, the poet joked, "Then you won't feed the crows on the cross." In reality, governors practiced moderation in denying burial, especially on the eves of festivals. This moderation often disappeared, however, for Christians, when their practice of taking relics became known. In response, some governors used soldiers to keep the believers from taking the bodies and then took the further step of rendering bodily remains entirely inaccessible. For example, the mutilated bodies of Lyon's martyrs were kept unburied for six days, then cremated and dumped into the Rhône River.[58]

The depiction of the soldiers' behavior at Jesus's crucifixion points toward (and perhaps helped perpetuate) the disaffection between the governors and Jews and early Christians.[59] This alienation is clearly discernible in a rabbinic

---

56. In private settings, a governor might minimize his military guard to avoid offense, but this could leave him vulnerable: note Flaccus's arrest at a dinner party in Philo *In Flacc.* 113.

57. E.g., Mark 15:15–26, Matt. 27:26–37; *Passio Perpetuae* 9 (an *optio* military orderly serving as prison guard; cf. *Passio Ss. Montani et Lucii* 4); *Passio Ss. Mariani et Jacobi* 5 (flogging, torture); *Passio Pionii* 21 and *Passio Ss. Montani et Lucii* 3 (immolation); Apul. *Met.* 10.34 (*ad bestias*). Cf. Philo *In Flacc.* 73–77. Of course, they could use force to protect life: in the short Greek version of the *Golden Ass* (pseudo-Lucian *Lucius, or The Ass* 56), when Lucius regains his human form in the crowded amphitheater, he begs the governor to hold him under arrest (ἔχειν με ἐν φρουρᾷ), lest the astonished crowd lynch him.

58. Petron. *Sat.* 111–12; Horace *Ep.* 1.16.48 (cf. Juv. 14.77). Deterrent effect: Marshall, "Symbols and Showmanship," 127; pseudo-Quint. *Declamationes minores* 274.13; Callistratus *Dig.* 48.19.28.15: "Most prefer to crucify infamous bandits in those places where they used to attack, so that after the punishment is exacted there, others may be deterred from those same crimes by the sight, and that the victim's relatives might have some solace"; cf. Tac. *Ann.* 14.44.3. Moderation, festivals: Philo *In Flacc.* 83–84, John 19:31, cf. Jos. *BJ* 4.317; the jurists are clement, *Dig.* 48.24, but they probably do not have provincial noncitizens in mind here. Relics: Euseb. *Hist. eccl.* 5.1.59–62 (late 170s AD); cf. the mid fourth-century Donatist passion of Maximian and Isaac (Maier ed., 259–75). See further Brown, *The Death of the Messiah*, vol. 2, 1207–11.

59. The cruelty of Pontius Pilate's soldiers toward Jesus: Mark 15:16–20; Matt. 27:27–31.

text that pillories provincial governors and their entire social stratum, as well as the troops these governors brought with them. It is a midrash on Deuteronomy 32:13–14, in which a third-century commentator has woven his own meaning into the words of the original ancient text (which I have italicized):

> *And he ate the produce of my field*: these are the four kingdoms; *and he made him suck honey out of the rock and oil out of the flinty rock*: these are the oppressors who have taken hold of the land of Israel and it is as hard to receive a farthing from them as from a rock, but tomorrow Israel inherits their property and they shall enjoy it as oil and honey. *Curds from the herd*: these are their consulars and governors; *fat of lambs*: these are their tribunes; *and rams*: these are their centurions; *herds of Bashan*: these are *beneficiarii* soldiers who take away (food) from between the teeth (of those who eat); *and goats*: these are their senators; *with the finest of wheat*: these are their matrons.[60]

Other rabbinic sources provide further insight into how third-century Jewish civilians experienced Roman rule when the governor and his soldiers came to town. One third-century entry from the Talmud relates to the exploitation Jews felt when the governor came to take advantage of offerings at local celebrations: "There is no festival without a patrol coming to Sepphoris…there is no festival without the governor or his retinue…coming to Tiberias."[61] This sort of complaint was common, as provincials saw their resources and hospitality abused by officials and soldiers, who are often associated with the governor. Pliny tells us that the province of Baetica successfully prosecuted not only its former governor, Caecilius Classicus, but also his "associates and ministers." Abuses of the *vehiculatio* transport system by these same groups, as noted above, generated official efforts to tighten the rules. In his glowing portrait of his father-in-law as a good governor, Tacitus paid careful attention to his proper staffing, meritoriously filling civil and military posts with free-born, honest men.[62]

---

60. Sifre Deut. 318, ed. Finkelstein, 359–60; trans. Isaac, *Limits of Empire*, 115.

61. B. Talmud *Shabbat* 145b; compare Tosefta (Mishnah supplement) *Betzah* ii 6, probably also from the third century: "A patrol of Gentiles came into town and the townspeople were afraid that the soldiers might harm them and therefore we prepared them a calf and we fed them and gave them drink and rubbed them with oil so that they would not harm the townspeople." Both translations from Isaac, *Limits of Empire*, 116.

62. Pliny *Ep.* 3.9: *socios ministrosque Classici*; Tac. *Agr.* 19. Agricola was governor of Britannia from 77–84.

The villagers of Skaptopara in Thrace were particularly hard pressed, it seems, situated as they were between two military camps and near a busy marketplace. Moreover, attractive thermal springs at the site drew in governors, imperial procurators, and soldiers, who forcefully demanded undue supplies and quartering. Unnamed governors had tried to stem the abuse, but their efforts apparently proved so ineffective that the villagers threatened to abandon the site.[63] In addition, both the elder and the younger Pliny relate the sad story of a tame dolphin in Hippo Diarrhytus, whose tricks drew so many visits from burdensome officials (including the governor) that the town decided to kill the poor animal.[64]

The perspectives offered by Judeo-Christian writers and other sources describing provincial life remind us that many provincials' experience of the governor, his hangers-on, and soldiers was marked by mistrust and fear of cruelty and exploitation. The typical provincial governor under the principate was no longer leading large numbers of troops in hopes of vying for a triumph, warring down proud little communities or populous tribes, as was more common in the republic. But even a small military escort attracted the notice, and opprobrium, of provincials. Plutarch, in his well-known statement about Greek discomfort with Roman rule, instructed the local Greek political elite to keep in mind that "You who rule *are* ruled, ruling a city subject to proconsuls, governors of Caesar.... This is not Sardis or Lydia of long ago" and that the Roman boots (κάλτιοι) poised over Greek heads belong to the governor or, by a different interpretation, the soldiers who are with him.[65]

When there was an atmosphere of provincial hostility, the governor's military guards would have been essential for providing security for him. This could be challenging at times. Suetonius, for instance, wrote that when Vespasian was proconsul of Africa, rioters in Hadrumetum pelted him with turnips.[66] Tacitus also mentioned the case of L. Piso, governor of Hispania Citerior, who was struck

---

63. *IG Bulg* 4.2236 (= Hauken no. 5, AD 238), esp. lines 21–164. See Meyer-Zwiffelhoffer, Πολιτικῶς ἄρχειν, 74–91, on governors' efforts to stem such abuses.

64. Pliny *NH* 9.26; Pliny *Ep.* 9.33. Hippo Diarrhytus (*BAtlas* 32 E2) = modern Bizerte.

65. Plut. *Prae. ger. reip.* 813e. Cf. 812–813d. The κάλτιοι of 813e have traditionally been assigned to soldiers, as in the 1936 Loeb: "you see the boots of Roman soldiers just above your head." But here, κάλτιοι seems to mean the half-boots worn in Rome, not the soldiers' *caligae*; qv. *calceus* in Lewis & Short; see further Talbert, *The Senate*, 219–20.

66. Suet. *Vesp.* 4.3. Cf. Dio Chrys. 32.71 on outrages in Alexandria against the Prefect of Egypt, and Philostr. *VS* 534. I believe that the *archôn* of Aspendus who is nearly immolated in *VA* 1.15 is meant to be a civilian authority, rather than a provincial governor, as some have assumed.

down by a lone assassin in AD 25.[67] In one explosive case, a governor's guards were the cause and the cure for a riot. Before the destruction of Jerusalem's Temple in AD 70, governors regularly posted extra military guards during major festivals. During Passover one year, one of the governor's soldiers keeping guard atop the Temple porticoes provocatively exposed himself to a huge mass of assembled Jews, thrusting out his buttocks and making obscene sounds. Enraged, the crowd started demanding that the governor, Cumanus, punish the soldier. When some started throwing rocks at the troops, Cumanus called in heavy reinforcements to restore order. But at what price? In terror when these soldiers arrived, thousands of people trampled one another to death in an effort to get away. Josephus highlighted this event as one of the signal troubles that led to the First Jewish War.[68]

The importance of soldiers attached to the governor went beyond their basic security functions to include administrative duties as clerks, notaries, and bailiffs—*officiales*, collectively, as they were at the service of the governor's staff or office (*officium*). These functions are well attested for soldiers who were detached from their larger units to serve the governor as *optiones* or *beneficiarii*—so named because the job brought the benefit (*beneficium*) of relief from certain military duties—and as *frumentarii* agents. These posts were often stepping-stones to the centuriate, and the men who served them were more educated and upwardly mobile than the average recruit.[69] Perceived as a more honorable and comfortable forms of military service, positions on the governor's staff were sought-after posts. Scholars have noted that some staff soldiers seemed to stay in governors' *officia* under various secretarial titles, becoming specialized bureaucrats more than warriors.[70] This may not be true of the ordinary, unlettered, and unskilled men who performed menial or dangerous tasks for the governor.[71] The process suggests that even if

---

67. Tac. *Ann.* 4.45; cf. Juv. 8.121–24. A prefect of Egypt may have been killed in an uprising during the reign of Antoninus Pius: see Alston's evaluation of the evidence, *Soldier and Society*, 77.

68. Joseph. *BJ* 2.224–27 (cf. 2.10–13), *AJ* 20.105–12; Sanders, *Judaism*, 138. Josephus seems to situate this episode early during Cumanus's tenure, which was from 48–52.

69. Note, e.g., the late-first-century career described in *ILS* 2118 (= *CIL* 12.2602), discussed below. See further Dobson, "The Significance of the Centurion," 403–4, and Breeze, "The Career Structure below the Centuriate." Later Christian martyr literature suggests that these *officiales* acted as adjutants in trials; see, e.g., *Passio Ss. Montani et Lucii* 20 (Valerian's persecution, 259) and *Martyrium Agapae* 3 (Great Persecution, 304).

70. E.g., *P.Mich.* 8.466 (Karanis, March 26, AD 107). Also Carrié, "Developments in Provincial and Local Administration," 310–11.

71. Hadrian's speech to the troops in Africa suggests that the troops posted out to the governor's *officium* would return to general duty; see below on *ILS* 2487 = Smallwood *Docs...Nerva* no. 328 (on which now note M. P. Speidel, *Emperor Hadrian's Speeches to the African Army: A New Text.*)

soldiers preferred to serve the governor directly, most *officiales* came from ordinary cohorts, not specialized units, and most would end up back in their home units, often with promotions. Marcus Carantius Macrinus was one success story. He enrolled as a regular soldier (*miles*) in the urban cohort stationed at Lyon but was made centurion in the same unit after serving in one governor's *officium* as *beneficiarius* and in another's as senior clerk (*cornicularius*).[72]

An important document from Hadrian's reign shows whence the governor received these staff soldiers. While on his great tour of the empire, Hadrian stopped in Lambaesis in Africa to review the troops of the *Legio III Augusta*. His speech to the men was subsequently inscribed on stone, and parts of his comments are very relevant to military policing. Addressing the chief centurions, Hadrian praised the execution of their cohorts' battle drills, despite the fact that they could have proffered a number of legitimate excuses had they performed poorly. The first potential excuse Hadrian enumerated was that "a cohort is presently absent because each year in turn a cohort is sent to the *officium* of the proconsul."[73] In provinces where no large units of Roman legionaries were stationed, *officiales* were commonly drawn from noncitizen *auxilia*.[74]

If the proconsul of Africa received an entire legionary cohort, as Hadrian remarked, to help him rule his province, then he could have had as many as five hundred or so soldiers with which to bolster his *officium*.[75] To be sure, not all of these soldiers were constantly with him, and on some social visits or personal errands, his entourage would be quite smaller than the total number of his staff. For example, on May 1, AD 165, the governor of Macedonia visited

---

72. *ILS* 2118 (= *CIL* 12.2602, late first century).

73. *ILS* 2487 Ab, (AD 128, = Smallwood, *Docs...Nerva* no. 328), lines 3–4: *cohors abest quod omnibus annis per vices in officium pr[ocon]sulis mittitur.* Other reasons include the fact that they had contributed several men to keep another legion up to strength, that they had recently changed camp twice and built a new one, and, most relevant to chapter 8 below, "because several diverse outposts (*stationes*) keep you far from one another" (line 6).

74. The second-century inscription edited by Oliver in "A Roman Governor Visits Samothrace," (*AE* 1967, 444) lines 32–37, lists the names of five *milites auxiliarii*.

75. In the same section of Hadrian's speech quoted above (*ILS* 2487 Ab), the emperor mentions the loss of four men from every cohort, drawn off to bolster another unit. Moreover, a unit's level of manpower on paper at any given time differed from the real number of men who were actually available. Duty rosters and enrollment lists from Dura Europus, Vindolanda, and Egypt reveal that the effectiveness and cohesiveness of cohorts must have been regularly compromised, as Hadrian himself suggested, by members drawn away for guard duty in distant posts (*stationes*), supply errands, special missions, and the influx of new recruits, not to mention the men who were injured, sick, or recently dead. See, e.g., *C.Pap.Lat.* 112 (= Fink *RMRP* 63).

a shrine to be inducted into a local cult, and the inscription memorializing the event gives a snapshot of the people with him, all or most of whom seem to be listed beneath the governor's name. The list includes four men designated as *amici* ("friends"), four *apparitores* (two lictors, two *viatores*), seventeen slaves belonging to the governor (with the names of a few belonging to his *amici* squeezed into the margin as an afterthought), and five soldiers—at least thirty-three people in his entourage.[76]

Most important for our purposes is that governors could dispatch any of the troops detailed to their *officium* for policing and security missions. As noted above, they might post soldiers to ensure the repair of buildings.[77] The enforcement of Valerian's edicts against Christians from 257–260 was driven by soldiers operating in civilian areas who arrested Christians and brought them to the governor. Policing specializations within governors' *officia* were developing around this time. The governor of Africa, for example, sent military staff from Utica to arrest Cyprian, the bishop of Carthage. We learn this from one of Cyprian's letters (his last), but our extant manuscripts differ on what *kind* of soldiers the governor sent. One manuscript reads *frumentarios*, which I strongly favor, since traveling to arrest prominent people was obviously one of their specialties. The other manuscripts have *commentarios* (*commentarienses* would be more correct), suggesting that the governor sent some of his senior secretaries to arrest the bishop. This is possible, as *commentarienses* are lightly attested in the third century doing police work, such as processing prisoners. (Their name connotes record keeping.) While I do not think that the governor sent *commentarienses* to arrest the bishop, one must admit that delineating duties within the *officium* is nigh impossible, particularly as opaque jargon proliferates into the fourth century. Occasionally, a figure not known for policing in our period enters the scene; one account has Bishop Cyprian arrested by two *stratores* ("equerries" or "grooms") of the governor. At least the bleak job of a *quaestionarius* is clear: interrogation and torture.[78]

---

76. Oliver, "A Roman Governor Visits Samothrace" (*AE* 1967, 444). The *amici* may have included his legates or quaestor, his top subordinates and social peers, or unofficial companions (*comites*), whom governors brought to provinces for companionship and counsel. Cf. *Samothrace* 2, I, 53, a similar but far less complete text from AD 124, which lists a legate, at least one lictor, and at least five slaves.

77. Ulp. *Dig.* 1.16.7.1 and 1.18.7.

78. Cypr. *Ep.* 81, adopting ms. µ's (Monacensis) *frumentarios* rather than *commentarios*. *Commentarienses* kept records; *commentarii* are day accounts; see Ulp. *Dig.* 48.20.6, instructing governors not to let *commentarienses* receive the personal effects of executed people; cf. *Passio Pionii* 21. The author of the *Acta proconsularia sancti Cypriani* (2.2) wrote that he was eventually arrested by two *stratores officii proconsulis* ("grooms of the governor's staff"). On

In terms of policing, among the most important *officiales* were the *speculatores*. In a purely military context, a *speculator* is a legionary scout or spy; in a domestic policing context, he served either as a bodyguard or an executioner. The former role was more common for *speculatores* who were serving the emperor directly (chapter 5 above). As members of governors' *officia*, *speculatores* were middle-ranking officers whom the sources usually describe as executioners. Cyprian was apparently killed in 258 near the governor's residence by a *speculator* of the governor's *officium*; it is remarkable how many different gubernatorial policing agents were involved in this one man's elimination.[79]

Pliny used soldiers to guard prisoners, as did other governors.[80] He also wanted to act on the requests of various subadministrators who felt the need for soldiers to help them with assorted missions and tasks. A "prefect of the Pontic shore" asked both Pliny and Trajan for more troops to help him perform his duties (the nature of which is unclear). He deemed insufficient his present force of ten *beneficiarii* (usually translated as "clerks"), two mounted guards, and one centurion. Trajan denied the request.[81] He again refused to allow Pliny to institute a military-policing presence in Juliopolis, although Pliny obviously thought the town's heavy traffic load merited one.[82] Trajan approved an extension of military policing in only one minor case (*Ep.* 10.27–28), a temporary transfer of two soldiers, presented to him as a fait accompli. It may have helped that the beneficiary was Trajan's freedman procurator,

---

stratores, see Ulp. *Dig.* 1.16.4.1; Jones (*LRE*, 1245) notes that only proconsuls are attested with *stratores* on their staff. The *Vita Caecilii Cypriani* (*CSEL* 3.1, xc–cx) ascribed to his deacon Pontius calls Cyprian's arresting officers (§15) just *milites* ("soldiers"). On *quaestionarii*, see, e.g., *Vet. Scholiast. ad Juv.* 6.480. On *officia* in general, see literature cited above (n. 54), esp. Austin and Rankov, *Exploratio*, 149–55. Cf. the arrest of Thecla in the fictional *Acts of Paul and Thecla* 31 (second century).

79. *Speculatores* as bodyguards: Suet. *Claud.* 35.1, *Galba* 18.1, *Otho* 5.2; Tac. *Hist.* 1.24–27, 1.31, 3.43; cf. *Suda* Σ 916. As military executioners: Sen. *Benefic.* 3.25 and *De ira* 1.18.4; Mark 6:27; Firmicus Matenus *Math.* 4.11.4; cf. *Martyrium Dasii* 12 (Diocletianic); Athanasius *Apol. sec.* (*contra Arianos*) 8; *Acta Alex.* II.A2.12 (= *P.Yale.inv.* 1536); *Acta Pauli, Martyrium Pauli* 5 (second century); *Vita (et sententiae) Secundi* (Perry, 72–74); and sv. pseudo-Zonaras's lexicon. The author of the *Historia Augusta* has them policing fellow soldiers like American MPs: *Pesc. Nig.* 10.6. Cyprian: *Acta procons.* S *Cypr.* 5.3–4; the *Vita Cypriani* (18) says that the executioner was a centurion.

80. Pliny *Ep.* 10.19; Rapske, *The Book of Acts and Paul*, 252; Eder, *Servitus Publica*, 87; cf. Krause, *Gefängnisse*, 306, noting the common corruption in prisons, which may have prompted Pliny's inquiry to Trajan.

81. Pliny *Ep.* 10.21–22. See Sherwin-White, *The Letters of Pliny*, 588–89, for possible duties of this *praefectus orae Ponticae*.

82. Pliny *Ep.* 10.77–78. *Pace* Sherwin-White (*The Letters of Pliny*, 666), Pliny's manifest sympathy suggests that the request probably originated from Juliopolis.

who wanted a stronger armed guard for a grain-provisioning mission to Paphlagonia.

Despite the fact that Trajan denied all but one of Pliny's requests to extend military policing, the evidence for military policing in several areas, from various sources, rises in Trajan's time and after. His hesitancy to use soldiers as police, perhaps because of greater military ambitions, seems not to be typical of his successors. Even if it were, we should entertain the possibility that what is particularly atypical about Trajan and Pliny's correspondence is the fastidiousness, on the face of it, with which they negotiated minor transfers of small numbers of troops. They both tried to portray themselves in the best possible light.[83] It is entirely probable that Pliny used soldiers as police more than he admitted to Trajan and only consulted him when he feared that he might get into trouble and that Trajan usually responded the way he did out of carefulness, because he was prompted to write responses that might be cited as problematic precedents later. Moreover, there was nothing special, or peculiar to Bithynia, about the mundane needs to which Pliny was responding. It is quite likely that governors routinely used soldiers in the ways Pliny was tempted to employ them.

Imperial Procurators

In his biography *Agricola* (§15), Tacitus imagined disgruntled provincials saying, "We used to have our kings one at a time, but now two are imposed, with a governor to savage our lives, a procurator our goods. Whether the two are in concord or discord with one another, it's equally deadly for their subjects, as both add insult to injury—the governor with his bands of centurions, the procurator with his slaves." The procurator referred to here would have directed the collection of provincial taxes, one of the many vital tasks of imperial procurators in the Roman Empire. Tacitus exaggerated the binary "kingship" of governor and procurator over the provincials, but despite their lower social status, imperial procurators were weighty figures, not to be taken lightly by the governor or anyone else. Their importance derived from essential functions they carried out for the emperors in Italy and the provinces;[84]

---

83. Noreña, "The Social Economy of Pliny's Correspondence"; cf. Stadter, "Pliny and the Ideology of Empire."

84. On the growth of procuratorial posts, see Eck, "The Growth of Administrative Posts," and Lo Cascio, "The Emperor and His Administration," 148–50.

accordingly, Ulpian urged proconsular governors to avoid interfering in the affairs of imperial procurators.[85]

The word *procurator* denotes someone who takes care of something for you, a manager or agent. In a public administrative context, a procurator was a nonsenatorial appointee chosen by the emperor and directly responsible to him. They were usually either equestrians or talented former slaves from the emperor's household (*familia Caesaris*). The class-conscious authors of our sources maligned the supposed haughtiness of the latter.

Duties delegated to imperial procurators varied, with many directly related to expenditures from or incomes to the imperial fisc: collecting tribute, provisioning the army, building roads, managing imperial estates, administering mines, even governing a handful of minor provinces. (Procuratorial governors, or "praesidial" procurators, are considered above, alongside their senatorial brethren.) With so many important procurators scattered throughout the provinces, the emperor could attempt to use them to counter potential threats. For example, Claudius's wife, Agrippina, eliminated a perceived enemy, the governor of Asia, through two procurators of imperial estates there.[86] When Agrippina's murderous son Nero started to suspect Galba's opposition from Spain, where he was proconsul, the emperor tried sending secret messages to his imperial procurators there, ordering Galba's death.[87] Later, Galba used his procurator in Africa to rid himself of Clodius Macer, the rebellious commander (*legatus*) who had cut grain shipments to Rome.[88]

Like governors, procurators became symbols of Roman rule for provincials who had not come to terms with their own subordination.[89] Procurators were also akin to governors in their propensity toward corruption and abuse,

---

85. Ulp. *Dig.* 1.16.9.pr. Compare the Saepinum-Bovianum dispute (*CIL* 9.2438, chapter 2 above), where the imperial freedmen seem eventually to get satisfaction. See further Tac. *Agr.* 9, *Ann.* 14.31–39 (difficulties between procurators and Suetonius Paulinus, governor of Britain), and Pflaum, *Les procurateurs équestres*, 157–60. In contrast, Burton, "Provincial Procurators," highlights evidence for procurators working closely with the provincial governor; cf. Septimius Severus's rescript to imperial-estate tenants at Tymion (AD 205 or 208), where he warns that his procurator will be able to call on the governor if illegal exactions continue: Hauken et al., "A New Inscription from Phrygia"; and Tabbernee and Lampe, *Pepouza and Tymion*, chap. 4.

86. Tac. *Ann.* 13.1. Tacitus claims that the victim, Junius Silanus, was poisoned at a banquet.

87. Suet. *Galba* 9.2 (cf. SHA *Hadr.* 5.6). This plan failed, of course and, according to Suetonius, even hastened Nero's overthrow, since Galba's detection of the plot forced him to react. Contrast Herodian 7.4–5, where procuratorial excess leads to the fall of the emperor they serve (Maximinus Thrax in 238).

88. Tac. *Hist.* 1.7; *Hist.* 4.49 shows that the actual assassin was a centurion.

89. E.g., Plut. *Prae. ger. reip.* 813e, 814d; cf. Tac. *Agr.* 15, cited above.

which "good" emperors were occasionally pushed to correct.[90] One important similarity that all procurators shared with governors was that they enjoyed a staff of soldiers at their disposal for security tasks.[91] For example, soldiers guarded mines and quarries, apparently to prevent the pillaging of supplies and to watch over the suspect workforce (often, though not always, slaves or condemned criminals who were there in the first place because they had broken the law).[92] A procurator in Egypt dispatched a soldier to a village to enforce a summons, issued on his own authority.[93]

Regarding soldier-police in the service of imperial procurators, Pliny's *Epistula* 10.27 to Trajan, cited above as the only case in which that emperor did not oppose Pliny's desire for greater military policing, suggests that the procurators received their military personnel from the governor. This relationship is not proof of procurators' subordination to the governor, although the latter enjoyed a much fuller number of soldiers. The two procurators in *Ep.* 10.27 (an equestrian and his subordinate imperial freedman) seem hard pressed to scrape together an escort of eighteen soldiers, even with Pliny's addition of two mounted guards from his own *officium*.

We turn now to a particularly important aspect of procuratorial jurisdiction, the management of imperial estates.[94] As Tacitus suggested in *Agricola*, procurators had slaves at their disposal to assist them in their duties. Procurators of some imperial estates in the west used two or more servile "woodland guards" (*saltuarii*) under the direction of the main slave overseer (*vilicus*) to police the estates, just as owners of private estates did (chapter 3 above).[95] On eastern estates, we occasionally hear of similar figures called "peace officers."[96]

---

90. E.g., Suet. *Dom.* 8.2 (cited as a good trait); *Epitome de Caes.* 42.21 (Trajan); SHA *Hadr.* 3.9 and 13.10; cf. *CJ* 8.40.3pr. (Sept. Severus and Caracalla), *Pauli sent.* 5.12.6.

91. Eck, "The Growth of Administrative Posts," 236, noting that procurators also had a staff of imperial slaves or freedmen alongside their military *officium*.

92. On military policing and mines, see Greene, "Industry and Technology," 747–50; Millar, "Condemnation to Hard Labour"; and esp. Hirt, *Imperial Mines*, 93–96, 185, 198–202 226–27, cf. 56–70, 168–97 passim, 268–69.

93. *P.Wisc.* 1.24, second or third century. A lacuna prevents us from knowing what kind of procurator this was.

94. For background, see Kehoe, *The Economics of Agriculture*, esp. chaps. 1, 3, and 7; and Mitchell, "The Administration of Roman Asia," 37–46.

95. Carlsen, "*Saltuarius*." Most attestations of *saltuarii* come from Italy; a few are from Africa.

96. *Eirênophylakes* or *eirênarchai* (not to be confused with the civilian police of chapter 3 above; *eirênarchai* on estates are actually attested first, in the late first century): *MAMA* 7.35; *SEG* 40.1232; Wolff, *Les brigands*, 236; Brélaz, *La sécurité publique*, 107–8, 228; Dmitriev, *City Government*, 206–7.

We see soldiers serving as police under procurators in an inscription discovered at Sülmenli, Turkey. It describes a drawn-out dispute between two neighboring villages on an imperial estate in early-third-century Phrygia. In this case, successive imperial procurators tried applying their full authority, and soldiers under their command, to establish the extent of each village's contested transport duties (*vehiculatio*, or, here, ἀγγαρεία). Essentially, the leaders of each village wanted its neighbor to provide more miles of service on the surrounding roads, thus hoping to spare themselves from providing draft animals and supplies for state traffic.[97] The first procurator decided that their transport duties would be proportional to the amount of tax each village paid and assigned one of his military attendants (an *optio*) to enforce the arrangement. Next, the inscription cites text from two letters or notices that this soldier gave to the villagers, reiterating obedience to the procurator and warning (line 29), "If you are negligent, you will be punished!"

Eventually, trouble returned, and in 213, the rival villagers met again before a new procurator, who tried to shore up the old agreement. According to the text, which is in the form of *acta* or official minutes, one village's representative then specifically requested a *stationarius*. The procurator replied, "I will grant a *stationarius*."[98] We will see in chapter 8 below that *stationarii* were almost always low-ranking soldiers on guard duty. We might conjecture that the *optio* previously deputized to safeguard the agreement did so from a distance. *Optio* is a rather high rank (second in command to a centurion), and the one we encounter here probably had other important duties. It seems that this time, some of the villagers actually wanted a soldier to stay with them, to help regulate the agreement closer to the ground level. Individual *stationarii* soldiers often served in towns this way for a year or two and then were rotated

---

97. Sülmenli = ancient Blaundos, *BAtl.* 62 B5. The principal edition remains Frend's 1956 "A Third-Century Inscription Relating to *angareia* in Phrygia" = Frend *JRS* 46. Zawadzki offered further points in "Sur une inscription de Phrygie." See also J. Robert and L. Robert's comments in *BE* 1958, 322, and 1961, 238. The villages Anossa and Antimacheia are otherwise unattested (probably *BAtlas* 62 E4). The fragmentary inscription preserves a multipart dossier. The first hearing (lines 1–19, date unknown) was held before the procurator Threptus. Lines 19–26 and 27–29 consist of two letters sent by Threptus's military orderly, the *optio* Symphoros. In 213, the contending parties had a second hearing (lines 30–33) before the procurator Philocurius, and there was yet another (lines 33–41) in 237 before the procurator Novellius.

98. Frend *JRS* 46, line 33: δώσω στατιωνάριον. It might seem surprising to have a Latin military term coming out of the mouth of an eastern villager, but it was first attested in Greek a hundred years before, under Trajan. In fact, the earliest attestations for *milites stationarii* are in Greek: *O.Claud.* 50–73, 80–82, a series of pass permits from Mons Claudianus in eastern Egypt; see chapter 8 below. Note also Mason, *Greek Terms*, 4.

out.[99] Other sources show *stationarii* oppressing people, taking property, and persecuting Christians, so it surprised the inscription's editor (a young W. H. C. Frend, who became one of his generation's greatest church historians) to see villagers requesting help from a figure whom he considered "notoriously an instrument of tyranny."[100]

In 237, the villagers met for a third time, before yet another procurator, who reinforced his predecessors' decisions. The inscription is more lacunose at the end, but this last procurator seemed to specify two members of his staff as enforcers of the arrangement.[101] While these three procurators had obvious trouble settling this dispute, by hearing the complaints and applying military staff to police the villages, they acted as authoritatively as peacekeepers in their domain as any proconsul in his province, even if they were freedmen. In other inscriptions, we see problems that parallel the worst facets of gubernatorial provincial maladministration, especially at the Saltus Burunitanus in Africa, in AD 181–182.[102] The problems that the peasants there were experiencing seem to have started with the procurators and lease holders forcing them to work beyond their labor requirements and seizing excessive amounts of their produce. The procurators, in collusion with violent and corrupt lease holders, then used soldiers to attack the villagers in order to prevent them from appealing directly to the emperor.

The peasants (*coloni*) who farmed imperial estates often did not have access to traditional organs of municipal organization, so one might view their civic status as precariously low. Economically, however, they were probably better off than many independent subsistence farmers.[103] Politically, the *coloni* in the Sülmenli *vehiculatio* inscription seem rather confident and persistent; one of them may even have threatened to appeal over the head of the procurator.[104] Of

---

99. E.g. (and explained in chapter 8 below), *IGRR* 3.812 and 4.1185; *ILS* 2052 and 9072; *AE* 1902, 89 and 1957, 218 (1981, 344); recall the *stationarii* in *CIL* 9.2438, the Saepinum inscription (chapter 2 below).

100. Frend, "A Third-Century Inscription," 52. Cf. Frend, *The Donatist Church*, 13.

101. The first is at Frend *JRS* 46, line 36: "Agathon the…" Frend suggested *optio*, but space at the left margin of line 37 could accommodate στατιωνάριος, the last-mentioned military functionary. A *tabularius* is also mentioned at line 39.

102. *CIL* 8.10570 (= *ILS* 6870, Hauken no. 1; cf. certain parallels in Hauken nos. 2, 3, and 6).

103. Note Kehoe, *Economics of Agriculture*, chap. 3.

104. Frend *JRS* 46, line 11, although the text is unclear. In some cases, it must have been dangerous for peasants on imperial estates to try to petition over the heads of their procurators and other estate managers. Indeed, in Hauken no. 1 (Saltus Burunitanus), the petitioners claim that the violence they suffered from soldiers was occasioned by this very attempt; they appeal to sympathy for their weakness but seem to know their rights well and are

the seven extant petitions to the emperor collected by Tor Hauken, four are from peasants on imperial estates, a fact that reveals more than the basic injustices they faced (namely, official corruption, violence from soldiers, illegal exactions, and requisitions of work animals).[105] It also suggests that imperial *coloni* felt a direct link and a right to appeal to the emperor, since they worked land owned by him and administered by his procurators. They were not powerless; when their straits were desperate enough, they threatened to disrupt imperial affairs by abandoning the estate altogether.[106] It was thus in everyone's interest to keep imperial estates pacified and calm.

Conclusion

The existence of institutional means to curb crime and impose order—namely, military police attached to the governors' *officia*—did not preclude instances of self-help, vigilantism, and negotiation. Sometimes governors are depicted as tolerant of noninstitutional means. Note, for instance, the aloof attitude of the proconsul Gallio when "the Jews" charged Paul before him in Corinth (Acts 18:12–17). He showed no interest in conflicts between Jews, about matters that were esoteric to him. Frustrated, Paul's accusers seized a synagogue official who was apparently allied to Paul and beat him in full view of the governor's court. Gallio did nothing, perhaps seeing the outburst of unregulated violence as another Jewish matter he had nothing to do with. Or perhaps he was not so disinterested but thought it best to allow Paul's agitated accusers to

---

assertive in demanding them. Hauken no. 6 makes it clear that the Araguanian petitioners were enabled only by the assistance of an educated ally who was familiar with the standard form of official documents and petitions (to which these *libelli* conform), and this must have generally been the case with any written appeal from civilians. Compare the situation in Egypt, where most petitions on papyrus were obviously drafted by professional scribes or modeled on ones that were. See further Connolly, *Lives behind the Laws.*

105. Hauken no. 1 (Saltus Burunitanus), no. 2 (Gasr Mezuar; very fragmentary), no. 3 (Aga Bey Köyü; the emperors' reply is lost; here, matters are so bad that the peasants threaten to abandon the estate, leaving it without a workforce; cf. Skaptopara no. 5), no. 6 (Aragua). Septimius Severus's reply to a petition from an imperial estate at Tymion in Phrygia (published in Hauken et al., "A New Inscription from Phrygia," and Tabbernee and Lampe, *Pepouza and Tymion*, chap. 4) warns (lines 11–12) that his procurator will intervene against illegal (?) exactions: *P]roc(urator) noster i[nte]rponet se adversum in/[licitas] exact[i]ones*; the remaining lines (13–16) seem to promise the governor's involvement, if needed. This text does not mention soldiers, although the lacunose final line could conceivably accommodate some military term. The stone bearing this inscription was found near Susuzören, which is about twenty miles northeast of Sül(ü)menli (ancient Blaundos, *BAtlas* 62 B5).

106. E.g., Hauken no. 1 (Saltus Burunitanus) and no. 3 (Aga Bey Köyü); cf. Lewis, *Life in Egypt*, 161–65.

vent their anger. Governors might also yield to popular pressure. The gospel accounts of Jesus's trial before Pilate suggest negotiation with the assembled rabble, which had nothing to do with the face value of Pilate's gubernatorial power on paper.[107]

Indeed, the governor could not be everywhere at once. When an angry mob initiated a night attack on Dio Chrysostom's house during a grain shortage, there was no governor, detachment of troops, or night watch to help him. Had the mob not abandoned its sortie, members of Dio's household would have had to fend for themselves as best they could.[108] In a stateless society, Dio would have had to come to terms with the rest of the community, or at least prepare for a real fight. But Dio did not rely on noninstitutional conflict resolution. At an assembly the next day, he gave his fellow citizens this thinly veiled threat: "Nothing which takes place in the cities escapes the notice of the governors ... just as family members of children who misbehave at home denounce them to their teachers, in just the same way the crimes of the cities' people are announced to the governors."[109] Thus, he employed the threat of retribution as a means of encouraging public order, although its actualization would depend on the governor's inclination to involve himself in a local dispute.

Dio's threat, furthermore, is based on the supposition that the governor would be determined to correct disorder and illegality. Some bad governors did not concern themselves much with this kind of work. But ultimately, no governor wanted to be seen as weak enough for a mob to manipulate or so distant that he could not protect his friends and vested interests. Nor was he a free agent; like the provincials he ruled, he himself was a subject of the emperor, too. Both emperor and provincials looked to the governor to keep his province pacified and quiet, and two important means toward this all-important end were his careful negotiation of local politics and his use of the soldiers attached to him to advance security and control. In the following pages, we will focus on the soldiers themselves.

---

107. There is no evidence outside the gospels for Roman governors releasing prisoners in the way Barabbas was freed (Mark 15:6–15; Matt. 27:15–26; Luke 23:18–25; John 18:39–40); it seems to be either a short-lived local peculiarity or an invention of Mark. A lengthy and unsatisfactory literature has grown around the topic; Brown's treatment is sensible: *The Death of the Messiah*, vol. 1, 787–800.

108. Dio Chrys. *Or.* 46, set in Bithynian Prusa during Vespasian's reign.

109. Dio Chrys. *Or.* 46.14. Cf. *Or.* 45.8 and Plut. *Prae. ger. reip.* 814.

8

"Military stations throughout all provinces": Detached-Service Soldier-Police

HISTORIANS SOMETIMES VIEW the *pax Romana* as a time when soldiers were relegated to distant frontiers, leaving civilians to enjoy the blessings of peace, with only minimal contact with the thousands of *milites* ("soldiers") who protected the empire from foreign threats. For instance, one historian has claimed that in contrast to republican times, soldiers during the principate "were a marginal group stationed in remote areas and involved in activities that were irrelevant to the daily lives of civilians."[1] This was not the case. Even during the early principate, numerous soldiers were scattered about Italy and the internal provinces, and Tacitus felt entitled to criticize lax *milites* who did most of their soldiering in luxurious eastern cities.[2] By the fourth century and later, many troops could still be found in the empire's major cities, where they could be called on to put down riots (in which they themselves occasionally participated).[3]

---

1. Cornell, "The End of Roman Imperial Expansion," 168.

2. Tac. *Ann.* 13.55 and *Hist.* 2.80.3; cf. Fronto *Ad Verum* 2.1.19 and *Principia historiae* 10–13 = Haines Loeb II, 148, 206–10. Pollard (*Soldiers, Cities, and Civilians in Roman Syria*, 3–5) and Cornell ("The End of Roman Imperial Expansion," 166–68) both claim that Tacitus himself knew very little about soldiers and soldiering, often relying on literary topoi to fill out his descriptions thereof. See further Parker, "Roman Legionary Fortresses in the East," and Wheeler, "The Laxity of Syrian Legions."

3. E.g., Libanius *Or.* 19 (fourth century, Antioch) and John Malalas 490–91 (Constantinople in 560); see further MacMullen, *Corruption*, 209–17. For members of the imperial guard participating in the great Nika Revolt of 532 in Constantinople, see *Chron. Pasch.* 626 and Procopius *De bello Persico* 1.24. See further Alan Cameron, *Circus Factions*; Liebeschuetz, *Antioch*, 124; and Nippel, *Public Order*, 110. In their treatments of the broad theme, however, Gregory ("Urban Violence") and Liebeschuetz (*The Decline and Fall of the Roman City*, chap. 8) both note the absence of soldiers or riot police in many cases of late-antique urban disorder. Riots were often allowed to run their course, and state response was often reactive and after the fact. Kelly ("Riot Control") intelligently argues that while emperors and governors were expected to make some kind of response to a riot, heavy-handed use of soldiers against civilians was often not in their interests.

We have already seen that emperors and governors relied heavily on soldiers to strengthen public order and state control among civilians in Italy and the provinces. The trend toward military policing started with Augustus's response to lingering disorders in Italy, where he "countered bandit attacks by distributing military stations in suitable locations."[4] From Tiberius on, military policing continued to expand under Augustus's successors, to such an extent that by circa AD 200, Tertullian noted in passing that "military posts are distributed throughout all provinces for the searching out of bandits."[5]

On its own, this one aside remark from an African Christian is worth little. Nonetheless, in this chapter, we will see that Tertullian's remark finds support from hundreds of other pieces of evidence. The numerous extant petitions from Egyptian civilians to outposted *milites* and centurions, for example, provide strong documentary evidence for the distribution of soldiers in civilian areas, where they performed a variety of security and administrative functions. Beyond the papyri, we have numerous epigraphic and literary attestations of various types of soldier-police—with more than a thousand references to one class of outposted soldiers alone, the *beneficiarii consularis*.

This chapter provides an overview of the various soldiers who were detached from their legions to perform police functions among civilians. We will begin with a consideration of the phenomenon of military "detached service," mainly by reviewing military-policing designations, such as *stationarius*, *regionarius*, and *beneficiarius*. Our chronological focus is the second and third centuries, when there was a marked increase in attestations of detached-service military policing, bringing with it a concomitant refinement of military-policing vocabulary. In many cases, we can only venture tentative observations, as the fragmentary nature of the sources makes differentiating and defining various types of soldier-police difficult. Moreover, we will note cases in which the duties of outposted soldiers crossed over into the realm of administering state services and institutions, although we will focus on tasks bearing on security and enforcement.

This increase in detached-service military policing constitutes a significant development in the evolution of the Roman Empire. A further goal of this

---

4. Suet. *Aug.* 32: *grassaturas dispositis per opportuna loca stationibus inhibuit* (chapter 4 above).

5. Suet. *Tib.* 37.1 (chapter 5 above); Tert. *Apol.* 2.8: *Latronibus investigandis per universas provincias militaris statio sortitur.* Barnes (*Tertullian*, 55) conjectures a date of 197/198 for the *Apologeticum.* We can compare Aelius Aristides' statement from the mid-second century (*Or.* 26.101, his glowing encomium on Rome) that security stations (*stathmoi* = Latin *stationes*) in remote regions supposedly made travel safe; cf. *Or.* 26.67.

chapter is to assess the intended functions and social impact of military police. The soldier-police discussed here operated under the notional command of superior authorities (most often the provincial governor), but our main aim is to investigate the lives and actions of outposted soldiers in their own right. We will see that during the late principate, these soldier-police shouldered heavy security and administrative tasks and came to exercise freer and greater authority than the policing functionaries we have looked at so far—the civilian officials and their attendants discussed in chapter 3 or the soldier-police under the direct command of emperors and governors in chapters 4 through 7. The greater scope and independence of military police brought about more numerous civilian-military encounters, many of which were marked by corruption and abuse of provincials.

The Army as Large-scale Police Institution

Before looking at the actions of soldier-police who were outposted in small numbers throughout the provinces, we must acknowledge that the army as a whole played a large-scale police role in the internal provinces of the empire. Of course, the empire's military history shows that legions could be pulled from the frontier to challenge (or even participate in) large-scale revolts and usurpations. Moreover, not all large military units were stationed on the frontiers; there were legions, auxiliary cohorts, and vexillations scattered about the empire. Under ordinary circumstances, the very presence of these units deterred large-scale disturbances of the peace in many provinces. Thus, in Egypt, the large legionary base at Nicopolis worked as an explicit threat against disorder in nearby Alexandria. Indeed, on more than one occasion, it was employed in reactive police actions, as in AD 66, when the prefect of Egypt employed two legions and extra auxiliary troops from Libya to put down unrest in that strife-prone city.[6]

Yet large legions and cohorts could be too bulky and impractical to provide security effectively in remote areas, and for this reason, units as small as fifty men, *vexillationes*, were sometimes dispatched to places that needed a military presence. To cite just one example, two vexillations from two different legions were sent to Salonae under Marcus Aurelius.[7] In fact, Brian Dobson has noted the increased use of vexillations during and after Marcus's reign, suggesting

---

6. Jos. *BJ* 2.490–97. It must also be noted that the legions could themselves become loci of disorder, as in the mayhem of 68–69. On disorder in Alexandria, see chapter 6 above.

7. *ILS* 2287 (= *CIL* 3.1980). See also Bishop, "*Praesidium.*"

that "they appear to assume greater importance as the army as a whole loses mobility."[8] This flexible trend toward using small detachments for ad hoc needs is reflected in the outposting of even smaller numbers of soldiers, who were dispatched to civilian areas to serve in temporary policing posts.

Beneficiarii consularis

We can deal with the military staff officers known as *beneficiarii consularis* rather briefly for two reasons. First, the hundreds of sources preserving information about them have been thoroughly treated in recent scholarship.[9] Second, it is now clear that contrary to earlier views, police work was not their primary duty; although they were soldiers, the *beneficiarius consularis* assignment was primarily administrative.[10]

In the late second century and throughout the third century, a system of government administrative posts, the *stationes*, emerged throughout most of the provinces and along some frontiers. As the omnipresent commanders of

8. Dobson, "The Roman Army" 19; see also Saxer, *Untersuchungen zu den Vexillationen*, esp. 123–24. For vexillations in general, see Goldsworthy, *The Roman Army at War*, 27–28; Keppie, *The Making of the Roman Army*, 197; Southern, *The Roman Empire from Severus to Constantine*, 156; and for vexillations in eastern cities, Isaac, *Limits of Empire*, 36–38, 125.

9. In the early twentieth century, von Domaszewski provided a valuable construction of the placement of *beneficiarii consularis* in the military hierarchy with his *Die Rangordnung des römischen Heeres*, updated in 1967 with a reedition by Dobson. Dise has contributed a monograph and a useful series of articles (see bibliography below), focusing especially on the middle Danubian provinces. An essential resource for the study of *beneficiarii* is provided by Schallmayer et al., *Der römische Weihebezirk von Osterburken*, vols. I and II. The first volume is a *Corpus der griechischen und lateinischen Beneficiarer-Inschriften des Römischen Reiches* (often abbreviated *CBI* or *CBFIR*), which was commissioned in response to two rich finds of *beneficiarii consularis* inscriptions discovered in the 1980s at Osterburken and at the site of ancient Sirmium. The second volume contains archaeological reports and synthetic papers presented at a 1990 conference at Osterburken. Ott subsequently published a revision of his 1993 Frankfurt dissertation, *Die Beneficiarier*; Rankov points out shortcomings of this monograph in his useful historiographical overview, "*Beneficiarii* (Military Staff Officers)," 681. In 2000, this fruitful scholarly activity reached its climax with the publication of Nelis-Clément's *Les beneficiarii: Militaires et administrateurs au service de l'empire*, which Rankov called "a masterly synthesis of virtually everything now known about these officers [which] gives the most complete picture available of any grade of Roman army soldier, on the one hand, and of the grass-roots working of Roman provincial administration, on the other. It is a hugely impressive achievement, and ought to explode once and for all the myth of Rome as an empire without bureaucracy" ("*Beneficiarii* and the Reality of Roman Bureaucracy," 524).

10. Dise, "A Reassessment of the Functions of *Beneficiarii Consularis*," 79–82, arguing against earlier views expressed by Hirschfeld ("Die Sicherheitspolizei," 595–96), and von Domaszewski ("Die Beneficiarierposten," 159 and passim), which were subsequently adopted by Robert, MacMullen, and other later historians.

these posts, the *beneficiarii consularis* were the sine qua non of this system. As their title suggests, *beneficiarii consularis* were originally closely attached to individual governors (*beneficiarius consularis* translates as "military staff officer of the consular," i.e., governor), but the provincial beneficiariate became a free-standing permanent institution not directly dependent on the provincial governors.[11] Privileged with higher pay and immunity from many burdensome camp chores, they were often rewarded for their skilled service with career promotions.[12] Their exact functions varied by region and local needs, with activities ranging from regulation of the traffic on roads, service as customs officers, and occasionally service as officials concerned with *annona* (grain provisions) and tax collecting. There is no evidence that they were closely linked to the state system of requisitioned transport (*vehiculatio*).[13]

Although some *beneficiarii* served in their provincial *stationes* for up to four years, terms of six months or one or two years were much more common. There are occasional indications of two *beneficiarii consularis* serving together in the same post, perhaps for the sake of training new arrivals and smoothing transitions. Otherwise, *beneficiarii consularis* appear as solitary figures. This may primarily be a result of the nature of our main body of sources, the nine hundred or so inscribed altars preserving individual dedications. It is likely that *beneficiarii consularis* were assisted in their administrative duties by a few local employees, or at least some slaves. It is certainly the case that they did not command any sort of units of police, *milites stationarii* or otherwise. Moreover, the *stationes* they typically served were not imposing fortresses and were not necessarily fortified at all or even fixed in one recognizable and specialized building. *Statio* need not refer to a particular structure where outposted *beneficiarii* did their work; it could just as well denote the general presence of a *beneficiarius consularis*, with whom certain travelers and traders would need to check in.

Not that these figures were mere papyrus pushers who garnered no respect. They were, after all, representatives of the Roman state and members of a quintessentially violent institution. Consider the special type of lance they carried as ceremonial symbols of their authority and reminders of their military status; archaeologists have found actual spear points from these weapons,

---

11. Dise, "The *Beneficiarii Procuratoris*," esp. 291. Dise argues that this transition occurred in Noricum soon after AD 170.

12. Ott, "Überlegungen."

13. Kolb, *Transport und Nachrichtentransfer*, 174–75.

which were commonly depicted in funerary reliefs of deceased *beneficiarii*.[14]
The very fact that soldiers were assigned to these various administrative tasks
may imply imperial concern to protect Roman interests in the provinces with
military authority and certainly indicates the possibility of direct coercion in
the enforcement of state regulations.

It seems that the duties of *beneficiarii* were flexible and shaped by local
needs. We know that *beneficiarii* did occasionally engage in police work. Tertullian noted that *beneficiarii* performed surveillance over workers in dubious
professions who were liable to the vectigal tax.[15] Tertullian was objecting to the
inclusion of Christians among these suspected groups, and *beneficiarii* are
also known to have been actively engaged in the persecution of Christians.[16]
Like many other soldiers and administrators in Egypt (and beyond), outposted
beneficiarii consularis received petitions from civilian victims of crime who
were hoping for redress.[17] Otherwise, we cannot be sure about any further
police functions. Austin and Rankov conjecture, on admittedly thin evidence,
that they may have regularly been involved in policing gold and silver mines.[18]

---

14. See the two papers by Alföldi, "*Hasta—Summa Imperii*," and "Vom Speerattribut." More
recently, see Eibl, "Gibt es eine spezifische Ausrüstung der Beneficiarier?" with excellent
illustrations (fuller than the plates of Nelis-Clément's *Les beneficiarii*, but note her photo-
graphs on 536, 538, 551–52, and 554). Also note Rankov, "The Governor's Men," 31–32; and
Nótári, "The Spear as the Symbol of Property and Power in Ancient Rome."

15. Tert. *De fuga* 13, discussed further below sub *curiosi*. He did not specify that this *beneficiarius* was *consularis*, but it was with this variety of *beneficiarius* officer that civilians would
most likely come into contact. Moreover, the activity of keeping tax records points to the
beneficiarii consularis, as we know that they participated in tax collection, at least in Egypt
(*P.Petaus* 34.7; *SB* 6.9409.3; *P.Oxy.* 14.1651.13, 20.2286.2, 36.2794.4, and 36.2797.2). Cf.
C.Th. 4.13.3 (AD 321) on the involvement of outposted soldiers in the collection of the vectigal tax.

16. *Passio Fructuosi* 1 (set in 259) and *Passio Agapae et al.* 3.1 (304), Lopuszanski, "La police
romaine et les chrétiens," 6–9; Nelis-Clément, *Les beneficiarii*, 220–27. *Beneficiarii* are specifically singled out in Euseb. *Hist. eccl.* 9.9a.7. The Christian sources, however, do not generally specify what type of *beneficiarius* were involved; there were various types of *beneficiarius*,
so not all of the concerned soldiers were necessarily *beneficiarii consularis*.

17. E.g., *P.Amh.* 2.77.27 (Soknopaiou Nesos, AD 139), *P.Lond.* 2.342, p. 173 (Soknopaiou
Nesos, AD 185), *PSI* 7.807.1 (Oxyrhynchus, AD 280), *P.Sijp.* 16 (Narmuthis, AD 115); *P.
Cair.Isid.* 62, 63, 139; Blumell, "Petition to a *Beneficiarius*"; outside of Egypt: *P.Bostra* 1; cf.
T.Vindol. 2.344. See further Rankov, "Die Beneficiarier in den literarischen und papyrologischen Texten"; Ott, *Die Beneficiarier*, 128; Nelis-Clément, *Les beneficiarii*, 227–43 (again, all
types of *beneficiarii* are covered here, not just *beneficiarii consularis*). On soldiers receiving
petitions, see Aubert, "Policing the Countryside"; and Peachin, "Petition to a Centurion"
(introduction to *P.Sijp.* 15).

18. Austin and Rankov, *Exploratio*, 196.

All in all, their work as police was quite secondary to their main administrative tasks. There is no evidence that they ever pursued bandits or criminals; it was probably not their *stationes* that Tertullian had in mind when he remarked that military stations were distributed throughout every province to counter brigandage.[19]

Milites stationarii: *Posts, service, and terminology*

In our overview of terminology and classifications of outposted soldier-police, it is best to turn now to the term *stationarius*, because studying the ancient usage of this word in some detail reveals many facets of military policing.[20] The casualness and flexibility with which some ancient sources use the word make a hard and fast definition elusive. Generally speaking, *stationarius* might possibly mean any person connected to a *statio*—usually "post" or "station," but this word itself can have several meanings. Furthermore, some *stationarius* references are clearly not from a military context.[21]

The word *statio* has a rich military pedigree, used by classical authors to describe the positions of troops on campaign. While writers such as Caesar, Livy, and Tacitus wrote of "soldiers at their post" or station (*milites statione*), they never used the word *stationarius*.[22] We have already met some references

---

19. *Pace* Hirschfeld, "Die Sicherheitspolizei," 595–96, followed by von Domaszewski, "Die Beneficiarierposten."

20. Petraccia Lucernoni's *Gli stationarii in età imperiale* (2001) is the leading study, valuably collecting all known *stationarius* references; little is said there about other police, but she laudably stresses the possibility and necessity of differentiating among various types of police in the Roman Empire, which are often muddled by modern scholars because of the difficult source material: "Si può innanzitutto osservare che lo *stationarius* si distingue dalle altre figure (*frumentarii, beneficiarii, kolletiones, curiosi*) con cui finora spesso era stato confuso, anche per l'esiguità e l'ambiguità della documentazione," 89. We will note that in some cases, unfortunately, she does not eliminate confusion between *beneficiarii consularis* and *stationarii*.

21. There are a few cases in which slaves are described as *stationarii*: *CIL* 2².847 has a matron doling out money to all of her household, with ten denarii "to each individual *stationarius* slave" (*item servis stationariis singulis*); see also *CIL* 2.2011. The *Zosimus Aug. n. stat.* of *AE* 1994, 299 can be expanded to *Zosimus Aug(usti) n(ostri) stat(ionarius)*, which would seem to denote an imperial slave or freedman; likewise, *CIL* 3.10308, the dedication of a certain [...] *limus stat.* [...]/[*p*]*ub.* might be from a public slave ([?] *limus stat(ionarius)...[p]ub(licus)*) of Intercisa in Pannonia Inferior, where the inscription was found. We cannot rule out a security function; perhaps these *servi stationarii* worked as private guards. The staff of two Italian trade offices (*stationes*) that represented the commercial interests of certain provincial cities are called *stationarii*: *OGIS* 595 preserves the appeal of Tyrian *stationarii* at Puteoli for aid from their mother city; see Sosin, "Tyrian *Stationarii*." Another commercial *statio* and *stationarius*, representing the cities of Noricum in Rome, is mentioned in *CIL* 6.250 (= *ILS* 3675).

22. E.g., Caes. *Gall.* 2.18.3, 4.32.1, 5.15.3, 6.37.3; Livy 3.2.8, 8.38.2, 10.43.14, 23.16.5, 28.1.8; Tac. *Hist.* 4.26.

to military *stationes* that have direct bearing on policing in Italy and the provinces. Appuleius, a soldier who was "in the station at Nicomedia," referred a complex case of a suspicious slave to Pliny when he was serving as governor of Bithynia-Pontus.[23] In addition, there are the military *stationes* established in Italy by Augustus and expanded by Tiberius (known from Suetonius's *vitae*), as well as the provincial counterbanditry stations mentioned by Tertullian (see above). In all likelihood, some of the soldiers associated with these *stationes* could be called *stationarii*. Pliny and Suetonius possibly shied away from this military neologism, because it never appears in the high-classical literary canon.

In fact, the earliest attested uses of the word *stationarius* occur in a strictly military context, in the Greek form στατιωνάριος (or στατιονάριος). The word is written on a series of twenty-seven pass permits on *ostraka* (scrap pieces of broken pottery used for writing material) found in the remote marble quarries of Mons Claudianus in Egypt's eastern desert. They date from 108–117, the last half of Trajan's reign. Issued by military officers to *stationarii* soldiers, the *ostraka* follow a set pattern: the officer's name and greeting to the *stationarii*, people whom the *stationarii* are to let pass, and the date according to the Egyptian calendar. For example: "Antoninus, Centurion, to the *stationarii*, greetings. Let pass two men. 20 Phaôphi."[24]

These military *ostraka* reveal a substantial element of detached-service military policing: the careful supervision of movement into and out of an area that was important to the emperor. The quarries of the Egyptian desert provided many of the marble columns that were transported to Rome for monumental imperial architecture. Unlike the labor force of many mines in the empire, the workers at Mons Claudianus were free, not condemned criminals or slaves. But the workers were not necessarily free from suspicion; the military surveillance there was probably primarily aimed toward safeguarding the long lines of supplies (which included luxury foodstuffs such as beer, eggs, meat, and parrot fish) from petty pilfering and the occasional nomad raid.[25]

---

23. Pliny *Ep.* 10.74: *Appuleius...miles qui est in statione Nicomedensi scripsit mihi.* Sherwin-White (*The Letters of Pliny*, 661) saw Appuleius as a *stationarius* from the auxilia; considering the arrested slave, he may be right. On the other hand, it is possible Appuleius was a *beneficiarius consularis*. This is one of the few cases in which a substantive inquiry from Pliny generated no extant response from Trajan in the dossier of their correspondence as we have it.

24. *O.Claud.* 60: Ἀντωνεῖνος (ἑκατοντάρχης) στατιωναρίοις χαίρειν. πάρετε ἄνδρ<α>ς δύο. Φαῶφι κ̄. See *O.Claud.* 50–73, 80–82; Van Rengen, "Les laissez-passer," 57–75. On this and other Latin military terms in Greek, see Mason, *Greek Terms*, 2–7 and passim.

25. See Kaper, ed., *Life on the Fringe*, esp. Bülow-Jacobsen, "Traffic on the Roads," 69–72; cf. Bagnall, "Army and Police," 69.

Ostraka like these are also important for understanding how outposted military guards were organized and rotated, a topic that will be discussed further below.

Our earliest epigraphic instances of *stationarii* also come from Egypt, the far southern town of Pselchis, to be exact. There, two outposted legionaries scratched their names into a sandstone cliff, creating brief texts akin to informal graffiti. In 149, Aurelius Herminianus entered his name three times, describing himself as an "armory supervisor, *stationarius*."[26] Two years later, one Tiberius Claudius described himself as "*stationarius* of the first legion" in a similar inscription.[27] It is striking that both men identified themselves, perhaps with some pride, as *stationarii*. In the context of other *stationarius* references, this suggests that they were detached from their legions for temporary guard duty on the frontier, a consistent function of soldiers designated *stationarii*, especially in the later empire.[28]

These first two sets of *stationarii* attestations from Egypt help delineate an important variation in the use of the word *stationarius*. Some soldiers were outposted in a particular place for this type of service for months or a few years and (like the soldiers down in Pselchis) explicitly thought of themselves as holding formal *stationarius* posts. But the anonymous soldiers from the Mons Claudianus *ostraka*, we will see, were probably serving very short terms of duty as outposted guards and were not necessarily specialized for this type of service. They probably did not think of themselves as a special class of soldiers. The term *stationarius* was applied to them by others, as a rather casual substantive adjective meaning "soldiers posted to guard duty." This same sort of loose terminology is applied by Ulpian in his description of the urban prefect's police duties in Rome, noting that to keep order at entertainments, the prefect "should also have *stationarii* soldiers placed in different places to protect the peace of the commoners' seating sections and to report to him what is happening and where."[29] Now these soldiers were just ordinary *milites* of the

---

26. *SB* 6146, 6147, 7979: ἀρμόρο(μ) κούστορ στατιωνᾶρις; Pselchis = *BAtlas* 81 C2.

27. *SB* 6143: Τιβέρις Κλαῦδις στατιωνᾶρις leg(ionis) α. See also *SB* 1584.

28. E.g., Amm. Marc. 18.5.3, describing guards on the eastern frontier; cf. *O.BuNjem* 2, 7–10, 25–26, 28 (AD 253–259). *Milites stationarii* in late antiquity: Petraccia Lucernoni, *Gli stationarii*, nos. 79–120; Hirschfeld, "Die Sicherheitspolizei," 598; Jones, *LRE*, index; and MacMullen, *Soldier and Civilian*, 55–65.

29. *Dig.* 1.12.1.12: *Quies quoque popularium et disciplina spectaculorum ad praefecti urbi curam pertinere videtur: et sane debet etiam dispositos milites stationarios habere ad tuendam popularium quietem et ad referendum sibi quid ubi agatur.* See chapter 5 above.

urban cohorts; *stationarius* here is a general adjectival description of their transitory guard chores at spectacles. *Milites stationarii* are not otherwise attested in Rome and do not figure in Rome's police apparatus the way they do in Italy and the provinces.

In fact, outside of Rome, there is ample evidence of regular, long-term *stationarius* posts. The legionaries who left the rupestrian inscriptions at Pselchis belong to this class. If some *stationarii* soldiers were specialized as such and served for very long periods, we have no direct evidence for it; terms of duty for a year or two seem to be the norm. While it cannot be ruled out that the two legionary *stationarii* from southern Egypt served together, the lapse of two years between their inscriptions suggests that one succeeded the other. Individual *milites stationarii* came and went; what was typically more permanent in a given locale was the post itself. In fact, two inscriptions from Asia Minor mention payment of a fine "to the stationarius at the time."[30]

So, our Tiberius Claudius and Aurelius Herminianus were at their posts temporarily, but the site of Pselchis may have had a permanent *stationarius* presence. They were two of any number of *stationarii* who served at Pselchis in the second century. Other inscriptions attest to the great importance of place in stationarial references, specified by the phrase "*stationarii* of" the communities or places where they were outposted, including Gorgorome in Galatia, Ephesus, Smyrna, and the banks of the Utica River in Africa.[31] We also know of *stationarii* in Italy, whose attachment to various communities is clearly stated.[32] Even some of the extremely brief *ostraka* sent to the very temporary *stationarii* at Mons Claudianus specify location, addressed to the *stationarii* "of the Porphyrites road" or "of the Claudianus road."[33]

Even though *stationarii* posts in the provinces were temporary assignments for detached-service soldiers, as usage of the term spread in the second

30. IGRR 4.1185 = TAM 5.1219 (Olympus in Lycia, ca. 200): στατιοναρίῳ τῷ κατὰ και[ρ]ὸν; Robert, *Études anatoliennes*, 285 (Tieion in Bithynia-Pontus) 9, l. 1: [τῷ κ]ατὰ καιρὸν στατι[οναρίῳ]. These funerary inscriptions will be discussed further below, as they pertain to the functions of *stationarii*. Cf. TAM 5.611 (Ioudda in Lydia, early third century), perhaps mentioning εἰωθότω[ν]...[...στατιωνα]ρίων, "customarily assigned *stationarii*."

31. AE 1972, 660 (second or third century; cf. AE 1972, 661), I. Ephesos 6.2319 (= ILS 2052, CIL 3.7136), I. Smyrna 382 (third century), and ILS 9072 (= CIL 8.25438, AE 1991, 1668; cf. AE 1954, 53), respectively.

32. ILS 9087 (= AE 1902, 89), a *stationarius muni/cipio Habae* [...; Haba is otherwise unattested and might mean Aveia (BAtlas 42 E4) or Heba (BAtlas 42 A3), the same post probably held by the praetorian *stationarius* in AE 1957, 218 (= AE 1981, 344; second or third century) Cf. CIL 9.2438 (quoted at the end of chapter 2 above) from Samnite Italy, mentioning the "*stationarii* and magistrates at Saepinum and Bovianum" (III, line 5: *stationari(i)s et magg(istratibus) Saepino et Boviano*).

33. ὁδοῦ Πορφυρείτου: O.Claud. 61, 62, 67, 80; ὁδοῦ Κλαυδιανοῦ: O.Claud. 64, 66, 68.

century, several outposted soldiers described themselves as *stationarii* in dedications or funerary monuments they dedicated to loved ones, apparently because they commissioned these inscriptions while they were serving as *stationarii*.[34] Likewise, when they died in service, they were called *stationarii* in the epitaphs found in the communities to which they were posted.[35]

Milites stationarii: *Status, connotations, and differentiation*

A careful reading of the evidence shows that the term *stationarius* could be used somewhat flexibly in the late principate but that it bore definite connotations of temporary guard or police duties by lower-ranking detached-service soldiers. In this way, the term differs significantly from those denoting more honored grades of service such as *beneficiarii* and *frumentarii*, with whom *stationarii* should never be confused. Because the details supporting these assertions are very technical in nature, I have set out my arguments in an appendix below.

Functions of Milites Stationarii *and Other Outposted Soldiers*

We have noted in passing that soldiers were detached from their military units and posted in small numbers at various points in Italy and the provinces for the purpose of providing some sort of police presence. The *milites stationarii*

---

34. *IG Bulg* 2.855 (near Marcianopolis in Moesia Inferior), *IG Bulg* 3.1336 (Bessapara in Thrace), *IGRR* 3.242 (= *MAMA* 8.340; near Kirili-Kassaba in Galatia), *I. Smyrna* 382 (third century), *AE* 1954, 53 (Thuburbo Maius, south of Carthage, post-177 AD), *CIL* 8.23120 (Thibica, modern Bir-Magra, in Africa Byzacena), *AE* 1922, 29 (Mauretania Tingitana; see below), *ILS* 9087 (= *AE* 1902, 89; Fossa in Samnite Italy), *AE* 1957, 218 (= *AE* 1981, 344; Heba in Etruria, approximately eighty-seven miles northwest of Rome, second or third century). The *L'Année Épigraphique* printing of *AE* 1922, 29 (= *ILAfr* 649, *IAM* 2.339), a *stationarius*'s simple memorial to his deceased wife, lists its provenance as "Azemmour?" although that city is in far western Morocco, on the Atlantic coast, an area the Roman Empire probably never contolled. Scholars today often cite this inscription as if the *stationarius* it mentions were stationed at Azemmour. This is not likely. Not only is this the only Latin inscription associated with the site, but the connection of the now-lost stone to Azemmour is also murky. By one local account, it was discovered near Azemmour; another account claims that it was brought there from le Gharb (i.e., Souk el Arba, *BAtlas* 28 C4). The latter site is obviously a more reasonable provenance, having yielded remains of a Roman camp and part of a military diploma (*IAM* 2.82). See Gascou's introduction to *IAM* 339, *Inscriptions antiques du Maroc* 2, 204.

35. *SEG* 35.724 (Beroia in Macedonia, late second or third century); *I. Ephesos* 6.2319 (= *ILS* 2052, *CIL* 3.7136, Ephesus); *ILS* 9072 (= *CIL* 8.25438, *AE* 1991, 1668; modern Henchir Techga on the northern Tunisian coast, near Hippo Diarrhytus); cf. *IGRR* 3.812 (Artanada, on the *flumen Calycadnus* in Cilicia). On *stationarii* in Asia Minor, see Brélaz, *La sécurité publique*, 254–63.

in the Egyptian desert must have been posted to guard the area, just as civilians in the Thebaid region of Egypt (where few Roman soldiers were present) were impressed into month-long terms of watchtower service and guard duty.[36] The soldier whom the Phrygian procurator posted as *stationarius* was clearly intended to safeguard a tenuous compromise between the villages of Anossa and Antimacheia, in dispute over transport duties (chapter 7 above).[37] In these cases, the need for rural security led to the posting of soldiers.

Soldiers such as the *stationarii* were typically outposted in response to pervasive security needs and difficulties in the provinces. We have encountered another case that illustrates how and why permanent military policing posts were established in civilian provinces: Pliny's request to Trajan for a centurion to be posted at Juliopolis, whose inhabitants wanted help because of the town's position and heavy traffic load.[38] The request, of course, was denied; Juliopolis was not the only town on a well-trafficked road, and in fact, its position near the provincial boundary would mean little in the way of additional regulations or special burdens.[39] Despite Trajan's rejection, however, the situation of communities such as Juliopolis probably contributed to the spread of military policing. Emperors and other responsible authorities would tend to look more favorably on extending the protection of soldier-police when compelling state interests were involved. The guarding of precious-metal mines, which were typically owned by the imperial fisc, is a significant example.[40] Soldiers, including *stationarii*, were employed as police in the enforcement of fundamental social mores, as in the persecution of Christians.[41] They were also called on to enforce the dichotomy between the free-born and slaves (chapter 2 above).

---

36. See chapter 3 above, and Bagnall, "Army and Police."

37. Frend *JRS* 46, discussed in detail at the end of chapter 7 above. The last part of the inscribed dossier shows that the agreement later broke down; if the police presence that the *stationarius* provided was not maintained, then it is possible that this was a contributing factor in the eventual failure of the 213 agreement. As noted above, an *optio* soldier was also involved in the dispute.

38. Pliny *Ep.* 10.77–78.

39. Talbert, "Rome's Provinces as Framework for World-View," 27–28: "If (travelers) chose to cross a provincial border, that was a routine matter, seldom of concern to a traveler or to the authorities, therefore. Consequently, we do not hear of efforts by the latter to mark or control provincial boundaries for policing or security purposes."

40. See, e.g., Austin and Rankov, *Exploratio*, 196; Dusanic, "Roman Mining," esp. 262–63; and Hirt, *Imperial Mines*, 93–96, 185, 198–202, 226–27, cf. 56–70, 168–97 passim, 268–69.

41. On *milites stationarii* in the persecutions, *Passio s. Mariani et Jacobi* 4 (Valerianic), *Passio SS Agapae, Irenae, et Chionae* 3.1 (Diocletianic), with Lopuszanski, "La police romaine."

It is tempting to think of Appuleius, the soldier who wrote to Pliny from "the *statio* at Nicomedia" about a possible runaway slave, as a *stationarius*, because the arrest of fugitive slaves (chapter 2 above) is one of the earliest and most clearly illustrated functions of *milites stationarii*.[42] Ulpian cited a late-second-century letter from Marcus and Commodus that mandated that *milites stationarii* help owners recapture their runaways.[43] Paulus added that "Harbor masters (*limenarchae*) and *milites stationarii* should hold arrested fugitive slaves in custody."[44] This is exactly what the *stationarii* mentioned in the Saepinum inscription were apparently doing in rural Italy when they detained transhumant shepherds.[45] Shepherds were seen as semibandit outsiders whose numbers often included escaped slaves, and the *stationarii* and local magistrates of Saepinum and Bovianum claimed that the people they attacked were runaway slaves who had stolen pack animals.[46] Their apparent overzealousness only attracted the attention of the praetorian prefects (and thus entered the historical record) because some of the affected flocks belonged to the emperor.

While it seems that the extension of military policing was usually aimed toward strengthening state control and protecting state interests, ordinary civilians clearly hoped that they would enjoy some incidental benefit. This is most clearly seen in the countless petitions that civilians sent to every variety of outposted soldiers, seeking redress when victimized by crime and support when entangled in legal difficulties. Most such documents are from Egypt, of course, and while we have examples from the early empire, the frequency of petitions to soldiers markedly picks up in the mid- to late second century.[47]

---

42. Pliny *Ep.* 10.74: *Appuleius...miles qui est in statione Nicomedensi.*

43. Ulpian *Dig.* 11.4.1.2. This chapter of the *Digesta* is discussed in detail in chapter 2 above.

44. Paulus *Dig.* 11.4.4 (= *Sententiae* 1.6.3). Lewis & Short's definition for *limenarcha*, "commander on the frontier," is incorrect. Note *P.Giss.* 1.10.4 (AD 118), *IG* 7.1826, and see further chapter 2 above. Despite Paulus pairing them with *stationarii*, limenarchs were not soldiers; Arcadius Charisius listed the office among civilian *munera*: *Dig.* 50.4.18.10; cf. *CJ* 7.16.38 (AD 294).

45. *CIL* 9.2438, III, lines 4–5 (quoted at the end of chapter 2 above).

46. On shepherds and brigandage, see chapter 2 above.

47. Campbell, *The Emperor and the Roman Army*, 434–35; Alston, *Soldier and Society*, 88–89; Peachin, "Petition to a Centurion," 81–82 (noting also increased use of documentary abbreviations). MacMullen, *Soldier and Civilian*, 53, placed this development too late, during the Severan era.

One example is the petition that two priests of an Egyptian cult addressed "to the local *stationarius*" after thieves attacked them and made off with some of their religious articles.[48] Egyptians often addressed these petitions to the nearest representative of the state; outposted soldiers in other provinces probably received similar requests for help, especially in areas with minimal civilian policing.[49]

It is striking that *stationarii* and other soldiers in Egypt received complaints about crime, because, as we have seen, Egyptian villages had fully developed civilian police institutions that were meant to handle local cases of crime.[50] These petitions probably generated some of the "orders to arrest" summonses discussed in chapter 3 above. Yet it is unlikely that the Roman government distributed soldiers in the provinces with the intention that they should become a fully fledged *police judiciaire*, and outposted soldiers did not appear to be jumping at chances to entangle themselves as referees in civilian conflicts. In fact, in the early years of the tetrarchy, Diocletian and Maximian mandated that "if anyone should think that he has suffered injury (*iniuria*) from somebody and should wish to make an official complaint, he should not direct it to the *stationarii*, but to the governor's office," further specifying that the complaint should be made in a formal petition (*libellus*) or deposition (*apud acta deponens*).[51] Despite imperial intentions and efforts to clarify official jurisdiction, soldiers came to be treated as if they had the legal jurisdiction to handle routine cases of crime, whereas this sphere traditionally belonged to

---

48. *SB* 6.9238 (Arsinoite, between 198–211): [τ]ῷ [ἐ]π[ὶ] τῶν τ[ό]πων σ[τ]ατιωναρίῳ. Literally, "to the *stationarius* of the places." There are not many papyri petitions or letters addressed to *stationarii* as such (indeed, *SB* 6.9238 is the only clear instance until the fourth century). Besides the relatively low status of *stationarii*, villagers also may not have been familiar with the latinate term, employing instead circumlocutions such as simply ὁ ἐπὶ τόπων ("he who is in charge of the area") for soldiers who would elsewhere be called a *stationarius* or *centurio regionarius*.

49. Petitioners sometimes besought multiple authorities in a scatter-shot fashion, hoping for success at some level, e.g., *P.Harr.* 2.200 (Philadelphia, AD 236), informing a centurion, a decurion, and the *stratêgos* of a theft. Outposted soldiers do not seem to have a formal, officially determined role in the judicial process. See Alston, *Soldier and Society*, esp. 88–93; and Peachin, "Petition to a Centurion" (92–94 for the meager evidence outside of Egypt).

50. On the balance between civilian and military police in late Roman Egypt, see Aubert, "Policing the Countryside."

51. *CJ* 9.2.8 (AD 284–292): *Si quis se iniuriam ab aliquo passum putaverit et querellam deferre voluerit, non ad stationarios decurrat, sed praesidalem, adeat potestatem aut libellos offerens aut querellas suas apud acta deponens.* Corcoran (*The Empire of the Tetrarchs*, 129) notes that this is presumably an extract from an imperial letter. See also Rivière, "Le contrôle de l'appareil judiciaire," 319; and cf. Bagnall, *Egypt in Late Antiquity*, 173.

recognized civilian authorities (such as local magistrates or civilian police, if not the governor). The special authority and status of soldiers meant a lot to civilians. It seems that when the emperors or governors placed soldiers among civilians for any kind of security measure, the popular desire for further protection resulted in police powers accruing to the soldiers. We have seen this happen, for instance, with the *vigiles* that Augustus instituted in Rome for the limited purpose of firefighting; but by the early third century, they had become involved in the repression of petty crimes (chapter 5 above).

To be sure, *stationarii* and other outposted soldiers had always had some involvement in the prevention and punishment of crime. We will see that centurions who commanded *stationarii* were apparently deputized to exercise this specific aspect of administration, attempting to provide security and rectify crimes in the areas under their responsibility. Such measures could benefit all civilians, the humble and the high-class alike. But a closer look at petitions reveals again the preeminent role of status, which well-positioned disputants would leverage against their opponents. As Richard Alston noted, petitioners "attempted to enhance their status, emphasising citizenship status or any other claim to importance they might have, since this might encourage more favourable and rapid treatment of their petitions. [This] shows a link between the perceived gravity of a case and the social status of the person involved."[52]

We find an interesting case of *stationarii*'s anticrime activity in a fragmentary tomb inscription from Olympus in Lycia, which includes the caveat that if anyone is caught disturbing the grave, he would have to pay the *stationarius* and the town's treasury a thousand denarii.[53] The inscription preserves no information about the deceased, but considering the penalty described in his epitaph, he may have been of local importance. Despite the private nature of the matter, state involvement here is not surprising; the basic concern for the sanctity of the dead became well established in Roman law.[54]

---

52. Alston, *Soldier and Civilian*, 91–92.

53. *IGRR* 4.1185 = *TAM* 5.1219 (ca. 200): καὶ ϛρατιοναρίῳ τῷ κατὰ και[ρ]ὸν Ἀτικᾶς χειλίας εἰς ἀρχεῖον, literally "Athenian drachmae," probably an archaism for denarii; denarii and drachmae were rated as equivalents: see Hauken, *Petition and Response*, 46–47.

54. *Dig* 47.12. Cf. *ILS* 8190 and the late-second-century Christian epitaph edited by Ramsay (*The Cities and Bishoprics of Phrygia* vol. 2, 722–23) and Calder ("The Epitaph of Aviricius Marcellus" = *BE* 1940, 159), which specifies that anyone who violates the tomb by placing another body in it must pay a fine both to the Roman treasury and to Hieropolis, the deceased's native city. The famous early first-century "Edict of Caesar" purchased in Nazareth shows imperial concern over tomb violation: *SEG* 8.13 = *FIRA* 1.69, Ehrenberg-Jones 322, *ARS* 133; see chapter 4 above.

Furthermore, a more complete inscription, which is parallel to the Lycian epitaph, provides further proof of this sort of enforcement of social mores. This
similar inscription from Tieion on the Black Sea opens with a fragmentary but
parallel warning relating to the payment of a fine "to the *stationarius* at the time"
and continues to reveal that an important member of the local elite was buried
there: "This [earth] has covered me, Julianus son of Chrestus, honorable ar[chon]
of the city for fifty years, but my brother, who is of the same name as me, endowed me as though I was still among the living, even after I had been buried
solemnly and gone down to Hades."[55] This case is a further suggestion that the
elite stratum of civilian society enjoyed first claims on the benefits of policing.

Frumentarii, kollêtiônes, stationarii, *and requisitions*

The provenances of both of the two grave inscriptions specifying payment of
fines to the *stationarius* were on important communication routes, where one
might expect some type of military presence. Olympus in Lycia is known to
have had a *beneficiarius* station.[56] Like Olympus, Tieion was situated on an
important road (running from Byzantium to the eastern frontier) and moreover was located at the mouth of the Billaeus River.[57] Outposted soldiers were
often placed along important transport and communication routes and
became increasingly involved in requisitioned transport.[58] Stopping points on

55. Robert, *Études anatoliennes*, 285 (Tieion in Bithynia-Pontus) 9:...[τῷ κ]ατὰ καιρὸν
στατι[οναρίῳ]. Πεντήκοντα ἔτη πόλεως φιλότιμον ἄρ[χοντα] Ἰουλιανὸν Χρήστου μ' ἥδε
κέκευθ[ε γαῖα ?] ἀλλά με ταρχυθέντα καὶ Ἅιδος ἐς κατ[αβάντα] ὡς ἔ(τ)' ἐνὶ ζῴοις ὄντ' ἐγέρησεν
ΑΙ [———] ὅς μοι ὁμώνυμός ἐστιν ἀδελ[φὸς.

56. *IGRR* 3.748 (= *CBI* 681). It is certainly possible that by "στατιονάριος," whoever made out
the Olympus epitaph meant the *beneficiarius consularis*, although, as I argue in the Appendix
below, ancient users of these terms tended not to equate them in the way that many modern
scholars do. Moreover, Austin and Rankov point out (*Exploratio*, 195) that many of the *stationes* of *beneficiarii consularis* were placed near other emplacements of troops.

57. Robert, *Études anatoliennes*, 285, on the Tieion (*BAtlas* 86 C2) inscription: "Il n'est pas
étonnant de trouver un *stationarius*, soldat romain chef de poste, à un endroit aussi important que Tieion dans le système des communications par ses routes et son fleuve."

58. Much of our information on soldiers and *vehiculatio* comes from official reaction to
abuses of the system, with soldiers often violating the limitations and regulations. See
Mitchell, "Requisitioned Transport," esp. 106, 111–12, 114–16. Pflaum had argued for a gradual militarization of the system (*Essai sur le* cursus publicus, esp. 143–48), and the third- and
fourth-century evidence bears out this view. Note esp. *C.Th.* 8.5.1 on *stationarii* as enforcers
of *cursus publicus* regulations; cf. *C.Th.* 4.13.2, and *C.Th.* 8.4.2 (= *CJ* 12.57.1, AD 315, with
further suggestions of soldiers' involvement in and abuse of the *cursus publicus*). See now
Kolb, *Transport und Nachrichtentransfer*, esp. 290–94; and "Transport and Communication,"
98–100. Evidence continues to emerge: note the recently edited inscription in Hauken and
Malay, "A New Edict of Hadrian."

what would become the fourth-century *cursus publicus* came to be clearly marked, showing authorized traveling soldiers and officials where they might expect a *mutatio* (a simple hostel where they could rest and change pack animals) or a *mansio* (a more elaborate and comfortable inn).[59] In the second and third centuries, *frumentarii* soldiers, in particular, are known to have been very active as message runners.[60]

Like *stationarii*, *frumentarii* seem to have been occasionally outposted as stationary military police, especially in the pre-Diocletianic province of Asia.[61] In such cases, perhaps these *frumentarii* might be called *stationarii*, but in the absence of explicit evidence, we should not presume so.[62] In fact, there are stark differences between the two. As we have noted, the *frumentarii* were a formal grade of soldier, with a headquarters in Rome, who circulated throughout the provinces as key go-betweens for emperors, governors, armies, and provincials. They are the only variety of military police to have a presence in all of the levels of policing carried out by soldiers—imperial, gubernatorial, and detached military policing. Moreover, unlike *stationarii*, who leave us with very little evidence of upward mobility, *frumentarii* were a relatively high grade of soldier who were often promoted directly to the beneficiariate and from

---

59. Private travelers could use elements of this infrastructure but would have to pay. On stopping places in the Peutinger map and itineraries, see Salway, "Travel, *itineraria* and *tabellaria*," 32; and Talbert, "Cartography and Taste," 127–28; "Rome's Provinces as Framework," 26–27; and now *Rome's World: The Peutinger Map Reconsidered*. On *mutationes* and *mansiones* in general, see Casson, *Travel in the Ancient World*, 184–204; Black, *Cursus Publicus*; Di Paola, *Viaggi, trasporti e istituzioni*; and Kolb, *Transport und Nachrichtentransfer*, esp. 209–13.

60. For the employment of *frumentarii* and other soldiers as official couriers, see Dio 79.14.1; 79.34.7; 79.39.3, Herodian 3.5.4; 4.12.6; 5.4.7–8 and .11; SHA *Hadr.* 2.6, *Maximus et Balb.* 10.3; cf. Tac. *Hist.* 2.73 and Jerome *In Abdiam* 18; *CIL* 3.2063 and 3.14191; *P.Mich.* 8.472, 487, 500–501, and 9.562; *P.Oxy.* 7.1022.24–46 and 55.3810.14–17. Rankov ("*Frumentarii*, the *Castra Peregrina* and the Provincial *Officia*," 180) thinks the main role of the *frumentarii*, in fact, was carrying messages between the emperor and provinces; on this function, see esp. Kolb, *Transport und Nachrichtentransfer*, 286–94.

61. *TAM* 5.611 (Ioudda, early third century), lines 2–3: εἰωθότω[ν] ταῖς [. . . /[στατιωνα]ρίων [κ(αὶ)] φρουμε[νταρίω]ν: "of the customarily assigned (?) *stationarii* and *frumentarii*." See also *ILS* 9474 (= *AE* 1907, 35); *AE* 1964, 231; *IGRR* 4.1368; Keil & Premerstein *Dritte Reise* no. 9 and no. 28. In the papyri, cf. *P.FuadUniv.* 14 (Memphis, third century), and *P.Mich.* 9.562 (Karanis, 119), a φρουμεντάριος 'Ρώμης' lease of agricultural land.

62. Roueché, "Rome, Asia and Aphrodisias," 115: "It seems fairly certain that when a *frumentarius* is named as responsible for a particular area—as in the case of the *frumentarii* at Aphrodisias—he is acting as, or in a manner similar to, a *regionarius* or *stationarius*—the standard titles for soldiers entrusted with peace-keeping in a particular area." The *centuriones frumentarii* at Aphrodisias (on which see below) would not be called *stationarii*, but she is right to draw the connection to *regionarii*, centurions responsible for the security of a given area.

there to the centuriate.[63] Despite some similarities in function (and reactions against their excesses), *stationarii* were not as distinctive, or distinguished, as *frumentarii* or *beneficiarii*.

In the third century especially, *frumentarii* and *stationarii* circulated in the provinces collecting resources from civilians, along with a more obscure third group, the *kollêtiônes*. Some of these collections could have been for requisitioning military supplies, although Hauken conjectures that a primary function of the *frumentarii* and *kollêtiônes* was to help local communities by providing muscle for the collection of local taxes and resources.[64] The excess and illegality with which these requisitions were exacted generated numerous complaints from provincials in the third century. In one inscription, *stationarii* and *frumentarii* are censured for "assaulting the town with intolerable burdens and damages," with the result that "having been completely exhausted by the immense costs of the outside visitors and by the great mass of *kollêtiônes*, it (the town of Iudda) is being deprived of its baths on account of this difficulty, and it is being deprived of the things necessary for life."[65] Another inscribed text, if restored correctly, preserves an unspecified official's response to civilian complaints against all three offending groups: "certain (?) exactions on their part [and on the part of the *stationari*]i and of the so-called *frum*[*entarii* and *kollêtiô*]*nes*. Hence I proclaim to them (?) ... that they abstain from their unauthorized (exactions?)."[66]

---

63. Breeze, "The Organisation of the Career Structure of the *Immunes* and *Principales*," esp. 268–69 (34–35 in the 1993 Mavors reprint).

64. Hauken, *Petition and Response*, 71. Recall Mitchell's opinion of civilian policing in Asia Minor (chapter 3 above), that it was primarily aimed at compelling peasants living around the city to pay taxes, *Anatolia*, vol. 1, 197.

65. *TAM* 5.611 (Ioudda in Lydia, modern Sacayak, early third century), lines 17–24: ἀνυποίστοις δὲ φορτίοις κ(αὶ) ζημιώμασιν ἐνσείοντες τὴν κώμην, ὡς συμβαίνειν ἐξαναλουμένην αὐτὴν εἰς τὰ ἄμετρα δαπανήματα τῶν ἐπι[δη]μούντων κ(αὶ) εἰ[ς τ]ὸ πλῆθος τῶν κολλητιώνων ἀπο[στειρεῖσθ(?)]α[ι] μὲν λουτροῦ δι' ἀπορίαν, ἀποστερεῖσ[θ]ε [δὲ κ(αὶ)] τῶν πρὸς τὸν βίον ἀ[ν]ανκέ[ω]ν.

66. *TAM* 5.154 (= *IGRR* 4.1368, near Saittai at Demirci, probably early third century), lines 2–4: τινας εἰσπράξεις παρ' αὐτ[ῶν καὶ παρὰ τῶν]/[στατιωναρί]ων καὶ τῶν καλουμένω[ν] φρουμ[ενταρίων]/[καὶ κολλητιώ]νων. ὅθεν προαγορεύω τούτῳ[(lege τουτοῖς?)]/...ἀπέχεσθαι τῶν παρ[αν]όμων. Note that the three groups are apparently distinguished from one another here. On similar complaints against *frumentarii*, cf. *TAM* 5.419 (= Hauken no. 7, from Kavacik in Lydia, to Philip the Arab, 247/248), line 7. The *frumentarii* who arrested nine imperial estate tenants in the Aga Bey Köyü inscription (ca. 200, Hauken no. 3, line 1) were probably attached to the imperial procurators. On *stationarii*, cf. *SEG* 37.1186, from Takina in Pisidia, 212/213, a rescript of Caracalla concerning illegal actions of soldiers. On *kollêtiônes* (discussed below), see also Hauken, *Petition and Response*, index; and Herrmann, *Hilferufe*, 34–36, 40. See further Meyer-Zwiffelhoffer, Πολιτικῶς ἄρχειν, 74–91.

This well-attested violence of corrupt outposted soldiers earned them much odium, ancient and modern. W. H. C. Frend, for instance, felt that the *stationarius* was "notoriously an instrument of tyranny."[67] We know that a few *stationarii* and *frumentarii*, however, were well enough liked by some provincials to have honorary inscriptions made on their behalf.[68] References to *kollêtiônes*, on the other hand, are wholly negative, with provincials consistently objecting to their unfair exactions. Our information on the *kollêtiônes* is so scant and one-sided that understanding who they were and how they operated is very difficult.

The use of the military term τάξις ("unit") to describe the arrangement of *kollêtiônes* shows that they were probably soldiers, rather than civilian officials who assisted soldiers in requisitions.[69] Matter-of-fact descriptions of individuals as *kollêtiônes* in official petitions from civilians might indicate that *kollêtiôn* was an official and widely recognized position.[70] But we have no case of a soldier calling himself a *kollêtiôn*, so, despite the separate mention of *kollêtiônes*, *stationarii*, and *frumentarii* in the inscription quoted above (*TAM* 5.611), *kollêtiôn* was likely a nickname that people applied to soldiers to describe their ad hoc duties as requisition agents. Unfortunately, we are not sure whence their name derives; conjectures include Latin *collectio* ("collecting," "gaining") or *collatio* ("collecting") or Greek κόλλα, κολλάω ("glue," "fasten").[71] *Collatio* seems most likely to me, considering the general economic and public revenue connotations surrounding this word.[72]

---

67. Frend, "A Third-century Inscription," 52. Cf. Rostovtzeff *SEHRE*, 411–12.

68. To *stationarii*: *IGRR* 3.812 (Artanada, on the *flumen Calycadnus* in Cilicia, quoted above); cf. *SEG* 35.724 (grave dedication from Beroia in Macedonia, late second or third century); two statue bases preserving dedications to *frumentarii* centurions, both found in Aphrodisias: *MAMA* 8.508 and *SEG* 31.905, for "serving honorably and bravely in the province of Asia" (ἀγνῶς καὶ ἀνδρ[ε]ίως ἀναστραφέντα ἐν τῷ τῆς Ἀσίας ἔθνει). The two nearly identical inscriptions both employ this phrase; Roueché ("Rome, Asia and Aphrodisias," 114–15) conjectures that they were set up simultaneously to honor a pair of *centuriones frumentarii*. (The second stone is lost, and the text from Sherard's notebook could conceivably be a garbled version of the first. Thus, one might object that we have firm evidence for only one *frumentarius* at Antioch, but this would probably be an unduly strict reading of the evidence.)

69. Keil & Premerstein *Dritte Reise* no. 28 (= Hauken no. 4, from Kemaliye in Lydia, ca. 197–211), lines 5, 18, 24.

70. E.g., *BGU* 23 (Soknopaiou Nesos, ca. 207, discussed below), a petition or deposition filed "against Pasión, the *dekadarchos' kollêtiôn*" (lines 4–6: κατὰ Πασίωνος κολλητίωνος δεκαδάρχου).

71. See Rostovtzeff, "*Synteleia Tironon*," 33; Robert, "Sur un papyrus," 114; Crawford (Thompson), "*Skepe* in Soknopaiou Nesos," 173.

72. For instance, the occasional monetary "gifts" that communities sent to Rome (e.g., the *aurum coronarium* or "crown gold," paid upon the accession of a new emperor) became formalized into regular taxes by the early fourth century, one of which was the *auri lustralis collatio*. See Potter, *The Roman Empire at Bay*, 397–98.

While the gathering of government revenues from provincials was nothing new, the evidence for more ambitious collection that we see in these provincial "cries for help" may be a result of the economic and military disorders that affected many areas of the empire in the third century. Moreover, rapid increases in military pay in the early third century vastly increased the state's need for revenue. Septimius Severus doubled the soldiers' pay; soon thereafter, his son Caracalla increased it considerably, and then, less than twenty years later, Maximinus raised it yet again.[73] This growth, on top of all of the empire's other needs (including provisions for the army, costs of transport, local taxes and fees), had to have been a major factor in the collections that outposted soldiers exacted from civilians.

A papyrus from circa 207 gives a rather full picture of the misbehavior of one of these *kollêtiônes*.[74] This document is a petition or deposition against Aiôn, a bullying *kollêtiôn* who serves a *dekadarchos* (a military official similar to the *regionarii* centurions, discussed below). This *kollêtiôn* was not only avoiding taxes and state service but was also extorting special emoluments from the villagers. Moreover, Aiôn was using his associates (whom he σκεπάζει "protects" like a modern mafioso) to prevent people from approaching the *dekadarchos* about these problems. He certainly was not the only *kollêtiôn* to abuse his powers and line his pockets, judging from the inscribed complaints. Considering what these sources show us about the *kollêtiônes*, Robert was probably right to emend κολληγίω(νι) in a papyrus list of taxes, bribes, and extortion (discussed below, p. 252) to κολλητίω(νι), that is, "to the *kollêtiôn*," named here as Hermias, recipient of one hundred drachmae.[75]

---

73. Basic legionary pay under Augustus had been nine hundred sesterces per annum, increased to twelve hundred by Domitian in the late first century. Within the four decades spanning the reigns of Septimius and Maximinus Thrax (193–238), basic legionary pay grew to be seventy-two hundred sesterces per annum. (There were about four hundred thousand men in the armed services at this period.) See M. A, Speidel, "Roman Army Pay Scales"; Mattern, *Rome and the Enemy*, 126–32; and de Blois, "The Military Factor in the Onset of Crises."

74. *BGU* 23, with Crawford (Thompson)'s valuable discussion "*Skepe* in Soknopaiou Nesos." On *kollêtiônes*, see further *P.Oxy.* 8.1100.19 (third century).

75. *SB* 6.9207, line. 7 (the previous line ends κολλ[......, with line 7 opening β (drachmae) ρ, thus "one hundred drachmae to two *kollêtiônes*" in addition to the one hundred for the *kollêtiôn* Hermaias?); Robert, "Sur un papyrus de Bruxelles," 114 ("Il y a eu une légère erreur de lecture: un *tau* pris pour un *gamma*." The two letters can, indeed, be difficult to distinguish in second-century papyri, e.g., *P.Oxy.* 75.5054, esp. line 12).

Curiosi

Writing in early-third-century Africa, Tertullian stated, "I do not know whether I should grieve or blush when in the notebooks of *beneficiarii* and *curiosi* for the vectigal tax (on infamous professions) Christians are included among tavern-keepers, doormen, bath-house thieves, gamblers, and pimps."[76] Uncertainty abounds concerning these *curiosi* (literally, "snoops" or "inspectors"). It might seem that they were private informants rather than soldiers, but by the fourth century, the term actually became an official description of a certain type of officer whose police duties included service as *cursus publicus* inspector.[77] As they took on greater police powers, Constantius and Julian attempted (unsuccessfully) to scale back their numbers, in response to popular hatred.[78] Tertullian may have been referring to an incipient form of this institution, and they are already mentioned in a military context in a third-century papyrus.[79] If Tertullian's remark does reflect an early phase of the later institution, then the term *curiosus* may have originated as a derogatory epithet from the reaction of the populace. But Tertullian used the Latin language very freely, so we cannot be sure exactly what type of officials he was referring to. The balance of evidence suggests that *curiosi* of our period (second and third centuries) were soldiers.[80] In any case, there are other known cases of soldiers' involvement in tax collection, including the tax on prostitution.[81]

---

76. Tert. *De fuga* 13: *Nescio dolendum an erubescendum sit, cum in matricibus beneficiarum et curiosorum inter tabernarios et ianeos et fures balnearum et aleones et lenones Christiani quoque vectigales continentur.* *Lanios* ("butchers") may be a possible reading for *ianeos* ("doormen"). Hirschfeld ("Die Sicherheitspolizei," 583) noted *ganeos* for *ganeones* ("gluttons," "debauchees") as another alternative (if not wholly satisfactory) reading.

77. *CTh* 6.29.2; Kolb, *Transport und Nachrichtentransfer*, 208 (and see index).

78 *CJ* 12.22 *De curiosis*, preserving imperial pronouncements from 355–395; see also Libanius *Or.* 2.58.18; *CTh* 6.27.23, 6.29, 12.10; Jones, *LRE*, 104, 129; Blum, *Curiosi und Regendarii*; and Paschoud, "*Frumentarii*," esp. 236–38. Paschoud sees them as specialized members of the *agentes in rebus* (the institution that succeeded the *frumentarii*) serving for one year (*CTh* 6.29.6). See also Athanasius's *Apologia contra Arianos* 74–75 on the κουριώσος τοῦ Αὐγούστου ("*curiosus* of the emperor"), whom Alexandrian Christian leaders petitioned in 355 after perceived mistreatment.

79. *P.Coll.Youtie* 2.74 (provenance unknown; third century, also mentioning a *frumentarius*; cf. *SB* 2253, a similar list from late-antique Oxyrhynchus.)

80. Some have conjectured that *curiosi* was a nickname for *frumentarii*, e.g., Lopuszanski, "La police romaine," 9. *P.Coll.Youtie* 2.74, though fragmentary, seems to list the two separately. Paschoud, "*Frumentarii*," does not equate *curiosi* with other groups.

81. *CIL* 3.13750 (= *IGRR* 1.860, Chersonesus); Sperber, "The Centurion as a Tax Collector" (on Tosefta *Demai* 6:3); Lopuszanski, "La police romaine," 6–13; and esp. McGinn, *Prostitution, Sexuality, and the Law*, 256–64. Cf. Tac. *Ann.* 4.72.

Regionarii *and other outposted centurions*

By both title and function, *regionarii* had much in common with the *stationarii*. Both were detached-service military police who were responsible for the security of the areas to which they were outposted. We must not follow other scholars in equating the two,[82] for there is a crucial difference. While *stationarii* were but regular *milites*, *regionarii* were centurions and thus fit into the broader context of centuriate policing in the empire. We have already seen that centurions performed important security missions for emperors and governors. They were also stationed among civilians in towns and in the countryside, where they took on large responsibilities for the administration of local security in the region (*regio*) of their responsibility.

The earliest attestations of *regionarii* centurions are from circa AD 100, at Vindolanda on Britannia's northern military frontier.[83] *Regionarii* are fairly well attested in Roman Britain; in fact, *centuriones regionarii* are one of the only types of police that are well attested in that province.[84] They are also known in the northern European provinces and beyond.[85] Other inscriptions preserve information about centurions being given responsibility over an area but do not employ the exact term *regionarius*.[86] We do not know if the designation *regionarius* denoted specific responsibilities beyond what was expected of other outposted centurions. At any rate, we have seen the motivation to create something like a new *regionarius* post in Pliny's letter requesting that Juliopolis receive what he called a *legionarius centurio* ("legionary centurion") on the model of the one at Byzantium.[87] By this he meant not a single outposted

---

82. E.g. MacMullen, *Soldier and Civilian*, 55–56.

83. *T. Vindol.* 250 mentions a *centurio regionarius* at Luguvalium and is probably the earliest reference (the document comes from Period 3 of the Vindolanda fortresses, ca. 97–102/103.) *T. Vindol.* 653 is a letter from a *regionarius*; *T. Vindol.* 255 may be also (see appendix of *corrigenda* in *The Vindolanda Writing Tablets* III, p. 157).

84. On *regionarii* in Britain, see, e.g., *RIB* 152 from Bath (probably second century) and 583 and 587, both from Ribchester (third century). British *regionarii* centurions are sometimes designated *praep(ositi) n(umeri) et regionis*; see Richmond's discussion in "The *Sarmatae*."

85. E.g., *CIL* 13.2958 (Agedincum in north Gallia Lugdunensis), *AE* 1944, 103, and 1950, 105 (Brigetio on the Pannonian frontier), *AE* 1953, 129 (Noricum, ca. AD 273), *IGRR* 3.301 (Pisidian Antioch).

86. E.g. *ILS* 1349 (= *CIL* 5.1838).

87. Pliny *Ep.* 10.77. Considering that Pliny wanted something identical, or very similar to, a *regionarius* centurion, perhaps the text of the letter originally read not *legionarium centurionem*, as we have it now in the single manuscript tradition that preserves Book X, but *regionarium centurionem*. See Brélaz, "Pline le Jeune." Cf. Brélaz, *La sécurité publique*, 264–67.

centurio but a detachment of *milites* led by a centurion, who would take up security responsibilities for the town. Rejecting the idea, Trajan clearly understood what he meant, describing the extant force at Byzantium as a *praesidium centurionis legionarii* ("a legionary centurion's garrison").[88]

As usual, our fullest information comes from Egypt, where an outposted centurion performing the role of *regionarius* was often called ὁ ἑκατόνταρχος ἐπὶ τῶν τόπων (a "centurion in charge of a region," literally, "over the places"). Like so many other soldiers and officials in Egypt, outposted centurions received petitions and requests for help from troubled civilians, such as one from a woman whose father and brother had disappeared on a hunting trip, raising the possibility of foul play.[89] We do not know the fate of this unfortunate family, but centurions seem to have been more able to follow up on crimes than were *stationarii* and other lower-status soldiers who sometimes received petitions.[90] Performing duties ranging from the processing of prisoners[91] to the hunting of Christians,[92] outposted centurions were among the most important elements of military policing in the Roman Empire. The considerable authority they wielded gave them greater flexibility and scope than most other police.

---

88. Pliny *Ep.* 10.78; *Ep.* 10.21 suggests one possible size and arrangement of such a centurion-led attachment: two cavalrymen and ten *beneficiarii*. For centurions in cities, see also Joseph. *BJ* 4.442.

89. *P.Tebt.* 2.333 (22 Dec., AD 216). Eusebius (*Hist. eccl.* 6.41.21, citing Dionysius of Alexandria, mid-third century) seemed to take it for granted that accused bandits would have a hearing before a centurion. Cf. *BGU* 2.522 (Soknopaiou Nesos, second century), *P.Gen.* 16 (= *Sel.Pap.* 2.289, Soknopaiou Nesos, AD 207), and many others. See Campbell, *The Emperor and the Roman Army*, 431–35. Alston (*Soldier and Society*, 86–96, with table 5.1) also offers a useful discussion, but he does not separate *beneficiarii* and centurions. See now the excellent study of Peachin, "Petition to a Centurion" (commentary on *P.Sijp.* 15). Centurions did take part in police and judicial processes, holding suspects, dealing with arbiters, writing reports. Centurions in Egypt often *seem* to be acting as judges, but Peachin points out (91) that a centurion did not formally give judgment unless he was officially appointed a *iudex datus*. Peachin also notes (84) that most petitions to centurions come from the northern Fayum region; the outposted soldiers guarding that area were probably the most accessible elements of Roman authority.

90. E.g., *P.Mich.* 6.425 (AD 198). Alston ("The Ties That Bind," 187) concludes from the papyri that an outposted centurion in Egypt "would only serve in a particular locality for a fairly brief period. Few centurions are attested [by name] in more than one petition."

91. E.g., Acts 23:17–23.

92. *Passio Mariani et Jacobi* 4, set in Africa during the Valerianic persecution: "And it was not a single *stationarius* soldier here and another there which was hunting us, as in other places, but a violent and relentless bunch of centurions" (*Nec ut aliis in locis unus hoc aut alius stationarius miles agebat sed centurionum violenta manus et improba multitudo*). Cf. Euseb. *Hist. eccl.* 4.17.

Organization, command, and effectiveness of outposted soldiers

Regionarii and other outposted centurions usually did not have to work alone. We have some attestations of centurions directly commanding *stationarii* in their anti-crime operations. For instance, we know of one centurion who was investigating a grain-export fraud and dispatched a *stationarius* to fetch some individuals for questioning.[93] We have seen that many *milites* nefariously took advantage of the freedom of action that detached service gave them. Outposted centurions generated the same sorts of complaints from harassed provincials but not as frequently.[94] Under the responsibilities of command, most outposted centurions seemed to uphold their own discipline, if not that of their subordinates. At least one *centurio regionarius* received praise for a job well done from the authorities of the community to which he was posted, honoring him for the maintenance "of justice and peace."[95]

Another important level of security in many areas was provided by watchtowers (*burgi* or *skopeloi*). Starting in the late first century, we see signs of an increase in the building of these structures not only on the frontiers but also near cities and in rural regions of the internal provinces (including some on private estates).[96] In the mid-second century, Antoninus Pius boasted of building twelve watchtowers, along with four military encampments (*praesidia*) and 109 guard posts (*phruri*), "for the sake of safeguarding the province of Thrace."[97] Sometimes soldiers served such watchtowers and guard posts, but very often they were manned by drafts of impressed

---

93. *P.Oxy.* 1.62. On centuriate command of *stationarii*, note also the centurions in the Mons Claudianus *ostraka* discussed above, who sent instructions to *stationarii*.

94. E.g., in Apul. *Met.* 9.39, the *vitis* staff that the soldier wields against the gardener suggests that Apuleius had a centurion in mind. Under some circumstances, Jews (Tosefta *Betzah ii* 6, see below) and Christians (*Passio Mariani et Jacobi* 4, above) expressed resentment against centurions, but this is a reflection of their marginalization and general alienation from the Roman state.

95. *IGRR* 3.301 (Antioch in Pisidia): ἐπιεικίας τε καὶ τῆς εἰρήνης; cf. the Aphrodisias dedications praising two *frumentarii* centurions (*MAMA* 8.508 and *SEG* 31.905, discussed above, for "serving honorably and bravely in the province of Asia").

96. See MacMullen, *Soldier and Civilian*, 37–42; Isaac, *Limits of Empire*, 136, 178–86; Austin and Rankov, *Exploratio*, 66; Sperber, *The City in Roman Palestine*, 121, 126–27, 154–55. On precedents from ancient Judaea, see Williams, *The Reach of Rome*, 17–18. Although they were exceptional, note the fascinating fortified water holes, watchtowers, and signal stations that the Romans constructed in Egypt's eastern desert from the late first century on, discussed by Zitterkopf and Sidebotham, "Stations and Towers," and Bagnall, Bülow-Jacobsen, and Cuvigny, "Security and Water."

97. *ILBulg.* 211 (= *AE* 1957, 279): *ob tutelam provinci(ae) Thraciae*; see also the very similar *AE* 1927, 168, and cf. *CIL* 3.3385; *RIU* 5.1127–37; *CIL* 8.2494–95, all from the mid-second to early third centuries. These inscriptions may somehow be related to the Hadrianic attempt to mark the boundary of Thrace and Moesia (on which see Talbert, "Rome's Provinces as Framework," 28), but the provenance of some falls well within the provincial boundary.

civilians, who were organized and supervised by centurions.⁹⁸ The involvement of Egypt-based centurions (and other commanders) in arranging military and civilian guard-post personnel has left us a number of revealing guard rosters on *ostraka*, which show us the variety of ways in which guards were posted and rotated.⁹⁹

Extant duty rosters (*pridiana*) from larger camps spell out assignments in much greater detail, telling us much more about the daily service of the soldier-guards in the *ostraka*. For instance, one roster from a fort in the Nile Delta during Domitian's reign consists of a complex grid outlining specific duties for thirty-seven different men over the course of at least ten days.¹⁰⁰ Some soldiers serve in one capacity for an entire week; others switch jobs daily, performing menial duties ranging from work in the armory, baths, or latrines to sweeping the barracks. Other tasks in the roster are parallel to the daily service of *stationarii* road guards at Mons Claudianus: *"via nico"* seems to mean that the soldier in question was posted as a guard on the road to Nicopolis; *"speclat"* means *speculator* ("guard"). Many entries beginning with *sta-* for *statio*, such as gate guard (*sta por*) or HQ guard (*sta principis*), relate to the internal security of the camp, with soldiers temporarily serving similarly to MPs in the modern American military.¹⁰¹ An entry reading *pagane* or *pagano cultus* has been interpreted as a "plainclothes" undercover operation.¹⁰² This

---

98. See esp. Bagnall, *The Florida Ostraka*, pp. 23–27; and "Army and Police." Also note *P. Fay.* 38, ca. AD 200, in which a centurion instructed the villagers of Taurinus to make sure their watchtower was adequately manned. On levies of *burgarii* watchtower guards in other parts of the empire, see *ILS* 8909 (AD 138, the earliest attestation) and, above all, *IGBulg.* 3.1690 (on which see Rostovtzeff, "*Synteleia Tironon*," and *SEG* 45.845 and 45.2214). *IGBulg.* 3.1690e contains a provision excepting a new emporium from having to provide *burgarii*. Scholars have come to no consensus on whether *burgarii* would be full soldiers, semimilitary local recruits, or ordinary civilians. By analogy with the Egyptian *skopelarioi*, the *burgarii* could have been peasants.

99. The most valuable are from the *Ostraka in the Amsterdam Collection* (*O.Amst.* 8–15; second century, provenance unknown; cf. *O.Florida* 24). One-day posts seem to have been the norm, but *O.Amst.* 8 (especially elaborate) and *O.Amst.* 13 show evidence for half-day posts, with alternating midday reliefs marked "ἄνω, κάτω." (Cf. Vegetius 3.8 on the division of days and nights into *vigiliae* ["watches"] for military lookouts.) *O.Florida* 26 is a list of guards batched together by month.

100. *P.Gen.Lat.* 1.v = number 9 in Fink, *Roman Military Records on Papyrus* (henceforth *RMRP*).

101. At one point (113), Fink calls soldiers at these *sta-* posts *stationarii*, even though the term is not attested this early, and his reference to MacMullen's *Soldier and Civilian* would lead the reader to much later sources.

102. *P.Gen.Lat.* 1.v = Fink *RMRP* 9, line 15. Fink (p. 113) points to Pliny, *Ep.* 7.25.6, as a parallel for *pagano cultus* as "plainclothes." Here, Pliny discusses a veteran who surprised him with his high level of refinement and culture. Pliny warns his friend Rufus, *sunt enim, ut in castris sic etiam in litteris nostris plures cultu pagano, quos cinctos et armatos et quidem ardentissimo ingenio diligentius scrutatus invenies*. Bagnall (*The Florida Ostraka*, p. 26) points out that ὁ παγανός usually means "civilian" in the Greek papyri (cf. Suet. *Aug.* 27.3).

interpretation is uncertain, but we have some attestations of soldiers operating under the guise of civilians.[103]

Some soldiers were given duties that took them far from camp. One entry in the same list of duties simply reads *insula*, presumably meaning the Alexandrian harbor island Pharos. C. Iulius Longus is cited as having left with someone, their destination lost. The next soldier on the list was placed at station for an entire week, it seems (the text is fragmentary), and another left for the granary at Neapolis. This last entry is widely spaced, filling the columns for most of the ten days. It is doubtful that he was on that assignment just for that week; rather, the writer was most likely indicating that he was already at the granary and was expected back no time soon.[104]

In fact, the other side of this same rich duty roster contains a list of soldiers on detached service.[105] Here, we have record of a soldier who left for the same granary in September or October 80 and did not return until January of the next year. One soldier left to make papyrus, another to dredge harbors. Others are sent away for guard duty, escorting grain convoys, or river-patrol service. Some of the exact dates are lost, but stretches of six months are not uncommon.[106] The constant trickle of men into and out of the cohort could not have helped this unit's sense of cohesion.

Indeed, throughout the empire, the outposting of *stationarii* and other detached-service soldier-police probably affected their home units negatively. A strength report from Trajan's reign likewise mentions requisition errands (for clothing, grain, horses, cattle) but also lists losses from deaths (accidental and in battle), vexillation service, transfers, scouting missions, service for an imperial procurator, and possible stragglers or deserters who could not be accounted for.[107] We can certainly understand now why Hadrian, in his speech to the *Legio III Augusta*, explicitly acknowledged the difficulties that detached service caused the legion, since it lost a different cohort each year to the

---

103. Philo *In Flaccum* 120, Joseph. *AJ* 18.55–62 (suggesting a favorite modus operandi of Pontius Pilate), and Epictetus *Diss.* 4.13.5; cf. Tac. *Hist.* 1.38, 1.85.

104. For commentary on *P.Gen.Lat* iv. part 5, see Fink *RMRP* 9, 106–14, and Davies, "The Daily Life of Roman Soldiers," 304, 321, 323. Compare Pliny's assignment of troops to accompany an imperial procurator on a mission to procure grain from Paphlagonia: *Ep.* 10.27.

105. *P.Gen.Lat.* ir. part 2 (Fink *RMRP* 10).

106. *P.Gen.Lat.* ir. part 2 (Fink *RMRP* 10). *P.Vindob.* L 112 r. (Fink *RMRP* 11) is a similar (but more fragmentary) list of men on detached service, and *P.Vindob.* L 4 (Fink *RMRP* 11bis) may be a list of their replacements.

107. *C.Pap.Lat.* 112 = Fink *RMRP* 63.

governor's *officium*, and many of the remaining soldiers served in "several diverse outposts (*stationes*) which keep you far from one another."[108]

In some situations, the stress that detached service inflicted on the legions could have deadly results, since weakening legions' cohesion and focus could undermine the army's fundamental purpose: winning battles against foreign enemies. This is the impression, at least, that Dio Cassius gives in his depiction of the great military disaster of AD 9, when Quinctilius Varus lost three legions in the Teutoburg Forest. Dio partially blamed detached service for the defeat: "Varus did not hold his military forces together, as is fitting in a hostile atmosphere, but distributed many of his soldiers to feeble communities who requested their help, so that he might guard certain parts of the land, round up bandits, or escort supply convoys."[109] Dio's statements, which have some echoes of Trajan's objections to Pliny's desire to use more soldiers as police, may reflect as much what he thought of detached-service military policing in his own time (the early third century) as what had gone on two hundred years previously.

Military men stationed in civilian areas were supposed to command respect, endowed as they were with the aura of state authority. But outposted soldiers sometimes performed poorly as police and failed to be effective agents of stability and security. In their perceived duty of rooting out banditry, the training, resources, and authority that the state invested in them was not always enough to keep bandits from the occasional win. In the Trajanic military-strength report from an unspecified unit, discussed above, listed among the numbers of the *θetati* ("dead") is a cavalryman who was "killed by bandits."[110] Dionysius, the bishop of Alexandria, claimed that he survived the Decian persecution because a party of civilians pretending to be bandits scared

---

108. ILS 2487 = Smallwood *Docs.... Nerva* no. 328 (AD 128) line 6: *quod multae quod diversae stationes vos distinent.* Note that Hadrian clearly differentiates between the cohort assigned to the proconsul (lines 3–4) and those soldiers doing detached service in *stationes*.

109. Dio 56.19.1: Οὔτ᾽ οὖν τὰ στρατεύματα, ὥσπερ εἰκὸς ἦν ἐν πολεμίᾳ, συνεῖχε, καὶ ἀπ᾽ αὐτῶν συχνοὺς αἰτοῦσι τοῖς ἀδυνάτοις ὡς καὶ ἐπὶ φυλακῇ χωρίων τινῶν ἢ καὶ λῃστῶν συλλήψεσι παραπομπαῖς τέ τισι τῶν ἐπιτηδείων διέδωκεν. Velleius Paterculus's account (2.117–18) does not substantially differ from Dio's analysis of the disaster's root causes, although Velleius focused on Varus's judicial activity, saying nothing about detached service. Velleius Paterculus served as a military officer under Augustus and Tiberius.

110. *C.Pap.Lat.* 112 = Fink *RMRP* 63, col. 2, line 10: a cavalryman *occisus a latron[i]bus*. The expression *thetatus* ("theta'd" for "dead" in Latin) comes from the initial letter of θάνατος, the Greek word for death. In *ILS* 5795 (Africa, ca. AD 153), lines 11–13, bandits attack and strip a veteran military surveyor. Phaedrus 5.2 (= Perry 524) has a bandit nearly defeat two soldiers (one of whom flees in terror). Cf. Arrius Menander *Dig.* 49.16.6.9, and Tac. *Hist.* 2.23, in which Martius Macer's gladiators rout a squad of auxiliaries loyal to Vitellius.

away his military captors.[111] A similar, albeit fully fictional, incident reminds us that aspects of the outposted soldier's job could spook even the brave, especially when their duties brought them into dark, unfamiliar places. Iamblichos's second-century novel *Babyloniaka* contained an episode in which a force of soldiers, in the course of burning a notorious cannibal bandit's house late one night, detect some fugitives from the law. The fugitives are able to escape when they claim to be ghosts of the bandit's victims, which frightens the soldiers into taking to their heels.[112]

Social Impact of Detached-Service Policing

When Tertullian commented (*Apol.* 2.8) on the distribution of soldiers in the provinces, he attributed a constructive purpose to them: to search out bandits. Some soldiers certainly engaged in this positive activity. We have already noted, for example, the praetorian cohort and detachment of twenty marines that helped a third-century *agens at latrunculum* fight bandits in Italy.[113] We know from Egypt's papyri that many civilians felt that the local outposted soldier might help them rectify problems in their lives. The state distributed skilled soldiers as builders, surveyors, and administrators, who played important parts laying down new roads, regulating traffic, and helping to settle boundary disputes.[114] People clearly hoped that the authorities would be able to provide them with security. Sometimes outposted soldiers performed their policing tasks too zealously, as perhaps the *stationarii* in Italy did when they arrested shepherds of imperial flocks (although here, theft was the more likely motivation; chapter 2 above). A lengthy tax record on papyrus mentions soldiers fighting bandits but also has them slaughtering people from various villages. This added to the social and economic disruption that already plagued the eastern Nile Delta in the second century.[115]

---

111. Euseb. *Hist. eccl.* 6.40; indeed, he was supposedly rescued a second time by civilians who bested a large centurion-led party: *Hist. eccl.* 7.11.22. If these stories have any truth (the circumstances of Dionysius's actions are very dubious), the soldiers' failures might reflect the lack of interest on their part in carrying out the persecution.

112. Iamblichus's *Babyloniaka* is lost, but its plot is fortuitously preserved in the ninth-century reading diary of Photios (*Bibliotheke* codex 94, 74b24–b31 for the episode here). Cf. Phaedrus 5.2 (= Perry 524).

113. *ILS* 509 (= *CIL* 11.6107), discussed in chapter 5 above. See Flam-Zuckermann, "À propos d'une inscription," and Riess, "Hunting Down the Robbers."

114. On boundary disputes, see, e.g., *CIL* 8.23910; on military surveyors, see Campbell, ed., *The Writings of the Roman Land Surveyors*.

115. *P.Thmouis* I, col. 99, on which see Alston, *Soldier and Society*, 83–86; de Blois "The Military Factor in the Onset of Crises," 500. The villagers seem to have been connected somehow with the so-called *Boukoloi* rebellion. Italian *stationarii*: *CIL* 9.2438 (chapter 2 above).

While many of the attested provincial reactions to military policing were very negative, these were mixed with positive ones, as with the few outposted soldiers who we know received honorary inscriptions from the communities they served.[116] The tenures of many *beneficiarii consularis* or *stationarii* were likely rather uneventful. By and large, most outposted soldiers probably engendered neither much popular antipathy nor much affection. Much of their time at their posts would have been spent in totally unexceptional and uninteresting occupations, watching over roads, towns, offices, or outposts.[117] In some cases, men probably saw a year or two on detached service as a welcome break from everyday life in the legion.[118] One can easily imagine, furthermore, that men who were detached from their legions and posted among civilians would be very interested in forming relationships with local women.

Augustus's ban on soldiers marrying lasted more than two hundred years, until it was lifted by Septimius Severus in 197. Nevertheless, throughout the first two centuries, it is clear that the ban did not prevent soldiers from having relations with civilian women, monogamous or otherwise. The legal appeals of soldiers show that many had started families with long-term partners.[119] While sizable civilian centers grew up around major legionary centers, detached service offered soldiers additional opportunities to meet women. One popular first-century story recounted the romance between a widow of Ephesus and a soldier guarding the crucifixion site of executed temple robbers. She had been starving herself to death grieving inside the tomb of her recently deceased husband, until the soldier kindly befriended her and eventually seduced her. After they became nightly lovers, the family of one of the criminals took advantage of the soldier's dereliction of duty and removed one body from the cross to bestow a more proper burial. When the soldier discovered this in the morning, he was about to anticipate punishment and disgrace by committing suicide when his clever lover suggested that they hoist her husband's corpse onto the cross instead. The reader is left with the impression that the characters in this yarn lived happily ever after.[120] A less happy tale was the

---

116. *IGRR* 3.812, *MAMA* 8.508 and *SEG* 31.905 (which is not to say that *all* members of the community agreed that these *stationarii* and *frumentarii* were good men).

117. See Bagnall, "The Roman Garrison of Latopolis," 143–44, for the despair of a lonely guard waiting to be relieved (ἀλλαγή as a change of personnel); cf. *P.Mich.* 3.203 (Pselchis, modern Dakkeh, in southern Egypt).

118. Cf. *P.Mich.* 8.466, showing a soldier's desire to be outposted to the governor's *officium*.

119. See Campbell, "The Marriage of Soldiers," and Phang, *The Marriage of Roman Soldiers*.

120. The story is known from two early sources: Phaedrus *App.* 15 (= Perry 543); Petron. *Sat.* 110–13. Phaedrus is entirely positive toward the lovers and offers no moral censure; the reaction of Petronius's characters is a bit more mixed. See further Pecere, *Petronio: La novella della Matrona di Efeso*, and Huber, *Das Motiv der "Witwe von Ephesus"*.

Jewish slander against Jesus, that he was born of an adulterous affair between Mary and a soldier named Panthera.[121] Aurelian apparently executed a soldier for committing adultery with the wife of a man who was lodging him; his biographer claimed that the emperor had the soldiers' legs tied to two different bent-back trees, ripping him in two from the crotch up. This punishment supposedly had the intended effect of terrorizing the other soldiers into behaving properly.[122]

Soldiers certainly frequented brothels and other zones of prostitution in civilian areas, as evidenced by many boastful graffiti from Pompeii.[123] There was usually nothing illegal or terribly socially problematic about soldiers buying sex from professionals. Rape is another matter. Throughout the centuries, rape has been a common problem in civilian-military relations, and it was likewise an unfortunate feature of detached service in the Roman Empire. It is hard to detect because of the social shame that attends rape; the Greek and Latin sources are rather reticent about it, aside from postcombat sacking of cities. Problems of status and definition create more obscurity. According to the *Historia Augusta*, Macrinus, tipped off by one of his *frumentarii*, severely punished billeted soldiers who had had sex with the maid of their host. Rape is not specified here; instead, the woman is maligned as being of ill repute, and as a slave, she lacked the status to prosecute anyone if she were the victim of sexual violence. The soldiers' actions were not lawful (Paulus *Dig.* 1.18.21), but Macrinus avenged the woman's owner, not the woman, and what most interested the biographer was the novel punishment (being stuffed into a freshly killed oxen), anecdotal of Macrinus's cruelty. In fact, it was probably low-status women who suffered most from sexual exploitation and rape (as we define it) at the hands of soldiers, especially after the third century, when soldiers were increasingly billeted in cities.[124] Rabbinic

---

121. *Panthera*, which means "panther," is an attested name (e.g., *CIL* 13.7514) but could be meant as a beastly nickname. See Origen *Contra Celsum* 1.28, 1.32–33, 1.69 (the only source, to my knowledge, that states that Panthera was a soldier, which the rabbinic sources do not specify; Origen's lengthy treatise amply quotes the reasoned anti-Christian sentiments of the second-century philosopher Celsus, who cited an unnamed Jewish source for this particular attack); Schaff, *History of the Christian Church*, vol. 2, 91; Stauffer, *Jesus and His Story*, 24; Brown, *The Birth of the Messiah*, 534–37; Tabor, *The Jesus Dynasty*, 59–72 (with overblown discussion of *CIL* 13.7514); Schäfer, *Jesus in the Talmud*, 17–21, 56, 98.

122. SHA *Aurel.* 7.3–4; cf. *Alex.* 52–53.

123. Phang, *The Marriage of Roman Soldiers*, 244–51; graffiti: e.g., *CIL* 4.2145 and 4.8767. On soldiers (esp. praetorians and marines) in and around Pompeii, cf. Ortisi, "Roman Military in the Vesuvius Area."

124. SHA *Macr.* 12.4; Tac. *Agr.* 31 refers to violation of civilian women; Phang, *The Marriage of Roman Soldiers*, 252–60; MacMullen, *Corruption*, 209–17; cf. Ziolkowski, "*Urbs direpta*." On differences between Roman and modern legal concepts vis-à-vis rape (falling somewhere between *rapina*, *stuprum*, and *vis*), see Robinson, *The Criminal Law of Ancient Rome*, 71–73; and *Penal Practice*, 162.

sources are more outspoken, reflecting the alienation and loathing that many Jews felt toward gentiles in general and Roman soldiers in particular. The disruptions caused by military patrols would have been a major part of Jewish-gentile interaction. Gentiles were thought to be so lacking in sexual self-control that some rabbis urged Jews to keep their male children far away from non-Jews.[125] Second- and third-century texts raise the issue of women who suffered sexual assaults from Roman soldiers; the mere presence of a large number of intrusive soldiers may have been enough to render priests' wives ritually unclean.[126]

Sexual crime is just one part of the mass of evidence for soldier-police engaging in sheer abuse and corruption. With the possible exception of the soldiery itself, there was no articulate class in the societies of the Roman Empire that did not feel some fear and loathing toward outposted military police. The attitudes of the early Christians, to take one provincial perspective, present a complex mixture. The authors of the New Testament generally took pains not to offend the Roman authorities, and Paul is depicted as having a number of respectful encounters with representatives of Roman power, including soldiers.[127] Soldiers are at least considered worthy of redemption: Jesus had a positive encounter with a centurion in Capernaum; in Mark's gospel, the centurion at Jesus's crucifixion was one of the first and few people to understand who Jesus was; finally, the first gentile convert accepted by Jesus's disciples was supposedly a centurion.[128] (It is noteworthy that the earliest Christians seem to have had a negative view of ordinary soldiers but a fairly positive view of their officers.) Yet there was never any clear atonement for the execrable enthusiasm of Jesus's military executioners, whereas the bandit dying by Jesus's side joins him in paradise.[129]

125. See Satlow, "Rhetoric and Assumptions," esp. 138.

126. Isaac, *Limits of Empire*, 117, citing y. Nedarim II.42d; y. Ketubot ii 26d; and m. Ketubot ii 9. Cf. Potter, *The Roman Empire at Bay*, 132; and the Midrash Rabbah Lamentations 1.16(45) = 4.19.22, on the threat of mass rape in a postcombat situation, which Pucci Ben Zeev connects to the Diaspora Revolt of 116–17: *Diaspora Judaism in Turmoil*, 116.

127. E.g. Acts 21:37–40.

128. Matt. 8:5–13 = Luke 7:2–10; Mark 15:39 ("Truly this man was God's son!"; cf. Matt. 27:54, Luke 23:47); Acts 10.

129. Mark 15; Matt. 27; Luke 23; John 19. Only in Luke does one bandit embrace Jesus: Luke 23:43. Later Christian myths made converts of Mark's centurion, of "Longinus" (the unnamed soldier who pierced Jesus's side with a spear in John 19:34), and even of Pontius Pilate; qv. in Cross and Livingstone's *Oxford Dictionary of the Christian Church*, and note the several legendary tales concerning the "good bandit" and Pilate in Ehrman and Pleše, *The Apocryphal Gospels*. Elitist classical sources did not place centurions above regular soldiers to the same degree as Christians; Persius (3.77) called them a *gens hircosa*, a tribe that stinks like goats. Cf. Horsfall, *The Culture of the Roman Plebs*, esp. app. 1.

Overall, the oral traditions that solidified into the gospels are critical of the soldiers and their malicious interactions with civilians. Jesus sent the demon whose name was "Legion" into a herd of pigs; it is easy to read this story as a muted attack on the soldiery, who were associated with pigs and pork.[130] When soldiers approached John the Baptist to ask what they should do, he told them only not to extort money from civilians.[131] There is scholarly debate regarding whether these soldiers are King Herod's or not, but that is largely a moot point. By the time the gospels reached their final form in the late first century, their audiences would have identified them with their own interactions with Roman soldiers. These texts spread far beyond their initial geographic setting, and later Christian writings echoed their objections to soldier-police treatment of Christians. Around 107, Ignatius wrote to Rome's Christian community, whither he himself was bound, in transit to his martyrdom after his arrest. He complained about the brutality of the soldiers guarding him, comparing them to wild beasts.[132] The next few centuries certainly saw no improvements in the relationship between outposted soldiers and Christians.

We find similar alienation and animosity in rabbinic texts from the late principate. One Mishnah supplement notes, "A patrol of Gentiles came into town and the townspeople were afraid that the soldiers might harm them and therefore we prepared them a calf and we fed them and gave them drink and rubbed them with oil so that they would not harm the townspeople."[133] We have already seen that the midrash on Deuteronomy 32:13–14 reveals how some Jews felt about the Romans' presence:

And he ate the produce of my field: these are the four kingdoms; *and he made him suck honey out of the rock and oil out of the flinty rock*: these are

---

130. Mark 5:1–20 = Luke 8:26–39; Crossan, *The Historical Jesus*, 313–18. (Noting the minimal Roman presence in the area in Jesus's time, Chancey is unconvinced: *Greco-Roman Culture and the Galilee of Jesus*, 55–56. Even so, one should consider the story's later resonance with its audience.) The symbol of the Tenth Legion, long stationed in the Levant, was a boar. This was the legion that took Masada, where pig bones have been found from their occupation. Note Roth, "The Length of the Siege of Masada," 91, and *Logistics of the Roman Army*, 26–32; and Ben-Yehuda, *Sacrificing Truth*; cf. Champlin, "The Testament of the Piglet," and Magness, "In the Footsteps of the Tenth Roman Legion."

131. Luke 3:14. On extortion (*diaseismos*), cf. *SB* 6.9207, the private expense account cataloguing official corruption, discussed below, p. 252.

132. *Ep. ad Romanos* 5.1; see also C. P. Jones, "A Note on Diogmitae."

133. Tosefta *Betzah* ii 6, probably third century. Cf. B. Talmud *Shabbat* 145b (third century): "There is no festival without a patrol coming to Sepphoris...there is no festival without the governor or his retinue...coming to Tiberias." Trans. Isaac, *Limits of Empire*, 116.

the oppressors who have taken hold of the land of Israel and it is as hard to receive a farthing from them as from a rock, but tomorrow Israel inherits their property and they shall enjoy it as oil and honey. *Curds from the herd*: these are their consulars and governors; *fat of lambs*: these are their tribunes; *and rams*: these are their centurions; *herds of Bashan*: these are *beneficiarii* soldiers who take away (food) from between the teeth (of those who eat); *and goats*: these are their senators; *with the finest of wheat*: these are their matrons.[134]

It is striking to find so many elements of Roman rule worked into this one concise expression of provincial discontent.

Of course, Christians and Jews had no monopoly on the fear and animosity felt toward soldier-police. What is most striking about the rest of imperial society's general wariness toward outposted soldiers is that the ill will was shared in common by the lowest and the highest strata of society. On the one hand, we have ample criticism of the greed and rapacity of soldiers from members of the senatorial literati, such as Tacitus and Cassius Dio.[135] Lawyers took it for granted that soldiers passing through an area would damage property and possibly harm its inhabitants.[136] Writers of more moderate means thought that soldiers were motivated mainly by the prospect of getting money from others, as when the apostle Paul asked, "Who ever serves as a soldier and pays his own wages?"[137] Among the lower classes, we have the humble Thracian villagers at Skaptopara, an otherwise advantageous site but sadly situated between two military bases. As a result, "Soldiers who are dispatched elsewhere leave their proper routes and show up here and likewise press us hard to furnish them quartering and provisions without paying anything."[138] The

134. Sifre Deut. 318, ed. Finkelstein, 359–60, ca. third century. Trans. Isaac, *Limits of Empire*, 115. (I have italicized the original words from Deuteronomy 32:13–14.)

135. E.g., Tacitus *Hist.* 1.46, 2.56, 3.76; Dio 79.26–28. On Dio and Herodian, see de Blois, "The Military Factor." This literary theme continued into later centuries: SHA *Aurelian* 7.5–8; cf. *Paneg. Lat.* 12(9).21.

136. *Dig.* 19.2.13.7. Here, Ulpian seemed to have large units in mind, but he also probably meant the reader to understand a domestic, peacetime setting, i.e., depredations by Rome's own men. Tenants who fled would not be liable for the damages if they had just cause to fear for their safety, which is not hard to imagine. See Frier, *Landlords and Tenants*, 96–98, 138–41.

137. 1 Cor. 9:7: Τίς στρατεύεται ἰδίοις ὀψωνίοις ποτέ; my trans.

138. *IG Bulg* 4.2236 (= Hauken no. 5, AD 238), lines 44–49: στρατιῶται ἀλλαχοῦ πεμπόμενοι καταλιμπάνοντες τὰς ἰδίας ὁδοὺς πρὸς ἡμᾶς παραγείνονται καὶ ὁμοίως κατεπείγουσιν παρέχειν αὐτοῖς τὰς ξενίας καὶ τὰ ἐπιτήδια μηδεμίαν τειμὴν καταβαλόντες. Hauken's trans., adapted.

petitioners from the imperial estate at Aragua complain that although they are not on a road or near a military encampment, soldiers also come to bother them.[139] In absolute terms, the villagers would have more to lose from the rapacity of wandering soldiers than a Tacitus or a Dio would. In any dealings with soldiers, it seems that all civilians feared getting robbed, cheated, or beaten.[140]

A number of official measures were enacted, which aimed to prevent abuse of civilians.[141] We do not need to dwell on the fact that these measures were insufficient to prevent the recurrence of unfair exactions by soldiers and officials. Since policing in the Roman Empire was often focused on preserving the interests of the state and cooperative elites, we should not take it for granted that there should be continuous efforts on the part of Roman authorities to protect the weak. It is true that the repetition of pronouncements against unjust military exactions reveals failure to solve the problem, but it also reveals continuous interest and investment of energy from the highest levels of the Roman state. At the same time, government measures against outposted soldiers' illegal exactions were not *solely* motivated by a desire to help lowly provincials. Concern over military discipline was certainly an additional factor, along with concern over how the representatives of the Roman state were perceived. Note the following missive, issued during the reign of Hadrian:

> Proclamation of Marcus Petronius Mamertinus, Prefect of Egypt. I am informed that without having a warrant many of the soldiers when traveling through the country requisition boats and animals and persons improperly, in some cases seizing them by force, in others obtaining them from the *stratêgoi* through favor or obsequiousness, the result of which is that private persons are subjected to insults and abuses and the army is reproached for greed and injustice. I therefore command the *stratêgoi* and royal scribes never in any case to furnish to any person without a warrant, whether traveling by river or by land, any contribution for the journey, understanding that I will vigorously punish anyone

---

139. *MAMA* 10.114 (= Hauken no. 6, AD 244–247).

140. The editor of *P. Yadin* 11 (AD 124), N. Lewis, thought he detected usurious abuse of a Jewish civilian at the hands of a centurion: *The Documents from the Bar-Kokhba Period*, 41; cf. Tac. *Ann.* 14.31.1. Also note 1QpHab III–XII for general resentment toward the greed of Roman soldiers (here, "the Kittim") in the Dead Sea Scrolls.

141. E.g., Ulp. *Dig.* 1.18.6.3 and 1.18.6.6; cf. 1.18.6.5, and 47.17.3.

who after this edict is discovered receiving or giving any of the aforesaid things.[142]

Evidence keeps mounting against the soldiers. A newly published inscription
from the province of Asia shows that Hadrian himself condemned these *vehiculatio* abuses in the strongest terms and tried to correct them:

Good fortune. Imperator Caesar Trajan Hadrian Augustus, son of the
divine Trajan, grandchild of Nerva, *pontifex maximus, tribunicia potestas*
for the thirteenth time, *consul* for the third time, *pater patriae, proconsul*
says: During the stay which I made among your people I had become
aware that the cities and the villages are being troubled more than the
rules allow by the soldiers who are travelling through. In order that
they shall know in the future what to keep themselves away from, that
you (shall know) what you have to perform and what (you shall) not
tolerate even if being requested, I found it necessary <to set forth>
(these matters) by an edict: (1) A wagon shall only be given to those who
have a diploma. He who uses the wagon shall pay what is fixed in the
diplomas. (2) No one shall have the right to take a guide since soldiers
do not need to leave the public roads, and since they do not leave they
have no need for anyone to show the way. In case the roads become
invisible because of a heavy snowfall, only then shall it be allowed to
take a guide. (3) It shall not be allowed to demand breakfast, dinner,
barley or fodder for free nor should anyone give these when called
upon. (4) But free lodging shall not be allowed for any soldier to take
while travelling on private business. But if someone is passing through
while on duty or if they are bringing the ruling power's money (χρήματα
τῆς ἀρχῆς κομίζοντες), or transporting prisoners or wild animals, public
lodgings shall be given only to them and provisions at the market price
which was effective ten days earlier. Then if anyone contrary to this
shall make an exaction or use force, the names of those who take shall
be sent to the provincial governor and my procurator (nothing is small,

---

142. *PSI* 5.446 (AD 133–137): Μᾶρκος Πετρώνιος Μαμερτῖνος ἔπαρχος Αἰγύπτου λέγει:
ἐπέγνων πολλοὺς τῶν στρατ[ι]ωτῶν ἄνευ διπλῆς διὰ τῆς χώρας πορευομένους πλοῖα καὶ
κτήνη καὶ ἀνθρώπους αἰτεῖν παρὰ τὸ προσῆκον, τὰ μὲν αὐτοὺς π[ρ]ὸς βίαν ἀποσπῶντας, τὰ δὲ
καὶ κατὰ χάριν ἢ θαραπείαν π[α]ρὰ τῶν στρατηγῶν λαμβάνοντας, ἐξ οὗ τοῖς μὲν ἰδιώταις ὕβρις
τε καὶ ἐπηρείας γείνεσθαι, τὸ δὲ στρατ[ι]ωτικὸν ἐπὶ πλεονεξίᾳ καὶ ἀδικίᾳ διαβά[λλ]εσθαι
συνβέβηκε. παρανγέλλω δὴ τοῖς στρατηγοῖς καὶ βασιλικοῖς ἀπαξαπλῶς μηδενὶ παρέχιν ἄν[ε]υ
διπλῆς μηθὲ ἓν τῶν (ε)ἰς παραπομπὴν διδο[μέ]νων μήτε πλέοντι μήτε πεζῆ βαδί[ζον]τι, ὡς [ἐμ]
οῦ κο[λ]άσοντος ἐρρωμένως ἐάν τις ἁλῷ μετὰ τ[οῦτο] τὸ διάταγμα λαμβάνων ἢ διδούς τι τῶν
[προειρη]μένων. Trans. from *Sel. Pap.* 2.221.

i.e., insignificant, which assists the cities for the future so they suffer
no harm) and shall be forwarded to me. Let it be posted.[143]

Despite so many official pronouncements, imperial literature gives us the impression that people felt that the mere proximity of soldiers meant that they
would soon be losing their pack animals, especially their donkeys.[144] Thoroughly understanding this aspect of detached-service soldiering helps us understand the literature of the period, which is peppered with bandits and
misbehaving soldiers. Consider the military jargon strewn throughout
Apuleius's *Golden Ass*, in which bandits act like soldiers—posting pickets, reporting casualties, holding levies, swearing oaths to Mars, and so on.[145] With
this over-the-top military language, I suggest that Apuleius's bandit tales are
often meant to evoke in the reader's mind not criminals but soldiers. The
transparent parody comes full circle when we finally meet a soldier and view
him up close—the centurion who tries to "requisition" the donkey at the end
of Book IX acts more like a bandit than a soldier. The novel's original readers
probably would have drawn immediate connections to real-life cases of outposted soldiers' misbehavior, perhaps even reading the mock-military bandit

143. Hauken and Malay, "A New Edict of Hadrian from the Province of Asia," lines 8–11,
35–42: κατὰ τὴν ἐπιδημίαν ἣ ἐπεδήμησα/τῷ ἔθνει ὑμῶν ᾐσθόμην τὰς πόλεις καὶ/τὰς κώμας
πλέον τῶν δικαίων ἐνοχλου/μένας ὑπὸ τῶν διοδευόντων στρατιωτῶν....(35) Καὶ ἄν παρὰ/
ταῦτα ἀξιώσωσίν τινες ἢ βιάζωνται [τὰ]/τῶν λαμβανόντων ὀνόματα τῷ τοῦ ἔθνο[υς]/
ἡγουμένῳ πεμπέσθω καὶ τῷ ἐπιτρόπῳ μ[ου]/(οὐδὲν δε μεικρόν ἐστιν τὸ βοηθῆσον ταῖς πό/
λεσιν πρὸς τὸ μηδὲν βίαιον παθεῖν) καὶ/πρὸς ἐμὲ ἐπιστελλέσθων./πρ[οτ]εθή[τω]. Hauken and
Malay's trans., quoted in its entirety. Soldiers may also have been blamed in the fragmentary
Tymion inscription (AD 205 or 208), but they are not clearly mentioned in the text's surviv-
ing portions; see Hauken et al., "A New Inscription from Phrygia," and Tabbernee and
Lampe, *Pepouza and Tymion*, chap. 4.

144. Phaedrus 1.15 and *App.* 10; Epict. *Diss.* 4.1.79; Apul. *Met.* 9.39, 10.1; Julian *Or.* 7.224a. Cf.
Petron. *Sat.* 82, on a soldier swindling a sword from a civilian; and *P.Fouad* 28 (Oxyrhynchus,
AD 59), an incredible petition to the *stratêgos* in which a veteran claims that he was kicked so
hard on the right shin by a donkey that a slave was leading that he nearly died (a topos of the
genre). The veteran claims that the slave fled and presents himself as having had no other
choice but to seize the ass that kicked him, which he still has in his possession. When the
slave reappears to get his animal back, the veteran sends this preemptive petition. In all likelihood, the veteran had acted similarly to the thieving soldier in Apul. *Met.* 9.39.

145. Military terms used in Apuleius's bandit tales, *Met.* 4.8–22, 7.4–10, include *castra*, *expug-
nare*, *dux*, *vexillarius*, *antesignanus* (soldier who fights before the standards), *sacramentum* (oath),
commilito, *militia*, *contubernalis*, *cohors*, *conferta manus* (close-packed formation; cf. *cuneus*), *ag-
minatim*, *speculatores* (scouts), *proelium*, *tirocinium*, *manipulus*, *stipendium* (pay), *viaticum* (travel
allowance), *castellum*, plus several references to Mars. This is Apuleius's own spin, rather than
something absorbed from the original Greek version. The Groningen commentators took the
military terms at face value, as straightforward descriptions of the way large bandit groups
would have operated: Hijmans et al., *Apuleius Madaurensis IV, 1–27*, app. 1.

narratives as veiled criticisms of the corrupt soldiery.[146] Note also the fact that
Apuleius describes his bandits as spirited, physically robust, lusty rustic
youths, just the type of men, in other words, that Roman military writers
thought should be enrolled into the legions. Cassius Dio, in fact, thought that
military recruitment was a primary means to keep young men from becoming
bandits in the first place.[147]

Others drew connections between criminal bandits and the soldiers who
were supposed to fight them.[148] Frankly, many soldiers *were* criminals. The
jurists spilled much ink on the issue of recruits or soldiers who were accused
of crimes, and Pliny and Trajan dealt with fugitive slaves who were almost illegally enrolled in the ranks.[149] By the late fourth and early fifth centuries,
emperors were permitting civilians to kill soldiers who were trespassing or
committing acts of highway robbery (*CJ* 3.27). Rome's soldiers were obviously
an imperfect instrument of law enforcement.

Conclusion

In praising the Roman Empire, articulate members of the provincial elite
recognized the great importance of Roman soldiers. Appian offered this
reflection:

> It has been nearly two hundred years from the establishment of the
> empire to the present time, during which the city of Rome has greatly
> been subjected to order, her revenues have grown exceedingly, and
> everything has advanced towards a steadfast, long-lasting peace and
> prosperous security.... They invest their empire with a ring of great

---

146. Compare Tac. *Agr.* 30 and the fourth-century *Testamentum Porcelli*, a lampoon of
crooked soldiers, on which see Champlin, "The Testament of the Piglet."

147. Vegetius *De re militari* 1.6; Dio 52.14.3, 52.27.5, 75.2.5–6, and Phang, *Roman Military
Service*, 156; cf. *Expositio totius mundi et gentium* 50 on the suitability of Thracians for
soldiering.

148. E.g., Varro *DLL* 7.3.19: "Bandits (*latrones*) are so named from *latus*, 'side,' since they
were at the king's side and carried swords at their sides, and since they were hired, later they
called them 'attendants' (*stipatores*) from *stipatio*, 'retinue.' Indeed, 'wages' in Greek is *latron*.
For this reason, the old poets sometimes call soldiers *latrones*. But now marauders of roads
are called *latrones*, because just like soldiers, they have a sword, or because they lie hidden
(*latent*) to carry out their ambushes." Cf. Festus p. 105 Lindsay, Serv. *ad Aen.* 12.7.

149. E.g., Papinian *Dig.* 48.2.22, Arrius Menander *Dig.* 49.16.4.8 and *Dig.* 49.16 passim;
Pliny *Ep.* 10.29–30.

(military) encampments, and they guard all this land and sea just as if it were an estate.[150]

By the time Appian was writing in the mid-second century, many soldiers were posted from the legions to the empire's interior. The functions they performed among civilians in the course of their detached service were important to the continued prosperity and security of the empire, but one might feel more comfortable viewing them from a safe distance. Considering the many problems that soldiers caused civilians, what is most surprising is the fact that the Roman state kept turning to them for policing needs, sometimes at the explicit request of civilians.[151] The several roles they played in provincial security and administration are a testament at least to their importance and usefulness to the state, if not always their uprightness and effectiveness.

---

150. Appian, *Praef.* 7: ...καὶ πάντα ἐν εἰρήνῃ μακρᾷ καὶ εὐσταθεῖ προῆλθεν εἰς εὐδαιμονίαν ἀσφαλῆ....τήν τε ἀρχὴν ἐν κύκλῳ περικάθηνται μεγάλοις στρατοπέδοις καὶ φυλάσσουσι τὴν τοσήνδε γῆν καὶ θάλασσαν ὥσπερ χωρίον. Cf. his contemporary, Aelius Aristides 26.67 and 101; and in the Constantinian era, *Paneg. Lat.* 12(9).21.

151. E.g., Pliny *Ep.* 10.77; Frend *JRS* 46, line 32.

9

Conclusion

THE ROMANS AND their empire's subject peoples had a range of institutional and noninstitutional approaches to handling conflicts and problems. We have treated the institutional end of this spectrum, especially policing. The scattered evidence reveals diverse police arrangements, and we can render this complicated variety more sensible by dividing it according to different levels: first, a fundamental dichotomy between civilian police (chapter 3) and soldier-police. Our focus has been the latter, further divided into three sublevels: imperial (chapters 4 through 6), gubernatorial (chapter 7), and military (chapter 8). These different levels cooperated in the recovery of runaway slaves (chapter 2); we know that governors were sometimes involved with civilian police; and *frumentarii* worked across all military-policing levels. Civilian and military police occasionally worked together during the persecutions. Otherwise, there is not much evidence for joint operations, and these policing levels were not particularly well coordinated. Moreover, there were defects at every level, from cruelty and greed to basic ineffectiveness.

It is all the more surprising, then, that during the first three centuries AD, scores of powerful Romans (emperors, governors, procurators, mayors, councilmen) chose to expand policing. There were republican-era antecedents, but by and large, they followed the example of Augustus, who was willing to create new institutions to help keep order throughout the Roman world (chapter 4). He was most concerned with Italy and, above all, Rome, of course. The growth of military policing spread from there. To be sure, nothing within the time and space of our focus would match Rome's eventual security complement of more than twenty thousand military police. Nearly all governors and procurators in the *pax Romana* would have been familiar with Rome, so they would have seen firsthand the advantages (and disadvantages) of having some kind of police force.

Perhaps the most important factor driving Roman military policing *outside* of Rome is the fact of an expensive, professional standing army. Everyone knew that the emperors' power ultimately rested on the army, which enjoyed the investment of massive state resources. Soldiers practiced a range of skills that could be helpful in running an empire. Lacking anything like ancient

China's large, highly trained bureaucracy, when daunted Roman rulers needed the help of responsible, able, disciplined agents, where else could they turn but to the soldiery? So, outside of combat (which most men never saw), soldiers contributed their skill as engineers and their talent as administrators and also their vigilance as guards. As we have seen, soldiers in the late principate increasingly took on policing responsibilities in the empire, complementing the diverse but limited civilian-policing institutions that were already there.

The frequent use of soldiers as police fits into a broader trend of administrative militarization during the late principate. This is not the only way to interpret the evidence, and not all scholars think that militarization is a valid or useful framework for this period. Jean-Michel Carrié, for example, sees the administrative and police work by soldiers more as evidence for bureaucratization within the military, rather than the militarization of policing and administration.[1] This is an interesting line of thinking, which brings the *beneficiarii* to mind (although they certainly had some police functions). Ultimately, though, the evidence for military policing is too vast to be explained away via redefinition. *Beneficiarii* remained soldiers, and while some men specialized in administrative assignments, many of the soldiers outposted for security tasks (such as *stationarii*) would have returned to regular service. Soldiers increasingly appear as enforcers of "orders to arrest" and edicts of persecution. They did not just regulate traffic or serve as governors' secretaries and messengers; they arrested or killed enemies of the state, processed prisoners, and guarded countless trouble spots. We see hints of the growth in policing by soldiers in first-century depictions of Jesus's arrest. In the earliest gospels, Jesus is taken by an armed rabble (*ochlos*, Mark 14:43, Matt 26:47). Luke (22:52) adds officials from the Temple guard. By the time John is finally written, a full-fledged military unit (*speira*) leads the arrest party (18:3, 18:12). When Origen was commenting on the gospel of Matthew in the third century, the arrest scene did not make sense to him without soldiers, so he referred his readers to John's account.[2]

By the end of the twentieth century, a scholarly consensus emerged that viewed early Roman imperial government as essentially passive, its bureaucracy as practically nonexistent, and its state institutions as having little impact

---

1. Carrié, "Police" and "Developments in Provincial and Local Administration."

2. Origen *Commentary on Matthew* §99. Dating the gospels cannot be done precisely; there seem to be early layers in John, but most scholars date its final form to the very late first century.

on a populace that largely relied on self-help. Usually, any one individual instance of policing, treated in isolation, can still fit within these views comfortably enough. But considering all elements of policing and public order together, the minimalist consensus loses much of its force. Augustus, his successors, and their underlings were increasingly willing to impose soldier-police on areas of civilian life that were hitherto barely touched by the military. But now thousands of military police worked in Rome itself, whose sacred boundary had excluded soldiers during the republic. In the provinces, soldiers fought bandits, arrested runaway slaves, secured roads, regulated traffic, carried messages, and received complaints from victims of crime. These developments were not planned from the start by some imperial mastermind or central power, but the accretion of policing experiments widened the prospect of state control throughout the vast territories that answered to Rome. Ineffectiveness and abuse of civilians by soldier-police threatened to undermine imperial power over Rome's subjects. Nevertheless, by the mid third century, Decius, Valerian, and the provincial governors who served them could even use these soldiers for novel interference in the religious lives of Roman citizens. Broadly viewed, Roman policing reveals a state that was much more ambitious and grasping than previously thought.

Emperors, governors, and procurators directly applied soldiers to various security challenges, but legionaries were not their only tools. Just as important as the direct use of soldiers was the overall management of public order. Rather than using soldier-police for every challenge they faced, emperors and other high officials negotiated with conflicting parties, balanced rewards with punishments, and issued threats. The higher classes were obviously advantaged in these processes, but society was not so unequal that the poor were stripped of any protection, however imperfectly realized their rights were. Victimized peasants thought it worth their while to petition outposted soldiers, governors, even the emperor himself. Moreover, new police institutions (say, watchtower guards organized by the local centurion or the *vigiles* in Rome) could benefit all law-abiding people, rich or poor. Public order and the rhetoric of peace and stability were threatened by corruption, despite frequent official efforts to reinforce proper conduct.

The trend of using soldiers as police has been the focus of these pages, which is not to minimize the importance of noninstitutional remedies or of civilian police. These three factors—self-help, civilian police, and military police—coexisted without being locked into a zero-sum game where an increase in one necessarily led to the decreased prevalence of others. But by scrutinizing the balance of these three forces, we can understand why the military element was growing rapidly in the late principate. One aggrieved party could render community self-regulation inoperative by appealing to the Roman authorities, and civilian police were hampered by limited authority and jurisdiction. When Roman governors or other *potentes* became involved in local problems, they faced the temptation to use soldiers at their disposal as police, if they thought that doing so could improve the situation. Any legionary or auxiliary grunt could conceivably find himself guarding a road or town for a single day, or a year or two, as a *miles stationarius*. Highly dependable and literate soldiers had better opportunities for ample travel (as *frumentarii*), for clerical work on the governor's staff (various *officiales*) or at semiindependent stations (*beneficiarii consularis*), and for high-level policing duties (*centuriones regionarii*). I imagine that the vast majority of soldiers who served ten or twenty years performed some kind of police duty at some point.

On the civilian side, it seems that almost any male could end up doing police work, broadly defined: a peasant farmer or a small boy could be impressed to serve as a watchtower guard or to man a town watch in an emergency. Guards' routines must often have involved drudgery, whether they were civilians or soldiers. On the whole, though, these were not bad jobs. Watching over a road is preferable to breaking rocks in a mine. Many police assignments—again, civilian and military—went to upwardly mobile, ambitious men, such as the *frumentarii* and *beneficiarii* soldiers destined for the centuriate. Provincial lictors probably strived for something akin to what we think of as middle class; junior magistrates such as eirenarchs and aediles aimed even higher. Even the slaves who served as estate bailiffs or *servi publici* were at the pinnacle of what anyone could reasonably hope to achieve as a slave.

Rome in the History of Ancient Law and Order

We should now widen our scope and ask where Roman policing fits into the broader swath of history. Here, I will also offer some tentative thoughts and bare outlines on other time periods and suggest avenues for further work.

To be sure, the Romans did not invent law enforcement. Early legal collections such as the *Code of Hammurabi* do not mention specialized police forces, but they do evidence state mechanisms of trial and punishment. By the time of the New Kingdom, Egypt had a significant paramilitary security force, the Medjay. Sources from numerous premodern civilizations reveal state measures against slave flight and marketplace cheating, with many official regulators combating the latter.[3] There is certainly sufficient raw material for

---

3. For documentation on these matters, see chapters 2 and 3 above.

comparative studies on each of these important topics, which could distinctly place these aspects of Roman policing in the wider context of global history.

At first glance, Greek civilization does not seem to offer much evidence for institutional policing. In the classical period, Athens offers the fullest evidence, including the use of public slaves and market officials (but not soldiers) as police. Virginia Hunter's intelligent book *Policing Athens* describes law and order there as driven by self-help and noninstitutional social control, similar to Nippel's analysis of Rome. There is room for another view. Edward Harris has argued that the power of public officials and the strength of formal law curtailed self-help, and I find his objections to Hunter's model convincing.[4] Material on policing in the Hellenistic kingdoms is very meager and scattered, with one major exception: Ptolemaic Egypt. For decades, this was a neglected topic. Now, John Bauschatz's careful analyses of the papyrological documentation present an impressive picture of Ptolemaic policing, which he argues was fairly effective and relatively untainted by corruption.[5] As case studies, Athens and Ptolemaic Egypt warn us not to assume a lack of institutional law enforcement in ancient states. To return to Roman civilization, the self-help, noninstitutional enforcement model is on much stronger ground for the republic than for the empire. But even for the republic, the level of policing and other state mechanisms of public order has probably been somewhat underestimated. As republican law and order is beyond our present focus, I leave this an open question for now.

The sources are not conducive to writing a narrative history of Roman policing, but we can at least compose a very tentative sketch. The traditional magistrates of the Roman republic held significant policing powers. None of these proved able to stabilize Rome during the crisis of the republic, which brought about riots, lynch mobs, and dubious novel expedients (the *SCU*, proscriptions, military dictatorship). Enough has been said above about Augustus, his various reforms and new institutions, and his transition from warlord to figure of peace. The transfer of power to and reign of his successor, Tiberius, was a vital test of the new state police. Here, one also sees the maturation of the principate and of petition-and-response governance, plus the gradual growth in military policing. Tiberius's dynastic successors used praetorians and other agents to counter perceived threats. Military-police units

---

4. See esp. Harris, "Who Enforced the Law in Classical Athens?"

5. Bauschatz, "Policing the *Chôra*," "The Strong Arm of the Law," "Ptolemaic Prisons," and "Archiphylakitai." We look forward to his forthcoming book. These works wholly supersede Kool's 1954 monograph *De Phylakieten*. On policing in other Hellenistic kingdoms, bits of evidence are treated in Jones, *The Greek City*; Brélaz, *La sécurité publique*; and Dmitriev, *City Government*.

were stationed in Ostia, Puteoli, Lugdunum, and Carthage—each of these probably involved imperial decisions, but details are lacking.

This brings us toward the end of the first century AD, during which we see fairly rudimentary civilian police forms, the slow spread of a handful of police units, soldiers occasionally carrying out police tasks, and larger army units responding to crises. The story of policing in the Roman world could have stayed on this track for several decades, but instead, it entered a period of creative, dynamic growth. There were new institutions such as the irenarchate and *milites stationarii*, which are first firmly attested during Trajan's reign (98–117) or just after it (*regionarii*, for example). Sources for some other figures attested before Trajan explode in the second and third centuries (*frumentarii, beneficiarii consularis*). There is no clear explanation for why this growth occurs at this time. If an emperor was the prime mover behind some of this expansion, we may be seeing the shadow of Domitian (r. 81–96). He was unashamed of his power and was interested and involved in provincial affairs. But the postmortem condemnation of his memory obscures the record.

The Jewish diaspora revolt at the end of Trajan's reign was tumultuous for many eastern communities (chapter 3); it may have encouraged the continued growth of policing. That trend was already established, and throughout the empire in the second and third centuries, soldiers became increasingly involved in provincial administration, sometimes in ways that were tangential to policing per se. With the waxing power of praetorian prefects, urban prefects, and other officials, Roman policing authority itself markedly expanded during the late second and early third centuries. Emperors, governors, and commanders continued to find useful reasons to outpost soldiers for security tasks as they began to face the challenges of the third century, with concomitant requisitions and persecutions of Christians.

The focus of our analysis ends with the mid-third century for various reasons. Texts illustrating Decius's and Valerian's ambitious persecutions in the 250s show what was probably the high point of imperial policing, when the police institutions that first appeared in earlier centuries were fully fledged. Evidence for the following decades is scant; we are able to discern near military and economic collapse in many areas. Policing changed over the course of the late third and fourth centuries, and the explosion of evidence for the fourth century alone merits its own volume. In the course of this book, we have noted some significant late-antique developments. We still see soldiers trying to keep the peace sometimes, especially in big, riot-prone cities. But some of the major military-police institutions were replaced by civilian ones: *agentes in rebus* supplanted the *frumentarii*, for instance (chapter 6); *curiosi* seem to be civilian inspectors by the fourth century (chapter 8); and civilian *riparioi* come to predominate in Egypt (chapter 3). Some military police disappear altogether, namely, all of the units in Rome (chapter 5). The needs and priorities of the late Roman state were different now, as was the structure of the army. While the army of the *pax Romana* was largely a peacetime force, military pressure on the frontiers was already a problem by the late second century. External threats became a serious menace in the third and fourth centuries, when civil war also consumed the lives and energies of thousands of soldiers.

I can do no more than offer a rough sketch of policing during even later centuries—here, too, there is much need for future work. In the west, the civilian and military police institutions of the principate disappeared with the decline of cities and the collapse of Roman power over the course of the fifth century. Early Germanic law codes feature stringent penalties for inciting or abetting runaway bondsmen, which is quite reminiscent of Roman concern over slave flight.[6] But gone are the institutional mechanisms of enforcement and fugitive recovery detailed in *Digesta* 11.4 (public slaves, magistrates, *limenarchae, stationarii,* governors; see chapter 2).

Policing in the early Byzantine Empire is easier to approach, for it offers a definite institutional history with the reassertion of imperial power in the east. Until their disappearance in the seventh century, *agentes in rebus* were under the command of the powerful *magister officiorum*. This "master of offices" served as both the head of civilian administration and the chief of the new imperial guard created by Diocletian or Constantine, the roughly six-thousand-strong *scholae Palatinae*. Initially elite battle troops, they became increasingly ceremonial and prestigious, their ranks filled by upper-class youths. By the reign of Leo I (457–474), the emperor's private security was handled by about three hundred *exkoubitores*. Throughout the empire, military officials and other strong men often hired soldiers as private retainers to protect their employers and intimidate their opponents. Provincial administrators of this period seem to have lacked the scope of action enjoyed by provincial governors during the principate. For instance, Justinian (r. 527–565) forbade them to hire or appoint civilians to fight bandits. (The fact that he also banned bishops from this practice shows their increased role in public life.) In addition to the soldiers who occasionally fought (or caused) disorder in Byzantine cities, the early-fifth-century *Notitia urbis Constantinopolitanae* mentions various elements of civilian policing in the new capital city: teams of volunteer

---

6. E.g., *Laws of the Salian Franks* (*Pactus Legis Salicae*) 39.1 (sixth century), and Rothair's mid-seventh-century *Lombard Law* 267, both edited by Drew.

firefighters (*collegiati*), public slaves (*vernaculi*), and night guards (*vicomagis-tri*). Overall law and order in Constantinople was the responsibility of the eparch of the city, a post analogous to the urban prefect of Rome in later antiquity.[7] We have here the same kind of experimental mix of civilian and military police seen in the principate. Despite vast changes, Byzantine history offers not only institutional parallels to earlier Roman praxis but even some basic continuity throughout Byzantium's long path to its final defeat in 1453.

Roman Policing: Toward a Final Assessment

Octavian Augustus initiated Rome's new police contingents to safeguard his own power and to make Rome's inhabitants feel more secure. These two motivations are not mutually exclusive. I must admit that trying to assess Roman motivations in general vexes me, because I assume that each reader will interpret the evidence through the lens of his or her own worldview. Much of this story looks like a Machiavellian approach to maintaining power (what could be more straightforwardly tyrannical than the praetorian guard?). Nouveaux Marxists will see elites fighting for their perpetual domination, manipulating the state to protect their economic power and social prestige.[8] Admirers of Rome will appreciate wide-scale policing as part of Rome's military and administrative grandeur. There is some evidence for all of these views—each is valid to some degree, because Roman policing was so multifaceted and complicated. Rome's admirers cannot ignore the corruption, brutality, and failure we often see in policing. Those inclined toward a darker view of policing must remember that ordinary people expected the powers-that-be to provide security, sometimes even asking for police in their area, and that the state did expend energy helping ordinary people and fighting corruption. In other words, the legacy of Roman policing is as mixed as the legacy of Rome itself.

The broad development of public order and policing from early Rome to the Byzantine Empire needs further work. This much is clear: during the first

---

7. Justinian's ban: *Nov.* 134.1–2. On policing and relevant officials in the early Byzantine Empire, qv. index of Jones, *LRE*, and see individual entries in *The Oxford Dictionary of Byzantium*, all written by A. Kazhdan, with the exception of "Boukellarioi" by E. McGreer. Also note Carrié, "Police," and Lenski, "*Servi Publici* in Late Antiquity." Dvornik's *Origins of Intelligence Services* is impressive for its remarkably broad scope (from the ancient Near East to Mongol China and early Russia), but his material on the Roman Empire is not always sound.

8. Note, e.g., Mitchell, *Anatolia*, vol. 1, 197, quoted in chapter 3 above. Yannakopulos writes in this vein as well in "Preserving the *Pax Romana*."

three centuries AD, leaders in the Roman Empire frequently embraced institutional policing as a way to keep order, enforce laws, and preserve their own power. I am not claiming that institutional policing was necessary or inevitable or the best course. We cannot even determine for certain if these policing experiments were, on the whole, successful—we have nowhere near the right amount or kind of data for such a conclusion. We can go as far as to say that it was not a total failure: the victimized Egyptian peasant who gives her petition to a centurion, the family tombstone that claims that a *stationarius* will help ensure the sanctity of the grave, the wise traveler who knows to stay close to a governor's security entourage... Numerous anecdotes and chance documents prove a general, widespread faith in institutional policing. That is clearly the path that the Roman state chose over noninstitutional means of enforcement, to the apparent gratification of some of the empire's subadministrators and ordinary inhabitants.

I will end, though, on a note of caution. Cases of noninstitutional self-regulation are less likely to enter our source record. Institutional means of enforcement were most readily available to elite minorities who spoke Greek or Latin. Thus, the historical record may be seriously skewed. The next step is a serious study of the other side of the coin, approaches to maintaining order that did not involve the Roman state.

Appendix: *Differentiating* Stationarii *from* Beneficiarii Consularis *and Other Detached-Service Soldiers*

Studying the detached-service soldiers brings with it certain difficulties in terminology. Out of all of the varieties of outposted soldiers whose duties touched on public order, *beneficiarii consularis* are most closely identified with the word *statio*, the term for the posts they served in the provinces. A common Greek expression for a *beneficiarius consularis*, στατίζων, is suggestive of these *stationes* (although the transliteration βενεφικιάριος is more common). In Latin, *stationarius* would seem to be a reasonable equivalent, and in fact, we know of many soldiers who were detached from their legions and outposted in the provinces, where they were called *stationarii*. It is not surprising, then, that the two are often confused. But there is no undisputable evidence that *beneficiarii consularis* and *stationarii* had anything to do with each other, and the word *stationarius* never appears in any of the hundreds of extant *beneficiarii* inscriptions. Oddly, detached-service *beneficiarii consularis* were outposted to a well-established system of *stationes*, which at first glance appear to serve a military policing purpose but, in fact, did not have much to do with public order at all. Conversely, *stationarii* soldiers' designation strongly suggests some tie to the provincial *statio* network of the *beneficiarii*, when, in fact, there was no such link. Rather, the purpose of *milites stationarii* was as focused on actual military policing as that of the *beneficiarii consularis* was focused on administrative tasks.

The challenges of military jargon, along with ostensible similarities in the service functions of *stationarii*, *frumentarii*, and *beneficiarii consularis*, have led many good historians to muddle these separate groups via inexact terminology.[1] By the

---

1. Examples of inexact terminology (especially relating to *stationarii*) include Calder, "Colonia Caesareia Antiocheia," 82; Rostovtzeff, *SEHRE*, 411–12; Pflaum, *Essai*, 166; Robert, "Sur un papyrus," 113; MacMullen, *Soldier and Civilian*, 52–56 passim; Fink, *RMRP*, p. 113; Russell,

fourth and fifth centuries, the extant sources on *milites stationarii* relate them more specifically to frontier guards, rural military police, and regulating officers of the *cursus publicus*.[2] In the second and third centuries, the term was not so fixed. Yet we can still draw certain distinctions. First, while many provincial *stationarii* likely had some sort of official contact with provincial governors, there is no firm evidence of governors directing soldiers who are explicitly called *stationarii*.[3] When scattered among various minor outposts, *stationarii* apparently acted freely. With one possible known exception, the elite detached-service soldiers who were most closely associated with the governor, his *singulares*, are never called *stationarii*.

The possible exception is *AE* 1937, 250, a brief dedication to Asclepius from a soldier named Zotikos, who styled himself κῆρυξ ἱππεὺς/σινγλάριος στα[....]/ριος: "herald, cavalry guard, *stationarius*(?)."[4] Michael P. Speidel suggests that he might be a *stator* ("guard"), citing *CIL* 3.12356 as a parallel, but στα[τιωνά]/ριος is a very good fit. Speidel notes further that Zotikos might be listing posts he has held not all at once but serially, as a sort of military *cursus honorum*.[5] Another, more likely possibility is that Zotikos was a cavalry guard, not in the provincial armies but originally in Rome, with the *equites singulares Augusti* that directly served the emperors alongside the praetorian guard (see chapter 5 above). In this scenario, Zotikos's service as a *stationarius* would be parallel to the common practice of dispatching praetorians for stationarial detached service in Italy and the provinces.[6]

Furthermore, the second- and third-century sources leave us with the firm impression that the *milites stationarii* of the late principate were low in rank. Although

---

"A Roman Military Diploma," 487; Bagnall, Sijpesteijn, and Worp, *Ostraka in Amsterdam*, 6; and Bagnall, "Army and Police," 84 n. 32. One could cite more recent examples. The most commonly confused are *stationarii* and *beneficiarii consularis*; we will see below that the authors of the seminal works on each (Petraccia Lucernoni, *Gli stationarii*; Nelis-Clément, *Les beneficiarii*) are not wholly agreed at properly differentiating the two.

2. See, e.g., Amm. Marc. 18.5.3; *CJ* 4.61.5, 12.1.6, 12.22.1, 12:57.1; *CTh* 8.5.1; and further documents cited in Petraccia Lucernoni's *Gli stationarii*, "Elenco prosopografico," nos. 69 and 79–116.

3. *Passio Mariani et Jacobi* 4 alludes to *stationarii* being used to pursue Christians in the Valerianic persecution, which might suggest gubernatorial direction. By analogy, the Phrygian imperial procurator of Frend *JRS* 46 (discussed at the end of chapter 7 above) agreed to post a στατιωνάριος to stabilize a conflict between two villages. In Italy, of course, there was no governor to supervise the *stationarii* there; the Saepinum inscription (*CIL* 9.2438; see chapter 2 above) suggests that the praetorian prefects might attempt to exercise some control over them in response to complaints of abuse, but it is notable that whereas the original complaints were made against the *stationarii* and the local magistrates, only the latter are admonished in the inscribed letter of the prefects.

4. *AE* 1937, 250; from modern Vasada in Galatia, of unknown date.

5. M. P. Speidel, *Guards of the Roman Armies*, 102.

6. See, e.g., *ILS* 9072 from Africa; *AE* 1981, 344, from Italy; *ILS* 2052 from Ephesus (= *I. Ephesos* 6.2319); cf. references to praetorians in Greek cities cited by Rigsby, "Graecolatina," 252.

some members of the privileged praetorian guard were outposted as *stationarii*, even these men seem to have enjoyed little prestige within their units. Judging from the epigraphic evidence, some *stationarii* felt that the temporary post brought them some distinction. Minor camp posts held by at least a few *stationarii* would have freed them from some of the physical hardships that the lowliest soldiers had to suffer. As *custos armorum*, the first *stationarius* we met with in southern Egypt enjoyed status as an *immunis*, granted immunity from certain unpleasant duties (*munera*). So did our herald Zotikos.[7] But there is no evidence that any *stationarii* ever reached the centuriate. Any onetime *stationarius* who did eventually gain higher rank found his past stationarial service too insignificant to list in later career inscriptions—this despite the fact that soldiers who never reached the centuriate still thoroughly listed modest honors and distinctions.[8] This is a major reason they must be strictly differentiated from upwardly mobile *frumentarii* and *beneficiarii consularis*, who commonly used these detached-service posts as career stepping-stones.

Our best indication of a *stationarius's* potential upward mobility (and it is only potential) is the *stationarius* honored by the community where he was posted, who was also described as the son of a centurion.[9] This same inscription has also caused confusion of the *stationarii* and *beneficiarii consularis*, for a single *beta* in this text has led to a crucial misinterpretation by some scholars: Ἀρτανάδα τῆς Ποταμίας ἐτείμησεν Γ. Ἰούλιον Οὐάλεντα β' στατιωνάριον, Ἰουλίου Οὐάλεντος ἑκατοντάρχου υἱὸν, ἁγνῶς ἀναστραφέντα, μαρτυρίας χάριν. The β' after Julius Valens's name is expanded by Petraccia Lucernoni and others (including Nelis-Clément) to β(ενεφικιάριον), thus suggesting promotion to *beneficiarius* or else providing false proof for the common misconception that *beneficiarii consularis* can be equated with *stationarii*.[10] That *beta* is not an abbreviation at all but is numeric. If Artanada were served by more than one *stationarius*, the *beta* could designate the honoree as "the second *stationarius*." But there is another clear, related alternative that we can confidently adopt: β' is part of Julius Valens's nomenclature here, standing for *Junior*, to differentiate father and son—both of them are mentioned in the inscription, and their names, after all, are identical. We can read: "Artanada of the River-district honored Gaius Julius Valens Junior, stationarius, son of Julius Valens, centurion, as testimony to his blameless conduct." Thus, the text has nothing to do with a *beneficiarius*, and Ott is right in noting that *beneficiarii* and *stationarii* never appear together *in statione*.[11]

---

7. Tarrunt. *Dig.* 50.6.7. (*SB* 6146–6147 and *AE* 1937, 250.)

8. See Lendon's discussion of *ILS* 2117 in *Empire of Honour*, 246–47.

9. *IGRR* 3.812 from Cilicia, of uncertain date.

10. Petraccia Lucernoni, *Gli stationarii*, pp. 38–39, 84; Nelis-Clément, *Les beneficiarii*, 357.

11. Ott, *Die Beneficiarier*, 34–35. One exception may be *P.Wash.Univ.* 2.80 (third century), which seems to be a record of payment to soldiers overseeing the transport of river freight.

If people in Roman times did, in fact, use the terms *beneficiarii consularis* and *stationarius* interchangeably, we would expect to find evidence of that in the petitions of Egyptian civilians. In fact, aside from vague addresses that could apply to any outposted soldier, there is very little evidence for civilians equating *stationarii* with *beneficiarii*. But in a fragmentary second-century papyrus, we do find another case of a στατιωνάριος β'. Petraccia Lucernoni again expands this to στατιονάριος β(ενεφικιάριος).[12] This is a repetition of the same error made with the Artanada inscription: the *beta* is once again numeric. This extraordinary document is someone's private account, listing various necessary payments. Interspersed with quotidian taxes and fees are payments to eight different civilian police officials or soldiers, in addition to a substantial sum of twenty-two hundred drachmae ὑ(πὲρ) διασεισμοῦ ("for extortion").[13] The whole text seems to be a testimony to official corruption, and the *beta* after *stationarius* would thus appear to be a petty bribe of two drachmae (perhaps exacted as a toll). Of all of the officials, the *stationarius* was apparently the cheapest to buy off—further anecdotal evidence of *stationarii*'s low status.

Nelis-Clément and others point to a late martyr text for proof of the supposed interchangeability of *beneficiarii* and *stationarii*. In the governor of Macedonia's judicial proceedings against Agapê and her companions, set in Thessalonica in 304, a report sent by a *stationarius* is read in court. The letter opens, "Greetings to you, my lord, from Cassander, *beneficiarius*."[14] But there is no reason to suppose that Cassander and the *stationarius* are one and the same; the *stationarius* merely conveyed the report written by the superior *beneficiarius*. This text does offer a rare glimpse of a *stationarius* working closely with a *beneficiarius* and a governor. However, the Great Persecution was an exceptional case, the account of Agapê's martyrdom is not necessarily fully historical, and the *stationarius*'s involvement here with the governor, at any rate, stands in contrast with the second- and third-century evidence that is our focus.

There is an understandable semantic logic in expecting *beneficiarii consularis* to be called *stationarii*. Yet *beneficiarii consularis*, although they served in *stationes*, were not normally called *stationarii*.[15] So, despite some flexibility in language, vagueness of vocabulary, and incomplete documentation, we cannot use these military-policing terms interchangeably. *Stationarii*, moreover, were neither as high-ranking nor as distinctive as the special units and offices of the *frumentarii* and the *beneficiarii*.

The papyrus clearly shows payments to a *kollêtiô* and at least one *stationarius*, and possibly *beneficiarii* (present only in the form of three *betas* serving as abbreviations).

12. *SB* 6.9207, (provenance unknown), lines 3–4: [...]/τιωναρίῳ β'. Petraccia Lucernoni, *Gli stationarii*, 64. Robert did not suggest Petraccia Lucernoni's restoration in his commentary on this document, "Sur un papyrus."

13. *SB* 6.9207, line 6.

14. *Passio SS. Agapae, Irenae, et Chionae* 3.1: Σοὶ τῷ ἐμῷ δεσπότῃ Κάσσανδρος βενεφικιάριος. Nelis-Clément, *Les beneficiarii*, 224–45.

15. *Pace* Nelis-Clément, *Les beneficiarii*, 75.

Bibliography

Absil, M. *Préfets du prétoire d'Auguste à Commode: 2 avant Jésus-Christ, 192 après Jésus-Christ*. Paris: De Boccard, 1997.

Adams, J. N. *The Latin Sexual Vocabulary*. Baltimore: Johns Hopkins University Press, 1982.

Albertini, E. "Addendum aux fragments des lettres d'Auguste." *Revue des Études Anciennes* 42 (1940): 379–81.

Alexander, M. C. "*Praemia* in the *quaestiones* of the Late Republic." *Class. Phil.* 80 (1985): 20–32.

———. "Law in the Roman Republic." In N. Rosenstein and R. Morstein-Marx, eds., *A Companion to the Roman Republic*, 236–55. Malden and Oxford: Blackwell, 2006.

Alföldi, A. "*Hasta—Summa Imperii*: The Spear as Embodiment of Sovereignty in Rome." *American Journal of Archaeology* 63 (1959): 1–27.

———. "Vom Speerattribut der altrömischen Könige zu den Benefiziarierlanzen." In *Limes Studien. Vor-träge des 3. Int. Limes-Kongresses in Rheinfelden/Basel, 1957*, 7–12. Basel: Institut für Ur- und Frühgeschichte der Schweiz, 1959, 7–12.

Alföldy, G. "*Bellum desertorum*." *Bonner Jahrbuch* 171 (1971): 367–76.

Alston, R. *Soldier and Society in Roman Egypt: A Social History*. London and New York: Routledge, 1995.

———. "The Ties That Bind: Soldiers and Societies." In A. Goldsworthy and I. Hayes, eds., *The Roman Army as a Community*, JRA Suppl. 34, 175–95. Portsmouth, R.I.: Journal of Roman Archaeology, 1999.

———. *The City in Roman and Byzantine Egypt*. London and New York: Routledge, 2002.

Amit, M. "Propagande de succès et d'euphorie dans l'empire romain." *Iura* 16 (1965): 52–72.

Anderson, G. *Sage, Saint and Sophist: Holy Men and Their Associates in the Early Roman Empire*. London and New York: Routledge, 1994.

Anderson, J. K. *Hunting in the Ancient World*. Berkeley and Los Angeles: University of California Press, 1985.

Ando, C. *Imperial Ideology and Provincial Loyalty in the Roman Empire*. Berkeley and Los Angeles: University of California Press, 2000.

von Armin, H. *Leben und Werke des Dio von Prusa*. Berlin: Weidmann, 1898.

Arzt-Grabner, P. "Onesimus erro: Zur Vorgeschichte des Philemonbriefes." *Zeitschrift für die Neutestamentliche Wissenschaft und die Kunde der Älteren Kirche* 95 (2004): 131–43.

Ash, R. "Severed Heads: Individual Portraits and Irrational Forces in Plutarch's *Galba* and *Otho*." In J. Mossman, ed., *Plutarch and his Intellectual World*, 189–214. London and Swansea: Duckworth, 1997.

———. *Ordering Anarchy: Armies and Leaders in Tacitus' Histories*. Ann Arbor: University of Michigan Press, 1999.

Aubert, J.-J. "Policing the Countryside: Soldiers and Civilians in Egyptian Villages in the Third and Fourth Centuries AD." In Y. Le Bohec, ed., *La hiérarchie (Rangordnung) de l'armée romaine sous le haut-empire*, 257–65. Paris: De Boccard, 1995.

Ausbüttel, F. *Die Verwaltung der Städte und Provinzen im spätantiken Italien*. Frankfurt: P. Lang, 1988.

Austin, N. J. E., and N. B. Rankov. *Exploratio: Military and Political Intelligence in the Roman World from the Second Punic War to the Battle of Adrianople*. London and New York: Routledge, 1995.

Badian, E. "The *Scribae* of the Roman Republic." *Klio* 71 (1989): 582–603.

Bagnall, R. S. "The Roman Garrison of Latopolis." *BASP* 12 (1975): 135–44.

———. "Army and Police in Roman Upper Egypt." *JARCE* 14 (1976): 67–88.

———. *The Florida Ostraka: Documents from the Army in Upper Egypt*. Greek, Roman, and Byzantine Monograph 7. Durham, N.C.: Duke University, 1976.

———. "Official and Private Violence in Roman Egypt." *BASP* 26 (1989): 201–16. Reprinted in *Later Roman Egypt: Society, Religion, and Administration*, with addenda, 2. Aldershot, U.K.: Variorum, 2003.

———. *Egypt in Late Antiquity*. Princeton, N.J.: Princeton University Press, 1993.

———. *Reading Papyri, Writing Ancient History*. London and New York: Routledge, 1995.

Bagnall, R. S., A. Bülow-Jacobsen, and H. Cuvigny. "Security and Water on the Eastern Desert Roads: The Prefect Iulius Ursus and the Construction of *Praesidia* under Vespasian." *Journal of Roman Archaeology* 14, no. 1 (2001): 325–33.

Bagnall, R. S., P. J. Sijpesteijn, and K. A. Worp, eds. *Ostraka in Amsterdam Collections*. Zutphen, Neth.: Terra, 1976.

Baillie Reynolds, P. K. "The Troops Quartered in the *Castra Peregrinorum*." *JRS* 13 (1923): 168–89.

———. *The Vigiles of Imperial Rome*. Oxford: Oxford University Press, 1926.

Baldwin, B. "Crime and Criminals in Graeco-Roman Egypt." *Aegyptus* 43 (1963): 256–63.

———. "Leopards, Roman Soldiers, and the *Historia Augusta*." *Illinois Classical Studies* 10 (1985): 281–83.

Ballance, M., and C. Roueché. "Three Inscriptions from Ovacık." In M. Harrison, *Mountain and Plain: From the Lycian Coast to the Phrygian Plateau in the Late Roman and Early Byzantine Period*, 87–112 (app. 2). Ann Arbor: University of Michigan Press, 2001.

Ballou, M. M. *History of Cuba; or, Notes of a Traveller in the Tropics*. Boston: Phillips, Sampson, 1854.

Barnes, T. D. *Tertullian: A Historical and Literary Study*. Oxford: Clarendon, 1971.

———. "Aspects of the Severan Empire, Part I: Severus as a New Augustus." *New England Classical Journal* 35 (2008): 251–67.

Barnstone, W., and M. Meyer. *The Gnostic Bible: Gnostic Texts of Mystical Wisdom from the Ancient and Medieval Worlds—Pagan, Jewish, Christian, Mandaean, Manichaean, Islamic, and Cathar*. Boston: Shambhala, 2003.

Barone-Adesi, G. "*Servi fugitivi in ecclesia*: Indirizzi cristiani e legislazione imperiale." *Atti dell'Accademia Romanistica Costantiniana* 8 (1990): 695–742.

Barrett, A. *Caligula: The Corruption of Power*. New Haven, Conn.: Yale University Press, 1990.

Barry, W. "Aristocrats, Orators, and the 'Mob': Dio Chrysostom and the World of the Alexandrians." *Historia* 42 (1993): 82–103.

———. "Popular Violence and the Stability of Roman Alexandria, 30 BC–AD 215." In N. Swelim, ed., *Alexandrian Studies in Memoriam Daoud Abdu Daoud (Bulletin de la Société Archéologique d'Alexandrie* 45), 19–34. Alexandria: Société Archéologique d'Alexandrie, 1993.

———. "Exposure, Mutilation, and Riot: Violence at the *Scalae Gemoniae* in Early Imperial Rome." *G&R* 55 (2008): 222–46.

Barth, M., and H. Blanke. *The Letter to Philemon: A New Translation with Notes and Commentary*. Grand Rapids, Mich.: Eerdmans, 2000.

Barton, C. A. *Roman Honor: The Fire in the Bones*. Berkeley and Los Angeles: University of California Press, 2001.

Bauman, R. *The Crimen Maiestatis in the Roman Republic and Augustan Principate*. Johannesburg: Witwatersrand University Press, 1967.

———. *Impietas in Principem: A Study of Treason against the Roman Emperor with Special Reference to the First Century A.D.* Munich: Beck, 1974.

———. *Crime and Punishment in Ancient Rome*. London and New York: Routledge, 1996.

———. *Human Rights in Ancient Rome*. London and New York: Routledge, 2000.

Bauschatz, J. "Policing the *Chôra*: Law Enforcement in Ptolemaic Egypt." PhD diss., Duke University, Durham, N.C., 2005.

———. "Archiphylakitai in Ptolemaic Egypt." *Syllecta Classica* 18 (2007): 181–211.

———. "Ptolemaic Prisons Reconsidered." *Classical Bulletin* 83 (2007): 3–48.

———. "The Strong Arm of the Law? Police Corruption in Ptolemaic Egypt." *CJ* 103 (2007): 13–39.

BeDuhn, J. D. "Magical Bowls and Manichaeans." In M. Meyer and P. Mirecki, eds., *Ancient Magic and Ritual Power*, 419–34. Leiden: Brill, 1995.

Behr, C. *Aelius Aristides and the Sacred Tales*. Amsterdam: Hakkert, 1968.

———, trans. *P. Aelius Aristides: The Complete Works*. 2 vols. Leiden: Brill, 1981.

———. "Studies on the Biography of Aelius Aristides." *ANRW* II.34.2 (1993): 1140–1233.

Bekker-Nielsen, T. *Urban Life and Local Politics in Roman Bithynia: The Small World of Dion Chrysostomos*. Black Sea Studies 7. Aarhus, Denmark: Aarhus University Press, 2008.

Bell, H. I. *Jews and Christians in Egypt: The Jewish Troubles and the Athanasian Controversy*. London and Oxford: British Museum and Oxford University Press, 1924.

———. "Acts of the Alexandrines." *Journal of Juristic Papyrology* 4 (1950): 19–42.

Bellen, H. *Studien zur Sklavenflucht im römischen Kaiserreich*. FAS 4. Wiesbaden: Steiner, 1971.

———. *Die germanische Leibwache der römischen Kaiser des julisch-claudischen Hauses*. Wiesbaden: Steiner, 1981.

Benaissa, A. "Sixteen Letters to Agoranomi from Late First Century Oxyrhynchus." *ZPE* 170 (2009): 157–85.

Bennett, J. *Trajan: Optimus Princeps*, 2nd ed. Bloomington: Indiana University Press, 2001.

Ben-Yehuda, N. *Sacrificing Truth: Archaeology and the Myth of Masada*. Amherst, Mass.: Humanity Books, 2002.

Bérard, F. "Le rôle militaire des cohortes urbaines." *MÉFRA* 100 (1988): 159–82.

———. "Aux origines de la cohorte urbaine de Carthage." *Antiquités Africaines* 27 (1991): 39–51.

———. "La garnison de Lyon à l'époque julio-claudienne." In Y. Le Bohec, ed., *Militaires romains en Gaule civile*, 9–19. Paris: De Boccard, 1993.

———. "Une nouvelle inscription militaire lyonnaise." *MÉFRA* 105 (1993): 39–54.

Berdan, F. F. "Crime and Crime Control in Aztec Society." In K. Hopwood, ed., *Organised Crime in Antiquity*, 255–70. London and Swansea: Duckworth and Classical Press of Wales, 1998.

Berkowitz, B. A. *Execution and Invention: Death Penalty Discourse in Early Rabbinic and Christian Cultures*. New York: Oxford University Press, 2006.

Bertrand-Dagenbach, C., A. Chauvot, M. Matter, and J-M. Salamito, eds. *Carcer: Prison et privation de liberté dans l'Antiquité classique*. Paris: De Boccard, 1997.

Bertrand-Dagenbach, C., A. Chauvot, J-M. Salamito, and D. Vaillancourt, eds. *Carcer II: Prison et privation de liberté dans l'empire romain et l'occident médiéval*. Paris: De Boccard, 2004.

Betz, H. D. "Fragments from a Catabasis Ritual in a Greek Magical Papyrus." *History of Religions* 19 (1980): 287–95.

———, ed. *The Greek Magical Papyri in Translation, including the Demotic Spells*. Chicago: University of Chicago Press, 1992.

Biezunska-Małowist, I. "Les esclaves fugitifs dans l'Égypte gréco-romaine." In *Studi in onore di Edoardo Volterra*, vol. 6, 75–90. Milan: Giuffrè, 1971.

Bingham, S. "The Praetorian Guard in the Political and Social Life of Julio-Claudian Rome." PhD diss., University of British Columbia, Vancouver, 1997.

———. "Security at the Games in the Early Imperial Period." *Echos du Monde Classique/Classical Views* 18 (1999): 369–80.

Birley, A. *Septimius Severus: The African Emperor*, 2nd ed. London and New York: Routledge, 1999.

———. "Q. Lucretius Vespillo (*cos. ord.* 19)." *Chiron* 30 (2000): 711–48.

Birley, E. "Septimius Severus and the Roman Army." *Epigraphische Studien* 8 (1969): 63–82, Reprinted in E. Birley, *The Roman Army: Papers, 1929–1986*, 21–40. Mavors 4. Amsterdam: Gieben, 1988).

Bishop, M. C. "*Praesidium*: Social, Military, and Logistical Aspects of the Roman Army's Provincial Distribution during the Early Principate." In A. Goldsworthy and I. Hayes, eds., *The Roman Army as a Community*, JRA Suppl. 34, 111–18. Portsmouth, R.I.: Journal of Roman Archaeology, 1999.

Black, D. "Crime as Social Control." *American Sociological Review* 48 (1983): 34–45.

Black, E. W. *Cursus Publicus: The Infrastructure of Government in Roman Britain*. British Archaeological Reports British Series 241. Oxford: Tempus Repartum, 1995.

Blänsdorf, J. "'Würmer und Krebs sollen ihn befallen': Eine neue Fluchtafel aus Gross-Gerau." *ZPE* 161 (2007): 61–5.

Blum, W. *Curiosi und Regendarii: Untersuchungen zur geheimen Staatspolizei der Spätantike*. Bonn: Habelt in Komm., 1969.

Blumell, L. "Petition to a *Beneficiarius* from Late Third Century A.D. Oxyrhynchus." *ZPE* 165 (2008): 186–90.

Boatwright, M. T. "Luxuriant Gardens and Extravagant Women: The *Horti* of Rome between Republic and Empire." In M. Cima and E. La Rocca, eds., *Horti Romani*, 71–82. Rome: ERMA di Bretschneider, 1998.

———. *Hadrian and the Cities of the Roman Empire*. Princeton, N.J.: Princeton University Press, 2000.

———. "Antonine Rome: Security in the Homeland." In B. Ewald and C. F. Noreña, eds., *The Emperor and Rome: Space, Representation, and Ritual*, 169–97. Cambridge, U.K.: Cambridge University Press, 2011.

Bodel, J. "Dealing with the Dead: Undertakers, Executioners, and Potter's Fields in Ancient Rome." In E. Marshall and V. Hope, eds., *Death and Disease in the Ancient City*, 128–51. London and New York: Routledge, 2000.

Bonfiglio, B. *Corruptio servi*. Milan: Giuffrè, 1998.

Bowersock, G. *Augustus and the Greek World.* Oxford: Clarendon, 1965.

———. *Greek Sophists in the Roman Empire.* Oxford: Clarendon, 1969.

———. "The Mechanics of Subversion in the Roman Provinces." In A. Giovannini and D. van Berchem, eds., *Opposition et résistances à l'Empire d'Auguste à Trajan,* 291–320. Geneva: Fondation Hardt, 1987.

———. *Martyrdom and Rome.* Cambridge, U.K.: Cambridge University Press, 1995.

Bowman, A. K. *Egypt after the Pharaohs.* Berkeley and Los Angeles: University of California, 1986.

———. "Provincial Administration and Taxation." In A. K. Bowman et al., eds., *CAH,* vol. 10, 344–70. Cambridge, U.K.: Cambridge University Press, 1996.

Bowman, A. K., and D. Rathbone. "Cities and Administration in Roman Egypt." *JRS* 82 (1992): 107–27.

Bradley, K. "Slaves and the Conspiracy of Catiline." *Class. Phil.* 73 (1978): 329–36.

———. *Slaves and Masters in the Roman Empire: A Study in Social Control.* New York: Oxford University Press, 1987.

———. *Slavery and Rebellion in the Roman World, 140 B.C.–70 B.C.* Bloomington: Indiana University Press, 1989.

———. *Slavery and Society at Rome.* Cambridge, U.K.: Cambridge University Press, 1994.

Braund, D. "Piracy under the Principate and the Ideology of Imperial Eradication." In J. Rich and G. Shipley, eds., *War and Society in the Ancient World,* 195–212. London and New York: Routledge, 1993.

Braund, S. M. *Juvenal Satires Book I.* Cambridge Greek and Latin Classics. Cambridge, U.K.: Cambridge University Press, 1996.

Breeze, D. J. "Pay Grades and Ranks below the Centuriate." *JRS* 61 (1971): 130–35. Reprinted in D. J. Breeze and B. Dobson, *Roman Officers and Frontiers,* Mavors 10, 59–64. Stuttgart: Steiner, 1993.

———. "The Career Structure below the Centuriate during the Principate." *ANRW* II.1 (1974): 435–51.

———. "The Organisation of the Career Structure of the *Immunes* and *Principales* of the Roman Army." *Bonner Jahrbücher* 174 (1974): 245–92. Reprinted in D. J. Breeze and B. Dobson, *Roman Officers and Frontiers,* Mavors 10, 11–58. Stuttgart: Steiner, 1993.

Brélaz, C. "Pline le Jeune interprète des revendications locales: L'*epistula* 10, 77 et le *libellus* des Juliopolitains." *Appunti Romani di Filologia* 4 (2002): 81–95.

———. "Les colonies romaines et la sécurité publique en Asie Mineure." In G. Salmeri, A. Raggi, and A. Baroni, eds., *Colonie romane nel mondo greco,* 187–209. Rome: ERMA di Bretschneider, 2004.

———. *La sécurité publique en Asie Mineure sous le Principat (Ier-IIIème s. ap. J.-C.): Institutions municipales et institutions impériales dans l'Orient romain.* Basel: Schwabe, 2005.

——— . "Les irénarques de la colonie romaine de Philippes." In M. Mayer i Olivé et al., eds., *Acta XII Congressus Internationalis Epigraphiae Graecae et Latinae*, vol. 2, 1217–19. Barcelona: Institut d'Estudis Catalans, 2007.

——— . "Lutter contre la violence à Rome: Attributions étatiques et tâches privées." In C. Wolff, ed., *Les exclus dans l'Antiquité*, 219–39. Paris: De Boccard, 2007.

——— . "Motifs et circonstances de l'ingérence des autorités romaines dans les cités grecques sous le Principat." In A. Baroni, ed., *Amministrare un impero: Roma e le sue province*, 109–43. Trento: Università degli Studi di Trento, 2007.

——— . "L'adieu aux armes: La défense de la cité grecque dans l'empire romain pacifié." In C. Brélaz and P. Ducrey, eds., *Sécurité collective et ordre public dans les sociétés anciennes*, 155–204. Geneva: Fondation Hardt pour l'Etude de l'Antiquité Classique, 2008.

Brélaz, C., with J. Fournier. "Maintaining Order and Exercising Justice in the Roman Provinces of Asia Minor." In B. Forsén and G. Salmeri, eds., *The Province Strikes Back: Imperial Dynamics in the Eastern Mediterranean*, 45–64. Helsinki: Finnish Institute at Athens, 2008.

Brennan, T. C. *The Praetorship in the Roman Republic*. 2 vols. Oxford: Oxford University Press, 2000.

Brown, P. R. L. "The Rise and Function of the Holy Man in Late Antiquity." *JRS* 61 (1971): 80–101. Reprinted with additional notes in P. R. L. Brown, *Society and the Holy in Late Antiquity*, 103–52. Berkeley and Los Angeles: University of California Press, 1982.

——— . *The Making of Late Antiquity*. Cambridge, Mass.: Harvard University Press, 1978.

——— . "The Rise and Function of the Holy Man in Late Antiquity, 1971–1997." *Journal of Early Christian Studies* 6.3 (1998): 353–76.

Brown, R. E. *The Birth of the Messiah: A Commentary on the Infancy Narratives in Matthew and Luke*. Garden City, N.Y.: Doubleday, 1977.

——— . *The Death of the Messiah: From Gethsemane to the Grave. A Commentary on the Passion Narratives in the Four Gospels*. 2 vols. New York: Doubleday, 1994.

Brunt, P. A. "Charges of Provincial Maladministration under the Early Principate." *Historia* 10 (1961): 189–227. Reprinted with addenda in P. A. Brunt, *Roman Imperial Themes*, 53–95, 487–505. Oxford: Oxford University Press, 1990.

——— . *Italian Manpower, 225 B.C.–A.D. 14*. London: Oxford University Press, 1971.

——— . "The Administrators of Roman Egypt." *JRS* 65 (1975): 124–47. Reprinted in P. A. Brunt, *Roman Imperial Themes*, 215–54, 514–15. Oxford: Oxford University Press, 1990.

——— . "Did Imperial Rome Disarm Her Subjects?" *Phoenix* 29 (1975): 260–70. Reprinted in P. A. Brunt, *Roman Imperial Themes*, 255–66. Oxford: Oxford University Press, 1990.

Buckland, W. W. *The Roman Law of Slavery: The Condition of the Slave in Private Life from Augustus to Justinian.* Cambridge, U.K.: Cambridge University Press, 1908.

Bülow-Jacobsen, A. "Orders to Arrest: P. Haun. Inv. 33 & 34 and a Consolidated List." *ZPE* 66 (1986): 93–98.

———. "Traffic on the Roads between Coptos and the Red Sea." In O. E. Kaper, ed., *Life on the Fringe: Living in the Southern Egyptian Deserts during the Roman and Early-Byzantine Periods*, 63–74. Leiden: CNWS, 1998.

Burrus, V. *Saving Shame: Martyrs, Saints, and Other Abject Subjects.* Philadelphia: University of Pennsylvania Press, 2008.

Burton, G. "Proconsuls, Assizes, and the Administration of Justice under the Empire." *JRS* 65 (1975): 92–106.

———. "The Issuing of *Mandata* to Proconsuls and a New Inscription from Cos." *ZPE* 21 (1976): 63–68.

———. "Provincial Procurators and the Public Provinces." *Chiron* 23 (1993): 13–28.

———. "Was There a Long-term Trend to Centralisation of Authority in the Roman Empire?" *Rev. Phil.* 72 (1999): 7–24.

Busch, A. W. "'*Militia in urbe*': The Military Presence in Rome." In L. de Bois and E. Lo Cascio, eds., *Impact of the Roman Army (200 BC–AD 476): Economic, Social, Political, Religious, and Cultural Aspects*, Impact of Empire 6, 315–341. Leiden: Brill, 2007.

Cadoux, T. J. Review of *Ricerche sulla* praefectura urbi *in età imperiale* by G. Vitucci. *JRS* 49 (1959): 152–60.

———. "The Roman *Carcer* and Its Adjuncts." *G&R* 55 (2008): 202–21.

Calder, W. M. "Colonia Caesareia Antiocheia." *JRS* 2 (1912): 79–109.

———. "The Epitaph of Aviricius Marcellus." *JRS* 29 (1939): 1–4.

Calderini, A., and S. Daris. *Dizionario dei nomi geografici e topografici dell'Egitto greco-romano.* 5 vols. Cairo: Società Reale di Geografia d'Egitto, 1935–1987.

Cameron, A. *Circus Factions: Blues and Greens at Rome and Byzantium.* Oxford: Clarendon, 1976.

Campbell, J. B. "The Marriage of Soldiers under the Empire." *JRS* 68 (1978): 153–66.

———. *The Emperor and the Roman Army, 31 BC–AD 235.* Oxford: Clarendon, 1984.

———. *The Roman Army, 31 BC–AD 337: A Sourcebook.* London and New York: Routledge, 1994.

———. *The Writings of the Roman Land Surveyors: Introduction, Text, Translation and Commentary.* JRS Monographs 9. London: Society for the Promotion of Roman Studies, 2000.

———. *War and Society in Imperial Rome.* London and New York: Routledge, 2002.

Canfora, L. *Julius Caesar: The Life and Times of the People's Dictator.* Trans. M. Hill and K. Windle. Berkeley and Los Angeles: University of California Press, 2007.

Carlsen, J. "*Saltuarius*: A Latin Job Title." *Classica et Mediaevalia* 47 (1996): 245–54.

Carrié, J-M. "Police." In G. Bowersock, P. Brown, and O. Grabar, eds., *Late Antiquity: A Guide to the Postclassical World*, 646. Cambridge, Mass.: Harvard University Press, 1999.

———. "Developments in Provincial and Local Administration." In A. K. Bowman et al., eds., *CAH*, vol. 12, 269–312. Cambridge, U.K.: Cambridge University Press, 2005.

Carter, J. M., ed. *Suetonius: Divus Augustus*. Bristol, U.K.: Bristol Classical Press, 1982.

Cassidy, R. J. *Paul in Chains: Roman Imprisonment and the Letters of St. Paul*. New York: Crossroad, 2001.

Casson, L. *Ships and Seamanship in the Ancient World*. Princeton, N.J.: Princeton University Press, 1971.

———. *Travel in the Ancient World*. London: Allen & Unwin, 1974.

Champlin, E. *Fronto and Antonine Rome*. Cambridge, Mass.: Harvard University Press, 1980.

———. "The Testament of the Piglet." *Phoenix* 41 (1987): 174–83.

Chancey, M. *Greco-Roman Culture and the Galilee of Jesus*. Cambridge, U.K.: Cambridge University Press, 2005.

Chaniotis, A. "Ritual Performances of Divine Justice: The Epigraphy of Confession, Atonement and Exaltation in Roman Asia Minor." In H. Cotton et al., eds., *From Hellenism to Islam: Cultural and Linguistic Change in the Roman Near East*, 115–53. Cambridge, U.K.: Cambridge University Press, 2009.

Chastagnol, A. *La Préfecture urbaine à Rome sous le bas Empire*. Paris: Presses Universitaires de France, 1960.

Clarke, G. Review of *The Mid-Third Century Persecutions of Decius and Valerian* by R. Selinger. *Bryn Mawr Classical Review*, October 12, 2002. http://bmcr.brynmawr .edu/2002/2002-10-22.html.

———. "Christianity in the First Three Centuries: Third-Century Christianity." In A. K. Bowman et al., eds., *CAH*, vol. 12, 589–671. Cambridge, U.K.: Cambridge University Press, 2005.

Clarke, J. R. *Art in the Lives of Ordinary Romans: Visual Representation and Non-Elite Viewers in Italy, 100 B.C.–A.D. 315*. Berkeley and Los Angeles: University of California Press, 2003.

———. *Looking at Laughter: Humor, Power, and Transgression in Roman Visual Culture, 100 B.C.–A.D. 250*. Berkeley and Los Angeles: University of California Press, 2007.

Claridge, A. *Rome: An Oxford Archaeological Guide*. Oxford: Oxford University Press, 1998.

Clauss, M. *Untersuchungen zu den principales des römischen Heeres von Augustus bis Diokletian: Cornicularii, speculatores, frumentarii*. PhD diss., Ruhr-Universität Bochum, 1973.

Coarelli, F. *Rome and Environs: An Archaeological Guide*. Trans. J. Clauss and D. Harmon. Berkeley and Los Angeles: University of California Press, 2007.

Coleman, K. M. "Fatal Charades: Roman Executions Staged as Mythological Enactments." *JRS* 80 (1990): 44–73.

Colin, J. *Villes libres de l'Orient gréco-romain et l'envoi au supplice par acclamations populaires*. Brussels: Latomus, 1965.

Connolly, S. *Lives behind the Laws: The World of the* Codex Hermogenianus." Bloomington: Indiana University Press, 2010.

Coogan, M. D., ed. *The New Oxford Annotated Bible with the Apocrypha/Deuterocanonical Books: New Revised Standard Version*, 3rd ed. Oxford: Oxford University Press, 2001.

Cooley, A. E. "Septimius Severus: The Augustan Emperor." In S. Swain et al., eds., *Severan Culture*, 385–97. Cambridge, U.K.: Cambridge University Press, 2007.

———. *Res gestae divi Augusti: Text, Translation, and Commentary*. Cambridge, U.K.: Cambridge University Press, 2009.

Corbier, M. "Fiscus and Patrimonium: The Saepinum Inscription and Transhumance in the Abruzzi." *JRS* 73 (1983): 126–31.

Corcoran, S. *The Empire of the Tetrarchs: Imperial Pronouncements and Government, AD 284–324*. Oxford: Clarendon, 1996.

Cornell, T. J. "The End of Roman Imperial Expansion." In J. Rich and G. Shipley, eds., *War and Society in the Roman World*, 139–70. London and New York: Routledge, 1993.

Cotton, H. "Some Aspects of the Roman Administration of Judaea/Syria-Palaestina." In W. Eck, ed., *Lokale Autonomie und römische Ordnungsmacht in den kaiserzeitlichen Provinzen*, 75–91. Munich: Oldenbourg, 1999.

Coulston, J. "'Armed and Belted Men': The Soldiery in Imperial Rome." In J. Coulston and H. Dodge, eds., *Ancient Rome: The Archaeology of the Eternal City*, 76–118. Oxford: Oxford University School of Archaeology, 2000.

Courtney, E. *A Commentary on the Satires of Juvenal*. London: Athlone, 1980.

Cox, C. A. "The *Astynomoi*, Private Wills and Street Activity." *Classical Quarterly* 57 (2007): 769–75.

Crawford (Thompson), D. "*Skepe* in Soknopaiou Nesos." *Journal of Juristic Papyrology* 18 (1974): 169–75.

Crawford, M., ed. *Roman Statutes*. 2 vols. London: Institute of Classical Studies, University of London, 1996.

Crone, P. *Roman, Provincial and Islamic Law*. Cambridge, U.K.: Cambridge University Press, 1987.

Crook, J. *Consilium Principis: Imperial Councils and Counsellors from Augustus to Diocletian*. Cambridge, U.K.: Cambridge University Press, 1955.

———. *Law and Life of Rome*. Ithaca, N.Y.: Cornell University Press, 1967.

Cross, F. L., and E. A. Livingstone, eds. *The Oxford Dictionary of the Christian Church*, 3rd ed. Oxford: Oxford University Press, 1997.

Crossan, J. D. *The Historical Jesus: The Life of a Mediterranean Jewish Peasant.* San Francisco: Harper, 1991.

Cumont, F. *Oriental Religions in Roman Paganism.* Chicago: Open Court, 1911.

———. *After Life in Roman Paganism.* New Haven, Conn.: Yale University Press, 1922.

Cunliffe, B. *The Temple of Sulis Minerva at Bath.* Vol. 2: *The Finds from the Sacred Spring.* Oxford: Oxford University, 1988.

Curran, J. *Pagan City and Christian Capital: Rome in the Fourth Century.* Oxford: Oxford University Press, 2000.

Damon, C. "Rhetoric and Historiography." In W. Dominik and J. Hall, eds., *A Companion to Roman Rhetoric*, 439–50. Malden and Oxford: Wiley-Blackwell, 2007.

Daube, D. "Some Comparative Law—*furtum conceptum.*" *Tijdschrift voor Rechtsgeschiedenis* 15 (1937): 48–77.

——— . "Slave-Catching." *Juridical Review* 64 (1951): 17–28. Reprinted in D. Daube, *Collected Studies in Roman Law*, vol. 1, 501–13. Frankfurt: Klostermann, 1991.

Davies, G. "Cremna in Pisidia: A Re-appraisal of the Siege Works." *Anatolian Studies* 50 (2000): 151–58.

Davies, R. W. "Police Work in Roman Times." *History Today* 18, no. 10 (1968): 700–707.

———. "The Daily Life of the Roman Soldier under the Principate." *ANRW* II.1 (1974): 299–338. Reprinted in R. W. Davies, *Service in the Roman Army*, 33–68. New York: Columbia University Press, 1989.

———. "Augustus Caesar: A Police Force in the Ancient World." In P. Stead, ed., *Pioneers in Policing*, 12–32. Montclair, N.J.: Patterson Smith, 1977.

De Blois, L. *The Policy of the Emperor Gallienus.* Leiden: Brill, 1976.

———. "The Military Factor in the Onset of Crises in the Roman Empire in the Third Century AD." In L. de Bois and E. Lo Cascio, eds., *Impact of the Roman Army (200 BC–AD 476): Economic, Social, Political, Religious, and Cultural Aspects*, 497–507. Leiden: Brill, 2007.

———. "Soldiers and Leaders in Plutarch's *Galba* and *Otho.*" In H. M. Schellenberg et al., eds., *A Roman Miscellany: Essays in Honour of Anthony R. Birley on his Seventieth Birthday*, 5–13. Gdansk: Foundation for the Development of Gdansk University, 2008.

Dench, E. *Romulus' Asylum: Roman Identities from the Age of Alexander to the Age of Hadrian.* Oxford: Oxford University Press, 2005.

Desideri, P. "City and Country in Dio." In S. Swain, ed., *Dio Chrysostom: Politics, Letters, and Philosophy*, 93–107. Oxford: Oxford University Press, 2001.

De Souza, P. *Piracy in the Graeco-Roman World.* Cambridge, U.K.: Cambridge University Press, 1999.

Bibliography

Dettenhofer, M. H. *Herrschaft und Widerstand im augusteischen Principat: Die Konkurrenz zwischen* res publica *und* domus Augusta. Hist. E. 140. Stuttgart: Steiner, 2000.

Di Paola, L. *Viaggi, trasporti e istituzioni: Studi sul* cursus publicus. Messina: DiScAM, 1999.

Dise, R. L. *Cultural Change and Imperial Administration: The Middle Danube Provinces of the Roman Empire.* New York: P. Lang, 1991.

———. "A Reassessment of the Functions of *Beneficiarii Consularis.*" *Ancient History Bulletin* 9, no. 2 (1995): 72–85.

———. "The *Beneficiarii Procuratoris* of Celeia and the Early Development of the *Statio* Network." *ZPE* 95 (1996): 286–92.

———. "Trajan, the Antonines and the Governor's Staff." *ZPE* 116 (1997): 273–83.

———. "Variation in Roman Administrative Practice: The Assignments of *Beneficiarii Consularis.*" *ZPE* 116 (1997): 284–99.

Dmitriev, S. *City Government in Hellenistic and Roman Asia Minor.* New York: Oxford University Press, 2005.

Dobson, B. "The Significance of the Centurion and 'Primipilaris' in the Roman Army and Administration." *ANRW* II.1 (1974): 392–434. Reprinted in D. J. Breeze and B. Dobson, *Roman Officers and Frontiers*, Mavors 10, 143–85. Stuttgart: Steiner, 1993.

———. "The Roman Army: Wartime or Peacetime Army?" In W. Eck and H. Wolff, eds., *Heer und Integrationspolitik: Die römischen Militärdiplome als historische Quelle*, 10–25. Cologne: Böhlau, 1986. Reprinted in D. J. Breeze and B. Dobson, *Roman Officers and Frontiers*, Mavors 10, 113–28. Stuttgart: Steiner, 1993.

von Domaszewski, A. "Die Beneficiarierposten und die römischen Strassennetze." *Westdeutsche Zeitschrift* 21 (1902): 158–221.

Dowling, M. B. *Clemency and Cruelty in the Roman World.* Ann Arbor: University of Michigan Press, 2006.

Drecoll, C. *Die Liturgien im römischen Kaiserreich des 3. und 4. Jh. n. Chr.: Untersuchung über Zugang, Inhalt und wirtschaftliche Bedeutung der öffentlichen Zwangsdienste in Ägypten und anderen Provinzen.* Hist. E. 116. Stuttgart: Steiner, 1997.

Drew, K. F. *The Lombard Laws.* Philadelphia: University of Pennsylvania Press, 1971.

———. *The Laws of the Salian Franks.* Philadelphia: University of Pennsylvania Press, 1991.

Drew-Bear, T. "Latin Terms in Greek: A Discussion." Review of *Greek Terms for Roman Institutions* by H. Mason. *Class. Phil.* 71 (1976): 349–55.

———. "Three Inscriptions from Asia Minor." In A. L. Boegehold et al., eds., *Studies Presented to Sterling Dow*, Greek, Roman, and Byzantine Monographs 10, 61–69. Durham, N.C.: Duke University, 1984.

Drinkwater, J. "Maximinus to Diocletian and the 'Crisis.'" In A. K. Bowman et al., eds., *CAH*, vol. 12, 28–66. Cambridge, U.K.: Cambridge University Press, 2005.

Drogula, F. K. "The Office of the Provincial Governor under the Roman Republic and Empire (to AD 235): Conception and Tradition." PhD diss., University of Virginia, Charlottesville, 2005.

Drummond, A. "Rome in the Fifth Century I: The Social and Economic Framework." In F. Walbank et al., eds., *CAH*, vol. 7.2, 113–71. Cambridge, U.K.: Cambridge University Press, 1989.

———. *Law, Politics and Power: Sallust and the Execution of the Catilinarian Conspirators*. Hist. E 93. Stuttgart: Steiner, 1995.

Duncan-Jones, R. *Structure and Scale in the Roman Economy*. Cambridge, U.K.: Cambridge University Press, 1990.

Dunn, J. D. G. *The Epistles to the Colossians and to Philemon: A Commentary on the Greek Text*. Grand Rapids, Mich.: Eerdmans, 1996.

Durry, M. "Juvénal et les prétoriens." *Revue des Études Latines* 13 (1935): 95–106.

———. *Les cohortes prétoriennes*. BÉFAR 146. Paris: De Boccard, 1938.

Dusanic, S. "Roman Mining in Illyricum: Historical Aspects." In G. Urso, ed., *Dall'Adriatico al Danubio: L'Illirico in età greca e romana*, 247–70. Pisa: ETS, 2004.

Duval, N. "À propos de la garnison de Lyon: Le problème de la composition de la garnison de Carthage." In Y. Le Bohec, ed., *Militaires romains en Gaule civile*, 23–27. Paris: De Boccard, 1993.

Dvornik, F. *Origins of Intelligence Services: The Ancient Near East, Persia, Greece, Rome, Byzantium, the Arab Muslim Empires, the Mongol Empire, China, Muscovy*. New Brunswick, N.J.: Rutgers University Press, 1974.

Echols, E. "The Roman City Police: Origin and Development." *Classical Journal* 53 (1958): 377–85.

———. "The Provincial Urban Cohorts." *Classical Journal* 57 (1961): 25–28.

Eck, W. *Die staatliche Organisation Italiens in der hohen Kaiserzeit*. Munich: Beck, 1979.

———. *Die Verwaltung des römischen Reiches in der hohen Kaiserzeit: Ausgewählte und erweiterte Beiträge*. 2 vols. Basel: Reinhardt, 1995–98.

———, ed. *Lokale Autonomie und römische Ordnungsmacht in den kaiserzeitlichen Provinzen vom 1. bis 3. Jahrhundert*. Munich: Oldenbourg, 1999.

———. "The Growth of Administrative Posts." In A. K. Bowman et al., eds., *CAH*, vol. 11, 238–65. Cambridge, U.K.: Cambridge University Press, 2000.

———. *The Age of Augustus*, 2nd ed. Trans. D. Schneider. Malden and Oxford: Blackwell, 2007.

Eck, W., A. Caballos, and F. Fernández. *Das Senatus consultum de Cn. Pisone patre*. Munich: Beck, 1996.

Eder, W. *Servitus Publica: Untersuchungen zur Entstehung, Entwicklung und Funktion der öffentlichen Sklaverei in Rom*. FAS 13. Wiesbaden: Steiner, 1981.

Edwards, C. *Death in Ancient Rome*. New Haven, Conn.: Yale University Press, 2007.

Ehrman, B. D., and Z. Pleše. *The Apocryphal Gospels: Texts and Translations.* Oxford and New York: Oxford University Press, 2011.

Eibl, K. "Gibt es eine spezifische Ausrüstung der Beneficiarier?" In E. Schallmayer et al., eds., *Der römische Weihebezirk von Osterburken II: Kolloquium 1990 und paläoboatische-osteologische Untersuchungen,* 273–97. Stuttgart: Theiss, 1994.

Eich, A. "Die Verwaltung der kaiserzeitlichen Armee: Zur Bedeutung militärischer Verwaltungsstrukturen in der Kaiserzeit für die administrative Entwicklung des Imperium Romanum." In A. Eich, ed., *Die Verwaltung der kaiserzeitlichen römischen Armee: Studien für Hartmut Wolff,* HABES 211, 9–36. Stuttgart: Steiner, 2010.

Eitrem, S., and L. Amundsen. "Complaint of an Assault, with Petition to the Police." *Journal of Egyptian Archaeology* 40 (1954): 30–33.

Elliott, T. "Epigraphic Evidence for Boundary Disputes in the Roman Empire." PhD diss., University of North Carolina, Chapel Hill, 2004.

Fagan, G. *Bathing in Public in the Roman World.* Ann Arbor: University of Michigan Press, 2002.

———. "Violence in Roman Social Relations." In Michael Peachin, ed., *The Oxford Handbook of Social Relations in the Roman World,* 467–95. New York: Oxford University Press, 2010.

———. *The Lure of the Arena: Social Psychology and the Spectators at the Roman Games.* Cambridge, U.K.: Cambridge University Press, 2011.

Fagan, J., and D. Wilkinson. "Guns, Youth Violence, and Social Identity in Inner Cities." *Crime and Justice* 24 (1998): 105–88.

Faraone, C. "Notes on Four Inscribed Magical Gemstones." *ZPE* 160 (2007): 158–59.

Faraone, C., and D. Obbink, eds. *Magika Hiera: Ancient Greek Magic and Religion.* Oxford: Oxford University Press, 1991.

Faulkner, R. O., trans. *The Ancient Egyptian Book of the Dead.* Austin: University of Texas Press, 1990.

Fear, A. T. "La *Lex Ursonensis* y los *apparitores* municipales." In J. González, ed., *Estudios sobre Urso: Colonia Iulia Genetiva,* 69–78. Seville: Alfar, 1989.

Fears, J. R. *Princeps a Diis Electus: The Divine Election of the Emperor as a Political Concept at Rome.* Rome: American Academy in Rome, 1977.

Fink, R. *Roman Military Records on Papyrus.* APA Monographs 26. Cleveland: Case Western Reserve University Press, 1971.

Finley, M. *Ancient Slavery and Modern Ideology.* New York: Penguin, 1980. Second edition, B. Shaw, ed. Princeton, N.J.: Markus Wiener, 1998.

Fitzpatrick, J. C., ed. *The Writings of George Washington.* 39 vols. Washington, D.C.: U.S. Government Printing Office, 1931–44.

Flam-Zuckermann, L. "À propos d'une inscription de Suisse (*CIL* XIII, 5015): Étude du phénomène de brigandage dans l'Empire romain." *Latomus* 29 (1970): 451–73.

Flower, H. I. *The Art of Forgetting: Disgrace and Oblivion in Roman Political Culture.* Chapel Hill: University of North Carolina Press, 2006.

Foster, B. R. "Agoranomos and Muhtasib." *Journal of the Economic and Social History of the Orient* 13 (1970): 128–44.

Foucault, M. *Power/Knowledge: Selected Interviews and Other Writings, 1972–1977.* C. Gordon, ed. New York: Pantheon, 1980.

Francis, J. A. *Subversive Virtue: Asceticism and Authority in the Second-Century Pagan World.* University Park: Pennsylvania State University Press, 1995.

Frankfurter, D. "Fetus Magic and Sorcery Fears in Roman Egypt." *GRBS* 46 (2006): 37–62.

Franklin, J. H., and L. Schweninger. *Runaway Slaves: Rebels on the Plantation.* New York: Oxford University Press, 1999.

Fraser, P. M. *Ptolemaic Alexandria.* 3 vols. Oxford: Clarendon, 1972.

Frederiksen, M. "The Republican Municipal Laws: Errors and Drafts." *JRS* 55 (1965): 183–98.

Freis, H. *Die cohortes urbanae.* Cologne: Böhlau, 1967.

Frend, W. H. C. *The Donatist Church: A Movement of Protest in Roman North Africa.* Oxford: Clarendon, 1952; revised 1985.

———. "A Third-Century Inscription relating to *angareia* in Phrygia." *JRS* 46 (1956): 45–56.

———. *Martyrdom and Persecution in the Early Church: A Study of a Conflict from the Maccabees to Donatus.* Oxford: Blackwell, 1965.

Frid, B. *Ten Uppsala Papyri.* Bonn: Habelt, 1981.

Frier, B. *Landlords and Tenants in Imperial Rome.* Princeton, N.J.: Princeton University Press, 1980.

Frisch, P. "Zum Edikt des Sex. Sotidius Strabo für Pisidien." *ZPE* 41 (1981): 100.

Fuhrmann, C. "Keeping the Imperial Peace: Public Order, State Control, and Policing in the Roman Empire during the First Three Centuries AD." PhD diss., University of North Carolina, Chapel Hill, 2005.

Fuks, A. "The Jewish Revolt in Egypt (A.D. 115–117) in the Light of the Papyri." *Aegyptus* 33 (1953): 131–58. Reprinted in A. Fuks, *Social Conflict in Ancient Greece,* 322–49. Jerusalem/Leiden: Brill, 1984.

———. "Aspects of the Jewish Revolt in A.D. 115–117." *JRS* 51 (1961): 98–104. Reprinted in A. Fuks, *Social Conflict in Ancient Greece,* 350–56. Jerusalem/Leiden: Brill, 1984.

Gager, J., ed. *Curse Tablets and Binding Spells from the Ancient World.* New York: Oxford University Press, 1992.

Gagos, T., and P. Sijpesteijn. "Towards an Explanation of the Typology of the So-called 'Orders to Arrest.'" *BASP* 33 (1996): 77–97.

Galinsky, K. *Augustan Culture: An Interpretive Introduction.* Princeton, N.J.: Princeton University Press, 1996.

Galsterer, H. "Municipium Flavium Irnitanum: A Latin Town in Spain." *JRS* 78 (1988): 79–90.

———. "Statthalter und Stadt im Gerichtswesen der westlichen Prozinzen." In W. Eck, ed., *Lokale Autonomie und römische Ordnungsmacht in den kaiserzeitlichen Provinzen*, 243–56. Munich: Oldenbourg, 1999.

Gamauf, R. *Ad statuam licet confugere: Untersuchungen zum Asylrecht im römischen Prinzipat*. Frankfurt: P. Lang, 1999.

Garnsey, P. *Social Status and Legal Privilege in the Roman Empire*. Oxford: Clarendon, 1970.

———. *Ideas of Slavery from Aristotle to Augustine*. Cambridge, U.K.: Cambridge University Press, 1996.

Gelzer, M. *Caesar: Politician and Statesman*, 6th ed. Trans. P. Needham. Cambridge, Mass.: Harvard University Press, 1968.

Gilliver, K. "The Augustan Reform and the Structure of the Roman Army." In P. Erdkamp, ed., *A Companion to the Roman Army*, 183–200. Malden and Oxford: Blackwell, 2007.

Giovannini, A., and M. Hirt. "L'inscription de Nazareth: Nouvelle interprétation." *ZPE* 124 (1999): 107–32.

Glancy, J. A. *Slavery in Early Christianity*. Oxford: Oxford University Press, 2002.

Goldsworthy, A. *The Roman Army at War, 100 BC–AD 200*. Oxford: Clarendon, 1996.

González, J. "The Lex Irnitana: A New Copy of the Flavian Municipal Law." *JRS* 76 (1986): 147–243.

Gowers, E. "The Anatomy of Rome from Capitol to Cloaca." *JRS* 85 (1995): 23–32.

Graf, F., and S. I. Johnston. *Ritual Texts for the Afterlife: Orpheus and the Bacchic Gold Tablets*. London and New York: Routledge, 2007.

Green, C. M. C. *Roman Religion and the Cult of Diana at Aricia*. Cambridge, U.K.: Cambridge University Press, 2007.

Green, P., ed. and trans. *Juvenal: The Sixteen Satires*, 3rd ed. London: Penguin, 1998.

Greene, K. "Industry and Technology." In A. K. Bowman et al., eds., *CAH*, vol. 11, 741–68. Cambridge, U.K.: Cambridge University Press, 2000.

Gregory, T. E. "Urban Violence in Late Antiquity." In R. T. Marchese, ed., *Aspects of Graeco-Roman Urbanism: Essays on the Classical City*, BAR 188, 138–61. Oxford: BAR, 1983.

Grimal, P. "Le modèle et la date des *Captivi* de Plaute." In P. Grimal, *Rome: La littérature et l'histoire*, CÉRF 93, vol. 1, 295–314. Rome: École Française de Rome, 1986.

Gruen, E. *Diaspora: Jews amidst Greeks and Romans*. Cambridge, Mass.: Harvard University Press, 2002.

Grünewald, T. *Räuber, Rebellen, Rivalen, Rächer: Studien zu Latrones im römischen Reich.* FAS 31. Stuttgart: Steiner, 1999.

———. *Bandits in the Roman Empire: Myth and Reality.* Trans. J. Drinkwater. London and New York: Routledge, 2004.

Gunnella, A. "Morti improvvise e violente nelle iscrizioni latine." In F. Hinard, ed., *La mort au quotidien dans le monde romain*,9–22. Paris: De Boccard, 1995.

Gustafson, M. "Condemnation to the Mines in the Later Roman Empire." *Harvard Theological Review* 87 (1994): 421–33.

———. "*Inscripta in Fronte*: Penal Tattooing in Late Antiquity." *Classical Antiquity* 16 (1997): 79–105.

Haas, C. *Alexandria in Late Antiquity: Topography and Social Conflict.* Baltimore: Johns Hopkins University Press, 1997.

Haensch, R. *Capita provinciarum: Statthaltersitze und Provinzialverwaltung in der römischen Kaiserzeit.* Mainz: Zabern, 1997.

———. "Kontolle und Verantwortlichkeit von officiales in Prinzipat und Spätantike." In A. Eich, ed., *Die Verwaltung der kaiserzeitlichen römischen Armee: Studien für Hartmut Wolff*, HABES 211, 177–86. Stuttgart: Steiner, 2010.

Hagedorn, U. "Das Formular der Überstellungsbefehle im römischen Ägypten." *BASP* 16 (1979): 61–74.

Halkin, L. *Les esclaves publics chez les romains.* Brussels: Société Belge de Librairie, 1897.

Halleux, R., and J. Schamp, eds. and trans. *Les lapidaires grecs.* Paris: Belles Lettres, 1985.

Hallof, K. "Die Inschrift von Skaptopara: Neue Dokumente und neue Lesungen." *Chiron* 24 (1994): 405–41.

Hansen, W., ed. *Anthology of Ancient Greek Popular Literature.* Bloomington and Indianapolis: Indiana University Press, 1998.

Hardy, E. G. *Roman Laws and Charters.* Aalen: Scientia Verlag, 1977. Reprint of *Three Spanish Charters and Other Documents.* Oxford: Clarendon, 1912.

Harker, A. *Loyalty and Dissidence in Roman Egypt: The Case of the* Acta Alexandrinorum. Cambridge, U.K.: Cambridge University Press, 2008.

Harries, J. *Law and Crime in the Roman World.* Cambridge, U.K.: Cambridge University Press, 2007.

Harris, E. "Who Enforced the Law in Classical Athens?" *Symposion 2005: Vorträge zur griechischen und hellenistischen Rechtsgeschichte* (2007): 159–76.

Harris, W. V. "The Roman Father's Power of Life and Death." In R. S. Bagnall and W. V. Harris, eds., *Studies in Roman Law in Memory of A. Arthur Schiller*, 81–95. Leiden: Brill, 1986.

———. *Dreams and Experience in Classical Antiquity.* Cambridge, Mass.: Harvard University Press, 2009.

Harrison, S. *Apuleius: A Latin Sophist.* Oxford: Oxford University Press, 2000.

————, ed. *Apuleius: Rhetorical Works.* Trans. S. Harrison, J. Hilton, and V. Hunink. Oxford: Oxford University Press, 2002.

Hauken, T. *Petition and Response: An Epigraphic Study of Petitions to Roman Emperors, 181–249.* Bergen: Norwegian Institute at Athens, 1998.

Hauken, T., and H. Malay. "A New Edict of Hadrian from the Province of Asia Setting Regulations for Requisitioned Transport." In R. Haensch, ed., *Selbstdarstellung und Kommunikation: Die Veröffentlichung staatlicher Urkunden auf Stein und Bronze in der römischen Welt,*, 327–48. Munich: Beck, 2009.

Hauken, T., C. Tanriver, and K. Akbiyikoğlu. "A New Inscription from Phrygia: A Rescript of Septimius Severus and Caracalla to the *Coloni* of the Imperial Estate at Tymion." *Epigraphica Anatolica* 36 (2003): 33–44.

Heinen, H., ed. *Menschenraub, Menschenhandel und Sklaverei in antiker und moderner Perspektive.* FAS 37. Stuttgart: Steiner, 2008.

Heintz, F. "A Greek Silver Phylactery in the MacDaniel Collection." *ZPE* 112 (1996): 295–300.

Heller, A. *Les bêtises des Grecs: Conflits et rivalités entre cités d'Asie et de Bithynie à l'époque romaine (129 a.C.–235 p.C.).* Pessac: Ausonius, 2006.

Henderson, J. *Telling Tales on Caesar: Roman Stories from Phaedrus.* Oxford: Oxford University Press, 2001.

Hengel, M. *The Zealots: Investigations into the Jewish Freedom Movement in the Period from Herod I until 70 A.D.* Trans. David Smith. Edinburg: T & T Clark, 1989.

Hennig, D. "Nyktophylakes, Nyktostrategen, und die παραφυλακὴ τῆς πόλεως." *Chiron* 32 (2002): 281–95.

Herrmann, P. *Der römische Kaisereid.* Göttingen: Vandenhoeck & Ruprecht, 1968.

————. *Hilferufe aus römischen Provinzen: Ein Aspekt der Krise des römischen Reiches im 3. Jhdt. n. Chr.* Göttingen: Vandenhoeck & Ruprecht, 1990.

Herz, P. "Finances and Costs of the Roman Army." In P. Erdkamp, ed., *A Companion to the Roman Army,* 306–22. Malden and Oxford: Blackwell, 2007.

Hezser, C. *Jewish Slavery in Antiquity.* Oxford: Oxford University Press, 2005.

Hidalgo de la Vega, M. J. "The Flight of Slaves and Bands of *Latrones* in Apuleius." In A. Serghidou, ed., *Fear of Slaves, Fear of Enslavement in the Ancient Mediterranean; Peur de l'esclave, peur de l'esclavage en Méditerranée ancienne (Discours, représentations, pratiques),* 325–36. Besançon: Presses Universitaires de Franche-Comté, 2007.

Hijmans, B., et al., eds. *Apuleius Madaurensis, Metamorphoses IV, 1–27: Text, Introduction, and Commentary.* Groningen: Bouma, 1977.

Hillebrand, S. "Der Vigintivirat: Prosopographische Untersuchungen für die Zeit von Augustus bis Domitian." PhD diss., Heidelberg University, 2006.

Hinard, F. *Les proscriptions de la Rome républicaine.* CÉFR 83. Rome: École Française de Rome, 1985.

Hirschfeld, F. *George Washington and Slavery: A Documentary Portrayal.* Columbia: University of Missouri Press, 1997.

Hirschfeld, O. "Gallische Studien III: Der praefectus vigilum in Nemausus und die Feuerwehr in den römischen Landstädten." *Sitzungsberichte der Wiener Akademie* 107 (1884): 239–57. Reprinted in O. Hirschfeld, *Kleine Schriften*, 96–111. Berlin: Weidmann, 1913.

———. "Die Sicherheitspolizei im römischen Kaiserreich." *Sitzungsberichte der Königlich Preussischen Akademie der Wissenschaften zu Berlin* (1891): 845–77. Reprinted in O. Hirschfeld, *Kleine Schriften*, 578–612. Berlin: Weidmann, 1913.

———. "Die ägyptische Polizei der römischen Kaiserzeit nach Papyrusurkunden." *Sitzungsberichte der Königlich Preussischen Akademie der Wissenschaften zu Berlin* (1892): 815–24. Reprinted in O. Hirschfeld, *Kleine Schriften*, 613–23. Berlin: Weidmann, 1913.

Hirt, A. *Imperial Mines and Quarries in the Roman World: Organizational Aspects, 27 BC–AD 235.* Oxford: Oxford University Press, 2010.

Hobson, D. "The Impact of Law on Village Life in Roman Egypt." In B. Halpern and D. Hobson, eds., *Law, Politics and Society in the Ancient Mediterranean World*, 193–219. Sheffield: Sheffield Academic Press, 1993.

Holmberg, E. J. *Zur Geschichte des* cursus publicus. Uppsala: Lundequistska, 1933.

Homoth-Kuhs, C. *Phylakes und Phylakon-steuer im Griechisch-römischen Ägypten: Ein Beitrag zur Geschichte des antiken Sicherheitswesens.* Munich: Saur, 2005.

Honoré, T. *Emperors and Lawyers*, 2nd ed. Oxford: Clarendon, 1994.

———. *Ulpian: Pioneer of Human Rights*, 2nd ed. Oxford: Oxford University Press, 2002.

Hopkins, K. *Conquerors and Slaves.* Cambridge, U.K.: Cambridge University Press, 1978.

———. "Rules of Evidence." Review of *The Emperor in the Roman World* by F. Millar. *JRS* 69 (1979): 178–86.

———. "Taxes and Trade in the Roman Empire (200 B.C.–A.D. 400)." *JRS* 70 (1980): 101–25.

———. "Novel Evidence for Roman Slavery." *P&P* 138 (1993): 3–27.

Hopwood, K. "Policing the Hinterland: Rough Cilicia and Isauria." In S. Mitchell, ed., *Armies and Frontiers in Roman and Byzantine Anatolia*, 173–87. Oxford: BAR, 1983.

———. "Bandits, Elites, and Rural Order." In A. Wallace-Hadrill, ed., *Patronage in Ancient Society*, 171–87. London and New York: Routledge, 1989.

———, ed. *Organised Crime in Antiquity.* London and Swansea: Duckworth and Classical Press of Wales, 1998.

Hornblower, S., and A. Spawforth, eds. *The Oxford Classical Dictionary*, 3rd ed. Oxford: Oxford University Press, 1996.

Horsfall, N. *The Culture of the Roman Plebs.* London: Duckworth, 2003.

Horsley, R. A., with J. S. Hanson. *Bandits, Prophets and Messiahs: Popular Movements in the Time of Jesus.* Minneapolis: Winston, 1985.

Horstkotte, H. "Die Strafrechtspflege in den Provinzen der römischen Kaiserzeit zwischen hegemonialer Ordnungsmacht und lokaler Autonomie." In W. Eck, ed., *Lokale Autonomie und römische Ordnungsmacht in den kaiserzeitlichen Provinzen*, 303–18. Munich: Oldenbourg, 1999.

Howe, L. L. *The Pretorian Prefect from Commodus to Diocletian (A.D. 180–305)*. Chicago: University of Chicago Press, 1942.

Huber, G. *Das Motiv der "Witwe von Ephesus" in lateinischen Texten der Antike und des Mittelalters*. Tübingen: G. Narr, 1990.

Hughes, S. "Fear and Loathing in Bologna and Rome: The Papal Police in Perspective." *Journal of Social History* 21 (1987): 97–116.

Hull, D. *Hounds and Hunting in Ancient Greece*. Chicago: University of Chicago Press, 1964.

Hunter, V. *Policing Athens: Social Control in the Attic Lawsuits, 420–320 B.C.* Princeton, N.J.: Princeton University Press, 1994.

———. "The Prison of Athens: A Comparative Perspective." *Phoenix* 51 (1997): 296–326.

———. "Plato's Prisons." *G&R* 55 (2008): 193–201.

Independent Budget Office, New York. "Police Staffing Levels and Reported Crime Rates in America's Largest Cities: Results of Preliminary Analysis." March 16, 1998. http://www.ibo.nyc.ny.us/iboreports/crimerep.html.

Isaac, B. *Limits of Empire: The Roman Army in the East*, 2nd ed. Oxford: Oxford University Press, 1992.

Jacques, F., and J. Scheid. *Rome et l'intégration de l'empire (44 av. J.-C.–260 ap. J.-C.). Vol. 1: Les structures de l'Empire romain*. Paris: Presses universitaires de France, 1990.

Jakab, E. *Praedicere und cavere beim Marktkauf: Sachmängel im griechischen und römischen Recht*. Munich: Beck, 1997.

Johns, C. *Dogs: History, Myth, Art*. Cambridge, Mass.: Harvard University Press, 2008.

Jones, A. H. M. *The Greek City from Alexander to Justinian*. Oxford: Clarendon, 1940.

———. "The Roman Civil Service (Clerical and Sub-Clerical Grades)." *JRS* 39 (1949): 38–55.

———. *The Later Roman Empire, 284–602: A Social, Economic, and Administrative Survey*. 2 vols. Norman: University of Oklahoma Press, 1964.

———. *The Criminal Courts of the Roman Republic and Principate*. Oxford: Blackwell, 1972.

Jones, C. P. "The Reliability of Philostratus." In G. Bowersock, ed., *Approaches to the Second Sophistic*, 11–16. University Park, Pa.: American Philological Association, 1974.

———. *The Roman World of Dio Chrysostom*. Cambridge, Mass.: Harvard University Press, 1978.

————. *Culture and Society in Lucian*. Cambridge, Mass.: Harvard University Press, 1986.

————. "A Note on *Diogmitae*." *Illinois Classical Studies* 12 (1987): 179–80.

————. "*Stigma*: Tattooing and Branding in Graeco-Roman Antiquity." *JRS* 77 (1987): 139–55.

Jordan, D. R. "A Survey of Greek Defixiones Not Included in the Special Corpora." *GRBS* 26 (1985): 151–97.

————. "New Greek Curse Tablets (1985–2000)." *GRBS* 41 (2000): 5–46.

Jordan, W. D. *White over Black: American Attitudes toward the Negro, 1550–1812*. Chapel Hill: University of North Carolina Press, 1968.

Jördens, A. "Das Verhältnis der römischen Amtsträger in Ägypten zu den 'Städten' in der Provinz." In W. Eck, ed., *Lokale Autonomie und römische Ordnungsmacht in den kaiserzeitlichen Provinzen*, 141–80. Munich: Oldenbourg, 1999.

————. *Statthalterliche Verwaltung in der römischen Kaiserzeit: Studien zum praefectus Aegypti*. Hist. E. 175. Stuttgart: Steiner, 2009.

Kaper, O., ed. *Life on the Fringe: Living in the Southern Egyptian Deserts during the Roman and Early-Byzantine Periods*. Leiden: CNWS, 1998.

Kasher, A. *The Jews in Hellenistic and Roman Egypt: The Struggle for Equal Rights*. Tübingen: Mohr, 1985.

Katzoff, R. "Sources of Law in Roman Egypt: The Role of the Prefects." *ANRW* II.13 (1980): 807–44.

————. "Prefectural Edicts and Letters." *ZPE* 48 (1982): 209–17.

Kazhdan, A., ed. *The Oxford Dictionary of Byzantium*. New York: Oxford University Press, 1991.

Kehoe, D. *The Economics of Agriculture on Roman Imperial Estates in North Africa*. Göttingen: Vandenhoeck & Ruprecht, 1988.

————. *Management and Investment on Estates in Roman Egypt during the Early Empire*. Bonn: Habelt, 1992.

————. "The Early Roman Empire: Production." In W. Scheidel et al., eds., *The Cambridge Economic History of the Greco-Roman World*, 543–69. Cambridge, U.K.: Cambridge University Press, 2008.

Kelly, B. "The Repression of Violence in the Roman Principate." PhD diss., Oxford University, 2002.

————. "Riot Control and Imperial Ideology in the Roman Empire." *Phoenix* 61 (2007): 150–76.

————. "Policing and Security." In P. Erdkamp, ed., *A Cambridge Companion to the City of Rome.*, Cambridge, U.K.: Cambridge University Press, forthcoming.

Kennedy, D. "Some Observations on the Praetorian Guard." *Ancient Society* 9 (1978): 275–301.

Keppie, L. *The Making of the Roman Army: From Republic to Empire*, 2nd ed. Norman: University of Oklahoma Press, 1998.

———. "The Army and the Navy." In A. K. Bowman et al., eds., *CAH*, vol. 10, 371–96. Cambridge, U.K.: Cambridge University Press, 1996.

Kissel, T. *Untersuchungen zur Logistik des römischen Heeres in den Provinzen des griechischen Ostens (27 v. Chr.–235 n. Chr.)* St. Katharinen: Scripta Mercaturae, 1995.

Kittredge, G. "Arm-pitting among the Greeks." *AJP* 6 (1885): 151–69.

Kleijwegt, M. *Ancient Youth: The Ambiguity of Youth and the Absence of Adolescence in Greco-Roman Society.* Amsterdam: Gieben, 1991.

Kokkinia, C. "The Governor's Boot and the City's Politicians: Greek Communities and Rome's Representatives under the Empire." In A. Kolb, ed., *Herrschaftsstrukturen und Herrschaftspraxis: Konzepte, Prinzipien und Startegien der Administration im römischen Kaiserreich*, 181–89. Berlin: Akademie Verlag, 2006.

Kolb, A. *Transport und Nachrichtentransfer im römischen Reich.* Berlin: Akademie Verlag, 2000.

———. "Transport and Communication in the Roman State: The *Cursus Publicus.*" In C. Adams and R. Laurence, eds., *Travel and Geography in the Roman Empire*, 95–105. London and New York: Routledge, 2001.

Kool, P. *De Phylakieten in Grieks-Romeins Egypte.* Amsterdam: Poortpers, 1954.

Kortus, M. *Briefe des Apollonius-Archives aus der Sammlung Papyri Gissenses: Edition, Übersetzung und Kommentar.* Giessen: Universitätsbibliothek, 1999.

Kotansky, R. "Incantations and Prayers for Salvation on Inscribed Greek Amulets." In C. Faraone and D. Obbink, eds., *Magika Hiera: Ancient Greek Magic and Religion*, 107–37. Oxford: Oxford University Press, 1991.

———. *Greek Magical Amulets: The Inscribed Gold, Silver, Copper, and Bronze Lamellae.* Part 1: *Published Texts of Known Provenance.* Opladen: Westdeutscher Verlag, 1994.

Krause, J.-U. *Gefängnisse im Römischen Reich.* HABES 23. Stuttgart: Steiner, 1996.

———. *Kriminalgeschichte der Antike.* Munich: Beck, 2004.

Kudlien, F. "Zur sozialen Situation des flüchtigen Sklaven in der Antike." *Hermes* 116 (1988): 232–52.

Kuhlmann, P. A. *Die giessener literarischen Papyri und die Caracalla-Erlasse: Edition, Übersetzung und Kommentar.* Giessen: Universitätsbibliothek, 1994.

Kurian, G. T., ed. *World Encyclopedia of Police Forces and Penal Systems*, 1st ed. New York: Facts on File, 1989.

———. *World Encyclopedia of Police Forces and Correctional Systems*, rev. ed. 2 vols. Detroit: Thomas Gale, 2006.

Lanciani, R. *Ancient Rome in the Light of Recent Discoveries.* Boston and New York: Houghton Mifflin, 1888.

Lane, E. "Sabazius and the Jews in Valerius Maximus: A Re-examination." *JRS* 69 (1979): 35–38.

Lattimore, R. *Themes in Greek and Latin Epitaphs.* Urbana: University of Illinois Press, 1942.

Laurence, R. *The Roads of Roman Italy: Mobility and Social Change.* London and New York: Routledge, 1999.

Lee, B. T. *Apuleius' Florida: A Commentary.* Berlin and New York: De Gruyter, 2005.

Lendon, J. E. *Empire of Honour: The Art of Government in the Roman World.* Oxford: Clarendon, 1997.

———. "Social Control at Rome." *CJ* 93 (1997): 83–88.

———. "The Legitimacy of the Roman Emperor: Against Weberian Legitimacy and Imperial 'Strategies of Legitimation.'" In A. Kolb, ed., *Herrschaftsstrukturen und Herrschaftspraxis: Konzepte, Prinzipien und Startegien der Administration im römischen Kaiserreich,* 53–63. Berlin: Akademie Verlag, 2006.

Lenski, N. "*Servi Publici* in Late Antiquity." In J.-U. Krause and C. Witschel, eds., *Die Stadt in der Spätantike—Niedergang oder Wandel?* Hist. E. 190, 335–57. Stuttgart: Steiner, 2006.

Lesquier, J. *L'armée romaine d'Égypte d'Auguste à Dioclétien.* Cairo: Institut Français d'Archéologie Orientale du Caire, 1918.

Levene, D. *A Corpus of Magic Bowls: Incantation Texts in Jewish Aramaic from Late Antiquity.* London and New York: Kegan Paul, 2003.

Levi, R. "Making Counter-Law: On Having No Apparent Purpose in Chicago." *British Journal of Criminology* 49 (2009): 131–49.

Levick, B. "*Concordia* at Rome." In R. Carson and C. Kraay, eds., *Scripta nummaria romana: Essays Presented to Humphrey Sutherland,* 217–33. London: Spink, 1978.

———. *Vespasian.* London and New York: Routledge, 1999.

Lewis, C. T., and C. Short. *A Latin Dictionary.* Oxford: Clarendon, 1879.

Lewis, N. *The Compulsory Public Services of Roman Egypt,* 3rd ed. Florence: Gonnelli, 1982.

———. *Life in Egypt under Roman Rule.* Oxford: Oxford University Press, 1983.

———. "The Romanity of Roman Egypt: A Growing Consensus." *Atti del XVII Congresso Internazionale di Papirologia* 3 (1984): 1077–84.

———, ed. *The Documents from the Bar-Kokhba Period in the Cave of Letters I: The Greek Papyri.* Jerusalem: Israel Exploration Society, 1989.

Liebeschuetz, J. H. W. G. *Antioch: City and Imperial Administration in the Later Roman Empire.* Oxford: Clarendon, 1972.

———. *The Decline and Fall of the Roman City.* Oxford: Oxford University Press, 2001.

Linderski, J. "The Surname of M. Antonius Creticus and the Cognomina *ex victis gentibus.*" *ZPE* 80 (1990): 157–64. Reprinted in J. Linderski, *Roman Questions (I),* 436–43.

———. *Roman Questions (I): Selected Papers.* HABES 20. Stuttgart: Steiner, 1995.

———. "*Imago hortorum*: Pliny the Elder and the Gardens of the Urban Poor." *Class. Phil.* 96.3 (2001): 305–8. Reprinted in J. Linderski, *Roman Questions II,* 337–41.

————. "*Isto vilius, Immo carum.*" *AJP* 123 (2002): 587–99. Reprinted in J. Linderski, *Roman Questions II*, 20–30.

————. *Roman Questions II: Selected Papers*. HABES 44. Stuttgart: Steiner, 2007.

Lindsay, J. *Daily Life in Roman Egypt*. London: Muller, 1963.

Lintott, A. *Violence, Civil Strife and Revolution in the Classical City 750–330 BC*. Baltimore: Johns Hopkins University Press, 1982.

————. *The Constitution of the Roman Republic*. Oxford: Clarendon, 1999.

————. *Violence in Republican Rome*, 2nd ed. Oxford: Oxford University Press, 1999.

Lissi Caronna, E. "Castra peregrina." In E. M. Steinby, ed., *Lexicon Topographicum Urbis Romae*, vol. 1, 249–51. Rome: Quasar, 1993.

————. "Castra praetoria." In E. M. Steinby, ed., *Lexicon Topographicum Urbis Romae*, vol. 1, 251–54. Rome: Quasar, 1993.

Llewelyn, S. "P. Harris I 62 and the Pursuit of Fugitive Slaves." *ZPE* 118 (1997): 245–50.

————. "The Government's Pursuit of Runaway Slaves." *New Documents Illustrating Early Christianity* 8: *A Review of the Greek Inscriptions and Papyri Published 1984–85* (1998): 9–46.

Lobur, J. *Consensus, Concordia, and the Formation of Roman Imperial Ideology*. New York: Routledge, 2008.

Lo Cascio, E. "The Emperor and His Administration." In A. K. Bowman et al., eds., *CAH*, vol. 12, 131–83. Cambridge, U.K.: Cambridge University Press, 2005.

————. "The Early Roman Empire: The State and the Economy." In W. Scheidel et al., eds., *The Cambridge Economic History of the Greco-Roman World*, 619–47. Cambridge, U.K.: Cambridge University Press, 2008.

Long, A. A. *Epictetus: A Stoic and Socratic Guide to Life*. Oxford: Clarendon, 2002.

Lopuszanski, G. "La police romaine et les chrétiens." *L'Antiquité Classique* 20 (1951): 5–46.

Lovato, A. *Il carcere nel diritto penale romano dai Severi a Giustiniano*. Bari: Cacucci, 1994.

Lyasse, E. *Le principat et son fondateur: L'utilisation de la référence à Auguste de Tibère à Trajan*. Collection Latomus 311. Brussels: Latomus, 2008.

Mackie, N. *Local Administration in Roman Spain, A.D. 14–212*. BAR 172. Oxford: BAR, 1983.

MacMullen, R. *Soldier and Civilian in the Later Roman Empire*. Cambridge, Mass.: Harvard University Press, 1963.

————. *Enemies of the Roman Order*. Cambridge, Mass.: Harvard University Press, 1966.

————. "Social History in Astrology." *Ancient Society* 2 (1971): 105–16. Reprinted in R. MacMullen, *Changes in the Roman Empire: Essays in the Ordinary*, 218–24. Princeton, N.J.: Princeton University Press, 1990.

———. *Roman Social Relations.* New Haven, Conn., and London: Yale University Press, 1974.

———. "Judicial Savagery in the Roman Empire." *Chiron* 1986, 147–66. Reprinted in R. MacMullen, *Changes in the Roman Empire: Essays in the Ordinary,* 204–17. Princeton, N.J.: Princeton University Press, 1990.

———. *Corruption and the Decline of Rome.* New Haven, Conn.: Yale University Press, 1988.

Magie, D. *Roman Rule in Asia Minor to the End of the Third Century after Christ.* 2 vols. Princeton, N.J.: Princeton University Press, 1950.

Magness, J. *The Archaeology of Qumran and the Dead Sea Scrolls.* Grand Rapids, Mich.: Eerdmans, 2002.

———. "In the Footsteps of the Tenth Roman Legion in Judea." In A. Berlin and A. Overman, eds., *The First Jewish Revolt: Archaeology, History, and Ideology,* 189–212. London and New York: Routledge, 2002.

Mann, J. C. "The Organization of *Frumentarii.*" *ZPE* 74 (1988): 149–50.

Marincola, J. *Authority and Tradition in Ancient Historiography.* Cambridge, U.K.: Cambridge University Press, 1997.

Marshall, A. J. "Governors on the Move." *Phoenix* 20 (1966): 231–46.

———. "Symbols and Showmanship in Roman Public Life: The Fasces," *Phoenix* 38 (1984): 120–41.

Mason, H. *Greek Terms for Roman Institutions: A Lexicon and Analysis.* Toronto: Hakkert, 1974.

Mason, S. "Contradiction or Counterpoint? Josephus and Historical Method." *Review of Rabbinic Judaism* 6 (2003): 145–88. Reprinted in S. Mason, *Josephus, Judea, and Christian Origins: Methods and Categories,* 103–37. Peabody, Mass.: Hendrickson, 2009.

Mattern, S. *Rome and the Enemy: Imperial Strategy in the Principate.* Berkeley and Los Angeles: University of California Press, 1999.

McGing, B. "Bandits, Real and Imagined, in Greco-Roman Egypt." *Bulletin of the American Society of Papyrologists* 35 (1998): 159–83.

McGinn, T. A. *Prostitution, Sexuality, and the Law in Ancient Rome.* New York: Oxford University Press, 1998.

Meeks, W. A. *The Origins of Christian Morality: The First Two Centuries.* New Haven, Conn.: Yale University Press, 1993.

Meiggs, R. *Roman Ostia,* 2nd ed. Oxford: Clarendon, 1973.

Melluso, M. "In tema di *servi fugitivi in ecclesia* in epoca giustinianea: Le *Bullae Sanctae Sophiae,*" *Dialogues d'Histoire Ancienne* 28, no. 1 (2002): 61–92.

Ménard, H. "L'insécurité dans la Rome impériale: Entre réalité et imaginaire." *Histoire Urbaine* 2 (2000): 59–71.

———. *Maintenir l'ordre à Rome: IIe–IVe siècles ap. J.-C.* Seyssel: Champ Vallon, 2004.

Meyer, E. "The Justice of the Roman Governor and the Performance of Prestige." In A. Kolb, ed., *Herrschaftsstrukturen und Herrschaftspraxis: Konzepte, Prinzipien und Strategien der Administration im römischen Kaiserreich*, 167–80. Berlin: Akademie Verlag, 2006.

Meyer, M., and R. Smith, eds. *Ancient Christian Magic: Coptic Texts of Ritual Power*. Princeton, N.J.: Princeton University Press, 1999.

Meyer-Zwiffelhoffer, E. Πολιτικῶς ἄρχειν: *Zum Regierungsstil der senatorischen Statthalter in den kaiserzeitlichen griechischen Provinzen*. Hist. E. 165. Stuttgart: Steiner, 2002.

Millar, F. *A Study of Cassius Dio*. Oxford: Clarendon, 1964.

———. "Paul of Samosata, Zenobia and Aurelian: The Church, Local Culture, and Political Allegiance in Third-Century Syria." *JRS* 61 (1971): 1–17. Reprinted in F. Millar, *Rome, the Greek World, and the East*, vol. 3 (2006), 243–74.

———. *The Emperor in the Roman World, 31 BC–AD 337*. Ithaca, N.Y.: Cornell University Press, 1977; reprinted with new afterword, 1992.

———. *The Roman Empire and Its Neighbours*, 2nd ed. New York: Delacorte, 1981.

———. "The World of the *Golden Ass*." *JRS* 71 (1981): 63–75. Reprinted in Millar, *Rome, the Greek World, and the East*, vol. 2 (2004), 313–35.

———. "Empire and City, Augustus to Julian: Obligations, Excuses, and Status." *JRS* 73 (1983): 76–96. Reprinted in Millar, *Rome, the Greek World, and the East*, vol. 2 (2004), 336–71.

———. "Condemnation to Hard Labour in the Roman Empire." *PBSR* 52 (1984): 123–47. Reprinted in Millar, *Rome, the Greek World, and the East*, vol. 2 (2002), 120–50.

———. "The Mediterranean and the Roman Revolution: Politics, War, and the Economy." *P&P* 102 (1984): 3–24. Reprinted in Millar, *Rome, the Greek World, and the East*, vol. 1 (2002), 215–37.

———. "A New Approach to the Roman Jurists." *JRS* 76 (1986): 272–80.

———. "'Senatorial' Provinces: An Institutionalized Ghost." *Ancient World* 20 (1989): 93–97. Reprinted in Millar, *Rome, the Greek World, and the East*, vol. 1 (2002), 314–20.

———. *The Crowd in Rome in the Late Republic*. Ann Arbor: University of Michigan Press, 1998.

———. *Rome, the Greek World, and the East*, 3 vols. H. M. Cotton and G. M. Rogers, eds. Chapel Hill: University of North Carolina Press, 2002–06.

———. "Redrawing the Map?" In Millar, *Rome, the Greek World, and the East*, vol. 3 (2006), 487–509.

Mitchell, M. "John Chrysostom on Philemon: A Second Look." *Harvard Theological Review* 88 (1995): 135–48.

Mitchell, S. "Requisitioned Transport in the Roman Empire: A New Inscription from Pisidia." *JRS* 66 (1976): 106–31, with plates VIII–X.

———. "The Requisitioning Edict of Sex. Sotidius Strabo Libuscidianus." *ZPE* 45 (1982): 99–100.

———. "Native Rebellion in the Pisidian Taurus." In K. Hopwood, ed., *Organised Crime in Antiquity*, 155–75. London and Swansea: Duckworth and Classical Press of Wales, 1989.

———. *Anatolia: Land, Men, and Gods in Asia Minor*, 2 vols. Oxford: Oxford University Press, 1993.

———. *Cremna in Pisidia: An Ancient City in Peace and in War*. London: Duckworth, 1995.

———. "The Admininstration of Roman Asia from 133 BC to AD 250." In W. Eck, ed., *Lokale Autonomie und römische Ordnungsmacht in den kaiserzeitlichen Provinzen*, 17–46. Munich: Oldenbourg, 1999.

Mitchell, T. "Cicero and the *Senatus Consultum Ultimum*." *Historia* 20 (1971): 47–61.

Modrzejewski, J. M. *The Jews of Egypt: From Ramses II to Emperor Hadrian*. Trans. R. Cornman. Princeton, N.J.: Princeton University Press, 1995.

Mommsen, T. *Römisches Staatsrecht*, 3rd ed., 3 vols. Leipzig: Hirzel, 1887–88.

———. *Römisches Strafrecht*. Leipzig: Duncker & Humblot, 1899.

Musurillo, H. *The Acts of the Pagan Martyrs: Acta Alexandrinorum*. Oxford: Clarendon, 1954.

———. *Acta Alexandrinorum: De mortibus Alexandriae nobilium fragmenta papyracea graeca*. Leipzig: Teubner, 1961.

———, ed. *The Acts of the Christian Martyrs*. Oxford: Clarendon, 1972.

Musurillo, H., and G. Parássoglou. "A New Fragment of the *Acta Alexandrinorum*." *ZPE* 15 (1974): 1–7.

Naiden, F. *Ancient Supplication*. New York: Oxford University Press, 2006.

Nelis-Clément, J. *Les beneficiarii: Militaires et administrateurs au service de l'empire (Ier s. a.C.–VIe s. p.C.)*. Bordeaux: Ausonius, 2000.

Nippel, W. "Policing Rome." *JRS* 74 (1984): 20–29.

———. *Aufruhr und "Polizei" in der römischen Republik*. Stuttgart: Klett-Cotta, 1988.

———. *Public Order in Ancient Rome*. Cambridge, U.K.: Cambridge University Press, 1995.

Nollé, J. "Marktrechte außerhalb der Stadt: Lokale Autonomie zwischen Statthalter und Zentralort. In W. Eck, ed., *Lokale Autonomie und römische Ordnungsmacht in den kaiserzeitlichen Provinzen*, 93–113. Munich: Oldenbourg, 1999.

Nordling, J. *Philemon*. Concordia Commentary Series. St. Louis: Concordia, 2004.

Noreña, C. F. "The Communication of the Emperor's Virtues." *JRS* 91 (2001): 146–68.

———. "The Social Economy of Pliny's Correspondence with Trajan." *AJP* 128 (2007): 239–77.

Norris, F. W. "Paul of Samosata: *Procurator Ducenarius*." *Journal of Theological Studies* 35 (1984): 50–70.

Nótári, T. "The Spear as the Symbol of Property and Power in Ancient Rome." *Acta Juridica Hungarica* 48 (2007): 231–57.

Oliver, J. H. "A Roman Governor Visits Samothrace." *AJP* 87 (1966): 75–80.

———. *Greek Constitutions of Early Roman Emperors from Inscriptions and Papyri.* Philadelphia: American Philosophical Society, 1989.

Olster, D. *Roman Defeat, Christian Response, and the Literary Construction of the Jew.* Philadelphia: University of Pennsylvania Press, 1994.

Oost, S. "The Alexandrian Seditions under Philip and Gallienus." *Class. Phil.* 56 (1961): 1–20.

Ortisi, S. "Roman Military in the Vesuvius Area." In L. de Bois and E. Lo Cascio, eds., *Impact of the Roman Army*, 343–53. Leiden: Brill, 2007.

Osgood, J. *Caesar's Legacy: Civil War and the Emergence of the Roman Empire.* Cambridge, U.K.: Cambridge University Press, 2006.

———. "*Nuptiae iure civili congruae*: Apuleius's Story of Cupid and Psyche and the Roman Law of Marriage." *Transactions of the American Philological Association* 136 (2006): 415–41.

———. *Claudius Caesar: Image and Power in the Early Roman Empire.* Cambridge, U.K.: Cambridge University Press, 2011.

Ott, J. "Überlegungen zur Stellung der Beneficiarier in der Rangordnung des römischen Heeres." In E. Schallmayer et al., eds., *Der römische Weihebezirk von Osterburken II: Kolloquium 1990 und paläoboatische-osteologische Untersuchungen*, 233–49. Stuttgart: Theiss, 1994.

———. *Die Beneficiarier: Untersuchungen zu ihrer Stellung innerhalb der Rangordnung des Römischen Heeres und zu ihrer Funktion.* Hist. E. 92. Stuttgart: Steiner, 1995.

Palme, B. "Die *Officia* der Statthalter in der Spätantike: Forschungsstand und Perspektiven." *Antiquité Tardive* 7 (1999): 85–133.

———. "Militärs in der administrativen Kontrolle der Bevölkerung in römischen Ägypten." In A. Eich, ed., *Die Verwaltung der kaiserzeitlichen römischen Armee: Studien für Hartmut Wolff*, HABES 211, 149–64. Stuttgart: Steiner, 2010.

Panciera, S. "Soldati e civili a Roma nei primi tre secoli dell'Impero." In W. Eck, ed., *Prosopographie und Sozialgeschichte: Studien zur Methodik und Erkenntnismöglichkeit der kaiserzeitlichen Prosopographie*, 261–76. Vienna: Böhlau, 1993.

———. "Le virtù del governatore provinciale nelle iscrizioni latine da Augusto a Diocleziano." In S. Demougin et al., eds., *H.-G. Pflaum, un historien du XXe siècle*, 457–84. Geneva: Droz, 2006.

Parker, S. T. "Roman Legionary Fortresses in the East." In R. Brewer, ed., *Roman Fortresses and Their Legions: Papers in Honour of George C. Boon*, 121–38. London and Cardiff: Society of Antiquaries of London, 2000.

Paschoud, F. "*Frumentarii, agentes in rebus, magistriani, curiosi, veredarii*: Problèmes de terminologie." *Bonner Historia-Augusta-Colloquium* 1979–1981 (1983): 215–32.

Passerini, A. *Le coorti pretorie.* Rome: Signorelli, 1939.

Peachin, M. "Which Philip?" *ZPE* 73 (1988): 98–100.

———. *Iudex vice Caesaris: Deputy Emperors and the Administration of Justice during the Principate*. HABES 21. Stuttgart: Steiner, 1996.

———. "Petition to a Centurion from the NYU Papyrus Collection and the Question of Informal Adjudication Performed by Soldiers (*P.Sijp.* 15)." In A. Sirks and K. A. Worp, eds., *Papyri in Memory of P.J. Sijpesteijn*, 79–97. Chippenham: American Society of Papyrologists, 2007.

Pecere, O. *Petronio: La novella della Matrona di Efeso*. Padua: Editrice Antenore, 1975.

Penwill, J. "Expelling the Mind: Politics and Philosophy in Flavian Rome." In A. J. Boyle and W. J. Dominik, eds., *Flavian Rome: Culture, Image, Text*, 345–68. Leiden: Brill, 2003.

Perry, B. E., ed. *Aesopica: A Series of Texts relating to Aesop or Ascribed to Him or Closely Connected with the Literary Tradition That Bears His Name*. Urbana: University of Illinois Press, 1952.

———. *Secundus, the Silent Philosopher: The Greek Life of Secundus*. Ithaca, N.Y.: Cornell University Press, 1964.

Peters, E. "Prison before the Prison: The Ancient and Medieval Worlds." In N. Morris and D. Rothman, eds., *The Oxford History of the Prison: The Practice of Punishment in Western Society*, 3–47. New York: Oxford University Press, 1995.

Petraccia Lucernoni, M. F. *Gli* stationarii *in età imperiale. Serta antiqua et mediaevalia* 3. Rome: Bretschneider, 2001.

Pflaum, H-G. *Essai sur le* cursus publicus *sous le haut-empire romain*. Paris: Imprimerie Nationale, 1940.

———. *Les procurateurs équestres sous le Haut-Empire romain*. Paris: A. Maisonneuve, 1950.

———. *Les carrières procuratoriennes équestres sous le Haut-Empire romain*. 4 vols. Paris: Geuthner, 1960–61.

Phang, S. E. *The Marriage of Roman Soldiers (13 BC–AD 235): Law and Family in the Imperial Army*. Columbia Studies in the Classical Tradition 24. Leiden: Brill, 2001.

———. *Roman Military Service: Ideologies of Discipline in the Late Republic and Early Principate*. Cambridge, U.K.: Cambridge University Press, 2008.

Phillips, C. R. "*Nullum Crimen sine Lege*: Socioreligious Sanctions on Magic." In C. Faraone and D. Obbink, eds., *Magika Hiera: Ancient Greek Magic and Religion*, 260–76. New York: Oxford University Press, 1991.

Phillips, D. A. "The Conspiracy of Egnatius Rufus and the Election of Suffect Consuls under Augustus." *Historia* 46 (1997): 103–12.

Pollard, N. *Soldiers, Cities, and Civilians in Roman Syria*. Ann Arbor: University of Michigan Press, 2000.

Pölönen, J. "Plebeians and Repression of Crime in the Roman Empire: From Torture of Convicts to Torture of Suspects." *Revue Internationale des Droits de l'Antiquité* 51 (2004): 217–57.

Potter, D. S. *Prophecy and History in the Crisis of the Roman Empire: A Historical Commentary on the Thirteenth Sibylline Oracle.* Oxford: Clarendon, 1990.

———. "Martyrdom as Spectacle." In R. Scodel, ed., *Theater and Society in the Classical World,* 53–88. Ann Arbor: Michigan University Press, 1993.

———. *Prophets and Emperors: Human and Divine Authority from Augustus to Theodosius.* Cambridge, Mass.: Harvard University Press, 1994.

———. "Emperors, Their Borders and Their Neighbors: The Scope of Imperial *Mandata.*" In D. Kennedy, ed., *The Roman Army in the East, JRA* Suppl. 18, 49–66. Ann Arbor, Mich.: Journal of Roman Archaeology, 1996.

———. *Literary Texts and the Roman Historian.* London and New York: Routledge, 1999.

———. *The Roman Empire at Bay: AD 180–395.* London and New York: Routledge, 2004.

Pucci Ben Zeev, Mi. *Diaspora Judaism in Turmoil, 116/117 CE: Ancient Sources and Modern Insights.* Leuven: Peeters, 2005.

Purcell, N. "The *Apparitores*: A Study in Social Mobility." *PBSR* 51 (1983): 125–73.

Raaflaub, K. A. "Searching for Peace in the Ancient World." In K. A. Raaflaub, ed., *War and Peace in the Ancient World,* 1–33. Malden and Oxford: Blackwell, 2007.

Rainbird, J. "The Firestations of Imperial Rome." *PBSR* 54 (1986): 147–69.

Ramsay, W. M. *The Cities and Bishoprics of Phrygia; Being an Essay of the Local History of Phrygia from the Earliest Times to the Turkish Conquest.* 2 vols. Oxford: Clarendon, 1895.

Rankov, N. B. "*Frumentarii,* the *Castra Peregrina* and the Provincial *Officia.*" *ZPE* 80 (1990): 176–82.

———. "Die Beneficiarier in den literarischen und papyrologischen Texten." In E. Schallmayer et al., eds., *Der römische Weihebezirk von Osterburken II: Kolloquium 1990 und paläoboatische-osteologische Untersuchungen,* 219–32. Stuttgart: Theiss, 1994.

———. "*Beneficiarii* (Military Staff Officers) and the Discoveries at Osterburken." *Journal of Roman Archaeology* 12, no. 2 (1999): 675–81.

———. "The Governor's Men: The *Officium Consularis* in Provincial Administration." In A. Goldsworthy and I. Hayes, eds., *The Roman Army as a Community, JRA* Suppl. 34, 15–34. Portsmouth, R.I.: Journal of Roman Archaeology, 1999.

———. "*Beneficiarii* and the Reality of Roman Bureaucracy." *Journal of Roman Archaeology* 15, no. 2 (2002): 524–27.

———. "The Origins of the *frumentarii.*" *Acta XII Congressus Internationalis Epigraphicae Graecae et Latinae* 2 (2007): 1169–72.

Rapske, B. *The Book of Acts and Paul in Roman Custody. The Book of Acts in Its First Century Setting,* vol. 3. Grand Rapids, Mich.: Eerdmans, 1994.

Raschke, M. G. "New Studies in Roman Commerce with the East." *ANRW* II.9.2 (1978): 604–1378.

Rathbone, D. "Poverty and Population in Roman Egypt." In M. Atkins and R. Osborne, eds., *Poverty in the Roman World*, 100–14. Cambridge, U.K.: Cambridge University Press, 2006.

Rawlings, P. *Policing: A Short History*. Uffculme: Willan, 2002.

Rea, J. R. "A New Version of P. Yale Inv. 299." *ZPE* 27 (1977): 151–56.

———. "Proceedings before Q. Maecius Laetus, Praef. Aeg., etc." *Journal of Juristic Papyrology* 19 (1983): 91–101.

Reardon, B. P., ed. *Collected Ancient Greek Novels*. Berkeley and Los Angeles: University of California Press, 1989.

Reiner, E. "Runaway—Seize Him." In J. G. Dercksen, ed., *Assyria and Beyond: Studies Presented to Mogens Trolle Larsen*, 475–82. Leiden: Nederlands Instituut voor het Nabije Oosten, 2004.

Reinhold, M. "Usurpation of Status and Status Symbols in the Roman Empire." *Historia* 20 (1971): 275–302.

Revell, L. *Roman Imperialism and Local Identities*. Cambridge, U.K.: Cambridge University Press, 2009.

Ricci, C. *Soldati delle milizie urbane fuori di Roma: La documentazione epigrafica*. *Opuscula Epigraphica* 5. Rome: Quasar, 1994.

Richardson, L. *A New Topographical Dictionary of Ancient Rome*. Baltimore: Johns Hopkins University Press, 1992.

Richmond, I. A. "The *Sarmatae, Bremetennacum Veteranorum* and the *Regio Bremetennacensis*." *JRS* 35 (1945): 15–29.

Riess, W. *Apuleius und die Räuber: Ein Beitrag zur historischen Kriminalitätsforschung*. HABES 35 Stuttgart: Steiner, 2001.

———. "Between Fiction and Reality: Robbers in Apuleius' *Golden Ass*." *Ancient Narrative* 1 (2000–01): 260–82.

———. "Hunting Down Robbers in 3rd Century Central Italy." In C. Wolff, ed., *Les exclus dans l'Antiquité*, 195–213. Paris: De Boccard, 2007.

Rife, J. "Officials of the Roman Provinces in Xenophon's *Ephesiaca*." *ZPE* 138 (2002): 93–108.

Riggsby, A. *Crime and Community in Ciceronian Rome*. Austin: University of Texas Press, 1999.

Rigsby, K. J. *Asylia: Territorial Inviolability in the Hellenistic World*. Hellenistic Culture and Society 22. Berkeley and Los Angeles: University of California Press, 1996.

———. "Graecolatina." *ZPE* 113 (1996): 249–52.

Rives, J. B. "The Decree of Decius and the Religion of Empire." *JRS* 89 (1999): 135–54.

Rivière, Y. "*Carcer et uincula*: La détention publique à Rome (sous la République et le Haut-Empire)." *MÉFRA* 106 (1994): 579–652.

———. *Les délateurs dans l'Empire romain.* BÉFAR 311. Rome: École Française de Rome, 2002.

———. "Recherche et identification des esclaves fugitifs dans l'Empire romain." In J. Andreau and C. Virlouvet, eds., *L'information et la mer dans le monde antique,* CÉFR 297, 115–96. Rome: École Française de Rome, 2002.

———. "Les batailles de Rome: Présence militaire et guerrilla urbaine à l'époque impériale." *Histoire Urbaine* 10 (2004): 63–87.

———. *Le cachot et les fers: Détention et coercition à Rome.* Paris: Belin, 2004.

———. "Encouragement, contrôle, lâchage et lynchage des agents du fisc impérial." In L. Feller, ed., *Contrôler les agents du pouvoir,* 329–42. Limoges: Presses Universitaires de Limoges, 2004.

———. "Pouvoir impérial et vengeance: De *Mars ultor* à la *diuina uindicta* (Ier-IVe siècle ap. J.-C.)." In D. Barthélemy et al., eds., *La vengeance 400–1200: Actes du colloque de l'Ecole Française de Rome,* CÉFR 357, 7–42. Rome: École Française de Rome, 2006.

———. "Le contrôle de l'appareil judiciaire de l'État dans l'Antiquité tardive." In J. Genet, ed., *Rome et l'état moderne européen,* CÉFR 377, 313–39. Rome: École Française de Rome, 2007.

Robert, L. "Études d'épigraphie grecque." *Rev. Phil.* 7 (1934): 267–92. Reprinted in L. Robert, *Opera minora selecta,* vol. 2, 1166–91. Amsterdam: Hakkert, 1969.

———. *Études anatoliennes: Recherches sur les incriptions grecques de l'Asie Mineure.* Paris: De Boccard, 1937.

———. "Sur un papyrus de Bruxelles." *Rev. Phil.* 17 (1943): 111–19. Reprinted in L. Robert, *Opera minora selecta,* vol. 1, 364–72. Amsterdam: Hakkert, 1969.

———. "La titulature de Nicée et de Nicomédie: La gloire et la haine." *Harvard Studies in Classical Philology* 81 (1977): 1–39.

———. "Documents d'Asie Mineure, VIII. Règlement impérial gréco-latin sur les hôtes imposés." *Bulletin de Correspondance Hellénique* 102 (1978): 432–37.

———, ed., with G. W. Bowersock, C. P Jones, J. Robert, and A. Vaillant. *Le martyre de Pionios, prêtre de Smyrne.* Washington, D.C.: Dumbarton Oaks, 1994.

Roberts, W. E. "A Study of *Concordia*: Changing Conceptions of Imperial Power and Responsibility in Late Antiquity." PhD diss., Emory University, Atlanta, 2003.

Robinson, O. F. *Ancient Rome: City Planning and Administration.* London and New York: Routledge, 1992.

———. *The Criminal Law of Ancient Rome.* Baltimore: Johns Hopkins University Press, 1995.

———. *Penal Practice and Penal Policy in Ancient Rome.* London and New York: Routledge, 2007.

Roller, M. B. *Constructing Autocracy: Aristocrats and Emperors in Julio-Claudian Rome.* Princeton, N.J.: Princeton University Press, 2001.

Rosenstein, N. *Imperatores Victi: Military Defeat and Aristocratic Competition in the Middle and Late Republic.* Berkeley and Los Angeles: University of California Press, 1990.

———. *Rome at War: Farms, Families, and Death in the Middle Republic.* Chapel Hill: University of North Carolina Press, 2004.

Rostovtzeff, M. "Die Domänenpolizei in dem römischen Kaiserreiche." *Philologus* 64 (1905): 297–307.

———. "*Synteleia Tironon.*" *JRS* 8 (1918): 26–33.

———. *The Social and Economic History of the Roman Empire,* 2nd ed. (*SEHRE*), rev. by P. M. Fraser, 2 vols. Oxford: Clarendon, 1957.

Roth, J. P. "The Length of the Siege of Masada." *Scripta Classica Israelica* 14 (1995): 87–110.

———. *The Logistics of the Roman Army at War.* Columbia Studies in the Classical Tradition 23. Leiden: Brill, 1999.

Roueché, C. "Rome, Asia and Aphrodisias in the Third Century." *JRS* 71 (1981): 103–20.

———. "Acclamations in the Later Roman Empire: New Evidence from Aphrodisias." *JRS* 74 (1984): 181–99.

Rowe, G. Review of *The Praetorship in the Roman Republic* by T. C. Brennan. *Bryn Mawr Classical Review,* August 21, 2001. http://bmcr.brynmawr.edu/2001/2001-08-21.html.

———. *Princes and Political Cultures: The New Tiberian Senatorial Decrees.* Ann Arbor: University of Michigan Press, 2002.

Russell, J. "A Roman Military Diploma from Eastern Pamphylia." *AJA* 95 (1991): 469–88.

Rutgers, L. "Roman Policy toward the Jews: Expulsions from the City of Rome during the First Century C.E." In K. Donfried and P. Richardson, eds., *Judaism and Christianity in First-Century Rome,* 93–116. Grand Rapids, Mich.: Eerdmans, 1998.

Rutledge, S. *Imperial Inquisitions: Prosecutors and Informants from Tiberius to Domitian.* London and New York: Routledge, 2001.

Saba, S. *The* Astynomoi *Law of Pergamon: Old and New Questions.* Forthcoming.

Sablayrolles, R. *Libertinus miles: Les cohortes de vigiles.* CÉFR 224. Rome: École Française de Rome, 1996.

———. "*Fastigium equestre*: Les grands préfectures équestres." In S. Demougin, H. Devijver, and M.-T. Rapsaet-Charlier, eds., *L'ordre équestre: Histoire d'une aristocratie (iie siècle av. J.-C.–iiie siècle ap. J.-C.),* CÉFR 257, 351–89. Paris: École Française de Rome, 1999.

———. "La rue, le soldat et le pouvoir: La garnison de Rome de César à Pertinax." *Pallas* 55 (2000): 127–53.

Saller, R. "Anecdotes as Historical Evidence for the Principate." *G&R* 27 (1980): 69–83.

———. "Corporal Punishment, Authority, and Obedience in the Roman Household." In B. Rawson, ed., *Marriage, Divorce, and Children in Ancient Rome*, 144–65. Oxford: Clarendon, 1991.

———. *Patriarchy, Property and Death in the Roman Family*. Cambridge, U.K.: Cambridge University Press, 1994.

Salmeri, G. "Dio, Rome, and the Civic Life of Asia Minor." In S. Swain, ed., *Dio Chrysostom: Politics, Letters, and Philosophy*, 53–92. Oxford: Oxford University Press, 2001.

Salway, B. "Travel, *itineraria* and *tabellaria*." In C. Adams and R. Laurence, eds., *Travel and Geography in the Roman Empire*, 22–66. London and New York: Routledge, 2001.

———. "Equestrian Prefects and the Award of Senatorial Honours from the Severans to Constantine." In A. Kolb, ed., *Herrschaftsstrukturen und Herrschaftspraxis: Konzepte, Prinzipien und Startegien der Administration im römischen Kaiserreich*, 115–35. Berlin: Akademie Verlag, 2006.

Sanders, E. P. *Judaism: Practice and Belief, 63BCE–66CE*. London and Philadelphia: Trinity, 1992.

Sandy, G. *The Greek World of Apuleius: Apuleius and the Second Sophistic*. Mnemosyne Suppl. 174. Leiden: Brill, 1997.

Sänger, P. "Die Eirenarchen im römischen und byzantinischen Ägypten." *Tyche* 20 (2005): 143–204.

Satlow, M. "Rhetoric and Assumptions: Romans and Rabbis on Sex." In M. Goodman, ed., *Jews in a Graeco-Roman World*, 135–44. Oxford: Clarendon, 1998.

Saxer, R. *Untersuchungen zu den Vexillationen des römischen Kaiserheeres von Augustus bis Diokletian*. Cologne and Graz: Böhlau, 1967.

Schäfer, P. *Jesus in the Talmud*. Princeton, N.J.: Princeton University Press, 2007.

Schaff, P. *History of the Christian Church*, 9th ed. 5 vols. New York: Scribner's, 1910.

Schallmayer, E., et al. *Der römische Weihebezirk von Osterburken I: Corpus der griechischen und lateinischen Beneficiarer-Inschriften des römischen Reiches*. Stuttgart: Theiss, 1990.

———. *Der römische Weihebezirk von Osterburken II: Kolloquium 1990 und paläoboatische-osteologische Untersuchungen*. Stuttgart: Theiss, 1994.

Scheid, J. *Res gestae divi Augusti: Hauts faits du divin Auguste*. Paris: Belles Lettres, 2007.

Scheidel, W., I. Morris, and R. Saller, eds. *The Cambridge Economic History of the Greco-Roman World*. Cambridge, U.K.: Cambridge University Press, 2008.

Schiffman, L. *Sectarian Law in the Dead Sea Scrolls: Courts, Testimony and the Penal Code*. Chico, Calif.: Scholars, 1983.

Schipp, O. "Der Raub freier Menschen in der Spätantike." In H. Heinen, ed., *Menschenraub, Menschenhandel und Sklaverei in antiker und moderner Perspektive*, FAS 37, 157–81. Stuttgart: Steiner, 2008.

Schuller, W. "Grenzen des spätrömischen Staates: Staatspolizei und Korruption." *ZPE* 16 (1975): 1–21.

———, ed. *Korruption im Altertum*. Munich: Oldenbourg, 1982.

Schulte, C. *Die Grammateis von Ephesos: Schreiberamt und Sozialstruktur in einer Provinzhauptstadt des römischen Kaiserreiches*. HABES 15. Stuttgart: Steiner, 1994.

Schumacher, L. *Sklaverei in der Antike: Alltag und Schicksal der Unfreien*. Munich: Beck, 2001.

———. *Stellung des Sklaven im Sakralrecht*. Stuttgart: Steiner, 2006.

Schwartz, J. "Dogs in Jewish Society in the Second Temple Period and in the Time of the Mishnah and Talmud." *Journal of Jewish Studies* 55 (2004): 246–77.

Scott, J. C. *The Art of Not Being Governed: An Anarchist History of Upland Southeast Asia*. New Haven, Conn.: Yale University Press, 2009.

Selinger, R. *Die Religionspolitik des Kaisers Decius: Anatomie einer Christenverfolgung*. Frankfurt: P. Lang, 1994.

———. *The Mid-Third Century Persecutions of Decius and Valerian*. Frankfurt: P. Lang, 2002.

Shaw, B. "Rural Periodic Markets in Roman North Africa as Mechanisms of Social Integration and Control." *Research in Economic Anthropology* 2 (1979): 91–117. Reprinted in B. Shaw, *Rulers, Nomads and Christians in Roman North Africa*. Aldershot: Variorum, 1995.

———. "Eaters of Flesh, Drinkers of Milk: The Ancient Mediterranean Ideology of the Pastoral Nomad." *Ancient Society* 13/14 (1982/83): 5–31.

———. "Bandits in the Roman Empire." *P&P* 105 (1984): 3–52.

———. "The Bandit." In A. Giardina, ed., *The Romans*, 300–41. Chicago: University of Chicago Press, 1993.

———. *Spartacus and the Slave Wars: A Brief History with Documents*. Boston: Bedford, 2001.

———. Review of *Apuleius und die Räuber* by W. Riess. *Ancient Narrative* 2 (2002): 268–79.

———. "Judicial Nightmares and Christian Memory." *Journal of Early Christian Studies* 11 (2003): 533–63.

Sheldon, R. M. *Intelligence Activities in Ancient Rome: Trust in the Gods but Verify*. London and New York: Frank Cass, 2005.

Sherk, R. K. *Roman Documents from the Greek East: Senatus Consulta and Epistulae to the Age of Augustus*. Baltimore: Johns Hopkins University Press, 1969.

———, ed. *Rome and the Greek East to the Death of Augustus*. Cambridge, U.K.: Cambridge University Press, 1984.

———, ed. *The Roman Empire: Augustus to Hadrian*. Cambridge, U.K.: Cambridge University Press, 1988.

Sherwin-White, A. N. *Roman Society and Roman Law in the New Testament*. Oxford: Clarendon, 1963.

———. *The Letters of Pliny: A Historical and Social Commentary*. Oxford: Clarendon, 1966.

Sinnigen, W. G. "The Roman Secret Service." *Classical Journal* 57 (1961): 65–72.

Slootjes, D. *The Governor and His Subjects in the Later Roman Empire*. Mnemosyne Suppl. 275. Leiden: Brill, 2006.

———. "Local *Potentes* in the Roman Empire: A New Approach to the Concept of Local Elites." *Latomus* 68 (2009): 416–32.

Smallwood, E. M. *The Jews under Roman Rule from Pompey to Diocletian: A Study in Political Relations*. Leiden: Brill, 1981.

———. "Philo and Josephus as Historians of the Same Events." In L. Feldman and G. Hata, eds., *Josephus, Judaism and Christianity*, 114–29. Detroit: Wayne State University Press, 1987.

Smith, M. *Traversing Eternity: Texts from the Afterlife from Ptolemaic and Roman Egypt*. Oxford: Oxford University Press, 2009.

Snell, D. *Flight and Freedom in the Ancient Near East*. Leiden: Brill, 2001.

Sosin, J. D. "Tyrian *Stationarii* at Puteoli." *Tyche* 14 (1999): 275–84.

Southern, P. *The Roman Empire from Severus to Constantine*. London and New York: Routledge, 2001.

Spaul, J. E. H. *Cohors 2: The Evidence for and a Short History of the Auxiliary Units of the Imperial Roman Army*. BAR 841. Oxford: Archaeopress, 2000.

Speidel, M. A. "Roman Army Pay Scales." *JRS* 82 (1992): 87–106.

Speidel, M. P. *Die Equites Singulares Augusti: Begleit-truppe der römischen Kaiser des 2. und 3. Jahrhunderts*. Bonn: Habelt, 1965.

———. *Guards of the Roman Armies: An Essay on the* Singulares *of the Provinces*. Bonn: Habelt, 1978.

———. "*Germani corporis custodes*." *Germania* 62 (1984): 31–45. Reprinted in M. P. Speidel, *Roman Army Studies*, vol. 2 (Mavors 8), 105–19. Stuttgart: Steiner, 1992.

———. "The Police Officer, a Hero: An Inscribed Relief from near Ephesos." *Epigraphica Anatolica* 5 (1985): 159–60. Reprinted in M. P. Speidel, *Roman Army Studies*, vol. 2 (Mavors 8), 190–91. Stuttgart: Steiner, 1992.

———. *Riding for Caesar: The Roman Emperors' Horse Guards*. Cambridge, Mass.: Harvard University Press, 1994.

———. *Emperor Hadrian's Speeches to the African Army: A New Text*. Mainz: Römisch-Germanisches Zentralmuseum, 2006.

Sperber, D. "*Calculo-Logistes-Hashban*." *Classical Quarterly* 19 (1969): 374–78.

———. "The Centurion as a Tax Collector." *Latomus* 28 (1969): 186–88.

———. "On Social and Economic Conditions in Third Century Palestine." *Archiv Orientální* 36 (1970): 1–25.

———. *The City in Roman Palestine*. New York: Oxford University Press, 1998.

Stadter, P. A. *Arrian of Nicomedia*. Chapel Hill: University of North Carolina Press, 1980.

———. "Pliny and the Ideology of Empire: The Correspondence with Trajan." *Prometheus* 32 (2006): 61–76.

———. "Biography and History." In J. Marincola, ed., *A Companion to Greek and Roman Historiography*, vol. 2, 528–40. Malden and Oxford: Blackwell, 2007.

Starr, C. "Epictetus and the Tyrant." *Class. Phil.* 44 (1949): 20–29.

———. *The Roman Imperial Navy*, 3rd ed. Chicago: Ares, 1993.

Stauffer, E. *Jesus and His Story*. Trans. D. Barton. London: SCM, 1960.

Ste. Croix, G. E. M. de. "Why Were the Early Christians Persecuted?" *P&P* 26 (1963): 6–38.

Stephens, S., and J. J. Winkler, eds. *Ancient Greek Novels: The Fragments: Introduction, Text, Translation, and Commentary*. Princeton, N.J.: Princeton University Press, 1994.

Stertz, S. "Pseudo-Aristides, ΕΙΣ ΒΑΣΙΛΕΑ." *Classical Quarterly* n.s. 29 (1979): 172–97.

———. "Aelius Aristides' Political Ideas." *ANRW* II.34.2 (1993): 1248–70.

Stewart, R. "The Textual Transmission of the *Sortes Astrampsychi*." *Illinois Classical Studies* 20 (1995): 135–47.

Stockton, D. *The Gracchi*. Oxford: Clarendon, 1979.

Stöver, H. D. *Die Prätorianer: Kaisermacher–Kaisermörder*. Munich: Langen Müller, 1994.

Strubbe, J. H. M. "'Cursed Be He That Moves My Bones.'" In C. Faraone and D. Obbink, eds., *Magika Hiera: Ancient Greek Magic and Religion*, 33–59. New York: Oxford University Press, 1991.

Swain, S. "The Reliability of Philostratus's *Lives of the Sophists*." *Classical Antiquity* 10 (1991): 148–63.

———. *Hellenism and Empire: Language, Classicism, and Power in the Greek World AD 50–250*. Oxford: Clarendon, 1996.

———. "Reception and Interpretation." In S. Swain, ed., *Dio Chrysostom: Politics, Letters, and Philosophy*, 13–50. Oxford: Oxford University Press, 2001.

Swift, L. J. "The Anonymous Encomium of Philip the Arab." *GRBS* 7 (1966): 267–89.

Syme, R. Review of *Les cohortes prétoriennes* by M. Durry. *JRS* 29 (1939): 242–48.

———. *The Roman Revolution*. Oxford: Clarendon, 1939.

———. "The Conquest of North-west Spain." In *Legio VII Gemina*, 83–107. León: Diputación Provincial, 1970. Reprinted in R. Syme, *Roman Papers*, vol. 2, 825–54. Oxford: Clarendon, 1979.

———. *The Augustan Aristocracy*. Oxford: Clarendon, 1986.

Tabbernee, W., and P. Lampe. *Pepouza and Tymion: The Discovery and Archaeological Exploration of a Lost Ancient City and an Imperial Estate*. Berlin: De Gruyter, 2008.

Tabor, J. *The Jesus Dynasty: The Hidden History of Jesus, His Royal Family, and the Birth of Christianity*. New York: Simon & Schuster, 2006.

Tajra, H. W. *The Martyrdom of St. Paul: Historical and Judicial Context, Traditions, and Legends*. Tübingen: Mohr, 1994.

Talbert, R. J. A. "Pliny the Younger as Governor of Bithynia-Pontus." *Collection Latomus* 168 (1980): 412–35.

———. *The Senate of Imperial Rome*. Princeton, N.J.: Princeton University Press, 1984.

———. "The Decurions of *Colonia Genetiva Iulia* in Session." In J. González, ed., *Estudios sobre Urso: Colonia Iulia Genetiva*, 57–67. Seville: Alfar, 1989.

———. Review of *Corruption and the Decline of Rome* by R. MacMullen. *Phoenix* 45 (1991): 85–87.

———, ed. *The Barrington Atlas of the Greek and Roman World*. Princeton, N.J.: Princeton University Press, 2000.

———. "Germanicus and Piso." Review of *Princes and Political Cultures: The New Tiberian Senatorial Decrees* by G. Rowe. *Classical Review* 54 (2004): 180–82.

———. "Cartography and Taste in Peutinger's Roman Map." In R. Talbert and K. Brodersen, eds., *Space in the Roman World: Its Perception and Presentation*, 113–41. Münster: LIT, 2004.

———. "Rome's Provinces as Framework for World-View." In L. de Ligt et al., eds., *Roman Rule and Civic Life: Local and Regional Perspectives*, Impact of Empire 4, 21–37. Amsterdam: Gieben, 2004.

———. *Rome's World: The Peutinger Map Reconsidered*. New York: Cambridge University Press, 2010.

Thomas, J. D. "Communication between the Prefect of Egypt, the Procurators and the Nome Officials." In W. Eck, ed., *Lokale Autonomie und römische Ordnungsmacht in den kaiserzeitlichen Provinzen*, 181–95. Munich: Oldenbourg, 1999.

Thurmond, D. L. "Some Roman Slave Collars in *CIL*." *Athenaeum* 82 (1994): 459–93.

Tomlin, R. S. O. "The Curse Tablets." In B. Cunliffe, ed., *The Temple of Sulis Minerva at Bath, Vol. 2: The Finds from the Sacred Spring*, 59–277. Oxford: Oxford University Committee for Archaeology, 1988.

———. "'The Girl in Question': A New Text from Roman London." *Britannia* 34 (2003): 41–51.

Torallas Tovar, S. "The Police in Byzantine Egypt: The Hierarchy in the Papyri from the Fourth to the Seventh Centuries." In A. McDonald and C. Riggs, eds., *Current Research in Egyptology* (I), BAR 909, 115–23. Oxford: Archaeopress, 2000.

———. "Los *riparii* en los papiros del Egipto tardoantiguo." *Aquila Legionis* 1 (2001): 123–52.

Torallas Tovar, S., and I. Pérez Martín, eds. *Castigo y reclusión en el mundo antiguo.* Madrid: CSIC, 2003.

Tost, S. "Schreiben eines Riparius an seinen Vorgesetzten." In B. Palme, ed., *Wiener Papyri als Festgabe zum 60. Geburtstag von Hermann Harrauer (P. Harrauer)*, 223–26. Vienna: Holzhausen, 2001.

Toynbee, J. M. C. *Death and Burial in the Roman World.* Ithaca, N.Y.: Cornell University Press, 1971.

Treggiari, S. *Cicero's Cilician Letters*, 2nd ed. LACTOR 10. London: London Association of Classical Teachers, 1996.

———. *Roman Social History.* London and New York: Routledge, 2002.

Urbainczyk, T. *Slave Revolts in Antiquity.* Berkeley and Los Angeles: University of California Press, 2008.

Valvo, A. "M. Valerio Messalla Corvino negli studi più recenti." *ANRW* II.30.3 (1983): 1663–80.

Van der Horst, P. W. *Philo's Flaccus: The First Pogrom.* Leiden: Brill, 2003.

Van Rengen, W. "Les laissez-passer." In J. Bingen et al., eds., *Mons Claudianus: Ostraca graeca et latina I (O.Claud, 1 à 190)*, 57–75. Cairo: Institut Français d'Archéologie Orientale du Caire, 1992.

Ver Eecke, M. *La république et le roi: Le mythe de Romulus à la fin de la république romaine.* Paris: De Boccard, 2008.

Vermès, G. *The Complete Dead Sea Scrolls in English*, rev. ed. London: Penguin, 2004.

Versnel, H. "Beyond Cursing: The Appeal to Justice in Judicial Prayers." In C. Faraone and D. Obbink, eds., *Magika Hiera: Ancient Greek Magic and Religion*, 60–106. New York: Oxford University Press, 1991.

Veuthey, J. L. "Le préfet à la répression du brigandage: Nouvelles données." *Études de Lettres* 2 (1994): 69–82.

Veyne, P. "*Cave canem.*" *Mélanges d'archéologie et d'histoire (MÉFRA)* 75 (1963): 59–66.

———. *Bread and Circuses: Historical Sociology and Political Pluralism.* Trans. B. Pearce. London: Penguin, 1990.

Vitucci, G. *Ricerche sulla praefectura urbi in età imperiale (sec. I–III).* Rome: ERMA di Bretschneider, 1956.

———. *Die Rangordnung des römischen Heeres.* Bonn: Marcus & Weber, 1908. Second edition, B. Dobson, ed. Cologne: Böhlau, 1967.

Wallace-Hadrill, A. "*Civilis Princeps*: Between Citizen and King." *JRS* 72 (1982): 32–48.

Wansink, C. S. *Chained in Christ: The Experience and Rhetoric of Paul's Imprisonments.* Sheffield: Sheffield Academic Press, 1996.

Watson, A. *Roman Slave Law.* Baltimore: Johns Hopkins University Press, 1987.

Watts, E. *Riot in Alexandria: Tradition and Group Dynamiics in Late Antique Pagan and Christian Communities*. Berkeley and Los Angeles: University of California Press, 2010.

Weinstock, S. *Divus Julius*. Oxford: Clarendon, 1971.

Weiss, A. *Sklave der Stadt: Untersuchungen zur öffentlichen Sklaverei in den Städten des römischen Reiches*. Hist. E. 173. Stuttgart: Steiner, 2004.

Wheeler, E. "The Laxity of Syrian Legions." In D. Kennedy, ed., *The Roman Army in the East*, *JRA* Suppl. 18, 229–76. Ann Arbor, Mich.: Journal of Roman Archaeology, 1996.

Whittaker, C. R. "The Revolt of Papirius Dionysius A.D. 190." *Historia* 13 (1964): 348–69.

Williams, D. *The Reach of Rome: A History of the Roman Imperial Frontier 1st–5th Centuries AD*. New York: St. Martin's, 1997.

Windley, L. *Runaway Slave Advertisements: A Documentary History from the 1730s to 1790*. Vol. 1: Virginia and North Carolina. Westport, Conn.: Greenwood, 1983.

Wiseman, T. P. *Clio's Cosmetics: Three Studies in Greco-Roman Literature*. Leicester: Leicester University Press, 1979.

———. "Lying Historians: Seven Types of Mendacity." In C. Gill and T. P. Wiseman, eds., *Lies and Fiction in the Ancient World*, 122–46. Austin: University of Texas Press, 1993.

Wolff, C. *Les brigands en Orient sous le Haut-Empire romain*. CÉFR 308. Rome: École Française de Rome, 2003.

———. "Le voyage et les juristes du *Digeste*." In M. G. Angeli Bertinelli and A. Donati, eds., *Le vie della storia: Migrazioni di popoli, viaggi di individui, circolazione di idee nel Mediterraneo antico; Serta antiqua et mediaevalia 9*, 319–39. Rome: G. Bretschneider, 2006.

Woodman, A. J. *Rhetoric in Classical Historiography: Four Studies*. Portland, Ore.: Areopagitica, 1988.

Woolf, G. "Roman Peace." In J. Rich and G. Shipley, eds., *War and Society in the Roman World*, 171–94. London and New York: Routledge, 1993.

Yannakopulos, N. "Preserving the *Pax Romana*: The Peace Functionaries in Roman East." *Mediterraneo Antico* 6 (2003): 825–905.

Yavetz, Z. *Plebs and Princeps*. Oxford: Clarendon, 1969.

———. *Julius Caesar and His Public Image*. Ithaca, N.Y.: Cornell University Press, 1983.

———. "The *Res Gestae* and Augustus' Public Image." In F. Millar and E. Segal, eds., *Caesar Augustus: Seven Aspects*, 1–36. Oxford: Clarendon, 1984.

———. "The Urban Plebs in the Days of of the Flavians, Nerva and Trajan." In A. Giovannini and D. van Berchem, eds., *Opposition et résistances à l'Empire d'Auguste à Trajan*, 135–86. Geneva: Fondation Hardt, 1987.

Zanker, P. *The Power of Images in the Age of Augustus.* Trans. A. Shapiro. Ann Arbor: University of Michigan Press, 1988.

Zawadzki, T. "Sur une inscription de Phrygie relative au *cursus publicus.*" *Revue des Études Anciennes* 62 (1960): 80–94.

Zedner, L. "Policing before and after the Police: The Historical Antecedents of Contemporary Crime Control." *British Journal of Criminology* 46 (2006): 78–96.

Zimmermann, M. "Probus, Carus und die Räuber im Gebiet des pisidischen Termessos." *ZPE* 110 (1996): 265–77.

Ziolkowski, A. "*Urbs Direpta,* or How the Romans Sacked Cities." In J. Rich and G. Shipley, eds., *War and Society in the Ancient World,* 69–91. London and New York: Routledge, 1993.

Zitterkopf, R. E., and S. E. Sidebotham. "Stations and Towers and the Quseir-Nile Road." *Journal of Egyptian Archaeology* 75 (1989): 155–89.

Zuiderhoek, A. "On the Political Sociology of the Imperial Greek City." *GRBS* 48 (2008): 417–45.

Zulueta, F. de. "Violation of Sepulture in Palestine at the Beginning of the Christian Era." *JRS* 22 (1932): 184–97.

New publications

I alert my readers (both here and at reasonable places in the notes above) to the following relevant works that were unavailable to me at the time of manuscript submission.

Brélaz, C. "Aelius Aristide (*Or.,* 50.72–93) et le choix des irénarques par le gouverneur: À propos d'une inscription d'Acmonia." In N. Badoud, ed., *Philologos Dionysios: Mélanges offerts au professeur Denis Knoepfler,* 603–37. Geneva: Droz, 2011.

Busch, Alexandra W. *Militär in Rom: Militärische und paramilitärische Einheiten im kaiserzeitlichen Stadtbild.* Palilia 20. Wiesbaden: Ludwig Reichert, 2011."

Kamen, D. "A Corpus of Inscriptions: Representing Slave Marks in Antiquity." *Memoirs of the American Academy in Rome* 55 (2010): 95–110.

Kelly, B. *Petitions, Litigation, and Social Control in Roman Egypt.* Oxford: Oxford University Press, 2011.

Lamoine, L. *Le pouvoir local en Gaule romaine.* Clermont-Ferrand, France: Presses Universitaires Blaise Pascal, 2009.

Ricci, C. *Soldati e veterani nella vita cittadina dell'Italia imperiale.* Rome: Quasar, 2010.

Rivière, Y. "Captivité et retour de captivité dans la Rome impériale." In *Circulations et frontières: Autour du 101e anniversaire de Fernand Braudel,* Cahiers du Centre de Recherches Historiques 42, 209–24. Paris: CRH, 2008.

Ruciński, S. *Praefectus urbi: Le gardien de l'ordre public à Rome sous le haut-empire romain.* Poznań, Poland: Adam Mickiewicz University, 2009.

Index of Ancient Sources

Velleius Paterculus
  2.57 98
  2.73.3 25
  2.90–93 95, 112, 120
  2.117f 227
  2.126 124
Vergil
  Aen. 6.535–627 46
  Ecl. 3.103 48
  Geor. 3.404 51
Vita Caecilii Cypriani
  15–18 193
Vita (et sententiae) Secundi *see Life of*
  Secundus Phil
Vitruvius
  6.5.2 50

Xenophon
  Cynegeticus 4–5 28
Xenophon of Ephesus
  Ephesiaca
  2.13 68
  3.95 68

pseudo-Zonaras *Lexicon*
  Spek. 193
Zosimus *Historia Nova*
  1.69f 156
  1.71 136

Index

CPSIA information can be obtained
at www.ICGtesting.com
Printed in the USA

9 780199 360017